Reforming the City

REFORMING THE CITY

The Contested Origins of Urban Government, 1890–1930

ARIANE LIAZOS

Columbia

University

Press

New York

Columbia University Press
Publishers Since 1893
New York   Chichester, West Sussex
cup.columbia.edu

Library of Congress Cataloging-in-Publication Data
Names: Liazos, Ariane, 1976– author.
Title: Reforming the city : the contested origins of urban government,
    1890–1930 / Ariane Liazos.
Description: New York : Columbia University Press, [2019] | Includes
    bibliographical references and index.
Identifiers: LCCN 2019015718 | ISBN 9780231191388 (hardback : alk. paper) |
    ISBN 9780231191395 (pbk. : alk. paper) | ISBN 9780231549370 (e-book)
Subjects: LCSH: Municipal government—United States—History. | Municipal
    government by city manager—United States—History. | City
    councils—United States—History. | City dwellers—Political
    activity—United States—History. | National Municipal League—History.
Classification: LCC JS323 .L53 2019 | DDC 320.8/5097309041—dc23
LC record available at https://lccn.loc.gov/2019015718

Cover design: Milenda Nan Ok Lee
Cover art: Charles Beard, *American City Government: A Survey of Newer
Tendencies* (New York: The Century Company, 1912)

For Marcelo, Georgia, and Aleco

Contents

Reforming the City

Introduction

Urban Reform, Coalitions, and American Political Development

When most Americans think of Ferguson, Missouri, they remember the events of August 9, 2014, when a white police officer fatally shot Michael Brown, an unarmed African American teenager. This incident ignited protests in Ferguson over police brutality, drew attention to the Black Lives Matter movement, and sparked national conversations about race and policing that continue to this day. Far fewer Americans, however, remember the role that the city manager and structures of Ferguson's government played in creating the conditions that led to the shooting. In the aftermath of the protests, the Civil Rights Division of the U.S. Department of Justice undertook a detailed investigation of Ferguson's government. Its report highlighted systematic racial bias in law enforcement procedures that were designed primarily to generate revenue for the city rather than to secure public safety. It also emphasized the role of the city manager and other officials in promoting these procedures. For these and other practices, the report concluded that the city violated the constitutional rights of African American residents.[1]

Soon after the report's publication, the chief of police, a municipal judge, and the city manager resigned, but Ferguson did not change its form of government.[2] On one level, the implication was that individuals—and not institutions—were the root of the problem. And yet in another example, an external investigatory body examining Norfolk, Virginia's government concluded the opposite. One hundred years earlier, with World War I looming, Norfolk was poised to become a major naval center. Boosters envisioned a period of rapid expansion but were concerned that the city would be unable to meet demands for new services. They called in specialists from the New York Bureau of Municipal Research to diagnose flaws in the city's organization and administration and propose solutions.[3] The resulting report of over five hundred pages provided a detailed description of nearly every facet of the city's government, noting inefficiencies in every department. In a striking parallel to the Department of Justice's report, it highlighted deficiencies of the police department, the police court, and the justices of the peace, concluding that their approach to raising revenues by imposing fees led them to issue groundless warrants.[4]

Despite this parallel, there are also essential differences in these two reports. In 1915, the New York Bureau of Municipal Research did not identify racism as a central concern. In fact, despite the fact that Norfolk's population was over one-third African American, the report largely avoided mentioning race. One of the rare moments when it did so was telling, claiming that "colored children" were jailed in deplorable conditions, much worse than those of white children.[5] Yet despite this silence, other sources from the time provide clear evidence of racially motivated police intimidation, spurious arrests, and unequal enforcement of laws in Norfolk and other cities in Virginia.[6] In 2015, in contrast, the Justice Department focused on race throughout its report, and some of its key recommendations to improve policing included training to reduce racial stereotyping and bias and efforts to promote more diversity in hiring.[7] While in 1915 the investigators avoided addressing institutional racism, in 2015 the Department of Justice addressed it directly and extensively.

Another key difference stemmed from the proposed solutions. While both reports recommended abolishing policing and judicial practices designed to generate revenue, the 1915 report went much further in proposing structural reforms, calling for a new charter to remake the city's organization and administration. It maintained that centralizing responsibility and authority under an individual such as a city manager would ensure a more efficient and impartial administration that would benefit the entire community.[8] The report's authors and many of their contemporaries promoted the view that structural reforms, particularly the establishment of city manager forms of government, would enable experts, above political

and personal motivations, to create what many called "good city government." Yet while the investigators of 1915 believed that a city manager form
of government would promote impartiality and efficiency, the Justice Department characterized the manager in Ferguson as exactly the opposite:
partial and inefficient.[9]

This book tells the story of how the forms of city government that now
dominate the urban landscape came to be. In doing so, it examines the silences and paradoxes of the movement that led to their creation. In
roughly thirty years, city government in the United States underwent a
massive transformation. An organization called the National Municipal
League (NML) and reform groups across the country spearheaded campaigns to restructure the governments of American cities, and in local
elections voters ratified charters that created new forms of representation
and systems of administration. In 1900, the sphere of self-government in
cities was circumscribed. The use of the initiative and referendum in local
elections was rare, and most cities were only allowed to undertake activities expressly permitted by state laws. By the 1930s, the initiative and referendum were widespread, and roughly one-third of states had passed
laws allowing "home rule" for cities.[10] Even more starkly, in 1900 city manager government did not exist. Urban areas were largely governed by
elected mayors and large, bicameral councils elected in partisan, ward-
based elections.[11] By the 1930s, nearly half of American cities were governed by small commissions and often administered by appointed city
managers, and over half of all commissions and councils were elected in
at-large, nonpartisan elections.[12] These features—provisions for direct democracy, nonpartisan elections, at-large elections (or a mix of ward-
based and at-large elections), and appointed city managers—continue to
be the most common elements of city government today.[13] How were reformers able to change the governments of American cities so dramatically
in only a few short decades?

Equally puzzling is the fact that many of these reforms did not achieve
what their original architects intended. Initially, promoters of city manager government, shorter ballots, and nonpartisan elections claimed that
these tools would increase interest in local government and make democracy workable in growing cities. In 1899, the NML issued an official program of reform focused on a variety of means to eliminate the influence
of parties in local affairs. One leader of the NML summarized this program

as an attempt to "organize municipal government" to bring about "the perfection of democracy." Another promised that it would ensure that citizens would control "public policy" in cities and "work out their own local destiny."[14] Twenty years later, Richard Childs, the principal architect of city manager government, promoted this plan as one that would enable democracy to flourish in the modern age. If citizens elected only small councils and did not have to vote for administrators, who would now be appointed by city managers, they would be informed about all candidates. Childs claimed that this system would make sure that councillors would not be beholden to special interests but rather "deal solely and directly with a free people."[15]

Today, political scientists continue to debate the overall impact of such changes, but there is a general consensus that many of these reforms lead to lower turnout in local elections, which in turn creates unrepresentative councils that pass policies that favor some residents over others. Removing parties from local politics, separating local from state and national elections, and delegating powers to appointed officials (such as city managers) rather than elected mayors all make citizens less likely to vote.[16] In recent years, participation in local elections reached a historic low, with less than one-quarter of registered voters showing up to the polls.[17] This state of affairs is not what Childs and many others envisioned. Why were these reformers so successful in altering the structures of local government but so wrong in predicting what these changes would accomplish?

We might also ask how much it really matters that turnout is low and local councils are often unrepresentative. While scholars continue to debate this issue, the story of Ferguson offers compelling evidence that it matters hugely. Ferguson was one of the first cities to adopt a city manager form of government in Missouri, with a small, nonpartisan council chosen in local elections held apart from national ones. In 2014, the population was 67 percent African American, but the mayor, five of six council members, the city manager, and the chief of police were all white, as were fifty of fifty-three police officers.[18] Ferguson, in short, provides a stark example of why we need to care about the institutions of city government. They determine who gets elected and how power is distributed among elected and appointed officials. They can also make it more or less likely for citizens to want to participate in local governance and feel that their voices matter.[19] The central question of this book is how reforms originally intended to make city government more accountable to voters ended up contributing to the creation of the systems in Ferguson and cities like it across the country. The answer lies in the story of the urban reform movement that swept through the country in the early twentieth century, particularly the diversity of its coalitions, the compromises made to maintain these coalitions, and the unintended consequences that resulted.[20]

Investigating Urban Reform: Sources, Scope, and Methods

Some of the earliest attempts to understand the motivations of these reformers argued for a near conspiracy. In the 1960s, historians claimed that there was a sharp difference between the professed ideology and actual practices of proponents of urban reform, suggesting that businessmen and professionals used seemingly democratic rhetoric to mask their real goals. For example, reformers attacked ward-based elections and party patronage as inherently corrupting, claiming that they prevented city government from representing the people's will and providing efficient services. In reality, this view claims, elites simply wanted to eliminate the ward system because it provided a voice for the largely immigrant working class in local politics.[21] This earlier scholarship has continued to be cited by major works in history and political science in recent years.[22] It also dominates accounts of early twentieth-century reform in political science textbooks today.[23]

Unquestionably, there is some accuracy in these arguments, but studies of individual cities suggest that the full story was far more complicated, demonstrating notable local and regional variations and offering examples of charter reform campaigns supported by diverse urban residents. In one instance, leaders of the African American community in Cincinnati, Ohio, joined with white reformers calling for a new charter. Both groups wanted to replace ward-based elections with a system of proportional representation. In another, ward politicians in New Brunswick, New Jersey, were leading proponents of a new reform known as the commission plan of government. And in the Southwest, reformers in many cities and towns secured the adoption of new charters by presenting urban reform as a way for residents to unite in support of local economic development.

Highlighting the complexity of urban reform, political scientist Amy Bridges characterizes it as developing from a "mixed assortment of motivations and goals, of efficiency and elitism, clean government and racism, the common good and exclusion."[24] Such accounts help us better understand the dynamics of Progressive urban reform in cities across the country, forcing us to ask why ward politicians and African American leaders supported reforms that eventually contributed to the effective disfranchisement of the working class and minorities.

This book is an attempt to answer this and other puzzling questions. In part, the answer may be that charters were more likely to be adopted when suffrage restrictions were in place, reducing the voting power of poor and minority residents.[25] But such restrictions cannot fully explain outcomes, because, as the accounts of reform in this book demonstrate, business leaders and suburbanites sometimes opposed new charters, and women's groups, union leaders, and African Americans sometimes supported them. Why did these latter groups support urban reform? Was the disempowerment of voters the real motivation of the original architects and most vocal proponents of urban reform? In other words, were they in fact conspirators, attempting to mislead working-class voters with false promises of democratic empowerment? Or were they instead political novices who did not understand what the true outcomes of their efforts would be? Did their reforms produce the intended results, at least in the short term?

These are not easy questions to answer. This study, like all works of historical scholarship, necessarily draws on the fragmentary records left by historical actors, and it must grapple with the silences and incomplete nature of these records. By examining academic debates about urban democracy, political battles over structural reform, and the resulting institutions created, this book offers an intellectual, political, and institutional history of urban reform. Adopting an interdisciplinary approach, I combine political history and the history of ideas with the insights of institutionalism and American political development in the social sciences. As a historian, I embrace the complex, contingent, and particular forces that shaped this unique historical moment, but I also draw on social scientists' insights regarding the importance of institutions and other forces that constrain and empower historical actors.[26] I draw from a diverse body of original source materials to trace the shifting alliances and complicated interactions among leading reformers in the NML, political scientists active in reform circles, and local political actors working for charter revision over a roughly forty-year period. I combine accounts of reform in five cities, a history of the NML, analyses of the works of the leading political scientists who were active in the NML, and quantitative data on changes in the structures of city government in over three hundred cities.

On the national level, by examining the NML's archival papers and publications and influential works of municipal political science, this book focuses on the NML and the bureaus of municipal research that were founded in cities as venues for applied social science. These organizations brought together leading reformers and political scientists who, despite their many differences of opinion, largely set the agenda for urban reform. These men (and a few women) met at yearly meetings, and their vast publications reached interested parties in cities throughout the United States. My account touches on the efforts of dozens of active officers and focuses more closely on the efforts of a few key leaders and political scientists who decisively shaped the NML's work.

On the local level, this book incorporates accounts of charter reform in five cities, detailing the interactions between local and national levels whenever possible. I rely heavily on local newspapers. Reformers, journalists, and editors often used urban newspapers as vehicles for the dissemination of "facts" to educate residents. Most residents, in turn, learned about local politics primarily through newspapers. As a result, newspapers partly set the political agendas of American cities.[27] The pages of local newspapers provide detailed accounts of campaigns to revise charters. Urban reform occurred within the context of broader discussions during the Progressive Era about the meaning of democracy and purpose of government. These discussions took place not only among political scientists and leading reformers at the NML's annual meetings but also among local reformers, politicians, and urban residents. Meetings to formulate new charters were akin to local constitutional conventions in which participants worked to create political institutions that embodied their understandings of democracy. They provide examples of a type of discourse that later scholars have termed a "public sphere" and a "community of discourse."[28] At meetings hosted by civic associations, on street corners, and in the pages of local newspapers, reformers (usually middle-class professionals), union leaders and members, officers of women's groups, business leaders, and politicians came together and discussed the meaning of democratic politics and government, as well as other matters of common concern.

Only by combining a variety of methodological approaches and diverse evidence—including local case studies, national debates, and quantitative data—can we come closer to understanding the full history of urban reform. The NML and other municipal organizations launched some of the first systematic investigations to gather data on American cities. Their efforts, combined with those of the Census Bureau, created records regarding state laws regulating cities, forms of city government (mayor-council, commission, or manager), electoral structures (partisan or nonpartisan elections, by ward or at large), public ownership of utilities and transit, spending on infrastructure, and much more.[29] Several political scientists and economists have made use of this type of data to offer conclusions regarding how and why reforms were adopted, sometimes making claims about the motivations of political actors based largely on statistical analyses.[30] In places I draw on their work, but at the same time I proceed from the conviction that quantitative studies alone cannot fully answer questions about human motivation and how and why structural reforms were adopted.

I began my research with national data to gain a sense of the broad patterns of reform, and my analysis of the forms of government in the 310 largest cities in 1930 confirms that regional variations were key: broadly speaking, most structural reforms were more likely to be adopted in the South and West and were less likely to be adopted in the Midwest and Northeast.[31] I then read historical accounts of many cities across the country to identify cities that followed the patterns most typical of their region. I discovered examples not only of campaigns in the South, Southwest, and West that led to the adoption of new charters but also of campaigns in the Northeast and Midwest where voters questioned the need for proposed changes. I selected five medium-size cities: Worcester, Massachusetts; Norfolk, Virginia; Toledo, Ohio; Fort Worth, Texas; and Oakland, California.[32] By the end of the 1920s, residents in Norfolk, Fort Worth, and Oakland adopted city manager charters with at-large elections, while residents of Toledo and Worcester had not, despite the efforts of reformers.[33]

Detailed accounts of campaigns to revise charters in these cities are essential to understanding the broader movement for urban reform.

Scholars of charter revision in the twenty-first century argue that it is not possible to understand the true nature of impassioned debates about local government, even today, without adopting a case study method that includes careful examination of the positions of both opponents and supporters of charter changes in specific cities. At the same time, a single case study alone cannot shed light on the national story. Multiple case studies must be compared in a search for patterns and common themes.[34] These methodological points apply not only to the modern study of charter change but also to its historical study, when the feelings involved in local debates reached levels that would surprise most contemporary readers. It is difficult today to understand the passion that animated participants of these debates, many of whom seem to have sincerely believed that the future of democracy was at stake in the formation of city charters. Moreover, my combined examination of local case studies, quantitative data, and national debates contributes not only to the scholarship on urban reform but also to broader questions regarding the development of political institutions in the United States, particularly the complex relationship between representative structures and the scope of activities undertaken by government.

The Movement for Urban Reform: Coalitions, Compromises, and Silences

Drawing on these methodologies and bodies of evidence, I begin by distinguishing between intentions and outcomes. Other studies rightly focus on longer-term outcomes of urban reform.[35] Yet, following the lead of James Kloppenberg, in this historical account I argue for the importance of unintended consequences and lost opportunities to secure alternative outcomes.[36] I also argue that the coalitions that marked this national movement for urban reform are key to understanding these unintended consequences.

To claim that there was a national movement is not to argue that it was neat or uniform but rather that a shared set of concerns drew together diverse individuals in coalitions.[37] Focusing on the networks of communication that brought reformers together and shaped the agendas they pursued locally demonstrates the powerful connections between the NML and local movements for reform and, as a result, that there is a national story to be told. At the same time, the connections remind us that historical change and institutional development are not simple or linear but rather complex, confusing, and even messy, marked by contestation and dissent. To make sense of the many seeming paradoxes of the movement for urban reform, we need to understand the formation of coalitions among seemingly disparate groups.

The diversity of individuals involved with the NML at first seems puzzling, ranging from passionate advocates of participatory democracy, some of whom even supported racial and gender equality, to equally passionate advocates of franchise restrictions, eugenics, and near-oligarchic views of government. Yet we need to remember that many Americans living at the turn of the twentieth century advocated multiple positions that today seem antithetical.[38] Moreover, contemporary scholarship now treats Progressive reformers more generally as diverse, unified by a commitment to some form of democratic self-government and a desire to harness science and expertise to improve modern life but deeply divided in many other ways. Some conceived of America's democratic community as largely white, Christian, and male, paternalistically working for the welfare of others. Others envisioned it somewhat more inclusively as a partnership among consumers and producers. Still others defined American national identity in pluralist terms, encompassing diverse races, ethnicities, genders, and religions.[39] Despite envisioning America's democratic community so differently, many of these individuals collaborated, working together to promote specific causes.

Clinton Rogers Woodruff, secretary of the NML during its first two decades, embodies a few of these seeming paradoxes. After studying at the University of Pennsylvania, he became a lawyer and briefly a member of the Pennsylvania legislature. He was active in numerous reform circles, serving as a leader in well over a dozen organizations advocating a dizzying array of causes, including, to name only a few, civil service reform, child labor laws, aid for Italian political prisoners, and international arbitration.[40] One study uses Woodruff as an example of an antidemocratic proponent of business interests, quoting him as describing structural change as "a simple, direct, businesslike way of administering the business affairs of the city." In this account (and many others), when reformers were interested in public welfare, they envisioned business leaders acting on behalf of a public that would not participate in decision-making processes.[41] Yet a more recent study of Progressives who worked to expand participatory democracy in cities celebrates Woodruff and his work as the president of the American Park and Outdoor Art Association. It describes him as someone who sought to foster participatory democracy by creating public spaces that would bring "people together into full and equal association" in order "to encourage interaction among different people and generate a democratic public."[42] Woodruff thus provides an example of a reformer who advocated views that today we might find contradictory, believing that the use of business models and the active engagement of a diverse citizenry would *both* improve city government.

Woodruff's own prolific analysis of urban reform helps us to understand the diversity of views held by the many Americans who joined coalitions in support of urban reform. He perhaps understood the movement's complexity better than many later scholars. One such historian, for example, contrasted "social reformers," who were more concerned with the welfare of urban residents, with "structural reformers," whose lack of faith in participatory democracy led them to believe that municipalities should be run by educated experts.[43] Yet Woodruff knew that there was no clear division between those who advocated the expansion of city government to promote popular welfare and those who advocated structural reform to make it more efficient. He identified the underlying motivation for both agendas: popular anger at the perception that corrupt (or inept) city governments sold contracts to private companies that provided poor and overpriced services to urban residents. According to Woodruff, "The question of public utilities . . . has in many places overshadowed all other questions." From "the street-railway situation" in Chicago to "the gas question" in Boston, the need to reform the present system for providing these services was "the one issue" that stirred people to action.[44] At the same time, he knew that desires to address the poor provision of services and also to expand the activities of city government generated interest in and support for structural reform. In addressing the NML, Woodruff noted that "the tendency to enlarge the scope of the city's functions . . . has unquestionably been the chief impetus of the movement" for early forms of city manager government.[45]

In offering these observations, Woodruff highlighted one of the most significant trends in American cities in the early twentieth century: the massive expansion of activities undertaken by city governments. Much of what many take for granted today as part of local government—public playgrounds, free kindergartens, clean water, and sewerage—first became widespread during these years. Though it is difficult to document the precise extent of this expansion, the increase in expenditures provides a sense of the scale of new activities undertaken. American cities nearly tripled their per capita expenditures between 1904 and 1930.[46] They roughly doubled spending on parks, recreation, sanitation, health, education, and charities from 1910 to 1921 alone.[47] Recent historical scholarship notes that cities played a prominent role in attempts to expand government in the Progressive Era. Public welfare had long been considered the province of local rather than state or national government, and with the rapid increase of urban populations, American cities, often inspired by European examples, experimented with new forms of governmental activism. Municipal courts, for example, were pioneers in the transformation of the criminal justice system, using law as a means of social control to regulate family life and public morality. Cities attempted to regulate many other areas of local life, monitoring sanitary conditions in the name of public health and licensing a variety of local businesses in the name of the public good. Yet such expansions were sometimes controversial, reducing the reach of the market and transferring many goods and services from the private to the public realm.[48] In many cities, however, prominent business leaders and journalists who had previously advocated a more laissez-faire approach to political economy came to support a more expansive role for government regulation or even ownership of municipal utilities in the name of the public interest and economic growth.[49]

I argue that these two trends—the expansion of governmental activities and the movement to refashion representative structures through charter revision—cannot be understood separately. Of equal importance was the movement for home rule for cities, marked by calls for greater local autonomy from state legislatures, that became popular in these years. Home rule encompassed the right of urban residents to decide on the scope of governmental activities and/or to draft and adopt charters.[50] To understand the origins of governmental institutions, we must pay close attention to sequencing and the convergence of historical trends.[51] Why did some cities adopt new charters and others reject them? When discussing charter revision today, political scientists continue to disagree, pointing to a variety of possible factors that influence voters' decisions: perceptions of crises, financial and otherwise; perceptions of corruption or incompetence; support or opposition of the press, business leaders, or political leaders; decisions of neighboring cities; regional variation; conflicting paradigms or beliefs about local government; demographics (size and composition of urban populations); economic development or a desire for growth; and continued strong perceptions that mayor- and manager-led governments represent fundamentally different values.[52]

Without denying the potential salience of these many factors, I argue that during the early twentieth century, the underlying, central issue that determined the success or failure of charter campaigns in cities throughout the nation was the ability of reformers to connect structural reform to functional expansion. The fact that charter reform became popular in these years was not coincidental. Its popularity hinged on the argument that restructuring electoral, representative, and administrative institutions would enable city governments to provide the services increasingly perceived as necessities of urban life. Closely related was the belief that urban residents should be allowed to determine their own fates without meddling from state legislatures. Decisions to undertake new activities always shaped and often directly caused efforts of reformers and politicians to experiment with new forms of representation. The question of what city government should do for residents went hand in hand with a reconsideration of how citizens should participate in urban politics and governance. In the case of charter reform, political actors with widely different understandings of democracy came together to argue for the reorganization of city government. Despite their many differences, they all wanted city governments to institute new programs, and they agreed that existing structures were preventing this from happening. They came together to propose structural reforms that would make functional expansion possible.

This connection between structure and function also provides the key to understanding the coalitions at play nationally in groups such as the NML and locally in cities across the country. Much of the variety among those who considered themselves urban reformers and the seeming contradictions among the diverse programs that they advocated can be reconciled by envisioning urban reform not as a singular, unified movement but rather as a series of shifting, dynamic, loose coalitions. This understanding of coalitions helps explain why individuals who celebrated participatory democracy and individuals who railed against the ignorance of urban voters both served as leaders of the NML and why labor and business leaders both at times supported the same charter reforms that promised to facilitate the expansion of city government.

While they lasted, such coalitions were often based on simultaneous desires for increased efficiency and expanded social welfare. Today many view these goals as contradictory, but Americans living a hundred years ago did not necessarily agree. The founders of municipal research bureaus believed that careful attention to reforming the administrative structures of city government would yield tax savings *and* improvements in social welfare.[53] A shared emphasis on efficiency and social welfare provides the key to understanding why leaders of working-class constituencies sometimes formed alliances with elite business leaders and professionals. Kenneth Finegold's comparative study of mayoral and council elections in New York, Chicago, and Cleveland demonstrates that the active presence of "experts" such as political scientists facilitated alliances among elite reformers, populist politicians, and members of the working class. These experts presented increased efficiency and the expansion of social welfare policies as inseparable, part of a unified and coherent vision, thereby appealing to multiple groups.[54] The same was often true in early charter campaigns, with populist politicians, union leaders, and officers in chambers of commerce forming unexpected alliances.

Similarly, varied groups and individuals advocated both "structural" and "social" reforms. Certainly, many emphasized one more than the other. Women's voluntary organizations, for example, tended to focus more on social welfare. Much of the contemporary scholarship on women's activism in American cities explores the differences between male and female reformers, and undeniably men dominated most efforts to achieve "good city government" while women dominated settlement work and other efforts to improve public health and urban living conditions.[55] Nevertheless, these differences did not preclude support for various structural and administrative reforms. Jane Addams, a national leader in the settlement house movement, celebrated the fact that "the most vigorous effort at governmental reform, as well as the most generous experiments in ministering to social needs, have come from the largest cities." Though not an active leader in the movement for charter revision, she served as a vice

president of the NML. She lamented the fact that current political structures prevented cities from becoming more of a positive force in the daily
lives of urban dwellers. According to Addams, many "carefully prepared
city charters" prevented cities from meeting the expanding "social needs"
of urban populations.[56] Particularly after the enfranchisement of women
in 1920, local women's groups emerged as prominent supporters of movements for charter revision.[57] Treating efficiency and welfare and social and
structural goals as separate prevents us from seeing the alliances among
groups and individuals who, at least for a time, came together to advocate
them as part of a unified platform.

The desire to keep these types of coalitions together led to the many
compromises and mutually agreed on silences that enabled local political
actors in cities across the country to adopt and adapt reforms in ways that
many of their creators did not necessarily intend. The NML's founders created the organization in 1894 as an impartial venue where all could come
together and express their views. They also believed that discussion, while
allowing for differences of opinion on many matters, would yield consensus on certain fundamental principles underlying "good city government."
For the political scientists who worked with the NML, this understanding
of the organization was essential. They wanted to effect change in the real
world without sacrificing their claims to academic objectivity. They hoped
to take the lead in efforts to refashion city government. But in doing so,
they struggled to balance seemingly contradictory goals, seeking to combine objective scholarship with active involvement in reform, to learn from
"real-world" politics while offering their own authoritative advice, and to
create democratic institutions that were responsive to the popular will but
also led by professional experts. The avowed neutrality of the NML enabled
them to shape reforms while maintaining their image as impartial experts.
Local reformers also celebrated the NML's professed expertise. Some decided to affiliate their local leagues directly with the national organization,
drawing on its resources and authority and sending delegates to annual
meetings.[58] Many more simply relied on their publications as authoritative sources of information and used them to present their own proposals
as scientific rather than partisan.

The NML reaped immense benefits from this image of neutrality and
expertise, becoming extremely influential, but the image was not easy to
maintain, and it was not without costs. Over and over the committees of

the NML, made up of prominent national reformers and political scientists, settled on compromise positions and refused to take a stance on controversial and potentially divisive topics, particularly the appropriate scope of activities for city government. In one of the clearest and most consequential examples, the authors of the first *Municipal Program* (1899), a statement on the ideal form of city government, decided not to take a position on the appropriate range of municipal activities. One issue was particularly controversial: whether cities should sell franchises to private companies for the provision of transportation and utilities or establish municipally owned systems. The program provided a detailed blueprint for the structures in cities in terms of the selection and duties of local officials. Yet it addressed the function of cities only in terms of the creation of an efficient administrative system to carry out programs, claiming individual cities should possess "a large measure of freedom in the determination of local policy."[59] The professed support for home rule allowed the NML to avoid controversy and maintain an alliance.

The avoidance of controversy by adopting compromise positions continued in the coming years. Several committees were unable to reach a consensus on the question of function, and NML publications advocated contradictory positions. In 1912, one critiqued municipal ownership and called for an increase in state regulation of private service providers; in 1914, another called for greater autonomy for cities to facilitate the establishment of municipally owned utilities.[60] By 1915, the NML endorsed a newer form of city government first called the "commission manager" and later "city manager" and then "council manager" plan, with a small elected council appointing a city manager as head administrator. As did the authors of the original program, the men who wrote *A New Municipal Program* relied on appeals to local autonomy to avoid taking a stance on municipal ownership. To maintain a unified position, they also agreed to include only "recommendations" that, for the manager plan to function democratically, it needed to include provisions for the initiative, referendum, and recall and for proportional representation in the election of city councils.[61] The debates continued in the following years: in the face of the rising popularity of at-large elections in the 1920s, a vocal and large minority wanted the NML to endorse only proportional representation. After a heated debate that resulted in a nine-to-eight vote in 1932, the committee that revised the earlier programs decided to declare at-large elections an acceptable alternative to proportional representation.[62] The result was that time and again, leading figures in the NML created frameworks that could be used by different groups, from labor organizations to chambers of commerce, for very different purposes.

These compromises also help us understand how such a diverse group of individuals agreed to support the NML—how individuals who seemed to have little in common came together. The contrast between James Carter and Horace Deming, both lawyers and leaders of the NML and New York's City Club, highlights this paradox. At the annual conference of the NML in 1899, Carter blamed corruption partly on the easily controlled votes of the "ignorant, less educated classes, the laboring classes, and . . . the criminal classes." Deming, in contrast, blamed urban problems on structural flaws and called for renewed efforts "to [make] city government a genuine representative democracy." Echoing Abraham Lincoln, he told his listeners, "City government must be a government of the people, by the people, and for the people."[63] Similarly, these compromises help us understand why L. E. Holden represented the Cleveland Chamber of Commerce at the next meeting of the NML, where mayor Samuel Jones of Toledo spoke to promote what he called "collective ownership for every form of public utility." Jones argued that "corrupt businessmen" rather than "corrupt politicians" were responsible for the "social distress of our cities." Notably, despite their divergent views, both men voiced support for allowing cities to make more decisions without the influence of state legislatures.[64] To maintain their coalition, the NML's leaders focused on such points of consensus and refused to take official positions on more divisive issues.

Silences regarding municipal ownership appear in existing historical records, with actors discussing and agreeing not to take positions or compromise on certain matters. Harder to uncover are the undocumented silences in the movement for urban reform, and there were many. Historians of groups marginalized in historical records remind us that we can never fully know what transpired in the past. Historical sources are not simply neutral records of past events but rather created documents that privilege some perspectives while excluding others. History is produced when historical actors create sources, written or otherwise; when archivists, librarians, and others gather and preserve sources; and, finally, when historians make use of these sources to create narratives of the past.[65]

These kinds of silences are present in the documentation of the move-ment for urban reform, particularly in terms of avoiding some of the most contentious political issues of the day: the suffrage rights of women and African Americans. Given the avoidance of these topics in written records, how can we understand the influence of ideas about gender and race on the restructuring of city government? In the pages that follow, I pay close attention to the few moments when they were discussed overtly. Yet at points I also situate charter reform within the wider discussions of these topics at the time that so often remained unaddressed in the records of urban reform. The vast majority of the officers and members of the NML were white men. Though the organization occasionally invited women and African Americans to contribute to conferences and publications, the first and second municipal programs and accompanying papers largely do not mention women, African Americans, or immigrants.[66] The NML's members included individuals with sharply contradictory views on the rights of women and African Americans, including A. Lawrence Lowell, who de-fended the disfranchisement of African Americans, and Moorfield Storey, the first president of the National Association for the Advancement of Col-ored People.[67] Similarly, leading figures in municipal reform circles in-cluded Charles Beard, an open and active supporter of woman suffrage, and Woodrow Wilson, who famously opposed woman suffrage when governor of New Jersey and only came to support it later in his presidency.[68] For the most part, to maintain a coalition, they seem to have avoided discussing these matters, agreeing to disagree.

Local newspapers also tended not to relate urban politics to the rights of women or African Americans, and they rarely documented the views of either group regarding charter reform. Regardless of these silences, there is clear evidence that racial, gender, ethnic, and class identity played important roles in discussions of city charters. Yet examining these roles in Worcester, Norfolk, Toledo, Fort Worth, and Oakland does not allow for simple conclusions. Conflicting views on these topics do not parallel con-flicting views on urban reform. In Norfolk, for example, white advocates and opponents of a proposed manager charter both supported the disfran-chisement of African Americans.[69] And after the adoption of this new charter, the first city manager received support from African American community leaders for his efforts to pave streets and improve public health in their neighborhoods.[70] Similarly, the gendered language of urban reform was something of a double-edged sword for women's inclusion in urban politics. Several scholars aptly note that the gendered language of business, professionalism, rationalism, and scientism often excluded women.[71] Yet at the same time, this language also offered potential benefits to some women. Mary Ritter Beard, for example, in a work published by the NML, claimed that the new focus of many reform groups on the administration of government (rather than electoral politics) would provide women with greater opportunities for "public service."[72] Opposition to parties, critiques of the immorality of urban machines, and appeals to a higher common good helped to create spaces for and a justification of greater involvement of women in public affairs. Many women, largely disfranchised in the early century, would benefit from moves away from electoral politics, as would expanding services and collaborations with voluntary groups in the name of the public good. In short, while many recent scholars argue that professionalized city government and civic organizations excluded African Americans and women, members of these groups at the time had different hopes for their potential.

What, then, were the consequences of this coalition of individuals who shared the conviction that structural reform was a necessary prerequisite for functional expansion but compromised on municipal ownership, direct democracy, and proportional representation and remained silent regarding the voting rights of women and African Americans? Their efforts resulted in the restructuring of government in hundreds of cities throughout the country. Yet for many of the individuals who promoted and supported charter revisions, the structures that they created yielded results that they may not have intended or envisioned.

Urban Reform and American Political Development

A framework for understanding urban reform that focuses on both structure and function offers key insights regarding the roles of cities in the development of American political institutions. American political development (APD) is a contemporary subfield of political science that examines the origins and growth of political institutions over time. Its practitioners often emphasize the historical and contingent nature of institutions such as Congress, federal bureaucracies, the judiciary, political parties, and even voluntary organizations.[73] Pioneering social scientists such as Theda Skocpol and Stephen Skowronek called for greater attention to the role of the state (a term used by scholars to signify government more broadly) in American politics and history, focusing on the roles of political parties and courts, as well as voluntary organizations and social movements, in building the capacity for governance.[74] More recently, historians such as William Novak and Brian Balogh have challenged the once widely held notion that the American state is somehow "weak" when compared with larger and more centralized and bureaucratic states in Europe. They note that, historically, American government was not weak so much as diffuse, indirect, and sometimes even seemingly invisible, based on often unclear divisions among public and private institutions. Government shaped civil society and business enterprises through regulation, taxation, land policies, and subsidies. Such indirect and decentralized structures and policies made state and local government extremely influential in the course of state development.[75]

Scholars in APD have devoted comparatively less attention to local than state and national levels of government, but for those who sought to expand the scope of government during the Progressive Era, cities provided opportunities to experiment with new programs, many of which were later adopted on the state and national levels. Turning their attention to cities, recent scholars in APD have begun to explore such key topics as the role of the local government in shaping economic development, the origins of social and welfare policies, the contested nature of national-state-local relations, and, importantly, the ways that civil society and reform movements shape the evolution of political institutions.[76] As a result of a distrust of centralized authority and celebration of local self-government, most Americans have historically been more comfortable with active states closer to home. Cities were the largest governmental presence in the daily lives of urban residents, the institution that made government real to them.[77] Additionally, while many reformers focused on national economic and political institutions, others who worried about the fate of popular sovereignty and democratic institutions turned their attention to the local level.[78]

This understanding of the importance of local government was captured vividly in *The Promise of American Life* (1909). Here, Herbert Croly, a prominent public intellectual, explained that the public was willing "to accept much more advanced ideas in this field of municipal reform than it is in any other part of the political battle-field." Celebrating the "vitality" and "progress" of cities, Croly emphasized the importance of the many "experiments" that looked to "an increasingly responsible municipal organization" to assume wider "economic and social functions." He felt that such advances would benefit the nation as a whole, concluding that "the American city will become in the near future the most fruitful field for economically and socially constructive experimentation; and the effect of the example set therein will have a beneficially reactive effect upon both state and Federal politics."[79]

Not only did many Americans view cities as innovators of new governmental functions, they also believed that cities were central to the future of democracy, sometimes relating the two. Frederic Howe, another prominent Progressive author, agreed with Croly, describing "the city" as "an experiment station, offering new experiences to the world." He also proclaimed cities "the hope of democracy." For Howe, urban democracy encompassed more than the right to vote, more than a "government by public opinion." It included a wider social vision in which the people of the city would consciously unite and work together to solve shared problems posed by urban living conditions. Urban politics, increasingly concerned "with the elevation of the standard of living, with equality of opportunity, [and] with the uplifting of life," anticipated "a movement for human society more hopeful than anything the world has known." The concept of home rule was central to this vision. Howe wrote of the rising move for "decentralization" that would prevent distant state legislatures from meddling in local affairs, declaring that "the problem with our cities is not too much democracy, but too little democracy." He defined the home rule movement as "a demand by the people to be trusted" to govern themselves.[80] It would, in short, be difficult to overstate the importance that many Americans living at the start of the twentieth century placed on cities.

Croly, Howe, and many of their contemporaries spoke of an expansion of "functions" to describe what political scientists today might call state building or state capacity. *Function* was not the only term they used to describe the new activities undertaken by local governments. They wrote of the "work" or "purpose" or "ends" of city government or, more simply, what a city "does" or "should do." But *function* was their preferred term to describe the new playgrounds and hospitals, lighting plants and trolley services, and I follow their lead. In using *structure* and *function* as shorthand for representative institutions and governmental activities, I use the terms as they did. Later social scientists would espouse a functionalism that held that political (and social) structures exist to fulfill societal needs. In such a model, institutions are often clear and rational responses to the changing demands of society.[81] In contrast, many early twentieth-century urban reformers and political scientists better understood that the legitimate function of city government was political and contested rather than the result of rational decision making and natural development.

Exploring the movement for urban reform in this context provides an excellent opportunity to expand our understanding of the development of political institutions. Prominent historians call for more empirical studies that treat state building as a dynamic process in which the boundaries of the government's power were debated and negotiated.[82] The subjects of this book engaged in this kind of contested process. As noted, some of the most heated debates in urban politics centered on the question of whether cities should provide utilities and transportation through programs of municipal ownership or through the sale of contracts or franchises to private companies. At the close of the nineteenth century, city councils typically granted franchises to private companies known as public service corporations to supply gas, electricity, and sometimes water and to construct and operate public transit systems. The problem was that, as the muckraking journalist Lincoln Steffens revealed to the nation, in return for granting these "special privileges," council members often received hefty kickbacks.[83] In the context of these revelations, most urban residents agreed that something needed to be done to reform this corrupt system.

The most vocal critics of the franchise system presented municipal ownership not only as the only solution to corruption but also as a means for creating a reinvigorated and expanded sense of democratic community. Municipal socialists and union leaders led the way, but a wide variety of left-leaning Progressive reformers and politicians—and urban voters—came to support the transfer of the provision of diverse goods and services from the realm of private enterprise to public enterprise. These forms of public ownership implicitly rested on the right of government to control certain aspects of the economy to improve the lives of urban residents.[84] While reformers certainly did not uniformly support municipal ownership, several leading figures in the NML connected it with democratic ideals. In *The American City: A Problem in Democracy* (1904), Delos Wilcox, an active participant in many NML projects and prominent "expert" on public utilities, argued that "the growth of cities" made "cooperation necessary through the expansion of city functions." Wilcox defined such cooperation as "democratic" and municipal ownership as "ultimate control by the whole people."[85] Charles Richardson, one of the original founders and later a first vice president of the NML, further explained the connection between municipal ownership and democratic community: "If we want the people to develop higher civic ideals we must enlarge the scope and importance of their city government."[86]

This connection was perhaps articulated most fully and passionately by Mayor Jones of Toledo. In 1900–1901, Jones attempted to reform the structure of Toledo's government in order to facilitate the implementation of his plans for a dramatic expansion of municipal ownership.[87] Invited to speak at the NML's annual convention in 1898, he declared to an audience of members, "Private ownership of public franchises is a high crime against democracy. It is contrary to the spirit of republican institutions. It is a city granting privilege to an individual to enrich himself, usually at the expense of the classes least able to bear it, the poor people."[88] Certainly, Jones was far to the left of most of his contemporaries, but it would be a mistake to assume that only figures like Jones, union leaders, and municipal socialists supported an expansion of municipal ownership. At times many Americans, including businessmen, agreed that local government needed to intervene and provide services when private enterprises were unable to do so effectively.[89]

While Jones and like-minded reformers viewed municipal ownership as the only viable path for state building, many of their contemporaries disagreed and were willing to expand local government through other means. There were many legal barriers to instituting programs of municipal ownership, most importantly a lack of home rule for cities. State laws typically limited the amount of money cities could borrow, making it difficult to raise the necessary capital to institute new programs. Historian Gail Radford notes that, as a result, many advocates of new programs turned to complicated hybrid systems of public-private enterprise to achieve their ends, today known as public authorities.[90] Such hybrid organizations may also partly have resulted from a wider historical trend of intermingling among the public sector, the private sector, and voluntary organizations.[91]

Recent scholarship in APD highlights the extent to which the boundary between public and private was particularly fluid in the early twentieth century. It demonstrates that many advocates of an expansion of functions were willing to "borrow" governing capacity from private companies and civil society if necessary. In this context, groups of organized citizens frequently attempted to persuade elected officials and administrators to expand the scope of government, performing functions that had once been carried out through voluntary associations or private businesses. They often offered their own services to help facilitate expansion, celebrating opportunities for volunteer citizens to lend service and professional expertise to aid in the growth of the state. The result was a sometimes confusing web of governmental, voluntary, and private initiatives. Political sociologist Elisabeth Clemens, highlighting the "indirect" nature of governance in America, characterizes the resulting state as an irrational one, describing it as "fragmented," "indirect," "delegated," "complex," and even "seemingly incomprehensible."[92] In short, such scholarship suggests that while some reformers vocally advocated municipal ownership, others attempting to expand the scope of government promoted a diverse and often unclear array of collaborations among governmental and private institutions, both voluntary and for profit.

The concept of a regulatory state also offered a path to expanding the reach of government. Progressive reformers laid the foundation for the regulatory agencies that would characterize much federal governance in the twentieth century, with administrative agencies designed to manage the economy in the public interest.[93] Moreover, business groups, including the U.S. Chamber of Commerce, often supported the creation of public and private regulatory agencies to establish rules for businesses competition.[94] William Novak highlights the importance of the concept of the public utility and public service corporation to the development of the idea of a regulatory state. He argues that the advent of the railroads—massive in size, scale, and infrastructure—sparked the transformation of various nineteenth-century legal ideas about public interests and public services. This "railroad problem," as it was often called, led to the development of more coherent intellectual and legal theories about the rights of the government to intervene in the economy through the regulation of public service corporations. Massachusetts and later Illinois pioneered centralized and more comprehensive state regulatory commissions that were successful, in part, because the alternative—"the threat of state ownership"— loomed large. Novak concludes, "In many ways, the modern American administrative and regulatory state was built directly on the legal foundation laid by the expanding conception of the essentially public services provided by corporations in the dominant sectors of the American economy: transportation, communications, energy supply, water supply, and the shipping and storage of agricultural products." He adds that the concept of a "public service corporation . . . yielded a new understanding of the relationship of the corporation and democracy in modern American resonances for regulation, administration, legislation, and adjudication to this very day."[95]

Much of this scholarship examines the federal and state levels, and this book contributes with a focus on the local level, specifically the ways that the movement for urban reform contributed to the ascendancy of regulatory models of state building. In the early twentieth century, there was widespread demand for cities to provide residents with more services, from utilities and transportation to public markets and recreation. Debates between proponents of municipal ownership and proponents of improved and expanded regulatory systems provide an example of conflicting views of appropriate models of state development. While the former advocated a form of state building that broke with the past, the latter promoted forms that were more in line with reigning models that relied on public-private partnerships. In their efforts to regulate public service corporations in American cities, they pioneered local- and state-level approaches to regulation. Moreover, as the evidence in this book suggests, the NML's compromise positions on municipal ownership, proportional representation, and direct democracy made this form of state building more likely, as did the work of diverse reformers in promoting the need for "experts in government." Faith in the apolitical expertise of professionals was necessary for the development of a regulatory state. And in the long run, the forms of city manager government promoted by the NML facilitated the election of local business leaders who increasingly favored franchises and limited regulation rather than municipal ownership.

This book also adds a new dimension to our understanding of APD by examining debates about competing forms of state building alongside debates about democratic participation and representation. While earlier studies of institutions often tended to neglect ideas, political scientist

Rogers Smith advocates greater attention to the connections among ideas and institutions in state development. Ideas shaped institutions when organizations and individuals mobilized to achieve specific ends.[96] There was an interplay among ideas, coalitions, and institutions: certain historical contexts sparked the formation of new ideas and goals, which in turn led to the formation of coalitions of individuals who worked to implement these ideas through the creation of new institutions of government and policies. These new creations modified the contexts, which in turn sparked the formation of new ideas, beginning the cycle again.[97]

This wider pattern regarding the interplay among ideas and political institutions applies to the movement for urban reform. At the start of the movement, a variety of contextual factors created a sense of urgency: a belief that existing urban institutions were failing, corrupted by the franchise system and unable to provide services to residents, combined with an equally firm conviction that cities, as a result of unprecedented growth, were essential to the future of American democracy. At this same moment, the NML and other reform organizations emerged and a new generation of political scientists came to believe that it was their duty to become involved in reform and shape political institutions directly. Together, these trends—the beliefs that existing urban institutions were failing, that an expansion of city government was necessary, and that reform organizations and activist political scientists had the potential to unearth solutions to these problems—sparked the formation of the coalitions that created a national movement for urban reform. These coalitions emerged nationally among academics and leading reformers in the NML and locally among diverse political actors. The former took the lead in the creation of the municipal programs and the latter in campaigns for charter reform in hundreds of cities across the country. Together, these were concrete and direct attempts to institutionalize new ideas about democracy. Along the way, ideas, goals, and coalitions shifted and proposed institutions were modified, but the fundamental question remained: What did it mean for city government to be democratic?

1

The Emergence of the Movement for "Good City Government"

Municipal Reform Associations, c. 1880–1900

I n January 1893, *Century Illustrated* magazine, a popular monthly magazine, published "The Cosmopolis City Club," a short story by Washington Gladden, a prominent minister and proponent of the Social Gospel (a movement to apply Christian principles to contemporary social and economic problems). Gladden's story begins with a meeting of five men—a factory owner, a lawyer, a schoolmaster, a carpenter, and a minister—in the public library in the city of Cosmopolis. They have gathered to discuss the prospect of obtaining funds from the city council to purchase books for the library. Reginald Payne, the lawyer, has relayed their request to council president O'Halloran and "Herr Schwab, of the ways and means committee." Reporting back to the group, he says their response is clear: "Millions for boodle, but not one cent for books." Tired of corruption and inefficiency, Sam Hathaway, the carpenter, declares it is time to act and form an "organization of the industrious and respectable people of this city, to secure good government." His friends agree, and they resolve to meet again in two weeks, each bringing ten associates, to form an organization dedicated to "intelligent and well-considered action upon municipal affairs."[1]

When the larger group assembles, they found the Cosmopolis City Club. The Club will not be a municipal party that runs candidates to compete with Democrats and Republicans in city elections, and the organizers agree to require members to sign "a declaration that in municipal affairs party politics should be ignored." They resolve that the Club will be "an educational more than a political association." As Payne explains, they will publicize their discussions and investigations, and, in so doing, "public opinion [will] be created and purified." Such "constant agitation" will "pressure . . . the managers of both parties" and "induce them to give us better candidates."[2] In short, the Club will function as an educator, guiding public participation in municipal affairs by providing citizens with information about local parties and public officials.

The following week, the Cosmopolis City Club holds its first meeting and elects Judge Hamlin president. In his acceptance speech, Hamlin quotes James Bryce's *American Commonwealth*, a well-known text on the political system. In one of the most widely cited passages, Bryce condemned city government as "the one conspicuous failure of the United States." Explaining this failure, Hamlin reminds his listeners that Bryce blamed not "the humbler classes," for they are "generally ready to follow when . . . patriotically led," but rather "the upper classes," whose "apathy and shortsightedness" prevent them from leading as they should. Hamlin wholeheartedly agrees. Corruption and inefficiency exist in cities because "the natural leaders of society"—the "educated men, the professional men, the active businessmen of our cities"—neglect their duty to lead. Working through the Club, Hamlin and his associates plan to fulfill their duty. Hamlin believes that their efforts will stimulate public interest and create popular demand for better city government.[3]

In cities across the country, urban residents formed dozens of similar groups in the 1890s, claiming, as the men in Gladden's story do, that they were fed up with inefficiency and corruption. In Norwalk, Connecticut, the founders of the Citizens' League declared that they came together to combat the growing influence of saloons in city politics, while the organizers of the Civic Federation of Galesburg, Illinois, claimed that they united after a "vicious element" stole an election to gain control of the city government in order to open a race track. Urban residents claimed to have organized municipal reform associations in response to local instances of electoral fraud and crooked and inept government.[4] Indeed, most accounts of the establishment of such associations leave the impression that local factors alone instigated their creation.

Yet the timing of their formation and the similarities of their structures and goals suggest otherwise. Electoral fraud and corruption did not suddenly, dramatically, and uniformly rise in cities across the country in the late 1880s and early 1890s. What was new, however, was the perception that something needed to and could be done to eliminate these problems. Civil service reform, challenges to the partisan press, and the rise of interest groups converged to weaken political parties across the nation.[5] At the same time, reformers increasingly viewed corruption in urban parties as entrenched rather than temporary and decided to form permanent organizations of their own to challenge parties as the leaders of public opinion in city matters. In their attempts to assert leadership, they faced competition not only from parties but also from citywide unions and business groups. Municipal reformers, however, did not only form local organizations to compete with local parties, business groups, and unions. Communicating through personal networks and reform-oriented newspapers and magazines, they came to know about the actions of peer groups in other cities. To learn from each other and to achieve wider influence and power, local reform groups joined together in larger federations, most notably the National Municipal League (NML).

In forming federations, municipal reform leagues helped to create a national movement for urban reform. Throughout American history, diverse membership associations seeking political power formed national or regional federations, paralleling the structure of the federal government and thereby underscoring the close interplay between civil society and state development.[6] During the Progressive Era, national federations devoted to single issues would become one of the most popular models of reform.[7] One of the forerunners of this type of organization, the National Civil Service Reform League (NCSRL), played an influential role in the formation of the NML, creating a model that municipal reformers emulated as they worked to form local, regional, and national networks. Through these networks, such organizations not only drew attention to problems cities were facing. They also facilitated the nationalization of municipal reform by bringing together individuals from across the country to discuss mutual concerns and experiences and form alliances. While they certainly recognized a level of diversity given the unique nature of specific local concerns, their decision to form translocal groups reflected their belief that cities were facing shared problems that had shared solutions. The result was a transformation in the ways that many Americans conceived of city government and local democracy, making it a national rather than local concern.

Previous studies of urban politics in these years provide a foundation to help us understand changing views of the appropriate roles of civic associations and voters in cities. Historian Robert Burnham notes that most early municipal reformers were native, Protestant businessmen and professionals. They tended to view cities as organic entities, composed of interdependent but inherently unequal groups.[8] The account in Gladden's story clearly echoes Burnham's characterization of reformers, marked by classism, nativism, and a sense of duty to the wider community. At the same time, historians Phillip Ethington and James Connolly both identify the seeds of what would later become pluralist conceptions of politics in cities of this time period. Champions of mid-twentieth-century pluralism later celebrated competing interests of diverse groups in the political sphere, rejecting the notion of any singular public good. In contrast, Ethington and Connolly note that earlier proponents of nascent forms of pluralism recognized the existence of diverse groups but still hoped to unite them in support of some form of unified public good.[9] Additionally, focusing specifically on the question of public discussion, historian Kevin Mattson argues that while some Progressives envisioned popular participation as the public approving of ideas determined by elite reformers, others advocated "democratic publics" in which all citizens came together to discuss mutual problems, deliberate, and educate each other.[10] Together, these studies help us to see this period as a transitional one marked by intense interest in forms of public participation in urban affairs.

This chapter builds on these insights in the context of a careful examination and comparison of the earliest municipal leagues. In doing so, it helps us to begin to understand what united coalitions and where divisions existed, even in these earliest years, and, as a result, the ideological and institutional foundations for the national movement for urban reform. The decisions to form both local and national municipal leagues were in part inspired by a set of convictions shared among many reformers. While their views varied in important ways, most of these men (and sometimes women) believed that democracy required more than simply voting in elections. Founders created municipal reform associations as institutions through which they could realize their idealized conception of leadership and popular participation in a democratic system. Almost all reformers, regardless of whether they espoused more elitist or inclusionary ideals, believed that the organizations they founded locally and nationally had the potential to function as mediums through which members could challenge the hold of parties on urban politics and create alternative ways to shape public opinion on matters pertaining to the governments of their cities.

Yet they soon discovered that even members of a single organization often disagreed. From the start, notable divisions emerged regarding the questions of who should be included in public discussions and the appropriate role of municipal associations. In one model, they functioned as venues to bring together diverse urban residents, including different classes and ethnicities and sometimes even races and genders, to discuss shared problems and jointly determine solutions. In another, they were vehicles for members of an elite "active class" to lead the masses in the formation of appropriate public opinion. Yet despite the presence of such divisions, almost everyone still adhered to the notion that a degree of consensus would result from some form of discussion and deliberation. In this context, leaders of reform groups, locally and nationally, began to search for ways to maintain coalitions, allowing for diversity of opinion on some matters while at the same time maintaining the need for consensus on others. The crucial questions were what matters would yield consensus and how they would achieve it.

The Origins, Spread, and Structures of Municipal Reform Associations

From the end of the Civil War through the early 1880s, when dissatisfied citizens came together to reform city government, they did so most often by organizing temporary committees. Only a tiny segment of residents participated in these committees, which were largely composed of elite businessmen and professionals. They typically emerged in response to exposures of corruption by the press, focusing on removing those culpable from public office and, in some cases, prosecuting them in the courts. After achieving these goals, the committees then dissolved until a new scandal surfaced. In Philadelphia, critics organized a Committee of Fifty-Eight, a

Committee of Sixty-Two, and a Committee of One Hundred in a period of less than twenty years. In perhaps the most well-known case, in 1871 outraged New Yorkers responded to revelations in the *New York Times* of the widespread theft of city funds by Boss William Tweed and Tammany Hall by forming the Committee of Seventy. After the Committee of Seventy brought down Tammany Hall, the most infamous ring in the country, its members disbanded. Thereafter, reformers in New York and elsewhere tended to form ad hoc committees during the municipal campaign season, disbanding after elections. These committees focused on exposing abuses and fraud by candidates and officeholders but did not develop positive programs of their own.[11]

This style of activism reflected a conception of politics that held that corruption resulted from the actions of a few dishonorable individuals rather than from larger, systemic problems. In the 1860s and 1870s, as scandal after scandal erupted in both parties, reformers described the groups responsible as "rings." A ring was a group of corrupt individuals who subverted the political system for personal gain at the expense of the public good. In contrast to *ring*, the term *machine*, which emerged in the late 1870s, suggested a highly organized branch of a party, usually in an urban area, controlled by self-interested, professional politicians. Although critics exaggerated their power and effectiveness, both the Democratic and the Republican Parties developed more elaborate structures after the Civil War. Machine imagery also relied on conceptions of social class, with bosses dominating easily manipulated masses of working-class voters.[12]

As the imagery of the ring gave way to that of the machine, so too did the temporary committee give way to the more permanent reform association. Municipal reformers, increasingly perceiving urban parties as tightly controlled machines, decided to fight such organizations with comparable organizations of their own. Initial attempts to form enduring reform groups began by the early 1880s. In one notable effort, Theodore Roosevelt, then a New York State assemblyman, organized the City Reform Club in 1882 to fight Tammany Hall, whose defeat at the hands of the Committee of Seventy had proved temporary.[13] As he later explained in "Machine Politics in New York City," an article published in *Century* magazine, without "steady work and much attention to detail," the "ordinary people" would "always be beaten by the organized army of politicians." He ridiculed those who refused to create formal reform associations because they believed instead that a "spontaneous uprising" of the people would defeat machines.[14] Gustav Schwab, a founding member of the German-American Reform Union, agreed, declaring, "Without organization, experience has taught us, we shall be powerless against our well disciplined opponents."[15]

By the late 1880s, one of the most readily available models of successful political organization was the movement for civil service reform, spearheaded by the NCSRL. The NCSRL united civil service reform associations across the country. Together, they combined forces and waged an educational campaign to garner mass support for the replacement of the patronage system with one based on merit and competitive exams. After several abortive beginnings in the 1870s, opponents of the spoils system formed the New York Civil Service Reform Association in 1880. This association inspired the formation of similar groups in over a dozen cities within less than a year. From its inception, the New York Association encouraged the establishment of "affiliated societies," hoping to coordinate efforts of local organizations and form a national movement. In 1881, working in conjunction with groups in Boston and Cambridge, Massachusetts, the New York Association organized and publicized a conference that brought together thirteen groups to form the NCSRL.[16] The NCSRL, according to a founding resolution, would serve "as a centre of correspondence" and facilitate "such united action as circumstances may demand."[17]

Several widely publicized successes on the federal and later state levels made civil service reform a well-known example of effective activism. The NCSRL was instrumental in the passage of the landmark Pendleton Act and subsequent state and national legislation through direct lobbying and publicity campaigns. According to an article in the New York Times, "The movement is designed not only to represent to the President the views of the associations regarding civil service, but particularly to impress the public with the nature and importance of this reform."[18] Leaders and members worked to foster massive public support to compel elected officials to pass favorable legislation. The assassination of President James Garfield at the hands of a disaffected office seeker provided just the propaganda tool they needed. They distributed pamphlets, wrote letters to candidates, offered prizes for essays, organized public addresses, and sent representatives to speak before congressional committees.[19] At every step, they made sure that newspapers printed articles detailing their work.[20] In the end, they achieved their goal of garnering public support for their cause in order to pressure politicians to reform the patronage system. Congressmen from districts with branches of the NCSRL were overwhelmingly more likely to vote for the Pendleton Act than those from districts without them.[21]

In short, these two perspectives—that urban parties were becoming highly organized machines and that the NCSRL and its affiliates were instrumental in the advancement of civil service reform—converged by the late 1880s to inspire the formation of a new style of municipal reform association. These factors were not the only reasons for the rising interest in city government, but they were central to why this interest took the form that it did.

Municipal reform associations spread rapidly in the 1890s. In 1895, in the first national study of municipal reform movements, William Tolman provided detailed information on over fifty local organizations.[22] Five years later, a leading authority on the subject declared that the number of organizations had quadrupled to approximately two hundred.[23] This explosion of local groups can only be understood fully when placed in the context of the larger history of voluntary associations in American history. The founders of most civic groups did not work in isolation, creating completely novel organizations. Rather, organizers of new groups built on familiar models of action.[24] The creators of municipal associations, aware of events transpiring in other cities, were no exception. Early reform groups were publicized in newspapers and popular monthly magazines, and they spread through personal contacts and networks. The result was that these groups, formed as part of a rising national interest in city government, shared similar languages, organizational structures, tactics, understandings of city politics, and goals.

The founding of the City Club of New York provides an example of a wider pattern. As noted, in the 1880s Tammany Hall regained control of city hall, and early efforts at organized opposition (such as Roosevelt's City Reform Club) never attracted large followings, remaining largely ineffectual. The founders of the City Club were determined to accomplish more, launching an aggressive membership campaign in 1892 that attracted over 650 prominent New Yorkers within months, drawing the attention of the press.[25] Many believed that one of the reasons machines were so successful was that they were social clubs as well as political associations, providing places for members to spend leisure time. As such, the City

Club was partly a social club, maintaining a clubhouse that included so-cial spaces as well as a library, reading room, and publication office. It was also intended to serve an educational purpose and provide a meeting space for members of various types of reform groups.[26] According to the articles of incorporation, the City Club provided a place to meet and exchange views for those who believed in "honesty and efficiency in the adminis-tration of city affairs," "in severing municipal from National politics," and "in procuring the election of fit persons to city offices."[27] Like civil service reformers a decade earlier, the organizers hoped that by bringing together reformers from different groups, they could educate each other and the public and garner support for their cause.

The City Club also encouraged the formation of like-minded associations and worked to unite such groups in federations. The Committee on Coop-eration with Affiliated Organizations was one of the most active in the City Club, and despite some internal disagreements, it took the lead in promot-ing the formation of a network of district-based good government clubs throughout the city to attract a wider base of support. Like the City Club, the good government clubs were founded on broad principles of nonparti-sanship and honest and efficient city government. Unlike the City Club, they were directly involved in electoral politics. While these good govern-ment clubs got off to a slow start, their successes in pressuring both parties to nominate more acceptable candidates in the fall elections attracted much attention. In 1894, the City Club organized the four existing clubs into the Confederated Council of Good Government Clubs, and by 1895, there were over twenty clubs with over ten thousand members total.[28] The City Club also initiated the creation of the Municipal League of the State of New York, a federation of nonpartisan organizations in cities throughout the state.[29] In working to combine the efforts of reform groups, the City Club's leaders hoped to achieve wider influence and power.

The influence of the City Club and good government clubs spread be-yond New York, illustrating a process by which dissatisfied residents in di-verse cities decided to form municipal reform associations. Through cov-erage in local newspapers and national magazines, citizens learned about the activities of reform groups in other urban areas, particularly in larger cities such as New York. In the summer of 1892, the *Chicago Daily Tribune*, in an article detailing the founding and structure of the City Club of New York, praised the Club, adding that there was an "urgent need for just such an organization . . . in Chicago." Writers at *Century Illustrated* magazine agreed that the City Club should be emulated "in all other large cities of the land."[30]

Personal networks also played an important role in the spread of the club model, as in Syracuse, where the Municipal Reform Club was founded in response to a direct appeal from the City Club for support for pending legislation pertaining to New York City in the state legislature. Personal networks may even have spread this model as far as Berkeley, California. According to Tolman's 1895 study, in Berkeley, "two or three recent comers from the Eastern States who were in touch with the movements for municipal reform there" met with local residents, who had previously viewed the state of municipal affairs as "hopeless," and founded the Good Government Club of Berkeley.[31]

Tolman's study provides further evidence that the club model originating in New York influenced the formation of early groups. Tolman was the secretary of the City Vigilance League of New York, an organization founded in 1892 to expose corruption among public officials that soon expanded its purpose to include wider studies of the social, economic, and political conditions in cities.[32] His *Municipal Reform Movements in the United States* was a national survey of fifty-six reform organizations. According to Tolman, the book aimed "to bring together, for comparison and selection, the salient and essential points of all the reform movements" so that those forming organizations in new cities could benefit from "the successful experience of other communities." The evidence presented suggested that this had already begun to happen. Most of the organizations were founded within a few years of each other, and their structures were similar.[33]

These structures demonstrated the desire to unite individuals and organizations in order to become powerful and enduring forces in urban politics. Of the fifty-six, only four went by the transitory name "committee of . . . ," most of the rest choosing to call themselves "city clubs," "municipal leagues," or "citizens' associations." The vast majority were governed by executive committees that appointed departments or standing committees to undertake the real work of the organizations. While most of the secretaries were volunteers, a few were paid professionals. Several of the groups worked to form wider networks, often organizing clubs on the ward level, much as the Confederated Council of Good Government Clubs did in New York. The Civic Federation of Chicago, for example, attempted to coordinate the efforts of a variety of civic organizations, and it likely inspired the organization of the Civic Federations of Galesburg, Illinois, and Detroit, Michigan.[34] In short, by the 1890s the municipal association was becoming a well-known model for dissatisfied reformers.

Competition for Leadership: Labor Unions, Commercial Bodies, and Rising Opposition to Parties

The expansion of central labor unions (CLUs), federations of local, mostly craft-based unions in cities, was somewhat analogous to the spread of municipal reform associations, particularly in terms of the emphasis placed on the value of organization. Gladden, in his fictitious account of the founding of the Cosmopolis City Club, actually claims that urban reformers learned the power and value of organization from unions.[35] Much as urban reformers claimed to have formed associations to combat increasingly organized partisan machines, CLUs maintained they needed to unite "to combat the ever growing encroachments of organized and consolidated Capital." In their constitutions and bylaws, most CLUs declared the importance of "organizing and concentrating" the efforts of individual unions and the working class more broadly.[36] Previously, individual unions joined together in committees, forming temporary coalitions to achieve specific goals. By the 1880s, however, these unions began to form more permanent federations and establish CLUs. Across the country, CLUs shared similar structures, typically consisting of five to ten elected officers and several standing committees. In some cases, representatives of CLUs joined together in state conferences, and by the end of the century, CLUs from seventy-nine cities had affiliated with the American Federation of Labor.[37] Union leaders, in forming CLUs, were following a similar path to organization in an effort to assert power.

In contrast, local commercial bodies lagged behind unions in forming regional, state, and national alliances. Though a national Board of Trade was organized in roughly 1870, it appears not to have been flourishing by the turn of the century, with only fifty members sending delegates to a national convention in 1903. In the new century, chambers of commerce increasingly replaced boards of trade as the primary business organizations in most cities. Chambers of commerce in larger cities began to attract national attention, with chambers in smaller towns looking to them for advice and emulating their activities. Many groups initiated contact with counterparts in neighboring cities and formed regional alliances, but it was not until 1912 that the Chamber of Commerce of the United States was founded.[38]

Even before the formation of this national organization, local commercial bodies asserted their right to lead in urban politics, becoming increasingly organized and enduring features in city life. Commercial bodies and CLUs justified claims to leadership in similar ways, claiming to be apolitical and uniquely suited to represent "the public" in matters pertaining to city politics.[39]

They also shared another key similarity: both advocated an expansion of municipal functions. Many CLUs included statements in support of a variety of reforms in their platforms, most often favoring public ownership of utilities.[40] Union leaders argued that public ownership of utilities and transportation would benefit both consumers (urban residents) and workers (public servants).[41] Similarly, as commercial groups undertook campaigns to attract outside investors to develop local infrastructure and facilitate economic development, they became deeply involved in the affairs of city government.[42] Commercial groups looked to municipalities to provide improved streets, sanitation, sewerage, water supplies, and harbor improvements. If they found local officials unwilling or unable to provide these amenities, organized groups of business leaders became involved in urban politics.[43]

In attempting to shape legislation and influence the actions of elected officials, CLUs and commercial bodies were experimenting with new forms of political activism. By the end of the nineteenth century, a variety of groups that felt frustrated and marginalized by mainstream party politics experimented with a form of organization once associated only with corrupt corporate interests: lobbying. Farmers, workers, and various women's groups pioneered lobbying and, in so doing, contributed to the legitimization of direct involvement in the policy process and to the birth of a new understanding of politics in which plural interests were a vital component of the democratic process rather than a perversion of the public good.[44]

In cities, unions embraced this form of group politics more openly than commercial groups and municipal associations. Yet although CLUs functioned primarily as unions, dedicated to collective bargaining and the advancement of workers' interests, their officers also aspired to broader leadership roles in their communities. Embracing a pluralist conception of politics, they openly worked to represent the interests of the working class as a distinctive group. While urban reformers often spoke of the need to direct public opinion as society's natural leaders, CLU officials spoke of the need "to mold public opinion in favor of Labor."[45] At the same time, leaders confidently asserted that their organizations were dedicated to the broader "public welfare" of their communities.[46]

Commercial bodies also declared themselves nonpartisan, claiming to speak for the welfare of entire cities. Their leaders and members tended to view themselves as uniquely suited to take the lead in city government. They presented their participation in city affairs as not merely beneficial to commercial interests, claiming that what was good for business was good for the entire community. One leader in the Cleveland Chamber of Commerce described recent efforts to achieve a more "progressive administration of affairs" in "the city's business" in these terms. He claimed that "businessmen" were "united in laboring for public benefits" and devoted to "the general welfare."[47] Frederic Howe, an active figure in reform circles, later described the Cleveland Chamber of Commerce in this light, commending its "non-political" yet "public" work to educate the community regarding "city affairs" and "civic obligation."[48]

Much like leaders of chambers of commerce and unions, the individuals who formed municipal associations experimented with new models of political activism, challenging parties and asserting leadership in urban politics. In municipal associations, while most reformers did not speak in pluralist terms in the 1890s, they embraced a model of political activism that celebrated the power of organized groups to shape the direction of politics without involvement in the Republican or Democratic Party. Disgusted with the actions of parties in city affairs, they felt marginalized from the major available institutional form of political participation. As such, if they wanted to affect the course of city government, they needed to organize alternative paths of leverage.[49]

In explaining their primary objectives, the organizers of most municipal associations claimed that they intended simply "to promote honest, efficient, and economical government."[50] Such statements, of course, implied that existing city government was the opposite—dishonest, inefficient, and wasteful. Accordingly, many groups began with efforts to uncover the root of these problems, operating as self-appointed watchdogs. This form of activism was popular before the 1890s, but it remained central to many organizations at the close of the century. In one example, the Citizens' Association of Chicago organized as a watchdog in 1874 and continued in this vein as late as 1893, declaring the need to keep "*the public advised* at all times of attempts to infringe their rights."[51] Newer groups formed in the 1890s also worked as investigatory agencies. Some, such as Saint Louis's Committee of Public Safety, focused on electoral fraud, scrutinizing allegations of irregularities in local elections. Another focus was abuses of power by elected officials. The *Nation* reported that the "true mission" of the City Club of New York was "the exposure of public abuses and the prosecution of official violators of the law."[52]

Most members of newer groups, however, felt mere exposure was not sufficient to bring about the changes they desired. In the past, reformers had believed that if they simply informed the public of transgressions, voters would respond by electing better candidates into office who would, in turn, create honest, efficient, and economical government. And so, often paralleling the decision to create more permanent organizations rather than temporary committees, many reformers also decided that they needed to offer constructive suggestions to improve city government rather than simply highlighting the shortcomings of the status quo. The question that remained was how they proposed to do so. These municipal reform associations were not law and order leagues, also popular in the 1890s, which were dedicated to ensuring the enforcement of the law, sometimes working with local officials but more often organizing their own investigations and raids. They also were not charitable or philanthropic bodies devoted to urban social reform, although many of their members were involved in such work. Urban reformers created distinct associations because they believed that there was a need for organizations exclusively dedicated to offering positive programs to improve city government.

For almost all municipal associations, the first step was the removal of parties from city affairs. Antiparty sentiment had existed in the United States since the early 1800s, playing on fears that corrupt "interests" would harm the republic. In the years after the Civil War, parties were powerful, dominating every level of government. At the same time, revelations of corruption in the Gilded Age sparked a new wave of antipartisanship.[53] As urban reformers' goals expanded beyond the exposure of corrupt individuals, they came to hold a larger, systemic problem accountable: the involvement of national and state parties in local politics. By the late 1880s, calls to separate local from state and national elections began to appear in the press, and by the early 1890s, the belief that parties had no place in local elections became popular in reform circles.[54] Clinton Rogers Woodruff of the Philadelphia Municipal League believed that despite their diversity in "form and methods," all organizations agreed that the first requirement for "true and permanent reform" was "the separation of state and national parties from municipal affairs, and the elimination of partisanship from municipal business."[55]

The aim of reformers—to unite urban voters across party lines—was based on an understanding of city government as apolitical, as a matter of administrative efficiency devoid of substantive divisions. Moorfield Storey, a prominent lawyer from Boston who would later become the vice president of the New England Anti-Imperialist League and the first president of the National Association for the Advancement of Colored People, articulated this rationale. He claimed that "the issues of national politics" were "entirely outside the questions" of city government. All "honest men" agreed on the need for "clean streets, good sewers, efficient police, a good fire department, the proper regulation of street railways, and other like questions." He believed that the presence of parties in local elections allowed party "henchmen" to create artificial divisions among voters in order to acquire the spoils of city government.[56]

This rejection of a legitimate role for parties in local politics begins to explain the strong ideological connection between urban reform and civil service reform. Most urban and civil service reformers shared a common aversion to the spoils system, claiming that it did not create popular accountability in the administration of government, as supporters maintained, but rather the corruption of party politics and a bureaucracy composed of inefficient and inept public servants. As a result, a central goal of many municipal reform associations was the establishment of a civil service system in city administration.[57] In Milwaukee, the Municipal League, when it formed in 1893, immediately commenced a campaign to expand the civil service system beyond the police and fire departments. In the face of great opposition from "the agents of machine in both parties," according to its president, their civil service bill died in a committee of the

Common Council.[58] This type of defeat solidified the desire to eradicate political parties from local politics by establishing nonpartisan elections. To do so—to marshal the power necessary to challenge such entrenched organizations, with ties to state and national parties—the leaders of local municipal reform associations decided to join forces and form a national alliance.

The Formation, Goals, and Tactics of the Early National Municipal League

Leaders of local reform associations decided to form the NML to achieve wider influence and power. Local parties had ties to state and national party organizations that provided resources far beyond the reach of a single, unattached local reform association. In much of American history, political institutions have favored groups and movements that coordinate endeavors at different levels of government.[59] Urban reformers aspired to this type of coordination. They emulated the NCSRL's federated model and founded the NML in 1894. In that year, the City Club of New York and the Municipal League of Philadelphia organized the National Conference for Good City Government in Philadelphia, where delegates of local organizations and other "invited guests" presented and discussed papers on the conditions of their home cities. Reformers agreed on the need to remove state and national parties from local elections and to stimulate public interest in city affairs. They also agreed on the need to coordinate local efforts through some sort of permanent national association.[60] Those who attended resolved to take the lead and organized the NML as a federation of local groups.[61]

The support of the NCSRL was evident through the active involvement of leading civil service reformers.[62] Soon after the passage of the Pendleton Act, which applied only to the federal administration, civil service reformers had turned their attention to dismantling the spoils system in states and municipalities.[63] As a result, the names of top civil service reformers were prominent among the one hundred leading reformers who officially endorsed the Philadelphia Municipal League's formal call for the First National Conference for Good City Government.[64] A history of the NCSRL in 1929 listed seven men as the key leaders of the civil service movement: George William Curtis, Dorman Eaton, Carl Schurz, Everett Wheeler, Charles Bonaparte, Richard Henry Dana, and William Dudley Foulke.[65] These men—lawyers, prolific authors, and reformers—were from the Northeast and active on behalf of a variety of causes. All except Curtis, who had died in 1892, signed the call for the conference and were actively involved in urban reform. Two were influential leaders in both the NCSRL and the NML. Bonaparte, great-nephew of Emperor Napoleon Bonaparte and lawyer from Baltimore, organized the Civil Service Reform Association of Maryland in 1881 and was one of the original founders of the NCSRL. He went on to serve on several committees and as chair of the council from 1901 to 1905. He was also a prominent early leader of the NML, chairing the executive committee from 1894 to 1903 and then serving as president from 1903 to 1910.[66]

Not only did many individual civil service reformers play a leading role in urban reform, but the NCSRL as an organization also provided direct aid to the NML in the early years.[67] In the 1890s, the NCSRL printed circulars soliciting new members for the NML and detailed reports of its conference for "Good City Government" in the pages of its own official journal, *Good Government*.[68] Representatives of the NCSRL also frequented NML's annual conference. In 1894, President Carl Schurz presented a paper titled "The Relation of Civil Service Reform to Municipal Reform," and Secretary William Potts offered a toast entitled "Civil Service Reform in City Government."[69] Over the years, the two organizations continued to support each other's work, collaborating on several joint committees on administrative topics.[70]

Not surprisingly, these two groups with shared memberships and resources often espoused similar views, regarding not only parties and patronage but also the roles of leaders, civic organizations, and public opinion in democracy. The campaigns spearheaded by the NCSRL, as noted, were founded on the conviction that the active work of a small segment of citizen leaders, united in reform organizations, had the power to educate and arouse public opinion to change political institutions. This model informed the efforts of many urban reformers. Yet reform circles were expanding in the 1890s, bringing together diverse individuals locally in cities and nationally at the NML's meetings. While they all attempted to assert some form of leadership, the meaning of leadership and their understanding of the role of public opinion in political processes varied widely. Some were committed to a vision of politics based on consensus, while others began to discuss groups as having legitimate, diverse, and sometimes competing interests. Some welcomed all Americans to participate in political debates, while others envisioned a more deferential role for most Americans, elevating their own role as natural leaders. Yet these divisions were often unclear, with members of the same groups and often individuals themselves articulating views that today we might find contradictory.

Most late nineteenth-century Americans agreed that in a democracy, public opinion ruled, but they did not agree on how that opinion was—or should be—formed. Some reformers, including Gladden, portrayed public opinion, good or bad, as the mere sum of individual opinions.[71] Others disagreed, arguing that some citizens played a larger role than others in the formation of public opinion. In *The American Commonwealth*, Bryce wrote that public "opinion does not merely grow; it is also made." For Bryce, while most Americans, busy with other concerns, only held "passive" views on public matters, "there is also the active class, who occupy themselves primarily with public affairs, who aspire to create and lead opinion."[72]

The founders of municipal associations tended to view themselves as members of this "active class." From their perspective, civic leaders like them, working through reform groups, were best suited to direct popular participation in city politics. Over and over, leaders of local associations officially declared their intention to foster public sentiment in line with their own views of good government. As the leaders of the Good Government Club of Berkeley explained, they aspired not only "to keep before our citizens the necessity of their interest in public affairs" but also "to discuss and shape public opinion upon all the questions which relate to the proper government of Berkeley."[73] Similarly, the leaders of the Civic Federation of Detroit planned to "shape public opinion on all questions relating to the municipal government."[74] The Citizens' Association of Albany hoped "to mold public sentiment from chaotic clamor into well-defined purposes of redress."[75] These groups and many others understood it to be both the right and the duty of reformers to instruct and organize the public as to proper courses of action.

On one level, these views were elitist, for though reformers believed in the power of public opinion in a democratic polity, theirs was a public opinion led by elites. Yet the depth of this elitism varied, even among leaders of a single organization. In one example, Edmond Kelly, an influential founder of the City Club of New York, expressed his hope that the affiliated good government clubs would welcome "men in every degree of wealth or poverty." In the same years, James Carter, president of the City Club, critiqued the "extreme development and application of the principle of democratic government" that allowed "ignorant and unthinking multitudes of different nationalities" to vote.[76] In a seeming paradox, one leader of the City Club welcomed members of the working class while another espoused classist and nativist views to justify franchise restrictions.

While some reformers envisioned the wider public as having a deferential role, others hoped to make their organizations more inclusive, to use them to bring together diverse urban residents in the name of better government. According to the president of the Milwaukee Municipal League, leagues should work "to protect and reinforce the true bond of popular fellowship and sympathy, by uniting as many as possible of all political faiths in the work; all reputable men who will subscribe a satisfactory pledge."[77] In this ideal, municipal reform associations functioned as venues where representatives of all groups came together as equals. This ideal was shared by other Progressive reformers who founded a variety of civic groups and public forms to create democratic public spaces.[78] In this context, some reform groups presented an alternative, more participatory understanding of civic associations as facilitating open discussion and communication.

The goal of inclusiveness was so integral to some that they described their organizations as "federations" to underscore the message that they were to be coalitions of diverse groups of urban residents and interests.[79] The Civic Federation of Chicago, founded in 1893, was the most well-known such group, serving as a model for similar federations in other cities, particularly in the Midwest.[80] Those who initiated the federation, including businessmen, female activists, labor leaders, and social workers, hoped that it would serve as a vehicle for improving not only city government but also urban life and intergroup relations more generally by facilitating communication and cooperation among Chicago's diverse residents.[81] They created an intricate, multilayered organization intended to represent as many groups in the city as possible, broken down into an executive committee of sixteen, a central council of one hundred divided into several standing committees, and thirty-four ward councils with subcommittees of their own.[82] In describing the federation to an audience at an NML convention, sociologist Albion Small of the University of Chicago argued that in combining groups that varied "greatly in specific purpose," the Federation recognized that only by coordinating activities could they "make up the total of successful municipal action."[83] In this model, the role of a civic federation was not to lead public opinion but to facilitate its formation by bringing people together to discuss mutual concerns.

In the NML's earliest years, many of its members and leaders presented its work in a similar light. Despite their clear support for nonpartisan local elections, leaders claimed that it simply provided a permanent venue for reformers from across the country to gather and exchange ideas. Their yearly Conference for Good City Government was integral to this mission.[84] The *New York Times* reported that the reformers meeting at the First National Conference for Good City Government in Philadelphia had decided to form a "permanent agency" to continue "the comparison of views, the exchange of experiences, and the discussion of methods." Within months they formed the NML.[85] In the years that followed, even though many individuals advocated nonpartisanship in their speeches, over half the papers at the NML conference were presented as reports on the "municipal conditions" of various locales, continuing the work of providing attendees with information about circumstances and events in other cities.[86] The introduction to the published proceedings of its fourth conference reminded readers that the NML sought only "to promote the free and full discussion of the difficult problem of municipal government, wisely avoiding any *ex-cathedra* utterances concerning questions upon which the best minds may, perhaps, differ."[87]

The organization's leaders also understood the NML to be a vehicle for raising awareness, intending their yearly conference to draw attention to the problems city government faced and remind urban residents of their civic duties. At the First National Conference for Good City Government, George Burnham Jr., president of the Municipal League of Philadelphia, said that reform was not possible without "an awakening of the public conscience" that would cause citizens to devote "serious attention to their political duties," while Carter celebrated the conference as just such a mark of "a rising tide of civic patriotism."[88] Indeed, the NML's leaders publicized the conference in the following months in these terms. The printed proceedings hailed the conference as "successful from every point of view," claiming that it had "awakened renewed interest" in urban reform, rousing "from apathy and indifference" those not previously involved and intensifying "the zeal of those already engaged in the work."[89]

Education was a central component of the NML's efforts. The leadership hoped to instruct members in how to proceed as reformers and serve their communities as leaders. Writers for the *Nation* described one conference of the NML as "invaluable," commending it for bringing together a certain "class of people" to discuss "the best means of bringing influence to bear on the voters in favor of better city government."[90] Woodruff, who became secretary of the NML in 1894, celebrated its role in "educating the active workers in new fields." The NML's constitution made this point even more clearly, highlighting the need "to multiply the numbers, harmonize the methods and combine the forces" of all who desired "united action and organization" in the name of good government.[91] In short, organizers hoped the NML's conference would bring together leaders of reform associations from different cities and then unify them in a national movement by discerning the best tactics for use on the local level.

While national leaders sought to instruct local leaders, local leaders sought to educate urban residents. At the Second National Conference for Good City Government, in 1894, Herbert Welsh, the son of a banker from Philadelphia who devoted his life to various reform movements, explained that the first task of "effective Municipal Leagues or associated Good Government Clubs" was "educational." Such education required that "the community . . . be instructed systematically and continuously—not spasmodically—by speakers, by pamphlets, through the columns of the press, by personal conversation, [and] by parlor meetings" regarding "the general needs of the city."[92] The Milwaukee Municipal League embodied this style of activism, for, according to its president, it began its efforts to expand the local civil service with a "period of education," of "agitation spent . . . issuing pamphlets and holding public meetings."[93] The Milwaukee League, like many of its counterparts across the country, worked to circumvent the party system and create a new style of political organization in which reformers garnered the pressure of public opinion through mass meetings, petitions, and the mobilization of the press.[94]

Although municipal reform associations were predominantly male, most of their members viewed women as powerful allies in their educational aspirations. As women were excluded from elections, their political activism relied on direct appeals to the public, often in the name of

expert research and investigation.[95] Many male and female organizations would later develop divergent goals.[96] In these early years, however, many men and women were united in a shared discontent with the
role of parties in city government. Women were a small but visible presence at the conferences of the NML, and every year the program included
a speech on the "woman's standpoint." These speakers claimed that
while men and women shared the same commitment to awakening a
deeper sense of civic duty, women were especially suited to educational
work because, without the right to vote, they were not tied to parties and
could act as "disinterested" citizens. The speakers also referred to city
government as a matter of "municipal housekeeping," a common expression that suggested that the primary task of cities and homes alike
was to create clean and safe environments.[97] This model presented city
government as apolitical and therefore not a legitimate subject of partisan contestation and political debate.

Women's municipal reform associations tended to emphasize the importance of education even more so than their male or gender-integrated
counterparts. Not only were women's groups particularly interested in city
government as it pertained to public schools, they also stressed the importance of the educational functions of their organizations. According to
Cornelia Frothingham, secretary of the women's Civic Club of Philadelphia,
"We women believe that serious permanent results can only be obtained
through *education*. And acting upon this belief, we intend to devote our-
selves to the collecting of such facts as bear upon the development of disinterested citizenship." The women's Civic League of New York agreed, declaring the "examination into the aims and functions of the city
government," "the gathering of intelligent reports," and "the suggestions
of schemes of improvement" to be among its central objects.[98]

With an emphasis on gathering "facts" and conducting "examinations,"
this educational style of political action paralleled the emergence of the
social sciences, together marking new ways of thinking about knowledge
and inquiry. Academic investigation increasingly was based on the premise that truth resulted from a process of real-world inquiry rather than one
of reasoning from theoretical abstractions. Yet while some scholars were
moving toward a pragmatic understanding of all truths as contextual,
most still believed that inquiry and discussion would yield consensus.[99] In
the realm of urban reform, although some characterized investigation as

an open-ended process, most believed that it would reveal a single truth that reformers would then convey to the public.[100] Groups such as the Municipal Club of Decatur, Illinois, and the Municipal League of Grand Rapids, Michigan, both declared their intent "to make a thorough and scientific investigation of the correct principles of local self-government . . . and to collect and publish all appropriate information on the defects and needs of our city government."[101] To accomplish this, many organizations even hired "experts" to conduct their investigations.[102] These investigations usually resulted in the "discovery" that the elimination of parties would eradicate corruption, and such findings were usually followed by concerted campaigns to educate the public about this fact.[103] Most reformers were open to exploring divergent views, believing that they needed to study real politics in order to discover solutions to the challenges city government was facing. But their willingness to listen and undertake investigations was still predicated on the notion that their efforts would unearth a singular solution on which all would agree.

Despite claims that the NML's purpose was simply to bring together urban reformers to share their experiences, it was clear from the start that yearly meetings were intended to do more than encourage dialogue and coordinate tactics. The NML's official stance of objectivity must be viewed alongside the conviction that reformers had already demonstrated the universal need for nonpartisan local elections. From this perspective, parties could play no legitimate role in urban politics because city government was an apolitical matter of administration. The starting point for all discussions, then, was that parties had to be eliminated, and it was in this context that reformers reconciled their professed openness with their agitation for nonpartisanship.[104] The NML's educative mission was a matter not just of promoting discussion but also of educating the wider public about the need to eliminate parties from local politics.

This model was successful in attracting members and building support for the elimination of parties as a starting point for urban reform. The NML quickly grew to be a national organization. In only five years, it quadrupled its membership, growing from twenty-eight organizations in 1894 to 129 in 1899. Moreover, although in 1894 northeastern cities were overrepresented, by 1899 western cities were actually overrepresented (table 1.1). The member organizations were overwhelmingly reform groups by 1899, although a small minority (12 percent) were commercial bodies. Only two

TABLE 1.1 NML Membership and Urban Areas by Region

	U.S. cities in 1900 (population 8,000+)	NML members in November 1899	NML members at founding in 1894
Totals[a]	546	129	28
Northeast	231 (42%)	59 (46%)	17 (61%)
Midwest	192 (35%)	34 (26%)	4 (14%)
South (includes D.C.)	92 (17%)	16 (12%)	5 (18%)
West	30 (5%)	19 (15%)	1 (4%)

Sources: Regions from "Census Regions and Divisions of the United States," U.S. Census Bureau, accessed April 11, 2019, https://www2.census.gov/geo/pdfs/maps-data/maps/reference/us_regdiv.pdf. Data on U.S. cities in 1900 from "Urban Population in 1900," *Census Bulletin* 70 (July 11, 1901): 2. NML membership data compiled from "National Municipal League," October 18, 1898, 5; "The National Municipal League," November 24, 1896, 2; "New Clubs in the Municipal League," April 24, 1895, 2; "National Municipal League," January 1, 1895, 3; and "Next Conference of Municipal League," November 16, 1894, 7, all in the *New York Times*. Also compiled from Executive Committee Minutes, Folders 62–67, Carton 1, National Municipal League Records, Archives of the Auraria Library, Denver; and "The National Municipal League," *Good Government: Official Journal of the National Civil Service Reform League* 14, no. 13 (July 15, 1895): 182.

Note: Northeast—Connecticut, Maine, Massachusetts, New Hampshire, New Jersey, New York, Pennsylvania, Rhode Island, Vermont; Midwest—Illinois, Indiana, Iowa, Kansas, Michigan, Minnesota, Missouri, Nebraska, North Dakota, Ohio, South Dakota, Wisconsin; South—Alabama, Arkansas, Delaware, District of Columbia, Florida, Georgia, Kentucky, Louisiana, Maryland, Mississippi, North Carolina, Oklahoma, South Carolina, Tennessee, Texas, West Virginia; West—Arizona, California, Colorado, Idaho, Montana, Nevada, New Mexico, Oregon, Utah, Washington, Wyoming.

[a] Total cities (546) includes one city in Hawaii (in the Pacific Region); total members (129; 28) includes the one national body (NCSRL).

were clearly women's organizations, but many of the other organizations likely admitted women.[105] (At the First National Conference for Good City Government, the participants unanimously voted to admit women to the NML.)[106] In short, by 1899 the NML had become a powerful, national network binding together local reform organizations from cities throughout the country.

In joining together in a national federation, the NML's member organizations not only made a statement that there was a shared, national interest in improving city government but also declared themselves representatives of that national interest.[107] Many other Progressive reformers would imitate this approach to organization and action. NML conferences were well attended and widely publicized, and countless other reformers dedicated to a wide variety of urban issues emulated the model of uniting local groups into national federations. By 1903, there were already at least three other national organizations dedicated to improving city government alone.[108]

The NML's leaders soon moved to nationalize city government further, deciding that the time for open-ended discussion was over and that they were ready to determine the best form of government for all cities. In 1895, Carter, then the NML's president, expressed his hope that they would come together and ascertain "the best method" of reform. The next year, he announced that the time had come to make "some definite and solid conclusions" and, based on "extensive information" and "the results of discussion and investigation," "recommend a suitable plan of practical action."[109] Others agreed, and in 1899 the NML determined its *Municipal Program*, a statement of ideal city-state relations and a model municipal charter intended to embody the universal principles of good city government.[110]

Municipal reform associations were not originally created to reform city charters.[111] As this chapter demonstrates, the early members first focused on ending corruption and eliminating parties in local elections, and they intended to do so largely through educational campaigns that would awaken greater public interest in city affairs. Yet as the NML's leaders struggled to do more than criticize existing problems and find points of agreement among a diverse membership, they increasingly turned to structural reform. To establish their claims to impartial leadership, their right to speak on behalf of the wider public, and their authority in matters pertaining to city government, reformers decided to enlist national experts in city government. They turned to leading figures in the nascent discipline of political science to help them produce model institutions for cities. What began as a movement to end corruption and awaken a higher sense of civic duty would soon become a movement for the structural reform of city government.

2

"Saved by the Scholar"

Political Science, the *Municipal Program*, and the National Municipal League, c. 1890–1900

n 1900, an editorial in the *New York Times* commended the National Municipal League's (NML's) recently published *Municipal Program* as "an experiment in the very best line of political education" that "deserves the highest praise." Contrasting the NML's work with that of previous urban reformers, the *Times* noted that the program was not narrow, dedicated to a single "cure-all" or "panacea," but rather the result of "the study, labor, and thought of many able and experienced men" working with great "patience and intelligence." The *Times* encouraged readers who hoped "to understand . . . the chief difficulties in our city management and . . . best reasoned ways of dealing with them" to purchase the program, "a really valuable set of suggestions regarding the more essential points" of city government.[1] The review, in short, celebrated not only the content of the *Municipal Program* but also the process by which it had been written, drawing together "able and experienced men" to study the problems city government faced and form a consensus regarding potential solutions. This process laid the foundation for the close ties that the NML fostered among reformers and political scientists.

The individuals selected to draft the *Municipal Program* embodied the NML's efforts to include both "practical men of affairs" and "students and investigators."[2] The "practical men" were Horace Deming, George Guthrie, Charles Richardson, and Clinton Rogers Woodruff, all lawyers and businessmen as well as active leaders in urban reform circles. The "students and investigators" were Frank Goodnow, professor of administrative law at Columbia University; Leo Stanton Rowe, professor of political science at the University of Pennsylvania; and Albert Shaw, editor of the *Review of Reviews* who held a PhD in political science from Johns Hopkins University.[3] Yet despite attempts to differentiate "practical" reformers and scholars, the line between public activism and academic scholarship was not yet clear. Woodruff, for example, was known largely as a reformer in his capacity as secretary of the NML, but he came to be regarded as an expert in academic circles, publishing dozens of articles and reviews in journals such as the *Annals of the American Academy of Political and Social Science*, *Political Science Quarterly*, and the *American Journal of Sociology*.[4] Moreover, not only did all seven committee members join the NML in the 1890s, six later joined the American Political Science Association (APSA).[5] In short, the division among professional political scientists and lay reformers, though emerging, was still permeable.

This chapter examines the evolving relationship among reformers and political scientists to explore the origins of several key concepts that would frame debates about urban political institutions for decades to come. Among political scientists, the emergence of what contemporaries termed the "realist" movement encouraged practitioners to use investigatory techniques to probe the real working of political institutions beyond what could be learned through the study of formal laws and official documents. Their scientific aspirations impelled them to act as unbiased observers, but this desire to focus on real politics inspired many to become involved in reform. Political scientists shied away from direct participation in partisan politics because they felt it would compromise their professed objectivity. Nonpartisan reform organizations such as the NML thus provided the perfect institutional form to realize their ambitions to be direct participants in and impartial analysts of political processes. As noted, the NML and local leagues in the 1890s repudiated partisanship. Their leaders intended to undertake objective investigations to discover the principles of "good city government" and then organize public opinion in support of reform. Attending conferences, presenting papers, and participating in discussions organized by municipal reform associations allowed political scientists to establish themselves as experts worthy of consultation. When the NML invited leading municipal political scientists to participate in the drafting of a municipal program intended to elucidate "the essential principles that must underlie successful municipal government" and devise "a working plan or system . . . for putting such principles into practical operation," they eagerly agreed.[6]

The creation of the *Municipal Program* was a turning point for both reformers and political scientists. Previous academic studies highlight its importance for both groups, some more critically and others more favorably. Early accounts tended to be largely celebratory, describing the program as an invaluable "political innovation."[7] More recent accounts are mixed. Political scientist Helene Silverberg argues that it created a framework to nationalize the movement for urban reform but also enabled discussions of political institutions to omit crucial questions pertaining to ethnic, racial, class, and gender identity and conflict.[8] Historian James Connolly characterizes it as the embodiment of a consensus view of politics that rejected the possibility of legitimate plural interests in urban politics.[9] On one level, elements of all of these assessments are true. At the same time, it is an oversimplification to present the individuals who created the program as believing that they would—or could—achieve consensus on all matters. Their own differences of opinion were far too evident. The central question was what topics needed uniform support and what topics could be left to the realm of uncertainty and legitimate difference of opinion. Reformers and politicians maintained a sense of shared purpose by avoiding discussions of the role of gender, ethnicity, class, and race in politics not because they were all uniformly opposed to woman suffrage or embraced nativism but because they disagreed on these topics. In avoiding these divisive issues, their discussions of "politics" came to center on the importance of the different branches and institutions of government, particularly administrative matters on which they could agree.

City government, with its perceived failings, complicated relation to state government, and importance in the growing field of administration, provided an ideal sphere for political scientists to participate in public political discussions. A close reading of the writings of Goodnow, Rowe, and Shaw—three of the leading political scientists involved in the formation of the *Municipal Program*—reveals a key difference of opinion over whether political scientists should focus on the structures of cities (i.e., their relation to the state, the powers of mayors and councils) or their functions (i.e., the construction of streets, the provision of utilities, etc.). While early discussions of function openly promoted the expansion of the range of governmental activities, political scientists gradually redirected discussions of function away from advocacy and toward the depoliticized realm of administration. Goodnow, who began in the subfield of municipal political science but soon became a leading figure in the discipline, famously defined the two purposes of government as politics, the expression of the state's will, and administration, the execution of that will.[10] This distinction allowed political scientists to focus on the creation of political and administrative structures that allowed for the expression and execution of that will.

The program followed Goodnow's lead, embodying a style of public activism that allowed political scientists to participate as neutral experts imparting their knowledge of apolitical fundamentals rather than as interested partisans advocating contested ideals. The program provided a detailed blueprint for the structures of cities in terms of the selection and duties of local officials. Yet, following Goodnow's lead, it addressed officials' functions only as they related to the creation of efficient administrative systems, claiming that its structural provisions provided councils with the necessary powers to decide on the appropriate scope of functions. While this decision partly reflected a commitment to local autonomy, it also provided a way for the committee that wrote the program to avoid potentially divisive issues, particularly that of municipal ownership of transit systems and utilities. Though most political scientists and members of the NML supported an expansion of the scope of city government, they differed greatly as to the nature and extent of that expansion. The ability to discuss function as a matter of administration thus facilitated the maintenance of a diverse coalition that could unanimously agree that the Municipal Program was based on "the essential principles" of city government.[11]

Political Science, Realism, and City Government

From the founding of their profession as an academic discipline, political scientists faced the dilemma of balancing commitments to scholarship and political activism. Inspired by the German model of higher education that encouraged students to pursue their own interests and engage in original research, many American scholars returned from studies abroad to establish graduate programs at universities in the United States in the late 1800s. John Burgess founded the most well-known and influential school of political science in 1880 at Columbia University. The program focused on scholarship but also aimed to prepare students to be public servants and leaders in America's democratic system. Concerned with the corruption of Gilded Age politics and interested in civil service reform, many political scientists intended to use their discipline to train personnel for administrative positions in government. At the same time, they also aspired to train scholars to carry out investigations and accumulate data to further the objective "science" of politics.[12]

Scientific aspirations were the foundation of the goal of impartiality. Adherents of scientism hoped that by employing the methodologies and concepts of the natural sciences, they could uncover facts about the political realm. For some, such an application required abandoning preconceived ideals and engaging in a mode of inquiry that was objective and dispassionate, stressing original research and the collection of empirical data. For others, it was part of an effort to discover fixed laws of politics. Initially, references to such laws derived from an application of Euclidian geometry and Newtonian physics to political life, but with the rising influence of Charles Darwin's theory of evolution, students of politics began to apply evolutionary rather than mechanical models.[13]

For many, adopting an evolutionary paradigm involved the use of a historical-comparative method. For much of the nineteenth century, American academics utilized a deductive approach to reasoning, determining political truths based on a priori principles. In contrast, by the later 1800s, many increasingly advocated an inductive approach in which scholars approached their subjects without preconceived notions about the generalizations that would arise from their analyses of evidence. They believed that only careful examination and analysis of historical documents and detailed comparisons with the governments of other countries (primarily European) could enable political scientists to establish generalizations about the real world of politics.[14] One important consequence of such studies was a newfound belief that political institutions were not fixed and ideal structures but rather dynamic. By gathering and examining the facts of historical development, political scientists hoped to uncover laws of progress.[15]

The historical-comparative method, however, was not the only one available, for as early as the 1880s a "realist" critique of the method had begun to emerge. Realism in political science further encouraged practitioners to make connections with the contemporary world of politics. Prominent figures such as Woodrow Wilson and James Bryce faulted proponents of the historical-comparative approach for getting lost in detailed examinations of official documents and manuscripts and consequently producing only descriptive accounts of formal institutions. Instead, they argued that political scientists needed to move beyond archival work and engage in a sort of fieldwork, observing and talking to real political actors in the contemporary world.[16] This methodological critique called for scholars to consider more than formal legal structures and turn their attention to the actual functioning of political institutions.

James Bryce's *The American Commonwealth* (1888), with its detailed descriptions of the institutions of American government, including the party system, was a forerunner of this realist style. Bryce was a British liberal politician and scholar who undertook extensive travels to compose a comprehensive account of contemporary political life in the United States. In his introduction to his massive three-volume work, Bryce presented his study as a work of political science in the realist style. He felt that new descriptions were needed periodically because of the rapid pace of change, with new problems, ideas, and institutions to be explored. As such, *The American Commonwealth* did not contain a historical treatment of its subject. Bryce's "chief aim" was contemporary—to present "a full and clear view of the facts of today." Yet Bryce still hoped to make a larger contribution that went beyond the moment in which he wrote, to uncover some of the "general truths in social and political science" and the "laws of political biology."[17]

The influence of *The American Commonwealth* on the discipline of political science was immense. Not only was it enthusiastically received by public and academic audiences alike, it quickly became the most popular textbook on American politics.[18] This popularity was likely due at least in part to Bryce's elevated vision of the proper function of academics. Bryce wrote that in America, neither "political arrangements nor . . . social and economic conditions" attracted the "best intellects and loftiest characters into public life." He recognized that popular opinion played a powerful role in the American system of governance, but he stressed the important role of an "active class" that led public opinion.[19] Who exactly were these individuals? When Bryce spoke at Johns Hopkins University as a visiting lecturer, he implored professors and students to realize "the need of the scholar in politics." Frederic Howe, then a doctoral student, later remembered that Bryce "said that America, with no leisure class devoted to statecraft, as in Great Britain, was to be saved by the scholar." Bryce inspired students to believe that, through their own "disinterested service," they could realize "the ultimate ideal" of "the scholar in politics," providing the necessary leadership to solve the "political ills" of the day.[20]

Bryce's appeal to scholars resonated with a special intensity in the emerging field of political science. With the founding of professional historical, economic, and sociological associations in the 1880s and 1890s, many scholars sought to distance themselves from conceptions of inquiry that equated investigation with reform.[21] This division came later in political science. The APSA was the last of the major social science associations to be formed (1903). As the study of politics took shape as a separate discipline—distinct from law, sociology, economics, and history—practitioners worked to determine the parameters of their work and the purpose of their profession. They confronted the dilemma of how to be both academics and leaders. They sought to produce objective, scientific scholarship and also to serve as public leaders, instructing citizens about their civic duties and guiding the course of political development.[22] Bryce envisioned schools of political science as analogous to schools of law, equally dedicated to academic scholarship and public practice.[23]

Newer visions of the state further encouraged direct involvement in public affairs. The concept of the state, originating in Continental Europe, helped to differentiate political science from other social sciences and law, providing it with a distinct subject matter. The state signified not simply the government but rather a more abstract conception of the political community of a nation.[24] For political scientists like Burgess, the state was the transcendent spirit of the people of a nation rather than something to be found in the institutions of the government.[25] Yet part of the larger move toward realism involved a desire to treat the state less as an indivisible, organic ideal and more as a tangible entity with distinct components.[26] Newer research thus centered on tangible and discrete topics such as public law, administration, and municipalities.[27] This understanding of political structures inspired many to attempt to become involved directly in this process of change, to have a role in shaping the future of state development.

There was often more than a small element of antidemocratic elitism in this understanding of the role of the scholar, for in elevating the importance of experts, some relegated the public to a circumscribed political role. Like Bryce, Woodrow Wilson, then professor of political science, argued that political scientists should serve as intermediaries between the American people and their elected representatives.[28] In both his academic work and his contributions to popular publications, Wilson publicized his views of the perils of excessive democracy.[29] He argued, "This vast and miscellaneous democracy of ours must be led; its giant faculties must be schooled and directed. Leadership cannot belong to the multitudes." He claimed that in America, "the sovereignty of the people" is really only a very limited sort of sovereignty, one that merely "passes judgment or gives sanction." In addition, the large scale of modern American democracy, according to Wilson, "necessitates the exercise of persuasive power by dominant minds in the shaping of popular judgments."[30]

The question that remained was how political scientists hoped to assume their leadership roles as the "dominant minds." For some, the expansion of administration provided the answer. By training civil servants and other specialists, political scientists hoped to shape this growing branch of the government through the propagation of the ideals of rational, disinterested service on behalf of the common good.[31] Many scholars, however, hoped to influence a far higher number of Americans. Textbooks and courses on American government in high schools, colleges, and universities would perform the task of educating Americans about their duties as citizens. Additionally, participation in the major movements of the day—for the initiative and referendum, the direct election of senators, reform of the civil service, and the restructuring of municipal corporations—also helped political scientists to realize their public aspirations.[32]

Yet such aspirations were complicated by the desire to be simultaneously involved in politics and impartial. The ways that political science defined *politics* and *political* were central to achieving this balance, and ideas about gender often played a central role. Some leaders of the discipline were vocal opponents of woman suffrage, but increasingly political scientists largely avoided this and other similarly controversial matters.[33] Not only did they avoid discussing voting rights for women, but most also ignored other instances of female presence in public affairs. Women's activism in voluntary and civic organizations, particularly in urban areas, challenged accepted notions of how one could participate in political processes, as previous understandings held that citizens could only participate through formal parties and elections. Political scientists, however, generally did not consider women's forms of activism to be political.[34]

Women's organizations in cities, claiming apolitical, nonpartisan status and a simple desire to further public welfare, had male counterparts in the municipal leagues and good government clubs of male reformers. Early political scientists implicitly accepted the claims of male reformers that these groups were nonpartisan and therefore nonpolitical. Accepting this definition was essential, for only if they were somehow apart from politics could political scientists justify their active involvement. As part of efforts to examine the more informal world of real politics, by the 1890s political scientists recognized the important function of parties, in terms of both their official structures and the unofficial bosses and rings that often controlled them.[35] Yet in their published treatments of urban politics, municipal political scientists largely continued to ignore the role of voluntary organizations.[36] As long as organizations such as the NML and its affiliates remained excluded from definitions of *political*, political scientists were free to attend their meetings, present proposals, and guide their activities. Participation in reform movements thus shaped the ideological content of political science, encouraging political scientists to continue to ignore the position of municipal reform organizations in urban politics.

Later historians of political science have debated the extent to which the realists were able to realize their methodological goals, either congratulating them for beginning the move away from exclusive attention to formal laws and institutions or criticizing them for arriving at a still narrow understanding of political factors.[37] Yet perhaps the more important questions are why political scientists included some factors and not others and what effect these inclusions and omissions had on their scholarship. It was obvious to many of their contemporaries that the proliferation of voluntary organizations, particularly those interested in matters of public policy, was creating new ways for citizens to participate in politics outside of partisan electoral processes.[38] Yet their own involvement in associations dedicated to urban reform prevented them from recognizing the political nature of such groups.

Realism and the Formation of the *Municipal Program*

The creation of the *Municipal Program* not only represented an attempt to fulfill political scientists' realist aspirations to shape the creation of new institutions of government, it also indicated that the ideals of realism were beginning to pervade reform circles.[39] As detailed earlier, local municipal reform associations and the NML pioneered a style of activism that would become prominent among a wide variety of Progressive reformers after 1900. Beginning with organization, often through voluntary associations in the name of the "people," reformers undertook investigations and gathered "facts," then analyzed the results, typically utilizing social science methodology, and finally embarked on campaigns of publicity, education, and lobbying.

The plans to create the *Municipal Program* epitomized this style, providing an opportunity to discover universal truths and educate the public about the requirements of good city government. Echoing sentiments expressed in his academic writings, political scientist Leo Stanton Rowe explained the need for such a program in speeches presented at the NML's annual meeting. He highlighted gaps between "political ideals and methods of political reasoning" and between "our civic and political standards" and "the conditions of city life." These gaps, according to Rowe, contributed to the failures of city government. He claimed that Americans experimented with forms of city government because of "the prevailing uncertainty as to the most effective organization of the municipality, as well as the great divergence of opinion on some of the fundamental questions of municipal policy."[40] Reform organizations, Rowe also noted, had not in the past addressed these problems because of their inability to move beyond "destructive criticism" and their failure "to furnish a positive basis for political reorganization." These limitations had resulted in a "growing distrust of the ability of reform movements to meet the practical problems of American political life." Rowe, however, was confident that the *Municipal Program* would put an end to such distrust.[41] Much as political scientists wanted to prove their usefulness, so did the NML, and the *Municipal Program* was its vehicle for doing so.

When Horace Deming, a founding member of the NML, first proposed developing a positive program at the annual conference in May 1897, he explained the rationale using the language of political science. Deming was a practicing lawyer and active leader in urban reform circles in New York. He also published several articles in the *Annals of the American Academy of Political and Social Science* and wrote a book on city government.[42] Much as realist scholars extolled the value of real-world inquiries that unearthed general principles, Deming spoke of the need to utilize the results of "experience and investigation" in order "to get into practical politics" by establishing the "fundamental principles" of city government. Describing the proposed program, Deming declared, it "shall embody the essential principles that must underlie successful city government and which shall also set forth a working plan or system, consistent with American political institutions and adapted to American industrial and political conditions, for putting such principles into practical operation."[43] Such sentiments reflected a faith that research and analysis would lead to a convergence of opinion and unearth "essential" points of agreement.

Yet even before the NML's committee began its work, some members voiced concerns that they would be unable to come to an agreement regarding "essential principles." Deming partly justified the value of a program by claiming that while the "actual framework" of city government varied tremendously, the "theory of the city under our American form of government is identical in every state." When Secretary Woodruff rose to second the resolution to begin work on a program, he added that he did so despite reservations, claiming, "I do not think that municipal conditions throughout this country are so uniform . . . , nor that any definite plan which might be devised by any body of men, no matter how wise, would fit all conditions." Regardless, he agreed that it was time to "find the certain particulars on which we all agree." Goodnow even joked about the divergence of opinions expressed. Complimenting one speaker's proposal while maintaining that he felt it "would be insufficient to obtain good popular government," he somewhat self-deprecatingly added, "but I suppose that all of us who have made a particular study of municipal reform have our own peculiar methods and ideas for reforming the present condition of things."[44]

Despite such concerns, the NML's official record proudly described the process by which the program was drafted as a deliberative one that yielded consensus. According to one published account, the members of the committee met several times to discuss drafts among themselves and also consulted the NML's membership and other experts and political scientists. Immediately after the formation of the committee in May 1897, its members divided themselves into topical subcommittees. In March 1898, they met again to hear the reports of the subcommittees. They next presented a draft to the wider membership in November 1898, proudly declaring that despite their "widely divergent training," "strong personal convictions," and "essentially different points of view," they were able to come to a "unanimous agreement that a 'Municipal Program' was feasible and practicable and by fair and full comparison of opinion were able to embody the result of their agreement in definite propositions."[45] After discussing the tentative provisions, Deming, with Goodnow's assistance, revised the draft. The committee then printed and sent copies of the amended draft to reformers and scholars throughout the country and met again to discuss criticisms and suggestions. At last, in November 1899 they presented the final draft, which they again unanimously supported, at a meeting in Columbus.[46] In spite of disagreements over minor points, the NML proudly declared that the expert committee had determined the "fundamentals" necessary for good city government and unanimously "adopted, ratified and approved" the *Municipal Program*.[47]

Despite this celebratory public narrative, a careful examination of the program itself, the accompanying explanatory papers, and the works of several key political scientists involved in its creation reveals an alternative interpretation. There was not as much debate and revision as the NML claimed. There are only minor differences between the original draft of the program first presented to the NML in November 1898 and the one finally published in 1900.[48] Moreover, despite claims in the press that the program was "not the work of any single author" and was not based on "any single theory," by and large, it was in fact founded on the writings of one political scientist: Frank Goodnow.[49]

/ and the Purpose of Government

l renown as a political scientist stemmed partly from
ı Bryce. Recognizing that much of *The American Common-wealth* consisted of general descriptions of America's political institutions, Bryce included a section titled "Illustrations and Reflections" to underscore his main arguments. The lead chapter in this section, written by Goodnow, supported Bryce's overview of machines with an account titled "The Tweed Ring in New York City."[50] Goodnow, although a relatively unknown lecturer in administrative law at Columbia University when he wrote this chapter, soon became one of the most influential political scientists in the country on the basis of his pioneering work in urban politics and administration.[51]

Goodnow's interest in municipalities developed out of his legal background. He graduated from Columbia Law School in 1882 and worked as a clerk for Judge John Dillon.[52] Dillon's published writings on city government played an integral role in the rise of municipal political science as a popular and dynamic subfield of the discipline. Dillon, a preeminent legal scholar, believed that municipalities were not autonomous political entities but rather subordinate creatures of the state. Dillon's rule, as it became known, permitted a limited sphere of action for city government by claiming that municipalities possessed only the powers expressly permitted or clearly implied by their charters. Previous legal doctrine had bestowed on state courts the power to review charters and determine the scope and structure of municipal law. Dillon's rule granted this right to state legislatures, making municipal law a political rather than a legal subject.[53] Goodnow, with his legal background and experience working for Dillon, was perfectly positioned to develop the academic field of municipal political science. He traveled to Europe to pursue further study. When he returned, he filled a vacant position in administrative law at Columbia's School of Political Science.[54]

Although Goodnow's early works did not suggest the Progressive politics he would later advocate, his methodological approaches marked him as an innovator within the discipline.[55] In Europe, he studied with scholars who believed there was a need to study more than formal institutions to understand the real workings of government, encouraging examinations of administrative structures.[56] His early articles on English local government demonstrate these influences, with their characterizations of English institutions not as an ideal system but as a somewhat haphazard amalgam of historical developments and innovations, with political changes following social and economic changes.[57] Yet while Goodnow's emphasis on the gaps that often separated formal and actual systems of government was provocative, his early works focused almost exclusively on the structures of government without discussing the objectives and functions of those structures. Not until 1909 would his work on city government more fully address social and economic forces in urban politics.[58] These omissions perhaps reflected Goodnow's intention to write as an objective academic, not a reformer, focused on only the most tangible institutions.

Goodnow's scholarship on municipalities was grounded in newer conceptions of the state and rising interest in administration. He viewed municipalities as part of the governmental system, and he began to explore the nature of the relationships among local, state, and national institutions. According to Goodnow, to discover "what the city really is," one must "treat the city rather as part of the governmental system than as an isolated phenomenon."[59] For Goodnow, administrative structures were crucial to these larger governmental systems. His views on administrative structures began to emerge in a series of essays on Prussian local government from 1889 and 1890. Goodnow explained that unlike in the United States, where municipal corporations were only authorized to undertake actions expressly granted in their charters, the Prussian system granted municipalities general powers to control their own affairs and regulated matters of common concern through central *administrative* rather than *legislative* control. Goodnow felt that this arrangement provided municipalities with autonomy to determine their own needs while enabling a central authority to control those functions that municipalities carried out on behalf of a central state.[60] This system allowed states to regulate only uniform administrative matters, retaining legislative decision-making regarding political matters for city councils.

Expanding on these interests, Goodnow published *Municipal Home Rule* in 1895. Although other academics had recognized the relations of states and cities as contributing to the shortcomings of city government, Goodnow was the first to undertake a detailed study of the topic.[61] With this book, Goodnow established himself as one of the foremost experts on the laws governing American cities. *Municipal Home Rule* remained an authoritative text for over twenty years.[62] Here, he rejected Dillon's rule and presented an alternative legal definition of municipalities in the United States. Goodnow believed that municipalities performed two functions, acting both as organizations for the satisfaction of local needs and as agents of the state. According to Goodnow, this dual nature provided the key to a fuller understanding of cities—on the one hand, private corporations devoted to the needs of local populations, and on the other, agents of the state concerned with the general welfare. In this context, he recognized the right of states to act in matters of a public and governmental nature. The problem was that legislatures had forgotten that municipalities also dealt with matters that were purely private and corporate, including "the powers to undertake and maintain public works of peculiar interest to them." When states attempted to regulate purely "local matters," they infringed "upon the domain of municipal home rule."[63] Therefore, while Goodnow dismissed those advocating complete home rule as naïve given the demands of modern government, he provided many reformers with a more sophisticated, nuanced basis for advocating a wider sphere of local autonomy.[64]

The definition of cities played an important role in determining the scope and subject matter of municipal political science. While Goodnow's argument for the dual nature of cities was provocative in that it directly challenged Dillon's rule, thereby justifying the need for a sphere of home rule, it was also narrow and legalistic. Critics felt that such a definition ignored the intangible quality of urban life, portraying cities as social and cultural organisms, communities of individuals bound together by a sense of civic pride.[65] And yet as the influence of the realist movement grew, a more divisive split among municipal political scientists emerged in the debate over structure versus function.

Goodnow, Shaw, and Rowe and the Debate Over Structure and Function

The debate over whether political scientists should focus on the structures of municipalities (i.e., their relation to the state, the powers of councils) or their functions (i.e., the construction of sewers, the provision of utilities) further illuminates the struggle to balance advocacy and objectivity.[66] These discussions were about not only the purpose of political science but also the purpose of government itself. Studies of functions emerged from the realist goal of examining the actual workings of government. At the same time, those who emphasized functions tended more openly to advocate a wider sphere of local activity. Other political scientists were concerned that public declarations in support of new governmental programs were not appropriate for objective scientists. Accordingly, those who wrote largely about structures of cities (particularly Goodnow) claimed the status of objective and scientific scholars and did not endorse or condemn the adoption of new programs.

Scholars focusing on functional expansion and scholars detailing structures both turned to European cities to frame their work as objective.[67] Scholars could argue that their proposals to reform the legal foundations of American cities were not unprecedented and radical but rather founded on centuries of European experiences. Rather than framing their work with abstractions from political theory and philosophy, they were able to utilize European examples in constructing arguments about the shortcomings and, in rare cases, the strengths of municipalities in the United States. They could cloak their prescriptive analyses in the language of comparative science, realism, and experience and even universalize their conclusions as fundamental to good city government everywhere.

An examination of the published scholarship by and debates among Goodnow, Shaw, and Rowe clarifies the tensions regarding structure and function, as well as between scholarship and advocacy. Their careers combined academic work and public engagement, but they did so in notably different ways. Goodnow, with his largely academic publications and position as a professor of administrative law, represented the legal and academic faction of municipal political science, focusing almost exclusively on structure. Yet he was active in reform politics as a founder of the City Club and later the New York Bureau of Municipal Research and an influential member of Theodore Roosevelt's charter commission in 1900.[68] Shaw was more of a public intellectual, and he openly advocated an expansion of municipal functions, critiquing scholars and reformers who focused only on structure. He combined a strong academic background with his work as editor of the *Review of Reviews* and publication of several books on European city government written for both popular and academic audiences. He was a member of over a dozen reform organizations in New York City. Despite the fact that he never held an academic position, he, like Goodnow, served as president of the APSA.[69] Rowe occupied a middle ground, with a strong academic career and a more open interest in functions. He too served as president of the APSA. Though he penned largely academic books and articles, he occasionally published articles in popular magazines.[70] Together, these three men engaged in debates about the scope of city government and municipal political science.

Rowe encouraged his peers to focus on the daily activities of government. He called for the study of a more "dynamic politics" that examined political institutions not in a vacuum but in their wider ideological, economic, and social contexts. In an essay that probed the nature of political science as a discipline, he insisted that scholarship "must go beyond the organized political forms." He highlighted the need to explore "the relation between institutions and ideas" and "the adjustment of such institutions to the needs of the community." At the same time, he urged fellow political scientists to pay close attention to "economic relations" and "new standards of conduct." The way to achieve this, Rowe concluded, was to focus on functions: "We must examine political institutions, primarily with reference to the functions they are intended to perform in a particular environment."[71]

Though Rowe's writings on municipalities were largely technical descriptions of administrative departments, he openly advocated the expansion of functions as part of his vision of democratic progress. For example, his study of Philadelphia's gas supply included detailed descriptions of complex legal structures but also underscored the "relation between municipal activity and social progress." He celebrated the effectiveness of public gasworks in English, Scottish, and German cities and even claimed that the "future of our democratic institutions" in America depended on the ability to "develop an equally efficient administration."[72] Rowe believed that the reorganization of formal structures was not sufficient. He stressed the importance of "social solidarity and civic responsibility" in urban public life and concluded "that the problem of city government" required "such a change in the life and thought of the people as will bring an increasing number of city services into organic, vital relations with the daily life, the pleasures and recreations of the whole population."[73] By making these claims in his writing in academic journals, Rowe located the functions of government, the more intangible moral aspects of democratic theory, and even open advocacy of an expansion of state capacity as part of the legitimate domain of political science.

Like Rowe, Shaw began with an organic conception of cities to argue for an expansion of functions. In *Municipal Government in Great Britain* and *Municipal Government in Continental Europe*, both published in 1895, Shaw wrote about European cities in moral and ethical rather than legal terms. He celebrated the growing spirit of collectivism, as well as the view of cities as "political and social organisms" to promote residents' welfare.[74] Shaw passionately argued for the need to focus on municipal functions. From his perspective, the "mechanism of municipal government is a secondary matter."[75] Shaw explained that while he had "tried to explain intelligibly the structure and working of the municipal machinery," he "considered it . . . no less essential . . . to describe the transformation of street-systems, and the measures by which death rates have been reduced." He argued that American reformers had "lost sight of the aims and objects of government in striving after good government as an end in itself." Excessively focused on "structure" and "mechanism," they "perpetually" reorganized local governments without devoting sufficient thought to their purpose. Shaw contrasted the endeavors of American reformers with those of the "Germans of our generation" who had "taken their old framework of city government as they found it" and "proceeded to use it for new and wonderful purposes."[76]

As this assessment suggests, Shaw used European models to support his call to reform American municipalities. Despite his claims that Americans "must deal with our own problems in our own way," Shaw clearly felt Americans had much to learn from European cities and believed that the challenges American and European cities faced were fundamentally "similar in all their essential characteristics." For these reasons, Shaw hoped that Americans would learn from "the lessons European cities have to teach." He hoped that "through the process of comparison and induction," Americans would be able "to establish certain fundamental principles and methods that must have place in the wide and permanent ordering of the affairs of any modern industrial community." For Shaw, these "fundamental principles" involved an expansion in the scope of city government, and he urged Americans "to adopt broader and more generous municipal programs."[77] Using these comparisons, Shaw framed what some contemporaries considered a radical expansion of municipal activities as proved by real-world European experiences.

Goodnow, though he also cited European examples, vehemently challenged Shaw's rejection of the importance of attention to structure. Goodnow and Rowe both published reviews of Shaw's two books. Rowe favorably assessed their value.[78] Goodnow, in contrast, offered praise but faulted Shaw for not recognizing the important structural differences between British and American municipalities that allowed the former to attain "good municipal government." He claimed that Shaw did not pay "sufficient attention" to the detriments of "the fact of continual legislative interference" in the United States.[79] Goodnow added that Shaw's critical attitude toward the interest of the American reformer in "structure and mechanism" detracted "from the value of both books." He highlighted Shaw's "tendency to look with indifference if not scorn on the details of municipal organization," pointing to the insufficient emphasis on the importance of the administration and "the relation of the Continental city to the central government."[80] From Goodnow's perspective, Shaw's discussion of the activities undertaken by European cities was incomplete without a careful consideration of the larger institutional context that made those activities possible.

For Goodnow, there could be no discussion of function without structure, for only with the correct structures could municipalities undertake the necessary functions. As he noted in *Municipal Home Rule*, Goodnow believed cities needed spheres of home rule, free from legislative interference by states, to perform the functions necessary for the welfare of local populations. He conceded that "proper organization of municipal institutions, selection of competent and upright municipal officers, and civic patriotism are all necessary." But Goodnow felt that without first ascertaining "the sphere of municipal government" and securing "an ample degree of local autonomy," "little progress in municipal government reform" would be possible.[81] As these statements suggest, while Goodnow did not focus extensively on functions, he did not dismiss their importance.

This approach appealed to many scholars, including open advocates of an expansion of city government like Rowe. Rowe admired Goodnow's work *Municipal Home Rule* and elsewhere for realizing his ideals of quality scholarship in political science. His review of *Municipal Problems* said as much, celebrating the two books as together "the first systematic attempt to determine the position of the municipality in our political system" and reserving for Goodnow "an exceptional place in the literature of American political institutions." Additionally, he admired Goodnow's recognition of the importance of "political ideas" and acknowledgment "that a change in the organization of our municipal governments rests upon a modification of our political ideas."[82] In short, even a figure like Rowe, who more openly advocated an expansion of city functions, admired and praised Goodnow's discussions of the structures of municipalities within the larger political system and the larger philosophies that shaped those relations.

In Goodnow's next project, he continued to focus on the distinction between structure and function, but he expanded this concept beyond municipalities to offer a more general theory of government. In 1900, with the publication of *Politics and Administration: A Study in Government*, Goodnow established himself as one of the leading political scientists of the day, reaching well beyond the subfield of municipal political science. Here, he distinguished the two main purposes of government: politics, the expression of the state's will, and administration, the execution of that will.[83] This theory directly stemmed from his previous work on municipalities, but its influence was so widespread that Goodnow was later credited with spearheading the field of public administration.[84] Goodnow's famous distinction also helped to depoliticize administration.

One of Goodnow's chief contributions was his claim that government needed to distinguish more carefully between the expression of the state's will and the execution of that will. In theory, the expression fell to the legislative branch and the execution to the judicial and executive branches. In practice, however, Goodnow realized that it was impossible to create completely separate organs to carry out these functions. As he explained, each branch of government was not "confined exclusively to the discharge of one of these functions" but rather was "largely or mainly" focused on "the discharge of one or the other."[85] In other words, for Goodnow, the distinction between politics and administration was a conceptual one, not a description of completely separate branches of government.

Goodnow applied this distinction to explain his somewhat complicated understanding of city-state relations. According to Goodnow's ideal, state legislative bodies should have the right to make state laws—a legitimate political function. Cities should be administrative bodies to the extent that they enforce state laws and therefore be subject to state regulatory boards regarding administrative matters. Yet Goodnow argued that cities should also perform a political function by determining local policies pertaining to local matters. To this end, they should have their own legislative bodies (councils) to determine local laws, and they also need administrative systems of their own (headed by mayors) to carry out local laws. In short, Goodnow again argued for the dual nature of municipalities: administrative agents of the state legislatures and political organizations via councils for the satisfaction of local needs.[86]

Contrasting this ideal situation with Goodnow's characterization of existing city-state relations clarifies his rationale for calling for a more careful distinction between politics and administration. Cities, as noted, currently possessed only those powers expressly granted by state legislatures. In the face of rising concerns about corruption associated with the spoils system and machine politics, state legislatures increasingly took powers away from city councils. The result, according to Goodnow, was that state legislatures, mayors, and other local administrators encroached on the determination of local policy, which should have been delegated to city councils. At the same time, the patronage of the spoils system allowed party politicians to let politics shape decisions that should have been purely administrative.[87] In short, Goodnow suggested that this confusing overlap between politics and administration and between state and local was largely responsible for the problems American cities faced. His call to distinguish political and administrative functions became the framework for both the redefinition of city-state relations and the reorganization of local government proposed in the Municipal Program.

Goodnow, Political Parties in Cities, and the Municipal Program

When the Municipal Program was published, political scientists understood Goodnow's influence and its potential to solidify a public role for political science. Henry Jones Ford began an article titled "Politics and Administration" by commending recent efforts "to apply the principles of political science to the solution of problems of government." He praised the use of scientific models, particularly "inductive methods," in such endeavors. To illustrate his claim, Ford pointed to "the practical study of problems of municipal government" by the NML and its recently published *Municipal Program*. Noting Goodnow's participation in the composition of the program, Ford suggested that *Politics and Administration* provided "the philosophical principles on which the program is based."[88] Ford was correct in recognizing the influence of *Politics and Administration*, and he could have added *Municipal Home Rule* and *Municipal Problems* as well. While the other members of the committee that drafted the program—particularly Rowe and Shaw—shaped its contents, and many details, particularly technical matters regarding indebtedness and accounting, originated from a variety of sources, the *Municipal Program* largely embodied Goodnow's theories on municipalities and their position in the governmental system.[89]

Reflecting its members' faith that careful research would yield universally applicable principles, the committee, while silent on potentially divisive details regarding municipal functions, forcefully and clearly asserted that its program successfully accomplished the NML's original goal of devising uniform structures.[90] The program offered a complex mix of greater state control and greater home rule for cities. It recommended uniform accounting, the submission of written reports to state controllers, and the creation of state boards to supervise cities in their roles as administrative agents of state laws. It reversed Dillon's rule, proposing that states grant cities "all powers not inconsistent with the general law" to provide "the widest possible discretion in determining the sphere of [municipal] activity." While it suggested that cities needed freedom to determine the scope of those activities, it also recommended uniformity in structures to allow them to do so. The program called for powerful councils to carry out municipal legislative functions and mayors to head municipal administrations, subject to the rules of civil service systems.[91] Goodnow's views regarding the distinct functions of government thus partly provided the basis for a consensus among reformers.

This consensus rested on Goodnow's views of political parties, which both challenged and solidified antiparty views among reformers. Goodnow, building on the work of Bryce, offered a new way to critique parties that did not rest on the anti-immigrant, class-based arguments of many earlier critics of machines. The involvement of parties in local elections appeared to reformers as perhaps the greatest source of urban political problems. Previously, critics had dismissed parties and machines as corrupt aberrations of an ideal republican government.[92] Bryce did much to change this line of analysis.[93] His account of urban politics and bosses quickly became one of the most cited sections of *The American Commonwealth*, particularly his contention that "the government of cities is the one conspicuous failure of the United States." Although Bryce argued that "ignorant" immigrant voters bore much responsibility for the failures of city government, his analysis also included a discussion of the structural flaws of political institutions, including parties. Challenging common misconceptions, he wrote, "It must not be supposed that the members of rings, or the great boss himself, are wicked men. They are the offspring of a system." He also argued that the interference of state legislatures in local matters, the lack of clear lines of responsibility and accountability, and the excessive number of elected positions all posed serious problems for cities. Greatly exacerbating these problems, however, was the party system itself, for the spoils system and other "opportunities for illicit gains arising out of the possession of office" were major factors in the growth of rings and bosses in American cities.[94]

Similarly, Goodnow provided a rationale to further distance antiparty sentiment from attacks on urban voters. While many of his contemporaries blamed universal suffrage for the election of incompetent and corrupt politicians, even in his earlier works Goodnow instead blamed "the imperfect character" of America's representative and partisan systems. He was no staunch defender of voting rights in these years, neither endorsing nor condemning movements to limit "universal municipal suffrage." His texts referenced attempts in the South to use "educational qualifications" to disfranchise the "large ignorant negro population" that posed "serious dangers to good government." Yet he also maintained that "universal suffrage ought not be held responsible for many of the evils for which it is made responsible, but which it is believed result from the imperfect character of all representative systems." Specifically, he pointed to the party system as an alternative culprit.[95]

Goodnow attempted to offer a balanced critique of political parties. He recognized the important role they played in America's system of divided powers, agreeing with others that parties coordinated America's otherwise fragmented political system.[96] Despite conceding such positive functions, Goodnow also stressed parties' limitations as representative bodies. He claimed that while they fulfilled vital public functions, because of their status as private organizations, they were not subject to state regulations.

As parties were left unchecked, members did not often have the power to control their actions or policies.[97]

Given this more nuanced understanding of parties, Goodnow's proposals to reform the status quo were similarly complex. Nationally, he proposed legal recognition and a variety of regulations of parties as political bodies, hoping to force them to be more accountable to members. His preferred model to ensure maximum accountability was the British parliamentary system. Yet given political realities, Goodnow suggested the more modest solutions of direct primaries, forced publicity of corporate and partisan financial records, and other measures to prevent electoral fraud.[98] In cities, Goodnow viewed parties' roles as more problematic, but he still felt that the solutions could not be as simple as reformers hoped. He faulted reformers for simply advocating separate local elections, arguing that it was unrealistic to expect an end to the influence of state and national parties in local elections. Instead, he maintained that a clearer demarcation between state and local government and between politics and administration would reduce opportunities for spoils and thereby partisan interest in local affairs.[99]

One of Goodnow's additional proposals would play a central role in the agenda of urban reform in coming decades and also what would become known as the Short Ballot movement. In *Municipal Problems*, he explained the problem of the "elective principle" in urban politics. He maintained that in large cities, "if a great number of offices is to [be] filled, many of which are . . . comparatively unimportant, even the most intelligent elector is apt to become confused and . . . vote the 'straight ticket' of the party." Additionally, he claimed that with the proliferation of municipal activities, in many new positions "technical skill" was "required." Although he remained a staunch advocate of a popularly elected representative council, Goodnow insisted that most city offices—"registers of deeds, sheriffs, country clerks, and coroners" and even in some cases mayors—ought to be appointed. In short, Goodnow, quoting a speaker from an NML convention, concluded, "Where you want skill, you must appoint; where you want representation, elect."[100]

The *Municipal Program*, following this theory, recommended that only the mayor and council be elected, and it also incorporated most of Goodnow's other suggestions for ways to weaken the influence of parties in local elections by fostering spheres of local autonomy. The program included provisions such as personal registration; nomination by petition; the use of alphabetical, nonpartisan ballots; a reduction in the number of elective positions; and the establishment of separate local elections. Also, by creating a merit system for local administrative positions, the program's creators hoped to eliminate the temptations of the spoils system, and by instituting a uniform and public system of accounting, they tried to make it impossible for politicians to disguise fraud and embezzlement.[101] The program thus contained a detailed plan to alter the structures that enabled parties to influence city politics, with the aim of making it easier for voters to make decisions according to local concerns without regard for partisan affiliation.

At first, some members of the NML voiced concerns that the program's antiparty measures were not strong enough. President James Carter cautioned that he saw "in the Municipal Program . . . a disposition to depreciate to a certain extent that degree of emphasis which the League has hitherto placed upon the notion that the interference of political parties in municipal affairs was the principal source of our trouble."[102] At the NML's founding in 1894, many speakers highlighted the interference of state and national parties in local affairs.[103] Five years later, as the NML's membership discussed the proposed *Municipal Program* at the annual conference, Carter reiterated this belief that partisan meddling was "the great principal source of the evils against which we contend."[104]

At this same conference, Goodnow tried to assuage such concerns by emphasizing his contrasting views of political parties. He agreed that the intrusion of state and national parties posed a problem and "that municipal matters" needed to "be determined on their own merits," but he believed that such intrusion grew out of "the natural and legitimate desire of political parties to further the objects for which they have been established" and "to strengthen their own organization and maintain power."[105] The choice of the words *natural* and *legitimate* to describe parties was undoubtedly shocking to many and presented a sharp contrast to Carter's characterization of parties as "the great principal source of the evils." The solutions offered by the program did not rely on such a monocausal explanation. As Delos Wilcox, a former student of Goodnow, explained to members, the committee maintained that there were nearly a dozen "principal causes" of misgovernment, including not only "partisanship" but also "interference . . . by State Legislatures," "the private control of public privileges," "an undeveloped civic consciousness," "indefiniteness of organization," and "undemocratic organization."[106] Goodnow and his peers redirected the NML's focus to a broader, structural assessment of the roots of urban problems.

Ironically, despite these efforts, Goodnow's views, based on scientific rather than moralistic critiques, provided the rationale for reformers in the NML and across the country to validate and even expand their opposition to political parties. They also provided the framework and language that would dominate NML publications for years to come, facilitating the maintenance of coalitions of reformers nationally and locally. The program built on the widespread anger concerning the spoils and the interference of state legislatures in city government, but it redirected it in two key ways. First, Goodnow provided reformers with a source of expert authority to validate their efforts to create civil service systems in local government. In lieu of older arguments about the moral shortcomings of party politicians, reformers could now speak of the need to make positions appointive rather than elective because they required technical skill rather than representation. Second, the program's emphasis on creating a sphere of local autonomy encouraged reformers to redirect their antiparty efforts to the movements for home rule that would become increasingly popular in the new century. The program provided a more realistic basis for home rule by justifying the exclusion of parties in certain realms of local activity and outlining specific provisions to accomplish this goal. The analytical tools of political science, as applied in the program, thus afforded a new way to defend antiparty sentiment and civil service reform as apolitical matters of applying the fundamental principles of government. In these ways, political scientists and reformers were able to oppose parties, bosses, and machines without openly making anti-immigrant, class-based arguments.

The program helped establish municipal political scientists as leading experts worthy of consultation on real-world matters of reform. Its enthusiastic reception in newspapers and academic journals alike solidified an acceptance of political scientists' participation in such public endeavors. Partly as a result of the extensive contacts that Goodnow, Rowe, and Shaw made with other political scientists in their work for the NML, they became leading figures in the establishment of the APSA only two years after the publication of the program.[107] Goodnow in particular became an established authority on the drafting of local charters, with dozens of local leaders from cities across the country writing to him and requesting advice.[108] His colleagues would later describe his career by celebrating his work as both a "purely academic investigator" and a "man of action" concerned with "social progress."[109] Shaw and Rowe also continued long careers that paired scholarship and public activism.[110]

The avowed neutrality of political science and the framing of the program as universally applicable also served an important purpose for the NML and its local affiliates. Nationally, the program established the NML as the leading authority. In a telling example, the Census Bureau began to gather urban statistics by expanding on the structural and administrative aspects of the program.[111] Locally, the program helped to establish the reputation of the NML and its affiliates. The founders of municipal reform associations, as noted, created these organizations to undertake educational campaigns and shape public opinion in opposition to parties and in support of good city government. Urban reformers attempted to use the program, with its exclusive discussion of structure, to gain support from a variety of local groups working to expand municipal activities, from business groups seeking to develop infrastructure for commercial expansion to social reformers seeking to create programs to improve public welfare. Citing the credentials of its authors, reformers presented the program as a universal system applicable to all cities. This claim, however, would not be accepted without dissent, with residents of cities across the country asserting their right to formulate their own unique structures of city government.

3

The *Municipal Program* and Early Campaigns for Charter Reform, c. 1895–1910

I n the pages of local newspapers, editorials echoed the image of the National Municipal League (NML) and city government promoted by its own leaders: through its conference and publications, it had demonstrated that urban problems were uniform and, with the *Municipal Program*, ascertained universal solutions. In Newport, Rhode Island, the *Daily News* celebrated the NML's efforts in spreading the "news of [each] victory for good government," fostering the "growth of reform organizations," and stimulating "a renewed interest in citizenship." It commended the NML for revealing that the "general situation was . . . substantially identical in all large cities in the Union." Over eight hundred miles away, in Fort Wayne, Indiana, an editorial in the *Morning Journal-Gazette* concurred, writing that discussions at the NML's conference "showed clearly that the many and serious defects recognized in American municipal institutions are practically the same throughout the country." It celebrated the *Municipal Program* as "one of the best pieces of constructive work ever done by an organization devoted to the improvement of municipal government." The editorial in Rhode Island offered even stronger praise, characterizing it as "the ideal of American municipal organization, the ultimate aim toward which municipal reform organization may strive."[1]

With the publication of the *Municipal Program*, reformers in cities increasingly cited the NML to present charter revision as an apolitical matter of applying universal rules of good city government. In local newspapers, sympathetic editors and journalists described the NML as a prominent, national leader driven only by a desire to provide unbiased information.[2] Editorials and statements by the NML's officers seemed to forecast a wave of adoptions of the program in cities, with urban reformers and politicians eagerly welcoming the "world's greatest" plan of city government. Examinations of campaigns to revise city charters, however, demonstrate that the story was more complicated. While the program shaped discussions throughout the country, its proposals often sparked debate rather than consensus.

While the authors of the program avoided some divisive topics to maintain a coalition within the NML, they also intentionally adopted other provocative positions, pushing Americans to reconsider certain common assumptions about the meaning of democracy and local self-government. As noted, a redefinition of city-state relations was the cornerstone of the program. One aspect of this redefinition appealed greatly to a wide range of people: the proposal to free cities from state control and enable them to institute new programs. The program's authors promoted it as a tool that would help cities expand the scope of their activities according to local desires, and they intentionally did not take a position as to what sort of new programs should be instituted. In contrast, the second major proposed redefinition of city-state relations was less popular. For while the authors declared that every city should have the right to determine the activities undertaken, they also argued that the structures of city government should be uniform and established by state laws. Cities were to be free to decide whether they should provide utilities and transportation, but the structures of the executive and legislative branches and the methods of electing and appointing officers were to be universal.

This chapter explores these two components of the *Municipal Program*—the expansion of home rule and the assertion of universal structures of city government. It also focuses on the rising interest in administrative centralization, combining accounts of campaigns for charter revision in Toledo, Ohio, and Norfolk, Virginia, with an analysis of debates among the leading figures in the formation of the program introduced earlier: political scientists Leo Stanton Rowe, Albert Shaw, and Frank Goodnow, as well as leaders in the NML, including Delos Wilcox, Horace Deming, and Clinton Rogers Woodruff. In Toledo and Norfolk, reformers moved to revise charters to centralize administrative authority. Under such plans, mayors typically gained control over administrative departments through the power to appoint and remove officers, a power that previously belonged to councils or state-appointed boards. Advocates hoped that concentrating administrative power would also concentrate responsibility and accountability, and though they spoke of councils as fulfilling legislative roles, they often neglected to define or enlarge those roles. Many pushed for a reduction in the size of councils and electing councillors at large rather than by ward.[3]

This chapter demonstrates that urban reformers at the turn of the century embraced the notion that structural reform would facilitate functional expansion. A wide variety of politicians and reformers justified proposed charters as simple matters of applying uniform structures that would allow cities to provide greater services. In Toledo, a left-leaning mayor wanted to expand social welfare programs; in Norfolk, the mayor and his reform-minded allies in the Chamber of Commerce wanted to develop infrastructure to improve the city's image and attract investors. Despite their different motivations, both mayors believed that the scope of municipal activities needed to expand, and, importantly, both attempted to revise their cities' charters to achieve their goals. Though supporters portrayed charter revision as a simple tool to create streamlined machinery to facilitate the implementation of expansive programs, critics felt that new charters had the potential to fundamentally alter the representative structures of city government, structures that determined who would control the shape of that expansion. The responses to proposed plans to revise the charters of Toledo and Norfolk reveal that while most Americans adhered to the general concept of local, democratic self-government, they did not agree on its meaning.

Some debates centered on the meaning of local self-government. While the NML's leadership declared that charter making was not an essential component of local self-government, many residents of Toledo and Norfolk disagreed. The daily business of city government in the Progressive Era was not autonomous or isolated but rather intricately intertwined with the politics of state legislative bodies.[4] The process of charter revision was no different, with state laws regulating the types of permissible structures and state legislative approval typically required for the adoption of new charters. When the dominant party in city politics differed from the dominant party in state politics, minorities in cities often looked to their allies in the state legislatures for support.[5]

Even those who agreed that individual cities should have the right to draft charters often disagreed about which residents should have the right to participate in that drafting. A variety of local constituencies challenged the right of urban party leaders and elected officials to write charters without accepting wider input from residents. Leaders of commercial organizations, labor unions, and local municipal reform associations all demanded that their voices be heard in local charter-making bodies, as did representatives of racial and ethnic minorities. In their minds, drafting charters was a cherished right of American citizens, an opportunity to create fundamental laws to embody their visions of democratic governance.

The need for and legitimacy of group representation continued in considerations of the provisions of proposed charters. The program's authors celebrated their work as democratic, highlighting the strength of a small council elected at large as the representative of the will of the people of the entire city. Could a small council elected at large represent the interests of all "the people"? Was it in fact more democratic to reduce the number of elective offices, allowing the mayor, as the administrative head of a city, to make more appointments, so that citizens would vote for individuals rather than "the party line"? Or were administrative centralization and a shorter ballot a threat to democracy?

The Scope and Purpose of Home Rule in the *Municipal Program*

Despite their emphasis on governmental institutions, the NML's leaders and members often maintained that structural reform alone would not solve urban problems. In discussing the details of the proposed program, Woodruff celebrated the efforts of "so many groups of men and women" who were "seeking in various ways to improve municipal conditions." At one convention, he explained that "no charter, no statute, no organization however carefully and ingeniously devised will compensate for the want of a deep, intelligent, abiding interest and participation in public affairs."[6] At the same time, many also believed that certain structures could foster this interest. The first vice president of the NML, Charles Richardson, a retired businessman from Philadelphia, explained that "good city government" required "the development of an active, continuous interest on the part of the intelligent voters" and that much of the program had "been designed for that express purpose."[7]

The architects of the program believed that establishing greater home rule would create conditions that would foster greater public interest in local politics by protecting and nurturing a sphere in which local concerns thrived apart from larger state and national concerns. Despite the fact that the *Municipal Program* would be called a "model charter" for years to come, it in fact consisted of a series of constitutional amendments and a municipal corporation's act intended to be passed at the state level. According to Rowe, the program proposed to "give to the municipality the widest possible discretion in determining the sphere of its activity" and "to assure to every city a large measure of freedom in the determination of local policy."[8]

While they did not endorse specific policies, the political scientists who shaped the program clearly supported some form of municipal expansion, envisioning government as a positive force in the lives of residents. Rowe spoke to members of the NML about the relationship between city government and "social evolution," arguing that each community needed to be able "to adopt, consciously, a policy favoring the growth of the new civic standards" and raising standards of living by "offering . . . new services or commodities."[9] Shaw echoed these sentiments, celebrating the work of "the people of European cities" in "using their municipal machines to accomplish results in the way of an improved life for their people."[10] Speaking to an audience of the NML's members, Goodnow questioned the rising "fashion . . . to speak of the city as a business corporation." He urged them to view cities as governmental institutions that undertook initiatives not to "derive a profit from them" but rather because "local social welfare demands that they shall be so assumed."[11] All three thus encouraged reformers to rethink certain popular assumptions in order to promote an understanding of government as an agent of public welfare.

Other leaders in the NML shared this vision of government. Richardson claimed that "the scope of our local governments must be so enlarged that they will affect the average voter as constantly and in as many ways as possible." He specified "that reformers should take every opportunity to urge the extension of municipal functions to all such matters as supply of light, water, street transportation, etc."[12] In more dramatic terms, Wilcox wrote,

> A city is brought into being by the sheer necessity of some positive co-operation. The growth of municipal self-rule marks the turning point in our general theory of government. Henceforth, government must more and more become positive co-operation for mutual service rather than for mere repression. Hence the Committee . . . have boldly proclaimed the government of cities is a positive and necessary good.[13]

A variety of the NML's constituents shared similar views of government. Many commercial organizations believed that it was the duty of cities to provide the local infrastructure necessary for commercial development. At the 1897 conference, NML member Riverson Ritchie, secretary of the Cleveland Chamber of Commerce, addressed the relationship between "Commercial Organizations and Municipal Reform." Ritchie detailed several areas in which the Chamber, as part of its effort "to promote the growth of commerce and industry," had encouraged the city's government to adopt "a policy of continuity in the execution of municipal necessities and enterprises." From the Chamber's perspective, this included creating or further developing "public grounds and roadways," "the water system," "public sanitation," "the harbor," and "modern facilities" for "vessels" and "cargoes."[14]

Other members desired to expand municipal functions for social and moral reasons. At the NML's annual conference in Indianapolis in 1898, two leading left Progressive mayors addressed this theme. Mayor Josiah Quincy of Boston, known for his innovative welfare programs, asserted that city government "should keep up with the growth of civilization and the development of the community." Comparing "the American city of to-day with that of twenty-five or fifty years ago," Quincy celebrated "the broader conceptions of the social ends" of city government.[15] Mayor Samuel Jones of Toledo more dramatically concluded that "the purpose of municipal government" was "that of ministering in every possible way to the social needs of the people." Jones declared himself in favor of not only municipally owned utilities but also streets, schools, gymnasiums, hospitals, asylums, parks, bands, lodging houses, reading rooms, and art galleries.[16] While most participants at the annual conference of the NML did not advocate as wide a degree of municipal ownership as Jones, they generally expressed support of some form of enlargement of public enterprise.[17]

Given such support for municipal expansion, the *Municipal Program*'s proposal to empower urban residents to determine the nature of that expansion served an important purpose. Public ownership of utilities and transit systems was controversial, with many viewing it as a form of municipal socialism. As a result, the program took no position on this issue. Goodnow explained to the NML's membership that "the powers which any city should exercise depend very largely upon local conditions. No general rule as to the extent of municipal powers can be laid down." Shaw agreed that while the program made it possible for cities to opt for public ownership, it was not appropriate for the committee to "advocate or to condemn any particular innovation or extension of municipal functions."[18] The program also did not offer much detail with regard to the composition of city departments. It discussed "the exercise of municipal functions" as a matter of "procedure," detailing methods for regulating franchises, keeping public accounts, and instituting merit systems.[19] In short, in discussing function purely in terms of the creation of efficient structures, the NML avoided controversy and marshaled unanimous support for the program.

While the program left the range of functions up to individual cities, it provided less freedom with regard to structure. It did not provide for a local right to frame charters. Perhaps in deference to the widely held conviction that this right was fundamental to home rule, it permitted residents of cities with populations of twenty-five thousand or more to do so. But given that the program's proposed state laws also required all cities to adopt relatively uniform systems in terms of elections, the sale of franchises, accounting, indebtedness, courts, and general organization, this stipulation did not leave much room for cities to maneuver.[20] Notably, despite this concession, the program's authors unanimously declared that there was no value in allowing individual cities to frame their own charters. Explaining their rationale, Shaw maintained that campaigns to revise charters were "almost never brought about for really broad and conclusive reasons of public policy" but rather to enable one group to "profit at the expense of some other set of individuals." He derided American reformers for "making and unmaking charters" while European reformers made do with existing structures and focused on more consequential matters. The committee members hoped that the program would afford

American reformers the same opportunity, for, according to Shaw, they agreed that "the main outlines of a municipal system should be uniform throughout all the towns of a State."[21] Yet while Shaw opposed allowing individual cities to draft charters because he felt structures were largely irrelevant, Goodnow opposed this privilege because he considered them extremely important. Goodnow believed that there were certain universal principles on which governmental institutions should be organized and that he and the committee had articulated them.[22]

This position was unconventional, for many Americans cherished the right to frame local charters. N. F. Hawley, a lawyer and secretary of the Minneapolis Charter Commission, defended this right in a response to Shaw, challenging the program on three fronts. First, he offered a pragmatic critique, suggesting that most Americans would be unwilling to accept predetermined charters. Explaining the popularity of charter revision, he quipped, "People seem to be as tenacious in their theories and forms of government as they are in their theological opinions."[23] Second, he suggested that the program, in proposing uniform charters imposed by state laws, might inadvertently lead to more interference by state legislatures.[24] And third, he questioned the assumption that authors of the program had in fact determined the ideal form of city government:

> The best form of charter under purely democratic institutions and free from aristocratic traditions and influence has not yet been demonstrated. It may somewhere be in practice, but the time has not yet come for its universal or even general recognition. In the meantime is it not best to permit the ideal or ultimate form of municipal government in this country to be evolved under the greatest municipal freedom?[25]

What did the NML's officers think of this difference of opinion? Unfortunately, there are few surviving minutes from internal meetings in these years to provide definitive answers. Only published accounts of the annual conference remain.[26] The yearly reports by Woodruff, with detailed summaries of the NML's major activities, provide clues. Speaking at the same convention where Shaw and Hawley disagreed about the program, Woodruff presented his summary titled "A Year's Advance." Though he discussed charter revisions and the expansion of municipal services, he focused on what he declared to be the NML's preeminent concern, discussing local autonomy in terms of "a consideration of municipal questions apart from State or national politics." When detailing the work of local affiliates, he celebrated their efforts to challenge political parties and political corruption: the efforts of the Municipal League of Philadelphia to highlight the corruption of elected officials; the work of the Richmond League for Good City Government to run nonpartisan tickets; and the decision of the Municipal Association of Cleveland to endorse candidates without regard for partisan affiliation.[27]

In his review the following year, Woodruff again discussed the importance of separating local from state and national issues, but there was a gradual, subtle shift in the way he discussed self-government. While he continued to note popular interest in municipal ownership, Woodruff devoted more time to detailing campaigns to reform city charters. Despite claiming the previous year that the program was intended to promote uniformity in city government, Woodruff now celebrated its influence not only in state bodies deliberating on local laws but also in the work of charter commissions in individual cities. While the tone of his remarks was often neutral, largely detailing events transpiring in specific cities, at times he seemed to be endorsing the notion that charter reform was part of home rule. He discussed state constitutions in California and Minnesota that allowed urban residents to appoint committees to draft their own charters, and he described charter campaigns in cities such as San Francisco, Spokane, Saint Paul, Duluth, Milwaukee, Wilmington, and Mobile. He characterized home rule laws and the resulting charter campaigns in positive terms, concluding, "The whole movement has been a healthy and a hopeful one and argues well for the future."[28]

Despite this deviation from the uniform charter proposed in the program, Woodruff still celebrated the influence of its authors. He noted that Goodnow, along with Deming and Shaw, had been invited to participate in the Greater New York Charter Commission, that President William McKinley had asked Rowe to join the Porto Rican Commission, and that in many other instances committee members had been asked to consult on charter commissions in cities, "advancing the principles embodied in the Program."[29] In short, Woodruff's remarks suggest that the NML's leadership promoted somewhat inconsistent views, simultaneously touting the professed universalism of the program's proposed charter while also embracing opportunities to shape charters drafted under home rule laws.

Charter Reform to Promote Municipal Ownership: Samuel "Golden Rule" Jones in Toledo, Ohio, 1897–1901

When the Republican Party in Toledo nominated Samuel Jones for mayor in 1897, its members did not understand the man they selected or anticipate the consequences of their decision.[30] In the 1890s, the Republican Party in Ohio was dominant and closely tied to business. Toledo was a rapidly expanding industrial center, marked by ethnic diversity and a reputation for gambling, prostitution, and drinking. Republican leaders nominated Jones, an outsider, to resolve a factional dispute. Jones was a relative newcomer to Toledo, known largely as a Christian businessman who promoted innovative but profitable labor methods.[31] Once he entered office, it became clear that Jones was not a typical businessman. Initially, he did not have a clear agenda or political philosophy. Nevertheless, the agenda that he began to form drew on his deep commitment to a sort of egalitarian communalism. His understanding of Christianity and American democratic ideals led him to support full equality among all men and women, whether "black or white, brown or yellow." Once in office, he came to view city government as a powerful tool for fostering community.[32]

Despite Jones's passionate belief in the potential of democratic government, he maintained that true democracy had never existed.[33] In his view, the major impediment to the realization of democracy in America's cities was the franchise system. He presented this system and municipal ownership as a choice between corruption and democracy. Jones viewed the sale of franchises on the local level as part of a larger, national problem that granted "special privileges" to the few at the expense of the many, including preferential tariffs, patents, and trusts.[34] A year after his election, he attended the NML's annual conference. There, after a discussion of the relative merits of the two systems, Jones declared, "Private ownership of public franchises is a high crime against democracy. It is contrary to the spirit of republican institutions. It is a city granting privilege to an individual to enrich himself, usually at the expense of the classes least able to bear it, the poor people." While many of his contemporaries blamed politicians for the corruption of city government, Jones insisted that businessmen driven by a desire for "success" and wealth were the real culprits.[35]

The following year, in *The New Right: A Plea for Fair Play and a More Just Social Order*, Jones proposed a dramatic expansion and redirection of city government. He insisted that if cities operated schools, police forces, and fire departments and constructed sidewalks, roads, and bridges, there was no reason that they should not also provide public transportation, water, lighting, heat, telephones, telegraphs, and even "free lectures, free music, free baths, free play-grounds, free gymnasia." He rejected the notion that the potential for corruption made municipal ownership unfeasible, noting examples of existing public programs that were well run.[36] Jones and his cohort of reformers in Ohio wanted cities to provide social and philanthropic activities currently supplied by private charities and political machines, believing that public recreation would function as a better deterrent to drinking and gambling than a punitive legal system. He felt that cities should devote less time to policing residents and more time to promoting public welfare, utilizing cooperation rather than coercion.[37]

For Jones, publicly owned utilities and transit systems were part of a larger vision of government as an agent of communal love rather than coercive power. Jones believed that municipal ownership provided opportunities for citizens to realize their love for their neighbors. He wrote that services provided directly by cities "are the fraternal forces that are unifying our life, that are bringing us together as members of one great family having one common interest and one common destiny."[38] Jones, like many of his contemporaries, was troubled by the loss of community that seemed to accompany modern urban life. In his factories, he sought to rebuild community by providing opportunities for recreation and fellowship among workers.[39] In a vision that many would call utopian, he offered "public ownership" as the way for "*the municipality, the state, and the nation [to] find a means of expressing its love for the people.*"[40] As mayor, he hoped to use city government to create a renewed sense of citizenship, patriotism, and community among Toledo's residents.

Jones believed that the only way to establish his program of municipal ownership in Toledo was through greater home rule and nonpartisanship. Like his peers at the NML, Jones believed that a rejection of parties and rise in independent voting would enable voters to focus on the needs of their local communities.[41] In the nineteenth century, many Americans were wary of centralization and more willing to accept governmental expansion on the local rather than state or national level. Active local government more closely aligned with republican ideals regarding self-government and individual liberty.[42] Jones, however, believed that cities would pave the way for public ownership in the states and nation: "The municipality is the nucleus of government. The state and the nation look to the municipality for their ideal."[43] For a time, Toledo's voters seemed to agree. In March 1899, Jones was reelected as an independent rather than a Republican, running on a platform of municipal ownership of utilities and protections of workers' rights.[44] At a convention of the NML, Woodruff celebrated Jones's election, stating that "his triumphant election by an overwhelming majority clearly indicated" support for nonpartisanship and municipal ownership among "the people of Toledo."[45]

Jones was optimistic that Toledoans would unite in support of his vision. In August, he asked the council to secure "REMEDIAL LEGISLATION, to enable the city through its legislative and executive departments to perform the functions that properly belong to it." He reminded his listeners that "State laws ... seriously hinder the progress of the city towards the scientific government of an ideal municipality." Specifically, he asked for support for a revision of the state code governing cities that would expand home rule to the largest degree possible without a constitutional amendment. Framing the issue as a moral one, he described the movement for home rule as a "great work for human emancipation." His goal was to provide "the Ohio municipalities" with "the necessary degree of liberty to allow the people of our cities to properly express their love for one another in or through government."[46]

Jones soon discovered that the state government was not the only or even the primary barrier to the realization of his vision. The previous administration, run by the local Republican machine, was marred by common accusations of corruption: taking payoffs for turning a blind eye to prostitution and gambling, rewarding supporters with patronage positions, and receiving kickbacks for selling valuable franchises. When Jones entered office, he discovered that Toledo's government was unwieldy and decentralized, run by a forty-five-member bicameral council elected by ward and fourteen boards and commissions. The mayor held little real power. One exception was the Police Board, appointed by the mayor. Jones worked with the Board to institute a civil service system and eight-hour workday. But in December 1899, when Jones attempted to prevent the sale of Toledo's municipal gas plant and block the extension of a franchise for electric lighting, the council blocked his efforts.[47] His independent candidacy won him a clear electoral victory but did not endear him to the party politicians who controlled the council. His firm nonpartisanship and refusal to bargain isolated him politically.[48]

After these defeats, Jones proposed to revise the city's charter to strengthen the office of the mayor.[49] His interest in structural reform developed through his contacts with national reform networks, but he adapted what he learned to conform to his own democratic convictions. While he did not directly cite the NML as his inspiration, the charter that he proposed in 1900 closely resembled the *Municipal Program* that was published the same year. Both enhanced mayoral powers of appointment; replaced large, bicameral councils with smaller, unicameral councils elected at least partly at large; instituted civil service provisions; reduced the role of parties in local elections; and maximized the sphere of home rule. Yet Jones's proposal differed in its advocacy of enhanced public participation in governance. He sought to offset the centralization of this form of "strong mayor" government with the inclusion of a provision to replace the mayoral veto of council bills, which he viewed as "undemocratic," with public referenda.[50] Jones wanted voters rather than the council to have the right to decide whether to grant franchises to private companies for the provision of utilities and transportation.[51] With the inclusion of this form of direct democracy, Jones likely believed that his plan could achieve the administrative efficiency necessary to expand the scope of city government while maintaining popular accountability.

Jones, echoing national reformers, presented his proposed charter as a simple mechanism for creating a more efficient and modern form of government to inhibit corruption. In a message sent to the council, Jones described Toledo's existing government as "cumbersome and antiquated," "primitive and inadequate," and "not adapted to the needs of a city the size of Toledo." Despite their recent differences, he insisted he felt only "cordial goodwill" for the council and expressed confidence in their "general integrity of . . . purpose." Notably, he did not mention franchises or municipal ownership and only alluded to the fact that the mayor was "a chief executive in name only." He did, however, claim that he had corresponded widely with officials from cities all over the country who concurred that "the party machine" was "the curse of American municipal politics." To address these problems, he proposed to revise the charter.[52]

Jones's views at times seemed contradictory: he criticized those who presented legal reforms as a panacea and simultaneously supported similar legal reforms. In supporting charter revision, home rule, and nonpartisan elections, Jones espoused a program similar to that of many prominent reformers in NML who believed the legal changes would yield better government. As he told Toledo's Common Council, "The problem of properly governing our cities is one that is commanding the most careful attention of the best minds of earth today."[53] Yet elsewhere, Jones critiqued such reformers, mocking the notion that "tinkering" with a few laws would yield "good government" without addressing economic exploitation.[54] Nevertheless, while he was primarily concerned with social reforms, his actions in 1899 and 1900 demonstrate his belief that legal changes would be necessary to achieve his social agenda. For Jones, the question was not whether to focus on social or structural reforms; rather, structural reforms provided the key to enacting his social agenda.[55]

Moreover, Jones's vision for the process of charter revision underscored his commitment to home rule and participatory self-government. Jones recommended the creation of a commission to draft a charter that would be voted on by Toledoans and then sent to the state legislature for approval. Cities in Ohio did not possess the right to draft charters. Officially, a uniform municipal code meant that cities of the same size shared the same system of governance. Unofficially, the state legislature intervened in urban affairs, passing individual bills based on narrow population grades to apply to specific cities. As a result, a popular referendum would not be binding, but Jones likely hoped that the legislature would approve a charter endorsed by Toledoans.[56] Regardless of state law, Jones consistently sought popular support for his reforms, including the proposed charter. He wanted the commission to represent all residents, and he worked to ensure that the charter would be created with publicity and public involvement.[57] Jones proposed that the presidents of Toledo's Central Labor Union (CLU) and Chamber of Commerce join him and the head of the council in appointing fifty members to a Charter Commission.[58] The resulting Commission was remarkably representative for the day. In addition to current city officials and business leaders, it included three women involved in education, the presidents of local unions, a bookbinder, a sheet metal worker, and an African American deputy county recorder. When a member of the Polish community complained that it had no representatives, the Commission later agreed to appoint one.[59] In short, while the *Municipal Program* influenced Jones, he also rejected several of the fundamental assumptions espoused by prominent figures in the NML: that local people should not have the right to draft their own charters and that any group had the right or ability to speak on behalf of all the people.

Charter Reform and Boosterism: The Good Government Association Versus the Municipal League in Norfolk, Virginia, 1904–1906

As in Toledo, the process of charter reform in Norfolk began when politicians attempted to restructure government to enable the city to undertake new programs. In the first years of the twentieth century, boosters in cities across the country worked to attract outside investors by providing modern infrastructures and services.[60] In Norfolk, a shipping center with a reputation as a "wide-open" town, the drive to modernize was urgent in 1904 with the Jamestown Tercentennial Exposition looming three short years away. As Mayor James Riddick stated, "With our city about to go on exhibition before the people of the whole world, it is particularly necessary for us to put our house in order." Riddick, a medical doctor lacking an extensive political background, would not play as active a role in charter reform as Jones.[61] He did, however, take the lead in promoting the expansion of Norfolk's government. Riddick celebrated recent advancements in public health due to improvements in sewerage and the establishment of a municipally owned waterworks. He highlighted progress in paving and lighting streets and regulating saloons. At the same time, he suggested that more needed to be done.[62] This desire to "boost" Norfolk through municipal expansion drew support from politicians, reformers, and labor leaders, sparking interest in adopting a new charter.

The other main impetus for a new charter was a change in state law. In 1902, Virginia adopted a new constitution with a revised article on the organization of the governments of cities and towns. Two years later, a member of Norfolk's Common Council introduced a resolution to revise

Norfolk's charter.[63] Norfolk's present charter now violated state laws in several ways, particularly by appointing rather than electing a number of officials.[64] Nevertheless, the move to adopt a new charter was also part of the move of the Good Government Association (GGA) to consolidate control of Norfolk's government.

The GGA began as a protest against the so-called Ring that dominated Norfolk's politics. Given the absence of a competitive Republican Party, the real contest in city elections was between these two factions in the Democratic primary. Under the rule of the Ring, Norfolk had become known for saloons, gambling, and prostitution. By 1902, with the support of organized labor, members of the GGA took control of the city councils, promising to reduce crime, institute honest elections, prevent the sale of franchises for political favors, and secure public control of utilities. That same year, Virginia's new constitution disfranchised African Americans and many poor whites. The loss of these voters hurt the Ring at the polls, and by 1904, the GGA controlled Norfolk's government.[65]

With the Jamestown Tercentennial Exposition approaching, the GGA worked with local commercial organizations to restore Norfolk's reputation, partly by embarking on a plan for beautification, particularly of streets, sidewalks, and parks.[66] Supported by fellow business leaders and professionals, councillors in the GGA worked to clean up the city, largely to attract investors. They collaborated with the Chamber of Commerce, which in 1904 petitioned the councils for the establishment of a municipal bureau of improvement. That same year, the Chamber took the lead in expanding the city's railway system. In 1905, the Chamber focused on the expansion of the city itself through consolidation with Portsmouth.[67] The *Virginian Pilot* commended such efforts, claiming that "Progressive cities everywhere have come to recognize the necessity of making themselves attractive, if not only as an end desired in itself, but as a means to their success and prosperity in a business way."[68]

The GGA initially formed alliances with unions. The CLU supported the GGA and regarded the upcoming Jamestown Exposition as beneficial for organized labor. The organizers promised to use union labor in building and construction projects.[69] Organized labor was active in Norfolk politics, and when an attempt to form a workingman's political club to nominate its own candidates for the councils faltered, the union members involved decided to back the GGA's candidates.[70]

While in Toledo Jones invited representatives of labor and business to participate in the drafting of a charter, in Norfolk the GGA attempted to insulate the process. As a result, it began to lose the support of organized labor and other groups, suggesting that for many individuals, democratic government began with the process of making the charter itself. Unlike Jones, Norfolk's politicians did not announce what type of revisions they supported from the start, claiming only that they wanted to revise the charter in accordance with new state laws. The councillors voted to create a commission to draft a charter, submit it to the councils for adoption, and then present it to the Virginia General Assembly for ratification. Predictably, the seven-person Charter Commission, including one member of the Select Council, two members of the Common Council, the city attorney, the city engineers, and two private citizens (both lawyers selected by the councils), was closely allied with the GGA.[71] In response, the CLU unanimously adopted a resolution requesting that the council appoint a representative of organized labor. The union member who proposed the resolution maintained that organized labor needed "representation along with other local interests," requesting that "someone conversant with the best interests of working people" be appointed.[72] The council denied the request, claiming that the current commissioners "were fully capable of representing all the interests of the community justly and fairly and that too many members would make it cumbersome and unwieldy." One councillor criticized the CLU for attempting to inject "party or factional politics in such an important body."[73] In so doing, the council rejected the notion that laborers had distinct interests that warranted representation.

The following month, the Charter Commission declared its sessions closed to the public, calling it "inexpedient" to allow access to its "deliberations," though it still accepted written suggestions from private citizens.[74] The press criticized this decision and reported information leaked from meetings.[75] Soon, disgruntled citizens claimed that the GGA was devoted not to reform but rather to consolidating power by any means. These citizens, declaring themselves representatives of the people, organized the Norfolk Municipal League to promote the adoption of a modern charter.[76]

The Norfolk Municipal League's founders and their allies used the organizational form of a municipal league to assert their authority as apolitical civic leaders interested only in good government and a revival of popular interest in local affairs. Shortly before its formation, an editorial in the *Virginian Pilot* explained that municipal leagues "are in existence in many of the largest and most progressive cities of the United States and the promoters of the proposed organization here aver that the time is ripe for the formation of such an association in Norfolk." At the Norfolk League's first meeting, in March 1905, President C. P. Shaw, a retired naval lieutenant, told listeners that to improve municipal government, many of the "larger cities of the country have organized municipal leagues." At their next meeting, the Norfolk League's members voted to adopt the constitution of "the famous Harrisburg league" and to affiliate with the NML. Within months, Shaw initiated plans to create a statewide league, sending appeals to newspapers and "prominent men" in towns and cities across Virginia to form leagues of their own. Echoing the NML's vision, the first declared purpose of the Norfolk League's constitution was "to induce citizens to take an active and earnest part in municipal affairs; to stimulate civic pride, cooperation and public spirit."[77]

The leaders of the Norfolk Municipal League built on the reputation of the NML and the *Municipal Program* to promote popular interest in charter reform and their leadership. The *Virginian Pilot* described the NML as a valuable source of unbiased information, depicting its officers and members as "earnest and sincere." It highlighted the NML's value, claiming that elected officials and other interested parties, increasingly aware of "the need for definite information," often wrote directly to the NML for advice. The newspaper recommended the *Municipal Program*, written by extremely "competent" men "free from all political prejudice," as "the league's greatest work, and indeed the world's greatest work of its kind."[78] Building on such praise, with the Charter Commission at work, the Norfolk League called on "all public-spirited citizens" to "unite to see to it that this charter should indeed be a 'charter of their liberties' and confer on the city in the highest possible degree the blessings of home rule." The Norfolk League recommended the *Municipal Program* as a model and presented copies to members of the Charter Commission. Shaw stressed that "the ablest experts" in the country had drafted the program, implying that the Charter Commission could do no better. He particularly emphasized the importance of the initiative and referendum, and he also sought the inclusion of a merit-based civil service.[79]

In response, the commissioners and others questioned the value of the *Municipal Program*. One commissioner commented, "We are trying to formulate a charter in accordance with the constitution of the state . . . such as may be applicable to the local conditions and not a charter based upon academic and theoretical views." An editorial in the *Norfolk Public Ledger* agreed, arguing that "there are some theories that are absolutely irrefutable from a standpoint of a theoretical argument that are untried and might not prove suited to local conditions."[80] While the leaders of the Norfolk League celebrated the academic credentials of the authors of the program, their opponents denigrated those same credentials, dismissing scholarly work as abstract and impractical.

Additionally, as self-declared public representatives, the Norfolk Municipal League's leaders assumed that they would be given access to the Charter Commission's sessions. The chair, however, maintained that while the Norfolk League's members were free to submit written suggestions like other private citizens, they would not be allowed to attend the closed sessions.[81] In response, Shaw launched a campaign against the "undemocratic secret sessions" of the Charter Commission. He claimed that secret meetings violated "the two fundamental principles on which all workable systems of representative government must be founded—that people are the sources of all power and that the majority must rule." When approached by the press, the commissioners refused to respond to Shaw's comments.[82] Despite the requests of the CLU and the Norfolk League, the commissioners did not view charter making as requiring public deliberation.

In short, the GGA's moves to initiate and control charter reform not only demonstrate a desire to use structural reform to facilitate the governmental expansion. They also resulted in vehement opposition from the CLU and the Norfolk Municipal League, opposition that confirms the conviction of NML members who challenged the *Municipal Program*: many Americans perceived the right to participate in the formation of city charters as a fundamental one and a vital component of self-government.

The *Municipal Program* as "Radical Democracy"

In contrast, the authors of the *Municipal Program* defined local self-government very differently: not as the right to draft charters but rather as the right to enact policies that reflected the popular will. As noted, the first step in achieving this goal was preventing state interference in local matters. The second was more clearly distinguishing between the mayor's administrative role and the council's legislative role. The program defined the mayor as the "chief administrative officer," with the right to appoint department heads and subordinate officers, subject only to a civil service system. It granted the council the right to formulate policies. The program intended this to be a wide grant of powers, including the right to establish city offices, make appropriations, levy taxes, regulate assessments, and investigate administrative departments.[83]

While reformers often described administrative consolidation as a strong-mayor form of government, the program's authors instead emphasized the powers of the council. They maintained that the program's inclusion of a powerful, representative local assembly was essential for the proposed system to function democratically. Given the pervasive distrust of city councils, most movements for charter reform by the 1880s focused on increasing mayoral administrative powers.[84] The program increased such mayoral powers, but only when paired with parallel increases in councils' legislative powers. When advocating powerful councils before the NML, Rowe joked that he was aware that "this implied plea for the rehabilitation of the local representative body will be received, in many quarters, with a smile." But he explained that "it is the only system which meets the requirements of modern democratic ideas."[85] In this way, the program's authors presented strong councils as fulfilling the need for representation of local opinion. (Despite this intention, later studies misrepresented the model proposed in the *Municipal Program* by characterizing it as a form of strong-mayor government.)[86]

The conviction that separating legislation and administration was essential explains why the program's authors did not view charter marking as a local right. As Goodnow explained, while "it has been felt that . . . free play might be given the people of the cities as to the details of their city charters, it was wiser to fix beyond the possibility of change the general principles which should lie at the base of municipal organization."[87] Therefore, in the formation of local charters, the program's provisions on the powers of mayors and councils left little room for variation.

The program's few discretionary structural provisions reveal the subjects that were sources of disagreement. The program's democracy was more representative than direct. In terms of representation, the program primarily recommended electing council members at large, though it did allow for individual cities to opt for proportional representation and enact measures for "direct legislation," presenting these choices as part of home rule.[88] The program, however, was far from neutral regarding the selection of council members, clearly favoring at-large elections. One committee member explained that at-large elections prevented gerrymandered districts.[89] And although Rowe explained that in larger cities residents might choose systems of ward-based elections, he believed that in "smaller cities there is no valid reason for district or local representation."[90] Moreover, the authors neglected to discuss either proportional representation or direct legislation in any depth when explaining the program.[91]

The fondness for at-large elections stemmed partly from the organic conceptions of cities still common among academics and reformers. Woodrow Wilson explained the connection between such conceptions and at-large representation in councils in a public lecture on city government in Baltimore in 1896: "Common interests should be determined by a common vote. A city is not a group of localities, nor an aggregation of interests nor a public works corporation, but an organism, whole and vital only when conscious of its wholeness and identity."[92] Most reformers agreed, claiming that ward representation led to the election of council members narrowly concerned with their own constituents rather than the good of the city as a whole. This preference for at-large elections also rested on the prevailing belief that despite the seeming diversity of opinion among urban residents, there nevertheless was a singular will to be represented in legislative bodies. The authors of the program agreed with this line of reasoning, critiquing ward-based elections.[93] Urban problems, according to Rowe, needed to "be considered from the standpoint of the community viewed as a unit."[94] The program thus reflected a belief in the existence of a singular will among urban residents and the assumption that councillors could—and would—represent the interests of all residents.

This belief is essential for understanding how the committee members viewed the program as a democratic form of government. They intended strong councils elected at large and the regulation of political parties to create a system consistent with what Wilcox called "the demands of radical democracy."[95] Deming articulated this view most directly in a talk titled "Public Opinion and City Government Under the Proposed Municipal Program." He argued that the council played an essential role in "representative democracy" because "public opinion" had to control the "conduct" of a city. He defined the program, with its provisions for home rule and a strong council, as a true "representative democracy" because it facilitated the conditions necessary to "develop an enlightened opinion" and enabled "a representative body, elected by the people, to determine local public policy."[96] The key assumption that Deming and others made was that there was only one "enlightened opinion," one "will of the people" to be represented by council members. Thus, while many provisions in the program were radical in comparison with established practices, they continued to be based on a conception of democracy that assumed that deliberation would yield consensus and a sense of common purpose.

Additionally, in a seemingly counterintuitive argument, several committee members claimed that reducing the number of elective offices made the program more democratic than existing forms of city government. A forerunner of the Short Ballot movement, the program drastically reduced the number of elective offices from the norm in most cities. In recommending that only the council and mayor be elected and that the mayor appoint all administrative positions, the program's authors attempted to make it easier for the public to control the administration by making clear whom they should hold accountable. If the administration was poorly run, the mayor was responsible, and, as he was only given a two-year term, the people could soon vote him out of office.[97]

While reducing the number of elective officers seemed to reduce the demands on voters, the program's authors and members of the NML who supported their work argued otherwise. They believed that the program created a form of government that would spark greater interest and involvement in city government. With its publication, Deming promised that, if adopted, the program would stimulate the public interest in local affairs necessary to solve urban problems. The program was designed in part to "compel the development of this interest." Its provisions for home rule and its version of mayor-council government forced citizens "to work out their local destiny" and provided them with "ample powers to manage the city's business."[98] And this, for the program's authors, was democracy.

Administrative Centralization and At-Large Elections as Undemocratic: Charter Reform in Toledo, 1901

The outcome of Jones's effort to secure a new charter demonstrates the local influence of the NML and its limits. Jones's popularity suggests that most Toledoans shared his vision of a more active city government that would better meet their needs. Yet they did not agree that administrative centralization and the creation of a small council elected at large were democratic. Toledoans may have wanted the city to provide more services, but they were unwilling to sacrifice what they perceived to be democratic control of government to achieve it.

While the NML asserted that urban conditions were so similar that charters should be uniform in all cities, in Toledo in 1901 the Charter Commission debated the appropriateness of models created elsewhere. When the Commission began its work, one member suggested that they adopt the "Cleveland Plan," a recent charter enacted in Cleveland to which they were, according to state law, now entitled, having moved to a higher population grade. But another member disagreed, arguing that the Commission should compare several models, including that proposed in the *Municipal Program*. Jones agreed, claiming that "Toledo should be a pacemaker, not a follower."[99]

Jones, as noted, hoped to modify the program by enhancing provisions for direct democracy with popular referenda on franchises and other council bills (rather than mayoral vetoes). Ironically, his desire for an inclusive process for drafting a charter led to weaker proposals for direct democracy. In his efforts to include diverse voices, Jones lost control of the process. Despite Jones's efforts to make the Charter Commission inclusive and deliberative, meetings were often marked by heated disagreements not about the content of the charter but rather about proper parliamentary rules of debate. Several members accused the chair of imposing a gag order to prevent them from voicing opinions and presenting alternative proposals.[100] Ultimately, a small Republican majority was able to push through a strong-mayor charter without Jones's plan to replace the mayoral veto with popular referenda. The charter created a seven-member council elected at large, granted the mayor extensive administrative control, established a civil service, and allowed popular referenda only on franchises.[101]

Despite the fact that the proposed charter was not what he had originally envisioned, Jones endorsed the Charter Commission's work as an improvement over the status quo. Many of his supporters, however, did not agree. Only twenty-three members of the Commission agreed to endorse the charter, and nineteen publicly declared opposition.[102] This division partly followed partisan lines, with most Republicans signing the charter and most of the Democrats signing the protest.[103] Yet the outcome also revealed the salience of racial, ethnic, and class identities in considerations of representation in government. All of the representatives of the Commission whose constituencies were otherwise ardent followers of Jones—the union members as well as the African American, German, and Polish members—voted against the charter. Leaders of Toledo's two largest federations of unions signed a public letter of opposition.[104] While they supported expanded public programs, they did not believe that this form of government was the way to create them.

Critics perceived the centralization of power in the office of the mayor to be not a simple matter of separating politics from administration but rather a dangerous attack on the principle of popular representation in government. L. W. Morris, a Republican judge in the common pleas court, wrote an article for the *Toledo Blade* to explain why he and other members of the Commission did not support the charter. He claimed that the position of the mayor was "UNDEMOCRATIC AND MONARCHICAL. It takes the government of the city out of the hands of the people and their duly authorized representatives and puts it into the hands of one man for a term of years." Morris added that it made the mayor a "dictator" and a "boss," concluding, "I believe that the American tendency to place municipalities under one man's management . . . shows, not only want of faith in the capacity of the people for self government, but great indifference as to results."[105]

Six days later, the *Blade* published a reply to Morris written by Julian Tyler, a Republican lawyer and one of the commissioners supporting the charter. Echoing the views promoted by the NML, Tyler claimed that their proposal separated the functions of the executive and legislative branches of city government, just as in the federal government. He denied that the mayor's administrative control would make him a despot since he had no legislative powers.[106] Morris, however, countered in another article that the mayor did have legislative powers in his rights to veto bills and recommend public improvements. He further claimed that the commissioners who supported the charter were using the theory of separation of powers to mask their real ends of granting the mayor absolute power. He even claimed that during their meetings, certain members of the Charter Commission referred to popular government as "nonsense" and equated the mayor with a czar.[107]

The proposed council sparked a similar debate. Those who opposed the charter claimed that a seven-member council elected at large did not provide for minority representation and voiced their preference for a much larger, ward-based body.[108] Morris's articles in the *Blade* explained why these commissioners felt that the charter did not provide for adequate representation. He argued that the proposed council "is not large enough to be fairly representative of the many import interests and sections . . . of a great and growing city like Toledo." In contrast, he advocated a council that provided "for minority representation, and for that of any great interest whether it be political, religious, social, mercantile, racial or industrial." Without such representation, a council, according to Morris, "is not only not democratic, but it lacks the very power of reflecting the popular will. Deprived of fair representation in council, the people are not granted even the appearance of participation in their own affairs."[109]

Tyler, in defending the council, presented a very different understanding of the nature of popular representation in legislative bodies, again echoing the views of the leadership of the NML. He believed that it was not fair for a person elected in only one ward to have the power to make legislative decisions that affected an entire city. The at-large system, he added, would make it possible "to elect men who will be truly representative of the entire body of the citizens, and who, while charged with the . . . duty of legislating for the best interests of the city as a whole, [will] protect and advance the interests of every part of it."[110] In short, in the pages of the local papers, Morris and Tyler articulated competing conceptions of representation. Their debates suggest that many Toledoans did not share in the views of democracy embodied by the *Municipal Program*: that administrative centralization would be offset by a strong council and that at-large elections allowed for representation of the will of the people.

The popular referendum on the charter suggests that the opinions of the voters of Toledo paralleled those of the charter commissioners, with working-class districts voting more heavily against the charter. The new charter failed to pass by a narrow margin of 49.4 percent to 51.6 percent.[111] Jones had originally hoped to make use of these features to implement social welfare policies that would have benefited members of the working class. Yet without strong support, he was unable to secure the inclusion of a popular referendum to replace the mayoral veto, and without the referendum, there was little in the Commission's proposal to convince the majority of Toledoans that city government would remain popularly accountable.

Elective Offices, Redistricting, and Civil Service: State Intervention in Charter Revision as Democratic, Norfolk, 1906–1907

The outcome of charter reform in Norfolk also demonstrated both the reach and limitations of the NML's influence. In Toledo, debates focused on the perceived excesses of the mayor's powers and the loss of representation in a council elected at large. In Norfolk, controversies centered on different topics, primarily the number of elective offices, redistricting, and the creation of a civil service. Yet as in Toledo, discussions surrounding proposed changes in Norfolk highlight differing views of the meaning of democratic self-government. Additionally, Norfolk's story highlights the importance of debates about race, minority representation, and state intervention in local affairs.

When the Charter Commission published its work in February 1906 after months of closed sessions, its proposed charter did not follow the recommendations of the *Municipal Program*, nor did it contain provisions for a civil service system, the initiative, and referendum as recommended by the Norfolk Municipal League, dismissed by the chairman as "not being of practical value."[112] Though the Charter Commission considered strengthening the mayor's administrative powers and other forms of administrative consolidation, it ultimately recommended the creation of a Board of Control.[113] The Board of Control would replace the six council-appointed boards that currently ran individual departments (streets, sewers and drains, water, police, health, and fire). It would centralize the city government, reducing the powers of the council, which would no longer manage departmental business in committee.[114]

With the announcement of this plan, President Shaw of the Norfolk Municipal League vehemently protested the lack of civil service provisions. A civil service system had already been introduced in Norfolk's fire department, and for a time it seemed that the Charter Commission would include provisions to expand it to include the police department.[115] During the commission's deliberations, Shaw had pushed for "the adoption of the competitive merit system" as part of a shift "from political to business methods," explaining that such a system would be the "death knell of the politicians, but the salvation of the taxpayer."[116] In doing so, he echoed Goodnow's assurances that enacting "civil service regulations" would eliminate "the temptation and the opportunity" for patronage.[117] In the face of Shaw's continued agitation, despite the charter commissioners' fears of the potential racial implications of a civil service system (African Americans would be eligible to apply for jobs), the councils amended the proposed charter to include one.[118]

Critics dismissed this amendment as an attempt to pacify those angered by the fact that the Board of Control was to be appointed. The editor of the *Norfolk Public Ledger* declared that "a limited and ineffectual civil service . . . does not lessen the desirability of having the board of control elected by the people."[119] Given the Board's vast powers, the method of its selection was essential in determining who would run Norfolk's government. The Charter Commission could not agree on this point. The public officials on the Commission wanted the Board appointed by the mayor, subject to approval by the council; the two private citizens wanted it elected.[120] In allowing the mayor to appoint this powerful Board, in theory, the proposed charter would remove administrative powers from the council. Yet opponents of the GGA viewed it as a political attempt to control Norfolk's government. With a sympathetic mayor in office, the GGA likely assumed that it would control the Board of Control.

The debate in the councils over which method to choose focused on the ability of the people to elect qualified candidates. While the authors of the *Municipal Program* argued that reducing the number of elective offices was democratic, opponents of the GGA did not agree. The GGA councillors claimed that the people would not choose those best qualified to run the city as it should be run, which in their view was as a business corporation. The Ring members defended the people's capabilities, insisting that if they could elect a competent mayor, they could elect a competent Board of Control. (Shaw of the Norfolk Municipal League wanted the Board elected by the councils using a system of cumulative voting to provide for minority representation.)[121] Many in Norfolk agreed with the Ring's members.

An editorial in the *Norfolk Public Ledger* warned that "the unfortunate tendency to centralization of power is a thing to be closely watched by the people," and one citizen described an appointed board as "a one man oligarchy."[122] Despite such protests, the GGA, firmly in control of the councils, secured an appointed board.[123]

Critics of the proposed charter then turned to the state assembly. Reformers in the NML typically portrayed state intervention in local affairs in a negative light, but groups that felt disempowered in Norfolk and other cities sometimes turned to state lawmakers to protect their rights. With the decision to insist on an appointed Board of Control, the GGA's popular support further eroded. It had come into office promising to make city government more responsive to the people, but its efforts to consolidate control through charter reform alienated many supporters.[124] The GGA had initially formed a coalition with labor in opposition to the Ring and in support of community preparedness for the Jamestown Exposition. Yet organized labor now questioned this alliance, which was a blow to the GGA given the power of unions in city politics.[125]

The ensuing events mirrored the view of city-state relations in the *Municipal Program*: cities had a right to determine their functions, but states had the right to regulate their structures. The CLU supported the appeal of the Ring's councillors to the Virginia General Assembly to amend the proposed charter with an elected board. Echoing the *Municipal Program*, at the Virginia Constitutional Convention in 1901, the Committee on the Organization and Government of Cities and Towns advocated an increase in the "powers of local self-government" granted to municipalities. But following the lead of "some of the best political scientists of the country," it applied that home rule only to the scope of municipal activities, favoring uniform structures in Virginian cities. The article pertaining to local government provided for a largely standard system, specifically permitting the General Assembly to amend or repeal city charters if it felt they violated these constitutional provisions. It also stipulated that several local officials who had previously been appointed now be elected.[126] This legal context, combined with the appeals of the CLU and the Ring, resulted in the state legislature agreeing with advocates of an elected board and amending the charter before passing it into law in February 1906.[127] In this context, many of Norfolk's residents likely viewed state intervention as enhancing local democracy. Norfolk's new charter provided for administrative centralization in the Board of Control, but state intervention ensured that the members of the Board would be elected.

The new charter was settled, but another controversial topic remained, again eliciting state intervention. Just as the GGA's councillors cited the state constitution to justify the need for a new charter, they also made use of it to defend their call to redistrict Norfolk. While in part this move was motivated by factional competition within the Democratic Party, it was also about race, citizenship, and representation. The Ring's previous dominance of Norfolk's elections partly relied on the support of African American voters. In 1901, the Ring easily defeated the GGA at the polls, winning a dramatic victory in the Fourth Ward, known for its large African American population, with a return of 1,224 to 16. With the adoption of new suffrage qualifications in the Virginia Constitution of 1902, the number of registered voters dropped by nearly half in Norfolk. In 1903, turnout in the Fourth Ward fell to 86. The Ring suffered several losses, and the GGA was well on its way to dominating city politics. Two years later, ostensibly because the reduction in the electorate affected wards unevenly, GGA councillors proposed to redistrict according to the distribution of voters rather than residents.[128]

This move sparked a debate about the appropriate basis of representation in councils that was fundamentally about race. The GGA's move to redistrict was widely understood as an attempt to gerrymander the city to solidify control of the council. GGA councillors argued that the current system unfairly overrepresented the Fourth Ward, and they proposed to abolish it and alter the boundaries of several other wards. Outraged, the Ring opposition maintained that the new constitution required districts to be made according to residents, not voters. At a Common Council meeting, one member of the Ring described the redistricting plan as the "dirtiest political steal." Despite the obvious motivations, the GGA faction maintained that it was only concerned with equitable representation. The architect of the redistricting plan claimed that it would provide "the people a more equal voice in the councils." At council meetings, both factions avoided mentioning race, but criticisms of the capabilities of African American voters surfaced in the local press. Critics of the Ring, accusing it of corrupt electoral practices, presented its African American supporters as unqualified for the duties of citizenship. In one editorial, the *Virginian Pilot* maintained that it was "nonsense" to speak of "the negro" as a legitimate "factor in government," asserting that as a "menial and an underling," he was "incapable of governing himself, much less . . . someone else." Further indicating the often unspoken racial motivation of the redistricting scheme, another editorial simply declared, "We all know what the Fourth ward is."[129]

This dispute was again resolved by state intervention. Though the GGA, with solid majorities in both councils, easily secured the passage of the redistricting bill, it was unable to gerrymander the Fourth Ward out of existence. The Ring challenged the measure in the state courts, which agreed that the bill violated the state constitution. When the GGA renewed its efforts with an attempt to circumvent an injunction that barred it from redistricting, the Ring sought the support of allies in the Virginia General Assembly. Despite the GGA's sending a delegation to Richmond, the Assembly passed a bill that prevented Norfolk from redistricting until 1909 at the earliest.[130] State intervention prevented the GGA from redistricting, just as it had blocked a charter without a popularly elected Board of Control.

The consequences of the GGA's maneuvering became clear during the first primary election under the new charter. Though many voters continued to oppose the Ring, wary of its ties to the liquor industry, the GGA's characterization of city politics as a "choice between honest, popular government and the bossdom of the political RING" no longer rang true.[131] Though the Norfolk Municipal League did not campaign against the GGA, it declared all candidates for the Board of Control to be suitable, implicitly rejecting the GGA's claims to the contrary.[132] In the primary, the Ring regained much of its lost ground in the council and won two of three seats on the Board.[133] As a result, the GGA did not control the many large-scale civic improvements undertaken in preparation for the Jamestown Exposition.[134]

In the end, incumbents in Toledo and Norfolk did not secure charter revisions to consolidate mayoral control over administrative departments, but their efforts shed light on several key trends in urban reform at the turn of the century. They help us understand the outcomes of efforts to secure new charters, particularly the importance of forming coalitions with local groups. There was almost universal agreement on the desirability of some kind of governmental expansion, from Jones's vision of massive public ownership in Toledo to the Chamber of Commerce's hopes to develop infrastructure to attract new businesses to Norfolk. Even though proponents portrayed charter revision as an apolitical administrative reform, when confronted with local political realities, they formulated strategies to secure their objectives, strategies that often required alliances. As detailed, although a wide variety of formal groups had always participated in city politics alongside parties, rising nonpartisanship generated opportunities for new styles of activism. In Toledo and Norfolk, political parties (and factions), municipal leagues, commercial organizations, and unions all asserted their right to participate in city politics. Proponents of charter revision often looked to these groups to support their efforts, and their ability to convince them to do so was crucial in determining the fate of proposed charters. Jones, as an independent, was isolated from both parties, and he did not have the support of a local municipal reform group, commercial organizations, or, in the end, unions. The GGA started out with allies among commercial organizations and unions, but the unwillingness of its leaders to include unions and the Norfolk Municipal League in the work of the Charter Commission alienated both. In short, failed coalitions led to failed charters.

At the same time, the accounts of these two cities also underscore the centrality of questions regarding "outside" influences in city politics, whether in the form of the intervention of state legislatures or appeals to the authority of the NML. Despite claims that the program embodied the ideal form of city-state relations, the meaning of home rule was contested. The outcome of charter reform, on one level, highlights the limited reach of the program, particularly the claim that home rule should not include the right to draft charters. Diverse residents in Norfolk and Toledo wanted their charters to be written locally. Many wanted to be involved directly, arguing that charter making was part of participatory self-government and refusing to defer to GGA officials, Republicans dominating a charter convention, or elite political scientists in the NML. As the movement for "home rule" gained momentum in the early twentieth century, the term increasingly became synonymous with state constitutional provisions granting cities the right to frame and adopt their own charters.[135] Yet the authors of the program were not wrong to associate home rule with control over the functions of city government, for the rising interest in home rule and charter revision stemmed from a more fundamental desire: as Jones predicted, "the franchise problem" became one of the central topics, if not *the* central topic, in urban political debates in the coming years.

4

"The Franchise Problem"

Home Rule, Charter Reform, and the Provision of Public Services, c. 1900–1915

Unique local conditions and personalities shaped the course of urban politics, but cities in the Progressive Era were far from isolated. Rather, by reading local newspapers and attending meetings of groups such as the National Municipal League (NML), urban residents often possessed detailed knowledge of events transpiring in distant cities. In Norfolk, with the debate about the new charter and Board of Control settled, urban reform remained prominent in the headlines, particularly the rising interest in municipal ownership in other cities.[1]

Across the country, the provision of utilities and transportation dominated city politics in the first decade of the twentieth century. City councils typically granted franchises to private companies known as public service corporations to supply gas, electricity, and sometimes water and to construct and operate transit systems. In return for granting these "special privileges," as the muckraking journalist Lincoln Steffens revealed to the nation in series published in *McClure's* in 1902 and 1903, council members often received hefty kickbacks. This series, so popular that it was reprinted in book form as *The Shame of the Cities* the following year, brought the depth and ubiquity of corruption in the process of granting franchises to a national audience. Steffens chronicled widespread "boodle" and "graft" in cities such as Chicago, Philadelphia, and Pittsburg. It was in Saint Louis, however, that Steffens described in greatest detail councillors being bribed by business leaders—"men of wealth and social standing"—for "special privileges" and "valuable franchises" from the city government.[2]

Steffens's understanding of the source of urban problems shaped the NML's developing agenda and the course of urban reform more broadly. With the publication of the *Municipal Program* in 1900, the NML had offered a model of ideal institutions and established leadership. In the next decade, discussions at national meetings revealed a struggle to set an agenda for the future of urban reform. In his annual address at the NML's 1902 convention, Secretary Clinton Rogers Woodruff chronicled scandals in diverse cities, explaining that this "question of the franchises of public service corporations" was increasingly receiving "a larger share of public attention."[3] Six years later, he wrote, "The question of public utilities . . . has in many places overshadowed all other questions." From "the street-railway situation" in Chicago to "the gas question" in Boston, the need to reform the present system for providing these services was "the one issue" that stirred people to action.[4]

In this climate, while interest in urban reform continued unabated, nationally and locally, discourse shifted. Increasing awareness of such relationships among public service corporations and elected officials fostered the development of a new understanding of the root of urban corruption that differed from earlier explanations. As noted, at the close of the nineteenth century, reformers focused on corruption resulting from machines and the spoils system. The NML's leaders, particularly the authors of the *Municipal Program*, added institutional critiques of the existing party system for encouraging state interference in local matters. In the new century, special privileges and the franchise problem took center stage. Rather than blaming the spoils system and politicians for promising city jobs in exchange for votes, reformers and other urban residents increasingly came to see collusion among party politicians and the businessmen who owned public service corporations as the source of corruption. Steffens was the most well-known spokesperson for this position, but numerous authors published books and articles to draw attention to the franchise problem.[5]

This understanding of corruption influenced discussions of two key topics among urban reformers: charter revision and home rule. As detailed earlier, the program's authors and many urban politicians presented charter revision and home rule as tools that would enable cities to institute new programs. With a rising awareness of the ways that the existing franchise system created opportunities for corruption, support for charter revision and home rule often took on a new sense of urgency. Attacks on the franchise system mirrored wider Progressive movements in the nation, portraying politics as battles of "the people" to put an end to systems that allowed for monopolies and special privileges.[6]

This chapter begins with an examination of the concept of home rule alongside simultaneous considerations of charter revision and potential solutions to the franchise problem. It explores debates at conventions in the first decade of the new century within the context of the broader discourse of urban politics, situating the NML's work in relation to that of other organizations and major works of leading public intellectuals, most notably Frederic Howe. The second section turns to the ongoing struggle within the NML regarding franchise reform. While continuing to defer to the principle of home rule to justify its lack of an official position, by the 1910s the NML simultaneously publicized two competing and in many ways incompatible solutions. One publication rejected municipal ownership as unfeasible and argued for state regulation of franchises through administrative commissions; another insisted that the right to choose between franchises and municipal ownership was an essential component of home rule and needed to be decided in local elections. These contradictions reveal a difference of opinion regarding the appropriate roles of the NML and professional experts in decisions about the provision of utilities and transportation. The final section returns to Toledo to examine the connections among these issues on the local level, where voters were offered a charter in 1914 explicitly designed to expand home rule and powers to regulate the sale of franchises and/or adopt programs of municipal ownership.

Examining urban reform with a focus on the evolving relationship among home rule, charter revision, and the franchise problem enables us to understand this moment in history as a pivotal one in the development of American political institutions. When urban residents and reformers discussed franchise reform, they considered the appropriate relationship between public and private enterprise and even the very purpose of government. Scholars such as William Novak and Elisabeth Clemens aptly note that federal, state, and even local government has historically expanded its reach through land grants, tariffs, franchises, subsidies, and a variety of other arrangements with private entities.[7] Additionally, studies by Gail

Radford and Carol Nackenoff and Julie Novkov point to the Progressive Era as a time when relations among public institutions and private enterprises were in flux, and they point to the importance of city government in institutional innovation.[8] This chapter builds on the insights of this scholarship in the context of debates over competing methods to provide public services in cities. Those who advocated reforms of the existing franchise system to eliminate opportunities for corruption wanted to continue with the prevailing model of public-private partnerships that dominated the nineteenth century. In contrast, those who advocated the adoption of a new system of municipally owned utilities and transit systems advocated a break with the past. Both groups, however, largely embraced a vision of the purpose of city government as not only negative, through the enforcement of laws, but also positive, through the provision of services and programs to improve the lives of residents.

At the same time, a focus on the connections among these three issues highlights another key question: the appropriate role of voters in expanding and increasingly technological governmental programs. For most supporters of home rule and charter revision, local autonomy was a means to an end. For some, this end was primarily the elimination of corruption and improvements in the provision of services, and, in some cases, the imposition of a predetermined vision of efficient government. A 1933 study of home rule movements highlighted this view, insisting that most home rulers were less concerned with "popular self-government" than with "good government" by the "the so-called, or self-called, good citizens."[9] This appraisal partly explains why some reformers, previously ardent supporters of home rule, began to turn to regulation by state administrative boards to reform the franchise system. Yet for others, the commitment to home rule reflected a commitment to local control that would enable urban residents to engage in discussions and make collective decisions regarding their governance. Howe perhaps best captured this vision in *The City: The Hope of Democracy*, describing the movement for home rule as "a struggle for liberty" and "a demand on the part of the people to be trusted."[10]

"A New Concept of Popular Government": Home Rule in Relation to Charter Revision and the Franchise Problem

Despite the fact that the *Municipal Program* originally declared that the right to draft charters locally was not part of home rule, charter revision and home rule increasingly became associated with each other—and franchise reform—in the new century. The national movement for home rule arose in the context of the rapid expansion of the scope of city government. Americans living in cities increasingly came to expect city government to do more than simply provide police protection and safeguard legal rights. Many cities extended public works programs in the more established realms of the construction and maintenance of streets, sewers, and public parks, and others began to experiment with the municipal ownership of utilities. City-owned water plants and sewer systems achieved widespread acceptance, with 54.2 percent of cities opting for municipal water plants by 1898.[11] Commercial leaders and city officials formed alliances with public health experts to advocate the availability of a clean and abundant public water supply as vital to making their cities attractive to newcomers and investors. Urban boosters thus typically supported the municipal ownership of water plants.[12] Water, more than other utilities, was considered a public good, vital to the health and safety of the community.[13] In the name of improving public health, cities also dramatically increased spending on garbage collection, street cleaning, sewerage, and water filtration and purification. Here, in municipalities, more than in any other level of government, Americans of the Progressive Era displayed a willingness to abandon a strict laissez-faire policy in favor of a more active government dedicated to the public welfare.[14] Nevertheless, other forms of municipal ownership were much less common. While over half of cities owned waterworks, public electric lighting plants spread more slowly (reaching 22.5 percent of cities by 1902), and gasworks and street railway systems remained rare.[15]

Despite these small numbers, the topic of municipal ownership attracted much interest. By the 1890s, academics and reformers such as Frank Parsons, founder and president of the National League for Promoting the Public Ownership of Monopolies and professor at Boston University, were already arguing that "the evils experienced from private monopoly," including high rates, poor services, and corruption, could be solved by the establishment of municipally owned utilities.[16] Proponents and opponents met and engaged in debates at a number of national forums. Focused on the franchise reform from its inception, the League of American Municipalities, composed primarily of elected officials, seemed to gravitate toward municipal ownership. Prominent supporters—reformers Parsons and Howe, leading Progressive mayors such as Toledo's Samuel Jones—regularly spoke at conventions and contributed to the *Bulletin of the League of American Municipalities*.[17] Yet perhaps in part because of its reputation for sympathizing with municipal ownership, the League of American Municipalities adopted an officially noncommittal stance on the subject.[18] In contrast, the leadership was able to agree on the issue of home rule and passed a resolution declaring it to be "the one absolutely vital measure needful for the prosperity, progress and moral well-being of the American city."[19]

Likewise, the Commission on Public Ownership of Public Utilities of the National Civic Federation produced a relatively noncommittal report after an expensive two-year study. The Federation was an investigatory and consensus-building reform organization designed to represent business, labor, and "the public" in opposition to socialists and the most conservative business groups. Several members of the NML were asked to participate in the Commission's work, including the political scientists instrumental in crafting the *Municipal Program*. As its secretary explained to an audience of the NML's members, the Commission "was not formed to advance any theories or to express opinions either for or against municipal ownership and operation" but rather "to ascertain the facts and present them in comprehensive and utilizable form."[20] Perhaps unsurprisingly, the report, published in 1907, offered a qualified endorsement for municipally owned enterprises in the realms of public health, safety, transportation, and infrastructure while also providing detailed recommendations for the regulation of franchises granted to private companies. Notably, the Commission on Public Ownership of Public Utilities also relied on the concept of home rule to avoid public disagreement, suggesting that the choice between the adoption of municipal ownership and the improvement of franchise regulation be left to each individual municipality.[21] In this way, both the League of American Municipalities and the National Civic Federation followed the model established by the *Municipal Program*.

While no city adopted the program in its entirety, it continued to be influential, particularly by contributing to the rising popularity of the belief in the need to separate politics and administration. Yet despite the program's definition of home rule as a matter of function rather than structure, home rule continued to be associated with charter revision. John Fairlie, political scientist at the University of Michigan and former student of Frank Goodnow, presented a report to the NML in 1908 highlighting the connection: "In those states where cities have authority to make their own charters the scope of municipal authority is clearly more extensive."[22] Home rule and charter revision, in short, seemed to go hand in hand with functional expansion.

Many Americans active in local politics believed there was an important connection between allowing cities to determine political structures and enabling them to embark on new and expansive programs. Supporters of home rule blamed the excessive interference of state legislatures for corruption and inefficiency in city government. They argued that state legislatures, dominated by rural districts, passed bills that disregarded the wants and needs of urban residents. This state of affairs, they claimed, violated the right to self-government. Many were particularly angered when state legislatures amended charters for what they believed to be political reasons. As outrage over such "charter tinkering" grew, home rule increasingly became synonymous with state constitutional provisions granting cities the right to frame and adopt charters.[23]

At the same time, defining home rule as the right to draft charters locally was closely connected to efforts to free cities to "experiment" with new functions. Howe articulated this vision vividly. Coming from a small town in Pennsylvania, he described his studies at Johns Hopkins with leading social scientists such as Richard Ely, Woodrow Wilson, James Bryce, and Albert Shaw as the time when he first "came alive." After graduation, he settled in Cleveland, Ohio, where he began working as a lawyer and became involved in urban reform under the administration of Mayor Tom Johnson. Johnson entered office on a platform of municipal ownership in 1901, the same year that Howe was elected to Cleveland's council.[24] Johnson was a contemporary of Samuel Jones of Toledo, and Howe, Johnson, Jones, and others became leaders of a civic revival in Ohio.[25] By 1905, in *The City: The Hope of Democracy*, Howe challenged those who dismissed the importance of charters. He believed that home rule needed to encompass both the right "to adopt . . . or amend the fundamental laws of the community" and "the right to determine what activities and powers shall be exercised," explaining that "democracy can best work out its problems when government is responsible, as well as responsive, to the immediate community which it serves." He celebrated diversity, writing that "home rule would produce variety in municipal administration rather than uniformity," and he described cities as "experiment stations of administration, taxation, and social betterment."[26]

Howe's celebration of the democratic potential of home rule was closely tied to his interpretation of the franchise system, which differed from the NML's and Steffens's interpretations in a few key ways. Woodruff celebrated Steffens's efforts to bring the problem of corruption to a national audience, and he framed the popularity of Steffens's exposés as an indicator of rising interest in urban reform and nonpartisanship, in line with the original vision of local autonomy espoused by NML leaders.[27] Yet Steffens himself offered a slightly different explanation for the popularity of his work, focusing on the role of business in a corrupt and inequitable system. Instead of highlighting electoral fraud, Steffens blamed the business community for its involvement in political corruption, writing that "the business man has failed in politics as he has in citizenship. . . . The commercial spirit is the spirit of profit, not patriotism; of credit, not honor; of individual gain, not national prosperity; of trade and dickering, not principle." Yet Steffens also blamed the apathy of voters who were aware of the situation but did nothing to alter it, and he hoped that his exposés would arouse a great sense of "civic pride" among "an apparently shameless people."[28]

Howe, in contrast, exculpated voters and democracy altogether. A close friend of Steffens, he insisted that "the corruption of our cities" was not due "to democracy, to the spoils system," or "to the indifference, if not the corruption of the voter." While many treated the "failures" of urban government "as the failures of democracy," Howe maintained that no American city had "a democratic government." He wrote, "What we really have in our large cities is a business-men's government, and a business-men's government rooted in privilege. Privilege has always been a source of corruption." In the typical city, a franchise corporation received "monopolies uncontrolled by law" by making a "bargain" and forming a "partnership" with a local party. Regardless of campaign rhetoric, elections were really about franchise grants. In short, Howe proclaimed that urban democracy had "been drugged by business interests."[29]

Support for municipal ownership, for Howe like Jones before him, was a matter not simply of improving public welfare but also of achieving a higher form of democracy. In part, Howe presented municipal ownership as a means to end the undemocratic "privilege of monopoly." Yet he maintained that it was not primarily a "monetary" question concerning "the relief of taxation" or "a profit or loss account." Nor was it a matter of "cheap water, gas, or electricity." Rather, it was a means to achieve a "higher civic life" and "political morality." He also believed that municipal ownership would lessen "class antagonism" by eliminating the temptation for businessmen to profit from city government and thus enabling them to take on their role as "natural leaders" dedicated to the service of the community.[30] Howe believed that home rule and municipal ownership had the potential to save democracy.[31]

Howe's views on municipal ownership stemmed from his larger economic understanding of urban problems. He presented his book as a primarily "economic interpretation of the city." He viewed economic conditions as the cause of corruption, inequality, and poverty, and he advocated institutional changes as solutions. His economic program encompassed not only an end to franchise privileges but also full employment and "taxing monopoly." For Howe, "it is the economic motive that makes municipal reform a class struggle," pitting "the few who enjoy privileges" against the "millions awakening to the conviction of industrial democracy."[32] In offering this assessment, Howe moved toward the social and economic views of Henry George, a prominent proponent of a "single tax" in which all profits from land, buildings, and corporations would be taxed for the benefit of the public.[33]

Such views made Howe's book popular, but they also positioned him to the left of many urban reformers. At the same time, he was active in reform circles, serving on the executive committee of the NML.[34] Woodruff carefully worded his review of *The City: The Hope of Democracy*, commending Howe for providing "an intelligent and forceful justification" for "the great growth of municipal functions." He presented Howe as a disciple of George and Johnson, and overall, he characterized the book as well-written propaganda: "It reads like the argument of an ardent partisan, rather than like the dispassionate analysis of a philosopher."[35] Howe did not conform to the dispassionate style employed by Woodruff and the political scientists and professionals in the NML. Yet his views were influential. Delos Wilcox, for example, wrote in a far more neutral tone but echoed Howe's views with his sympathy for municipal ownership and home rule.[36]

In contrast, opponents of municipal ownership voiced concerns that city government was becoming too large, encroaching on domains better left to private industry. One critical account of the "craze of municipal ownership" conceded that cities needed to provide water, streets, sewers, education, and police and fire protection. But it drew the line at these "public necessit[ies]," arguing, "The municipality should not encroach upon public utilities service to individuals any more than it should undertake to furnish individuals with bread and meat, with clothing or newspapers; no more than it should conduct hotels, restaurants, theaters or the opera. Doing so, it invades the exclusive domain of private enterprise."[37] Similarly, others cautioned that diverting funds to new enterprises might prevent cities from performing existing (and legitimate) functions. In some instances, they used gendered imagery to associate municipal ownership with women to portray it as dangerous and irresponsible (figures 4.1 and 4.2). In these and other ways, critics of municipal ownership argued for a continuation of more limited government, challenging efforts to redefine the scope of municipal action.

Yet many of the NML's leaders and members echoed Howe's belief in the need for more active government and its potential to spark a democratic revival. In 1905 and 1906, Leo Stanton Rowe returned to present two papers at annual conventions, one titled "The Relation of Municipal Government to American Democratic Ideals" and another titled "Municipal Ownership and Operation—The Value of Foreign Experience." His goal was to promote greater understanding of municipal ownership and emphasize "the tremendous power of the city in furthering social welfare." He began with a historical and sociological (rather than ethical or moral) justification for the need to expand municipal functions. While in the past local governments largely enforced the law and protected individual liberty, in recent years "the concentration of population and the growth of great industrial centers have brought into the foreground a mass of new problems." He explained that while those who clung to "the political ideas of the eighteenth century" believed that "private effort" could solve these problems, almost every "student of American city life" recognized the need

The Neglected Family

FIGURE 4.1 "The Neglected Family"

F.T. Richards, "The Neglected Family," *Concerning Municipal Ownership* 8, no. 2 (February 1915): 36.

FIGURE 4.2 "The Siren"

"The Siren," *Concerning Municipal Ownership* 8, no. 8 (August 1915): 182.

for "an extension of municipal functions . . . to grapple with the problems which cannot be solved without organized action."[38]

Rowe emphasized the importance of structural changes to make this expansion possible. He explained that "a readjustment of the machinery of government" required the acceptance of mayoral control of the administration and a smaller council confined to legislative functions (in other words, the model outlined in the *Municipal Program*). He detailed the inefficiencies of large councils and the blurring of administrative and legislative tasks, and he chastised those who clung to existing systems as the only possible forms of democratic government. He maintained that his proposals would create greater "popular control over the city government." He predicted that municipal ownership would spread and concluded, "The American people must . . . develop a new concept of popular government, in which the prominent factor will not be the election of officials but rather that control or organized public opinion over the administration of public affairs which is, after all, the essential element of a vigorous democracy."[39]

When Rowe spoke of "the American people," he relied on a conception of politics common in his day. In the first decade of the twentieth century, many reformers hoped that a sense of unity would emerge out of the seemingly intractable divisions in American cities. But they did so in ways that were diverse, complicated, and sometimes inconsistent.[40] Rowe, for example, simultaneously called on NML members to "depend upon a great number of voluntary organizations representing different elements in the community" while cautioning them not to assume that any one "represent[s] the opinion of the community as a whole."[41] Moreover, at least a few members of the NML were becoming more rather than less open to the need to include a greater diversity of voices. In 1899, one officer blamed electoral corruption on the "ignorant, less educated classes, the laboring classes, and . . . the criminal classes."[42] Ten years later, the NML invited Grace Abbott, a resident of Chicago's Hull House and director of the League for the Protection of Immigrants, to speak. Abbott stated that "the leaders of these newer immigrants should be drawn into the general reform movements of our cities," and she urged listeners to realize that "our Anglo-Saxon ancestors did not possess a monopoly of all political wisdom and our community life might become richer by an appreciation of the contribution which others among us might make."[43] According to the official record, her comments were well received, drawing praise from several members, including the secretary of the New York Tax Reform Association, the president of the Boston Art Club, and a Civil War veteran from Wisconsin.[44] Yet even those who were more welcoming of diverse groups and ideas typically believed that discussion would yield consensus. As Wilcox wrote, "The mixture of races may in the end develop a more intelligent and virile citizenship than is found in any one of the constituent peoples."[45]

This goal of consensus was central to many reformers who supported home rule, for while they believed that unity was possible, many key figures argued that face-to-face discussions among diverse individuals were essential to create it. Howe and Woodruff, despite their differences, both believed that urban reform required the creation of spaces and institutions that promoted engagement and deliberation. Howe attempted to implement his democratic ideals not only by serving on Cleveland's council but also through his later leadership in the People's Institute and the People's Forum in New York, working to create opportunities for academics, public intellectuals, and reformers to engage in conversations with urban residents. Similarly, in addition to his work with the NML, Woodruff was president of the American Park and Outdoor Art Association. In this capacity, he worked to create parks, town halls, and other meeting spaces for citizens to come together and discuss matters of common concern.[46]

While the NML focused more extensively on charter and franchise reform, under Woodruff's leadership its members also discussed and publicized Edward Ward's movement to create "social centers" as spaces for citizens to gather and discuss a variety of topics. Ward defined social centers as places where "people may and will gather . . . , across different lines of opinion, creed and income, upon a common ground of interest and duty, just as neighboring citizens." Woodruff celebrated Ward's work to foster communal interactions as "a source of information and inspiration to the growing list of workers for democratic municipal government" and highlighted the importance of social centers in facilitating the growth of "that sound public sentiment without which there can be no true and permanent success in the matter of self-government."[47]

In short, despite the seeming simplicity of the concept of home rule, its meaning was far from clear. Early advocates of home rule understood city charters to be fundamental laws representing a homogeneous and unified public will and rejected the possibility of legitimate heterogeneous interests.[48] Yet by the first decade of the twentieth century, while elements of this view remained, others focused on ways to facilitate discussion among a diversity of urban residents.

Competing Solutions to the Franchise Problem: Municipal Ownership Versus State Regulation

In 1905, Charles Bonaparte, the second president of the NML, offered his views on the appropriate scope of the league's activities in "The Field of Labor of the National Municipal League." Bonaparte was a lawyer from Baltimore who had been an active leader in a variety of organizations for municipal and civil service reform for thirty years. In 1905, Theodore Roosevelt appointed him secretary of the navy; a year later, he became attorney general.[49] Bonaparte believed that for the NML to function as "an instrument of active good," it "must and will be given up to the pursuit of those ends about which all its members think alike." Echoing his predecessors, he reiterated the belief that the scope of the "functions" of government should be determined on the basis of the needs "of each community." He explained that certain topics were "suitable for discussion . . . but . . . altogether inappropriate for determination by the League." In short, he felt that it was not appropriate for the NML to take an official position as to whether cities should own transit systems. Rather, it should only provide advice on how to best implement municipal ownership if the voters chose to do so.[50]

Despite Bonaparte's stance, the records of the NML's annual meeting leave the clear impression that, overall, many prominent leaders favored municipal ownership. For several years, Woodruff reported on the rising popularity of municipal ownership as a positive trend. In 1903, he characterized the "deep hold" of the "municipal ownership movement" on "the urban population of this country" as "a healthy and an auspicious sign."[51] In 1904, he again discussed its widespread support among voters, and in 1905 he suggested that it was perhaps the most popular line of reform in American cities over the past decade.[52] Though Woodruff framed his remarks as simple reports of events transpiring in cities, his comments were marked by an undercurrent of sympathy, if not support.

Yet when Woodruff and others discussed municipal ownership, they did so carefully, going to great lengths to avoid seeming partisan. The first step was often framing the provision of utilities and transit as legitimate public services. In a striking example, in 1909, at a round table luncheon at a convention in Cincinnati, lawyer Walter Fisher, vice president of the NML and president of the Municipal Voters League of Chicago, led a discussion regarding public ownership of transit systems. He began by citing a recent decision of the Supreme Court declaring that railroads provided a public service and therefore performed a "function of government." In this context, he stated that there was "nothing radical, nothing doctrinaire or theoretical" in concluding that "government has turned over to private agencies those things which are properly functions of government." The audience applauded this statement.[53] Such comments clearly indicate support for publicly owned transit systems, and yet Fisher did not directly state such support. Why were men like Woodruff and Fisher so reluctant to advocate municipal ownership?

One possibility is the emergence of an alternative solution to the franchise problem. While home rule and municipal ownership remained popular, many political scientists, professionals, and reformers began to promote state-level administrative commissions. They argued that appointed commissions could eradicate corruption and inefficiencies by regulating the sale of franchises by municipalities. The leadership (and likely membership) of the NML was deeply divided regarding the implications of such regulatory boards for home rule and local democracy.[54] Two parallel projects reveal the depth of that division. In 1910, the executive committee voted to create the Committee on Franchises to review papers presented at recent conferences and recommend a course of action. They appointed several men to the Committee, including Delos Wilcox.[55] Wilcox had studied with John Dewey at the University of Michigan and Frank Goodnow at Columbia and aided in drafting the *Municipal Program*. By this time he was a well-known expert on public utilities and franchises in New York, serving as chief of the Bureau of Franchises of the Public Service Commission for the First District and later deputy commissioner of water supply, gas, and electricity.[56] The NML also invited Clyde King of the University of Pennsylvania to select the most important papers presented by "qualified experts" and publish them in an edited volume.[57] King also studied at the

University of Michigan and the University of Pennsylvania. In addition to his work as a political scientist, he later held a number of state and then national administrative positions.[58] King and Wilcox, in short, had similar educational and professional backgrounds and engaged in similar projects for the NML. Yet their assessments of the franchise problem led them to starkly different conclusions.

In 1912, in an NML publication entitled *The Regulation of Municipal Utilities*, King concluded that municipal ownership was unfeasible; in 1913, Wilcox presented the report of the NML's Committee on Franchises at the annual meeting, declaring that urban residents should be free to adopt municipal ownership under systems of home rule. King praised administration by state boards as a way to prevent corruption in the sale of franchises. Wilcox warned that state regulation could deny citizens their right to self-government. In the report, Wilcox noted that the NML had "always been friendly to the idea of municipal home rule" and argued that "the powers of municipalities to control local utilities . . . are being seriously curtailed or taken away entirely."[59]

In a stark contradiction, King maintained that state regulation provided the ideal method to end the corruption of the existing franchise system. He believed that municipal ownership would ultimately prove unsuccessful because publicly owned enterprises required more extensive regulations than private endeavors.[60] He also explained that several legal limitations reduced the viability of municipal ownership. First, King noted that courts often held that cities could exercise only those powers expressly granted them by state constitutions or legislatures. Given that less than half of American cities had been granted the right to own and operate utilities by the states, municipal ownership, for most, was not a practical option. Second, through both constitutional and statutory law, most states limited the amount of debt that cities could incur, thereby making it impossible to raise funds to undertake public programs. Citing these reasons and others, he thus concluded that regulation by "expert public service commissions" provided a more efficient and more viable resolution. According to King, "Under a scheme of competent regulation . . . the municipality will probably rarely, if ever, have occasion for resorting to municipal ownership and operation."[61]

Additionally, a few speakers at NML conventions assured members that state boards would not compromise home rule. Joseph Eastman, secretary of the Public Franchise League of Massachusetts, told members that the residents did not view the existence of a state commission as a threat. He detailed the work of the Massachusetts Public Utilities Commission in regulating railroads and companies that provided electricity, light, gas, and telephone services, framing the Commission's work as an apolitical "division of labor" that was in no way "a violation of the principle of 'home rule.'" He justified the existence of state commissions by stressing their accountability: the citizens of Massachusetts elected "good governors" who in turn "appointed able and courageous men."[62]

King presented the work of state commissions in a somewhat different light, depicting commissioners as professional experts with specialized knowledge rather than accountable public servants. King argued that existing regulations failed because neither courts, nor legislative bodies, nor the public had the time, knowledge, skill, and training to supervise public service corporations. Municipally owned utilities would not solve this problem because they required even more management and administration. The best solution, he maintained, was to create permanent commissions of trained professionals to oversee the granting and ongoing enforcement of franchises.[63] Reformers such as Howe and Parsons heralded the use of the initiative and referenda either to grant franchises or (preferably) to establish municipal ownership. They believed that returning control to the people would destroy a system that granted unfair special privileges.[64] Yet King and others, emphasizing the specialized, technical nature of the provision of public services, rejected this line of reasoning, hoping to remove the granting of franchises from the political process and relocate it in the administrative realm.

Wilcox, who somewhat perplexingly authored two chapters in King's edited volume, articulated an alternative view, questioning the notion that expert boards could or should make choices for urban residents. Speaking for the NML's Committee on Franchises, Wilcox insisted that allowing decisions regarding the provision of utilities to be made locally was an important component of democratic self-government. He explained that in order to awaken and sustain "the active and intelligent interest of the voters," "the control of all public functions should be localized as much as possible" and "the entire machinery of government [should] be kept close to the people for whose benefit it has been created." He warned that state regulation made municipal ownership more difficult to implement.[65] His fears of state regulation and support for municipal ownership grew in the coming years, and his expression of his views became more forthright. A decade later, he wrote a pamphlet warning that state legislatures and commissions alike were not able to regulate public service corporations. He declared that most Americans were blind to the "all-permeating danger of private mindedness in control of the affairs of cities" that threatened the future of "urban democracy."[66] For Wilcox, it was state regulation rather than municipal ownership that was simply unfeasible.

In short, while advocates of municipal ownership and state boards both desired to bring greater efficiency and expertise to city government, they fundamentally disagreed on how best to achieve these goals. Their many differences highlight the dangers of portraying reformers as a uniform group.[67] And yet despite their differences, King and Wilcox agreed on one fundamental matter: the necessity of expanding the reach of city government to address the needs of rapidly growing urban populations. King, in a subsequent publication sponsored by the NML titled *Lower Living Costs in Cities*, described a shift from a limited vision of urban government in the nineteenth century to one marked by a more expansive list of "things done collectively" in the twentieth century, including the provision of "light," "heat," "transit," "recreation," and "food."[68] Similarly, Wilcox, when discussing the evolution of "civic cooperation," maintained that "the growth of cities" created "conditions of life" that "conspire[d] to make cooperation necessary through the expansion of city functions," including the distribution of food, the "establishment of parks, playgrounds, and other means of public amusements," and the provision of jobs to the unemployed.[69] Both men, in short, expressed a positive understanding of government. Their divergent views regarding state regulation and municipal ownership were disagreements over means, not ends.

"The Free City": Toledo and Brand Whitlock, 1912–1914

It is not difficult to connect these debates among political scientists and leading reformers to events transpiring in cities throughout the country, particularly in the case of Toledo. In 1912 and 1913, while King and Wilcox were offering contrasting views regarding the potential of state boards,

Mayor Brand Whitlock was leading a campaign to bring home rule and municipal ownership to Toledo. Whitlock spoke at NML conventions and knew Howe and Steffens personally, and in his crusade to make Toledo a "free city," he presented home rule and charter revision as means to destroy the corrupt franchise system and establish municipal ownership. Diverse Toledoans, unsatisfied with local streetcar services in particular, found his arguments convincing. At the same time, Toledo's story complicates the visions espoused by Whitlock and leaders of the NML. While Toledoans overwhelmingly advocated greater local autonomy, the process of drafting a new charter highlighted competing understandings of the role of city government in regulating people's private lives.

For years, Toledoans had complained that the Toledo Railway and Light Company provided poor services and charged excessive fares. When the company bribed councillors to secure an extension of its franchise in 1904, Mayor Samuel Jones vetoed the ordinance in one of his last official acts. After his death, supporters continued Jones's program by forming the Independent Party that called for home rule, greater democracy, and an end to corruption. Whitlock, the Independents' mayoral candidate, was a lawyer, writer, and close friend of Jones. He was elected in a landslide in 1905.[70] As mayor, Whitlock continued Jones's efforts to replace Toledo Rail-Light with a municipal streetcar system, and to do so he first fought for home rule.

Whitlock's political career was founded on his commitment to a vision of home rule that echoed the NML's early nonpartisan stance and aspects of the democratic convictions of Steffens and Howe. At the annual convention in 1903, Woodruff described the need to separate local from state and national politics as "oft-repeated gospel of the National Municipal League" and celebrated Jones's reelection as evidence of rising nonpartisanship.[71] After Jones's death, Whitlock gave a speech at the 1907 convention titled "The Evil Influence of National Parties and Issues in Municipal Elections," offering largely the same message. Echoing Steffens, he claimed that "the trusts, the railroads, the street-car companies and other privileges" ruled cities. Like Howe, he maintained that "democracy has not yet been fully tried" because cities lacked true home rule.[72]

Five years later, Whitlock led efforts to secure a home rule amendment. During the Ohio Constitutional Convention, municipal Progressives worked to secure an amendment that would enable cities to undertake new initiatives. Opponents feared that granting cities autonomy would make it impossible for the state to limit the sale of alcohol. To avoid entangling home rule with the "liquor question," supporters carefully crafted an amendment to grant cities the right to adopt charters and enact ordinances that did not conflict with state laws, specifically mentioning the right to own and operate utilities.[73]

The *Toledo Blade* portrayed the proposed amendment as making possible new positive roles for cities. One editorial maintained that each city needed to "fit its government to its own peculiar needs" by adopting "changes, betterments and experiments."[74] Another contrasted the vision of government held by the delegates of the constitutional convention of 1850, who had drafted the current constitution, with that of the delegates of 1912. The former "erected barriers and imposed restrictions," while the latter "tore down barriers and granted permissions." The proposed amendment would "empower the cities to do many things that are now expressly forbidden" and "set free" the cities.[75] Utilizing the rhetoric of the day, they portrayed home rule as a tool for the "people" to end the unjust "privileges" secured by "the interests" (public service corporations and their paid lobbyists, depicted as affluent males) (figure 4.3).

Progressives at the convention considered this amendment a vital component of their larger program, and the campaign to secure home rule drew together reformers and their union allies in opposition to "the interests." The Ohio Manufacturers' Association and the Ohio State Board of Commerce opposed the new constitution. The *Toledo Union Leader* reported that the Ohio Federation of Labor supported the proposed amendments and urged local central labor unions (CLUs) to campaign for them to counter "big business and its allies."[76] In 1911, prominent reformers in Ohio had formed the Progressive Constitutional League to secure the inclusion of the initiative, referendum, and home rule along with other Progressive measures in the new constitution. Whitlock was elected president, and he soon helped form the Ohio Municipal League, which took the lead in drafting the home rule amendment in early 1912.[77] To promote the amendment, the Ohio Municipal League appealed to local public officials and civic organizations throughout the state.[78] Partly as a result, despite the opposition of public service corporations, the convention adopted the home rule amendment by a strong majority, including a provision allowing cities to own and operate utilities.[79]

WHO'S AFRAID?

FIGURE 4.3 "Who's Afraid?"

"Who's Afraid?," *Toledo News Bee*, August 24, 1912, 1.

Working to garner support in Toledo for the amendment before the statewide referendum, Whitlock related home rule to American democracy more broadly. He maintained that "no reform . . . is of more importance than of home rule," which would make "democratic government" a reality. Under the present system, cities did not enjoy "self-government." He explained, "the street car company and the gas company, the electric lighting company, the railroad"—"the Interests, Privilege"—had "found a way of ruling cities in its own interests" and "took for its own selfish use and aggrandizement, the things which belong to the people of the city." Securing popular control over the provision of municipal services was the first step in a wider movement to redeem American democracy, for, according to Whitlock, "if things are to be set right in this country, they must be set right in the cities first."[80] Perhaps swayed by such rhetoric, Toledo's voters adopted the home rule amendment and all of the Progressive amendments in September 1912.[81]

After the amendment passed in the statewide election, Whitlock turned his attention to securing a new charter for Toledo. Within days, he declared his intention to recommend that Toledo's council move for a new charter. Like many of his contemporaries, Whitlock greatly admired European systems of local government. In order to assist Toledo in drafting a charter that would serve as "a model to other cities," Whitlock decided to go to Europe and undertake a "systematic inquiry."[82] He spent October and November visiting cities in Ireland, Scotland, England, France, Belgium, and Germany and writing a series of articles to be published in a syndicate of newspapers that included the *Toledo News Bee*.[83] Though Whitlock originally declared that he would focus on structures, his articles highlighted new functions undertaken by European cities under publicly owned programs.[84] Whitlock commended Europeans for operating successful and profitable public programs and celebrated the expansive spirit of cities such as Glasgow, which extended municipal ownership beyond utilities to include street railways, telephones, parks, art galleries, museums, and libraries.[85] Emphasizing the importance of local autonomy, Whitlock wrote that German cities, "practically supreme in all that concerns their own affairs," had extended "municipal activity" to levels "wholly unknown to us."[86] Upon his homecoming in December, Whitlock worked with the Ohio Municipal League to draft model charters for Ohio's cities.[87]

Meanwhile, in Toledo, despite the efforts of a few zealous reformers, there was little evidence of widespread interest in charter reform. The home rule amendment allowed cities to call for the election of a commission, by either a two-thirds vote of the council or a petition signed by 10 percent of voters, to draft a charter to be submitted to a popular vote.[88] When the council hesitated to call for the election of a commission the following spring, citing the expense and suggesting that they wait until the general election in the fall, local members of the Ohio League of Municipalities and the German American Alliance, supported by the *News Bee*, began circulating a petition.[89] Though they claimed to have collected several thousand signatures, when the council called a "mass meeting" to discuss the matter, only twenty to thirty people attended. At the meeting, a delegation from the local branch of the Socialist Party voiced opposition to charter revision.[90] The *Toledo Union Leader* declared that there was no need for a new charter given that Toledo already had home rule and the right to adopt municipal ownership by popular election.[91]

Widespread interest only emerged when city leaders directly connected charter reform to home rule and municipal ownership. While Toledo's council was considering calling for a special election, Ohioans were debating the precise relationship among the three. As councils began considering extensions of municipal functions under home rule, a difference of opinion emerged as to whether the amendment was self-executing. Some argued that before municipalities could acquire home rule, they had to adopt new charters, while others maintained that municipalities already possessed home rule. To resolve the matter, Toledo's city solicitor orchestrated a test case by asking the council to fund "a municipal moving picture house," which it would only have the right to do if home rule were in effect. The *News Bee* explained that if the courts ruled that "the city does not now have those home rule powers, then if the people voted against a new charter they would be voting against home rule for Toledo."[92]

In May, the state supreme court ruled that home rule was not automatic and that cities could only do what their current charters expressly permitted. The tide turned in favor of charter revision. Toledoans were outraged, criticizing the courts for not adhering to the clear intent of the voters to enact home rule immediately. The *Union Leader* railed against the courts for attempting to stay "the rising floodtide of true democracy," urging readers to continue the "fight for the public ownership of things used in common."[93] Whitlock advised that the best course of action was to begin efforts to secure a new charter, and the council, in a unanimous vote, called for the election of a Charter Commission in November.[94]

Despite widespread support for a new charter, the work of the Charter Commission elected in 1913 highlighted divisions among Toledoans regarding the role of city government, particularly in terms of addressing vice. While Howe and others believed that cities would unite without outside influences, urban residents often disagreed passionately. As mayor, Whitlock angered local Protestant leaders with what they perceived to be his lenient and permissive attitude toward gambling, drunkenness, and prostitution. Whitlock believed that government should eradicate the causes of crime rather than punish offenders. In *On the Enforcement of Law in Cities* (1910), he argued that the best way to prevent "the existence of vice and crime" was to enact reforms that would end systems that granted "monopolies and privileges to a few . . . by denying common rights to the many," thereby reducing "them to a condition of involuntary poverty." The first step was to end the franchise system and enact municipal ownership. Yet Whitlock had grander visions for city government, hoping to use taxation to eliminate extreme wealth and poverty and fund educational and cultural programs.[95] Whitlock thus situated a critique of the franchise system in a larger context, portraying city government as able to promote economic, social, and political equality.

Whitlock's views elicited passionate support and opposition. He was popular with immigrants and other members of the working class, and their votes were crucial in his electoral victories.[96] In 1913, however, Whitlock decided not to seek reelection, and the Independent Party splintered, running two mayoral candidates. As a result of Whitlock's reputation for moral permissiveness, the Guardians of Liberty and other anti-Catholic organizations backed the Republican candidate. The Republicans swept into office, winning every seat on the council and all city offices. The mayoral contest overshadowed the election of the Charter Commission.[97] The Republicans won the majority of seats on the Commission, but Whitlock and other Independents won the remaining seats.[98] The next month, Whitlock left Toledo and the Charter Commission behind when Woodrow Wilson appointed him ambassador to Belgium.[99]

In his absence, though the Commission adopted many reforms that Whitlock would likely have favored, it adopted others that conflicted with his views. The proposed charter established home rule, thereby making municipal ownership possible. It included provisions for direct democracy, specifically calling for referenda on franchise grants and/or plans for municipal ownership. It also included a version of the "federal plan." Implicitly following the recommendations of the Municipal Program, the proposed charter attempted to distinguish administration and legislation. While it retained a ward-based system of selecting councillors, it instituted nonpartisan nominations and elections and a system of preferential voting. To make the administration efficient and accountable, it empowered the mayor, as the administrative head, to appoint and remove directors of all departments. It also created the City Planning Commission for future physical development, the Commission on Publicity and Efficiency to investigate departments and publish the Toledo City Journal, and a civil service commission. These departments extended city government into new areas, beyond the maintenance of basic infrastructure and police and fire protection. The new Department of Public Welfare included divisions of health, labor, parks and boulevards, charities and corrections, and playgrounds, recreations, and amusements.[100]

Leaders of local Protestant organizations advocated other forms of expansion. They had attended meetings of the Charter Commission, asking that the regulation of dance halls and "provision for municipal censorship of all public entertainments and amusements" be included.[101] The Commission complied, and as one commissioner explained, under the proposed charter, "authority is given to council to regulate recreations, amusements and entertainments, and to define and suppress all things detrimental to the health, morals, safety, comfort and welfare of the people."[102] The charter empowered the commissioner of playgrounds, recreations, and amusements to supervise and control public and private social venues.[103] Such proposals were not likely to appeal to working-class voters, who often questioned public interference in their private lives.

Despite the potential working-class opposition to these proposals, the commissioners courted the support of organized labor. Although no labor candidates had been elected to the Commission, an official delegation from the CLU regularly attended meetings and was, for the most part, cordially received.[104] When the Commission finished its report, it asked for the CLU's support in campaigning for the charter before the popular election.[105] While the CLU's membership ultimately voted to oppose the charter as an organization, this decision was hardly a foregone conclusion given that it contained many reforms supported by organized labor. Municipal ownership was the second plank of the CLU's platform.[106] Unions in Toledo supported home rule, the federal plan, ward-based council elections, and direct democracy. Yet they also opposed nonpartisan elections, and many leaders were concerned about the mayor's wide appointive powers and a clause that allowed the council to amend or repeal ordinances passed by popular referenda.[107] In encouraging members to reject the charter, union leaders emphasized that it had been written by businessmen and professionals.[108] A member of the Socialist Party disparagingly referred to the commissioners as "a bunch of corporation lawyers, their doctors and a federal judge" at a meeting of the CLU.[109] Others, however, dissented. One of the official delegates of the CLU to the Commission publicly supported the charter, arguing that labor candidates would have an easier time getting elected in nonpartisan elections.[110]

Regardless of such debates, the topic that most captivated the CLU and most of Toledo in 1913–1914 was public transit. After years of failed negotiations with city officials and disputes over high fares, poor services, and overcapitalization of company stock, all parties in the city elections of 1913 opposed a renewal of the Toledo Railway and Light Company's franchise and declared their support for municipal ownership of utilities and streetcars—if favored by the people in a popular vote.[111] The newly elected council refused to renew the franchise and passed an ordinance allowing the company to charge no more than a three-cent fare after its current franchise expired in March 1914.[112] A legal standoff ensued, and while the courts were considering the matter, several local groups organized to resolve the situation directly.[113] The Commerce Club attempted to negotiate with the company directly, concerned that the dispute was generating "undesirable notoriety" and hampering efforts to advertise the city.[114] Business leaders formed the Toledo Citizens' Franchise Association to broker a compromise.[115] At the same time, the Municipal Ownership League began circulating a petition calling for a special election to enact an ordinance for the issuance of bonds to fund the construction and operation of municipally owned streetcars and electric, light, and gas plants. Upon receipt of a petition signed by nine thousand voters, the Board of Election called for a vote in August.[116] The measure passed, but even before the vote, the Toledo Citizens' Franchise Association and others declared that the election was unconstitutional, and by fall, the council was still considering a franchise, claiming that municipal ownership was not possible at present.[117]

The Charter Commission drafted its charter during the same months that the battle against Rail-Light was raging, and the outcome of the charter campaign can only be understood in this context. After the adoption of the home rule amendment in 1912, Toledo's service director voiced his hope that "under a new charter Toledo should be able to do more things for itself instead of contracting jobs out," such as building bridges and operating an asphalt plant.[118] Soon after the publication of Whitlock's series of articles on European cities, those attending a public meeting to discuss a new charter said that they wanted any revisions to establish municipally owned "street car, heating and lighting systems" and "public bath houses and laundries."[119] When the Charter Commission took up the issue, it was no surprise that it drafted provisions for strict regulations of public service corporations and provided for the option of municipal ownership by popular referendum.[120] In short, union leaders, the business leaders on the Charter Commission, and elected officials all advocated improved regulation of franchises and even the possibility of municipal ownership. The charter was a tool to achieve these goals.

The local press used support for municipal ownership to promote the charter. Portraying it as the fulfillment of the independent movement, the News Bee claimed that the charter established "practically every principle of good city government for which Toledo voters struggled." These principles included home rule, nonpartisan elections, direct democracy, a more "carefully guarded" process of granting franchises, and the option of municipal ownership.[121] With the council claiming that municipal ownership was not currently possible, the fact that the new charter would make it so was a powerful argument. As William Renz, president of the German-American Alliance, succinctly stated, "We cannot have municipal ownership, for which the people voted, until we get a new charter."[122] These arguments were persuasive to many voters, and the charter was adopted with 56 percent of the vote.[123]

Yet the adoption of the charter did not end the controversy surrounding streetcar services. Soon after he left office, Whitlock wrote a memoir that discussed his efforts to help create "the free city." He was confident that home rule would end the reign of public service corporations and usher in a new era of municipal ownership.[124] Whitlock was wrong. In 1920 the voters, by a two-to-one margin, granted a franchise to the newly formed Community Traction Company and, by the same margin, rejected a bond proposal to establish a municipally owned transit system. The new franchise included two of the key provisions that Toledoans had long demanded: lower fares and greater regulations. These regulations, however, embodied the complexity of city politics, mixing several strands of reform. Rather than deferring to a state board, Toledoans opted for local control: the mayor would appoint an unpaid Board of Street Railways Control, and the Board would in turn appoint a street railway commissioner who was "charged with the duty of protecting the rights of the public," accountable to the Board and the mayor but paid by the new Community Traction Company.[125] Perhaps many Toledoans wanted lower fares, greater protection of their rights, and improved regulations more than municipal ownership.

Toledo's history, when considered alongside debates at the NML, helps us better understand the development of American political institutions. National reformers and urban residents all wanted municipalities to secure better services for inhabitants but disagreed about how best to do so. Figures such as Howe, Wilcox, and Whitlock portrayed municipal ownership as the only solution, as part of a larger crusade to safeguard and expand democracy. They believed that the majority of urban voters shared their vision and that with home rule, expansive systems of municipal ownership would be enacted. Others disagreed. Reformers, political scientists like King, and, in the end, Toledo's voters supported improved regulation of the existing franchise system. Historian William Novak's study "The Public Utility Idea and the Origins of Modern Business Regulation" demonstrates that in the late 1800s, the rapid expansion of railroads initiated debates that led to a transformation of legal understandings of public services. The result was the emergence of more comprehensive legal justifications for government regulation of private companies that provided public services. Novak argues that these state regulatory commissions laid the foundation for "the modern American administrative and regulatory state," which he characterizes as a notable expansion of state power over corporations and markets.[126]

This chapter's accounts of debates at the NML and in Toledo add to this story. The regulatory vision was opposed not only by proponents of a free market but also by supporters of municipal ownership. Many Americans for a time viewed public ownership as a viable alternative to the franchise system, an alternative that was a much starker deviation from nineteenth-century models of governance, and resisted government by expert commission. Moreover, the depth of popular dislike of the existing franchise system also helps us better understand the popularity of charter reform and home rule. While this outrage may not have ushered in a wave of municipal ownership, it generated support for home rule and charter revision, two reforms that would fundamentally reshape the development of political institutions in American cities and metropolitan areas.

5

The Commission Plan, c. 1900–1915

While the inclusion of charter making as part of home rule was a major challenge to the *Municipal Program* of the National Municipal League (NML), what became known as the commission plan would be an even greater test. After a hurricane destroyed much of Galveston, Texas, in 1900, a group of local businessmen petitioned the state legislature for an emergency measure to replace the mayor and council with a small commission to help rebuild the city. Pleased with the results, civic leaders elected to retain the commission, and a new plan of local government was born. A small body of five to seven commissioners, working for the city full time, replaced the mayor and council, taking over administrative and legislative duties. Elected at large in nonpartisan elections, commissioners typically each headed an individual department (streets, police, etc.). Other cities in Texas soon adopted this Galveston Plan, and when reformers in Des Moines, Iowa, modified it in 1907 by including provisions for the initiative, referendum, and recall, the Des Moines Plan attracted national attention. In newspapers and magazines, promoters claimed that they had finally found a way to concentrate power and responsibility while maintaining popular accountability. By 1910, ninety-two cities had adopted the commission plan, and over the next five years, an additional 331 followed.[1]

The commission plan challenged not only the characterization of the *Municipal Program* as an ideal form of city government but also one of the NML's most cherished goals: the creation of a unified body of opinion among political scientists and leading reformers. For while the NML's leadership was able to garner largely unified support for the *Municipal Program*, its officers and members were unable to reach consensus regarding the commission plan. For some, it provided a solution to many of the problems that had long plagued city government. The consolidation of powers created clear accountability, which in turn promised greater efficiency and facilitated governmental expansion. Proponents typically viewed provisions for direct democracy as sufficient safeguards to offset the centralization of power and maintain accountability. For others, this centralization seemed dangerous and, perhaps more importantly, a violation of one of the most fundamental principles of government: the separation of administration and legislation.

Such divisions among reformers were often absent in early historical accounts of urban reform, which tended to present commission government and other structural reforms as tools used by business leaders to gain control of city government.[2] Certainly, class divisions were factors in many campaigns for commission government. In cities across the country, business and professional organizations often initiated moves to adopt commission charters. Yet these charters in many cases would not have been adopted without such groups forming alliances with other local political leaders, most often union officials and/or party politicians.[3] Why would working-class constituencies support reforms that would reduce their own power in city politics? And why was this new form of government so popular? To answer these questions, this chapter combines an examination of debates about commission government among prominent leaders and members of the NML, national data on the adoption of commission charters, and a comparison of campaigns to secure commission charters in three cities. Together, this evidence demonstrates that national reformers and local businessmen were not united in support of the commission plan. Instead, anger over the franchise system and regional political and economic variations together explain why and how commission government spread.

An awareness of the extent of popular outrage over the corruption of the franchise system is key to understanding the dynamics of the coalitions that supported commission government. Its popularity was due in large part to the belief that it would enable cities to maintain greater popular control over the provision of utilities and transportation, whether through improved regulation or municipal ownership, thereby enabling cities to undertake new programs. Campaigns for the adoption of commission charters differed from the earlier efforts to secure administrative consolidation by increasing mayoral powers. As explained previously, opponents of strong-mayor charters were concerned about the antidemocratic implications and possibilities for corruption that could potentially accompany administrative centralization, and rising anger over the perceived corruption of the franchise system was a major factor in the popularity of home rule and municipal ownership. The rapid spread of commission government is part of this same story. With the publication of Lincoln Steffen's exposés and revelations of corruption involved in the granting of franchises to private companies, popular anger exploded.[4] In this context, despite the fact that the commission plan centralized power to a far greater degree than strong-mayor charters, there was not as much resistance to the plan on these grounds. Moreover, reformers promised that the initiative, referendum, and recall would offset centralization and facilitate greater popular control over the provision of utilities and transportation.

Regional political and economic variations, state laws, and unique local circumstances all played important roles in decisions to adopt or reject commission charters, but ultimately all of these variables were closely related to the root issues of franchise reform and the expansion of municipal services. A variety of Progressive reforms were often more successful in western states, where political parties were less entrenched and powerful. Western states were also more likely to allow cities greater degrees of home rule. These factors created a context in which it was easier for organized groups to secure the adoption of commission charters, and they were more likely to do so when they were able to frame commission government as a path to franchise reform. This chapter compares two successful campaigns to secure commission charters in Fort Worth, Texas, and Oakland, California, with an unsuccessful campaign in Worcester, Massachusetts. This comparison suggests that commission charters tended to be adopted when reformers were able to harness popular anger and form alliances with other groups. In Worcester, an entrenched two-party system and strong state regulatory system prevented reformers from convincing voters, who were for the most part satisfied with municipal services, to abandon the mayor-council form. In contrast, in western and southwestern cities such as Oakland and Fort Worth, residents were initially more united in their anger toward public service corporations, typically seen as outsiders and often tied to large railroad conglomerates. As a result, unions and commercial organizations formed alliances to work for commission charters. Street-railway systems, vital to economic development and the primary means of transportation for most workers, connected these groups and took center stage in campaigns for commission government.

Accounts of these three cities also demonstrate the continued influence of national reformers and political scientists in shaping the discourse of reform. Despite the fact that they did not fully endorse commission government, politically active urban residents continued to appeal to the NML and prominent academics to justify their agendas. The movement for commission government sparked debates that involved an incredible diversity of Americans. According to an article in the *American City*, one such debate pitted "a Polish washerwoman and the president of the W.C.T.U. [Woman's Christian Temperance Union]" against "a day cleaner and a college professor," with "the president of the Consumers' League and a high school professor" serving as judges.[5] In Worcester, Oakland, and Fort Worth, leaders of chambers of commerce, trades assemblies, fraternal orders, improvement clubs, and the Democratic, Republican, Progressive, and Socialist Parties all debated the merits of this new form of government. Fort Worth's mayor quoted Steffens, and reformers in Oakland called on an "expert" from the University of California at Berkeley to draft a commission charter for their city. Debates raged among reformers in the NML and in cities across the country. Was commission government idealistic or practical? Would it finally enable urban residents to rein in public service corporations?

The Commission Plan: Accountability or Oligarchy?

In the early years, the popularity of commission government was in large part due to the belief that its combination of centralization of power and democratic accountability would facilitate municipal expansion without corruption. Even before the creation of commission government, the initiative, referendum, and recall were associated with increased control over the process of granting franchises and/or the establishment of municipal ownership. As early as 1899, Frank Parsons, a public intellectual known for his passionate support of municipal socialism, made this connection.[6] He carefully distinguished "public ownership" from "government ownership." While the latter could exist under a corrupt spoils system, the former required "the merit system of civil service and the initiative and referendum" in order "to prevent private monopoly by abuse of . . . power."[7]

When first publicizing the Des Moines Plan, supporters highlighted direct democracy as essential to controlling the provision of public services. In Des Moines, John Hamilton, a reporter and editor at the *Des Moines Daily News*, promoted the commission plan and was instrumental in its passage.[8] He later championed commission government in *The Dethronement of the City Boss* (1910). Echoing Parsons, he wrote that both "private ownership of . . . public services" and "municipal ownership" were "attended with great dangers so long as the civil service of our cities was on a spoils basis." He maintained that Des Moines' new charter eliminated these dangers with a commission elected at large, direct democracy, and popular votes on franchises.[9]

The association of commission government with direct democracy and expanded services proved to be partially correct, at least in the short run. As of 1914, roughly 94 percent of commission-governed cities had some provisions for direct democracy.[10] And, according to a study by the Census Bureau, commission-governed cities undertook more debt and spent more on public service enterprises than "unreformed" cities with mayor-council forms of government.[11] Through the 1910s, the commission plan was associated with greater public control of the provision of utilities and streetcar services and with the expansion of services. The commission plan's popularity was tied to its pairing with nonpartisan, at-large elections, civil service systems, and measures for direct democracy.[12]

Within the NML, discussions focused not only on whether direct democracy could offset commissioners' immense powers but also on whether it was wise to combine executive and legislative powers in a single body. At a conference in 1910, Ernest Bradford started the discussion by presenting the results of his "Comparison of the Forms of Commission Government in Cities." He studied political science at the University of Wisconsin, worked as a fellow at the University of Pennsylvania, and, in 1907, became a statistician and economist for the U.S. Department of Commerce.[13] Bradford praised the plan, claiming that it facilitated improvements in the provision of services and "greatly aroused public interest in municipal affairs." He agreed with the popular view that commissions were simultaneously more powerful and more accountable.[14]

The responses to Bradford's paper suggest that support for commission government derived not solely from class background but rather from differences of opinion regarding centralized powers. Ansley Wilcox, who came from a more elite background than Bradford, feared that this new system was oligarchical. He studied at Yale and Oxford before beginning a law practice in Buffalo, New York. He was active in civil service and urban reform and a close friend of Theodore Roosevelt.[15] Wilcox began by highlighting the "many things upon which we all agree": the need for "publicity," "direct nominations," "a short ballot," "the merit system," "home rule," and "the simplest form of city charter, which will fix responsibility directly upon those who possess power." They differed regarding whether commission government was the best way "to accomplish these results." For Wilcox, the commission plan was "an elected oligarchy": "It creates a combination of five men, who initiate everything, pass upon everything, carry through everything and then certify everything." After he spoke, a man named Charles Sumner from Missouri, presenting himself as "a representative of organized labor" and "a real democrat," defended the commission plan, maintaining that provisions for direct democracy were safeguards against "autocracy." Undeterred, Wilcox again spoke against commission government. When it became clear that consensus would not be reached, the chair moved to adjourn, concluding by commending the NML for providing "accurate information" on divisive topics.[16]

When an NML committee published its study of the commission plan the following year, the results were the same: an attempt to highlight points of consensus to mask underlying disagreement regarding the overall advisability of the plan. The committee included Bradford; the NML's secretary, Clinton Rogers Woodruff; Richard Childs, secretary of the National Short Ballot Organization; and Charles Beard and William Bennett Munro, professors of political science and Columbia and Harvard Universities, respectively. The committee's "analytical study" concluded that the plan was a "relative success" compared with "the older forms" and that commission-governed cities manifested "a striking increase in efficiency and a higher standard of municipal accomplishment." It also claimed that "the relative success of commission government results primarily because it is more democratic (i.e., sensitive to public opinion) than the old form." The committee cited two essential "democratic features": the unification of legislative and executive functions to prevent the evasion of "full responsibility," and a shorter ballot. It also included the initiative, referendum, and recall and nonpartisan elections as "useful" and "desirable" though not "indispensable" features.[17]

Yet despite this praise, the committee offered only a qualified endorsement, and the report detailed several disagreements. While the members recommended the plan for cities of one hundred thousand people and under, some expressed reservations about its use in larger cities. Several maintained that commission government could only be successful in such cities with ward-based elections (or plans for proportional representation) and "radically" larger commissions. Others felt that the at-large feature and smaller size could be retained given the safeguards provided by the initiative, referendum, and recall. The committee also disagreed as to whether individual commissioners should be appointed to head departments (i.e., water departments, street departments, etc.). While some felt that provision was an essential component of the commission plan's fusion of executive and legislative powers, others insisted that the commission really remained a popularly elected representative body.[18] These disagreements reflect a lack of consensus regarding whether such a small body could in fact effectively represent and govern a large urban area.

The fusion of executive and legislative branches was the subject of greatest division in academic circles. In his 1912 textbook on city government, Munro explained that this aspect of the plan marked "a radical disregard of [the] time-honored theory . . . of checks and balances." Yet he also maintained that "the plan puts an end to that intolerable scattering of powers, duties, and responsibilities" in forms of city government with divided powers. Munro dismissed those who called the commission plan "oligarchical, undemocratic, and un-American" because of this fusion of powers.[19] Hamilton and other political scientists agreed, insisting that direct democracy replaced checks and balances among the different branches of government.[20]

Others, however, disagreed. One article published by the American Academy of Political and Social Sciences warned that "checks and balances of power in government that have been adopted as the result of the experience of ages cannot safely be cast aside" and that concentrating executive and legislative functions would grant commissioners "absolute power."[21] Moreover, Frank Goodnow's popular distinction between politics and administration held that these two functions should be separated when possible.[22] The commission plan's fusion of branches violated this distinction. Beard, who was a former student of Goodnow, wrote elsewhere about the importance of "the separation of politics from administration."[23]

Despite these concerns, commission government continued to spread, particularly in cities with greater autonomy. As the movement for home rule increasingly focused on charter reform, it became associated with commission government. According to Hamilton, cities that adopted commission charters were marked by "a determination of the city to rule its own affairs."[24] States dealt with the desire of cities to adopt commission charters in a variety of ways that fell into two general categories: some allowed cities to determine charters largely independently, while others retained legislative control (table 5.1). These laws varied by region, with states along the East Coast, both North and South, the least likely to allow autonomy of cities (29 percent) in comparison with eastern central states (78 percent) and states west of the Mississippi River (91 percent) (table 5.2). Regional variation in state laws seems to have been consequential: states west of the Mississippi were home to a disproportionately large number of commission governed cities (table 5.3).[25] These differences suggest that state home rule laws were important factors in understanding the adoption of commission charters.

Regional variation in state laws and commission government developed partly from differences in political and economic development. In the late 1800, political parties in eastern states were more elaborately structured and deeply entrenched. While eastern parties typically mobilized large memberships in competitive elections, western parties, allied with railroads and mining companies that dominated local economies, did not need to mobilize to remain in power. Progressive reformers in these states were able to harness the electoral power of new groups of voters without strong preexisting partisan loyalties. Opponents of partisan politics and the spoils system were more successful in demonizing established parties

TABLE 5.1 **States Laws Regarding the Adoption of Commission Charters, 1918**

States where state legislatures allowed cities to adopt charters independently			States where state legislatures controlled the adoption of charters		
Constitutional home rule charters	Optional model charters	Permissive or general option charters	Special charters	Obligatory, self-executing charters	No commission laws or cities
Arizona	Massachusetts	Alabama[a]	Florida	Alabama[a]	Connecticut
California	New York	Arkansas	Georgia	Missouri[a]	Delaware
Colorado	Ohio	California	Maine	Pennsylvania	Indiana
Michigan	Virginia	Idaho	Maryland	Utah	New Hampshire
Minnesota		Illinois	North Carolina		Rhode Island
Missouri[a]		Iowa	West Virginia		Vermont
Nebraska		Kansas			
Ohio		Kentucky			
Oklahoma		Louisiana			
Oregon		Mississippi			
Texas		Missouri[a]			
Washington		Montana			
		Nebraska			
		Nevada			
		New Jersey			
		New Mexico			
		North Dakota			
		South Carolina			
		South Dakota			
		Tennessee			
		Texas			
		Washington			
		Wisconsin			
		Wyoming			

Source: Data on state laws from Tso-Shuen Chang, *History and Analysis of the Commission and City Manager Plans of Municipal Government in the United States,* University of Iowa Monographs, Studies in the Social Sciences 6 (Iowa City: the University, 1918), 99–157.

[a] Several states appeared in more than one of the six subcategories, but only Alabama and Missouri had laws that fell in both of the two broader categories, allowing some cities to adopt commission charters independently while passing obligatory laws requiring other cities to adopt commission charters. Nevada, Texas, Idaho, Tennessee, Massachusetts, and New York all initially allowed individuals to adopt the commission plan through special charters passed by state legislatures but soon passed general laws allowing cities to adopt commission charters without state legislative approval.

TABLE 5.2 State Laws Regarding the Commission Plan by Region, 1918

Region[a]	Percentage of states allowing independent adoption of commission charters	Percentage of states controlling the adoption of commission charters
East	29 (5 of 17)	71 (12 of 17)
East Central[b]	78 (7 of 9)	11 (1 of 9)
West[b]	91 (20 of 22)	5 (1 of 22)

Sources: Data on state laws from Chang, History and Analysis, 99–157; regional classifications from Bureau of the Census, Fourteenth Census of the United States Taken in the Year 1920, vol. 1, Population (Washington, D.C.: Government Printing Office, 1921), 46.

[a] Regions defined by combining several categories according to the Census of 1920. East includes "New England," "Middle Atlantic," and "South Atlantic." East Central includes "East North Central" and "East South Central." West includes "West North Central," "West South Central," "Mountain," and "Pacific." ("Pacific" did not yet include Alaska and Hawaii, which were not yet states.)

[b] Alabama and Missouri excluded because they had laws falling into both categories.

TABLE 5.3 Adoption of Commission Charters, Numbers of Cities, and Urban Population by Region, 1920/1922

	Percentage of cities adopting commission charters by 1922	Percentage of total U.S. cities in 1920	Percentage of U.S. urban population in 1920
East	25 (109 of 444)	42 (1,169 of 2,788)	49.5
East Central	26 (117 of 444)	27 (755 of 2,788)	27.7
West	49 (218 of 444)	31 (864 of 2,788)	22.8

Sources: Data on adoptions of commission charters from Bradley Robert Rice, Progressive Cities: The Commission Government Movement in America, 1901–1920 (Austin: University of Texas Press, 1977), 113–25; data on cities and urban population from Bureau of the Census, Fourteenth Census, 52–56.

as "the interests" and securing the adoption of Progressive reforms such as state-level direct primaries and direct democracy.[26]

In western cities, reformers were also more successful in securing the adoption of commission charters that typically weakened political parties through nonpartisan, at-large elections and the initiative, referendum, and recall in local matters. Particularly in the Southwest, weak party organizations combined with a lack of available local capital to enable business

leaders to act as reformers and successfully secure the revision of charters. Organized groups of businessmen had access to resources and were
able to attract outside investments from state and local governments and
from private investors in other parts of the country, thereby making it possible to attract local support despite certain antidemocratic consequences
of the reforms they sought.[27] Additionally, in the West, a wide variety of
urban residents (not just businessmen and investors) supported plans to
expand and develop their cities and promote economic development.[28] Promoters of the commission plan often promised that it would enable cities
to promote local control of economic development.

Such regional political and economic variations and the resultant dis-
parities in state laws begin to explain why reformers in some cities were
more successful than others in building coalitions based on the promise
that commission government would improve and expand the provision of
services. This argument was more convincing in cities with some combination of the following variables: weak state regulatory boards, dissatisfaction
with public service corporations, the absence of a competitive two-party
system, and cooperation between commercial and labor organizations.
That these variables were more common in the Southwest and West accounts for much of the greater popularity of the commission plan in these
regions.

Fort Worth, 1900–1907: The Commission Plan and Public Service Corporations

At the end of the nineteenth century, Fort Worth was primarily a retail
center for farmers and cattle dealers; after 1900, packinghouses came to
the city, attracting manufacturing plants. In the following decade, the
city's population nearly tripled, reaching over seventy-three thousand by
1910.[29] A friendly state legislature in Austin granted a commission charter
to Galveston's neighbor and rival Houston in 1905, and by 1907 five other
cities had requested similar charters.[30] As Fort Worth grew, the city needed
to provide new services and often relied on public service corporations to
do so. Local business leaders and reformers turned to charter reform as a
means to prevent these corporations from controlling the city's government and ensure the provision of the roads, sidewalks, water, and transpor-

tation necessary for continued growth. They worked to garner support by playing on popular distrust of public service corporations and the franchise system.

Mayor T. J. Powell played an essential role in generating support, and through his ties to national networks he brought the rhetoric of reform to Fort Worth. In local papers, he presented an expanded sphere of city government, subject to popular control, as an essential component of democratic self-government in the modern era. Powell, an attorney and former newspaperman, campaigned as an opponent of "rings" and "machines."[31] As a member and later an honorary vice president of the League of American Municipalities, Powell came into contact with prominent supporters of public ownership, from Frank Parsons to Toledo's mayor Brand Whitlock, also an honorary vice president.[32] In an article published in the *Fort Worth Telegram*, Powell argued for municipal ownership of "essential services": "The urban resident . . . must have light, water, transportation, [and] communication with other things that are a daily necessity." He believed that the provision of services dominated city politics, and he worried that, with continued growth, politicians would be tempted by the "great value and power" of franchise grants. He also celebrated the democratic implications of allowing the people to adopt municipal ownership, referencing the Declaration of Independence in portraying the referendum as a tool to return to a government deriving its "just powers from the consent of the governed." Finally, elevating the importance of "the problem of the city," Powell declared, "Upon its solution rests . . . the perpetuity of democratic institutions in this country."[33]

During his administration, Powell battled with Fort Worth's council over plans to amend the charter. He and his allies feared that public service companies would soon control the council. In 1900 and 1901, Powell, backed by the newly formed Board of Trade and endorsed by various federations of unions, unsuccessfully attempted to convince the council to revise the charter.[34] Renewing efforts in the fall of 1904, supporters of charter reform organized a Civic League and citizens' clubs in several wards, modeled after the Chicago Civic League. They recommended amendments to the current charter, including at-large council elections and the election of most administrative positions currently appointed by the council. Franchise regulation continued to take center stage. Not only did they propose a tax of at least 2 percent on the gross earnings of all public service corporations, they also sought referenda on all franchises. The councillors, however, rejected most of these proposals. One insisted that it was absurd to hold referenda, claiming that "it is our business to issue franchises." Powell responded by vetoing the council's proposals, declaring that he would continue "working for referendum . . . in the aid of pure and honest government." With the Board of Trade and the Trades Assembly (of unions) supporting him, the council backed down and included a mandatory referendum on franchises along with several other minor reforms among the amendments to be sent to the state legislature.[35]

Despite the adoption of the amendment providing for referenda on franchises, continued fears of domination by public service corporations influenced the upcoming election. Powell did not seek reelection. In the Democratic primary, though both candidates made similar promises to improve streets and sidewalks and construct additional schools, the candidate with ties to the Northern Texas Traction Company, a public service corporation that at the time held several franchises for street railways, was soundly defeated by County Judge William Harris.[36]

Powell was out of office but continued to be influential, allied with Mayor Harris. Together, they began a renewed campaign, attempting to organize local organizations to challenge the council and secure the adoption of a commission charter. Another standoff ensued. In 1906, the *Telegram* printed articles celebrating the successes of Galveston's experiment, and the Board of Trade promoted commission government.[37] Powell, now acting as a private citizen, attempted to bypass the council by organizing a Citizens' Charter Committee composed of thirty-five delegates from various organizations. Harris supported Powell and invited the Committee to meet in his office. The Committee proposed a charter that would replace the mayor and councillors elected by wards with five commissioners elected at large. The council countered by forming its own charter revision committee, proposing several amendments but retaining the mayor-council form. The council then called for an election for voters to choose between the charter of the Citizens' Committee and the council's amendments. Harris declared that the council had no legal right to call for an election, but critics accused the Citizens' Committee of trying to secure the passage of its charter at the state capital without the people's approval at home. In a compromise, the state legislature passed the charter of the Citizens' Committee in early 1907 with an amendment stipulating that it would only become law if approved by the voters of Fort Worth.[38]

Though a struggle between businessmen-reformers and ward politicians was a factor in this confrontation, franchise reform was central.[39] Regional economic conditions partly explain why voters in southwestern cities were more likely to support commission (and later city manager) charters. Southwestern cities in the early twentieth century lacked capital, and the segments of local business communities who supported charter reform typically presented themselves as leaders capable of attracting outside resources from both state and national government and private companies. They claimed that under new charters, cities would be able to provide the lighting, paved streets, sewers, water supplies, and public transportation necessary to attract workers and employers.[40] In Fort Worth, the officers of the new Board of Trade were these leaders. Within one year of its founding, the Board had organized committees on water, lights, parks, public grounds, education, city ordinances, city finances, the state legislature, and advertising. By 1907, it had nearly five hundred members. To attract outside investors, it printed pamphlets advertising Fort Worth and worked with the Home Factory and Industrial Association. To obtain favorable rates and conditions, it lobbied against railroad corporations at the state legislature. And to limit the power of public service corporations, it led the efforts of the Citizens' Charter Committee to secure a commission charter.[41]

The Board of Trade's success in securing a commission charter was partly due to the coalitions it formed. In the weeks before the election, it worked with the mayor, the Trades Assembly, and a network of ward-level civic leagues to promote the charter as an instrument for regulating franchises and expanding services. Mayor Harris urged residents to pay their poll taxes and vote for the charter. Leaders of the Board of Trade and the Trades Assembly spoke at meetings organized by the civic leagues.[42] In its list of reasons to vote for the charter, the Sixth Ward Civic League not only made general statements about creating "a more truly representative government" and fighting "special interests" but also specifically addressed the ways in which it would improve the regulation of franchises.[43] Organized labor in the city had long favored referendums on franchises and municipal ownership of utilities. The delegates from the Trades Assembly who had participated in the deliberations of the Citizens' Committee publicly supported the charter and urged members to vote for it in the upcoming election.[44]

In attempting to garner support, reformers did not emphasize theoretical arguments for at-large elections or concentrating legislative and executive functions but rather highlighted specific ways that the charter would enable the city to provide more services. Harris underscored the fact that it would enable the city to raise funds by allowing it to take on more debt than was currently allowed by state law. It permitted an additional $150,000 worth of bonds annually, and Harris maintained that such funds were necessary to carry out several pending projects, including constructing additional schools and paving streets in poor condition.[45]

Municipal ownership of utilities was popular in many circles in Fort Worth. The *Telegram* had long published articles on municipal ownership in cities throughout Texas and Europe, noting its profitability.[46] Unions favored public ownership of utilities, as did former mayor Powell, now a candidate for Congress.[47] Fort Worth currently owned a water plant, a fact celebrated by boosters, and various groups sought to establish a municipal garbage plant and a city market house for the sale of produce in 1906. Yet despite popular support (630 citizens signed a petition favoring a market house while only 72 signed a petition against it), these proposals were not enacted.[48]

Despite internal disagreements, the Citizens' Charter Committee ultimately included several clauses expanding opportunities for municipal ownership, and champions of these clauses cited them as reasons for voters to support the charter. The charter provided for the option of municipal ownership of all utilities and directly established a municipal lighting plant. Additionally, it granted commissioners what the *Telegram* described as "absolute control over the street and sidewalks and the ground under them, and the air above them," and allowed the city to charge public service corporations providing transportation, telephone and telegraph service, lighting, and electricity for their use (and to compel property owners to pay for the paving of streets adjacent to their properties). Yet the charter also limited commissioners' powers, denying them the right to sell any property or utilities owned by the city without a popular referendum.[49]

The inclusion of these provisions suggests that businessmen in the Board of Trade did not control the Citizens' Committee and compromised with other groups to secure their support. As a member of the Citizens' Committee, Captain B. B. Paddock, founder, secretary, and director of the Board of Trade, attempted to omit the "public ownership" clauses but faced stern opposition from other committee members. These clauses were included in the final version.[50] Campaigning at the Eighth Ward Civic League in March 1907, union leader C. W. Woodman, a delegate from the Trades Assembly to the Citizens' Committee, promised listeners that "the new charter will pave the way for municipal ownership of public utilities when the city is ready for them."[51]

While the charter allowed for municipal ownership, it also proposed improved regulations of the existing franchise system, again sparking controversy. The charter included strict regulations of the granting of franchises and the activities of public service corporations, particularly streetcar companies. Even though representatives of these companies had requested a meeting with the Citizens' Committee to voice objections to proposed "radical" provisions, the final charter granted commissioners powers to regulate speeds, fares, and the construction and maintenance of tracks. It also provided for several new taxes on public service corporations. Additionally, the decision to make referenda on franchises optional rather than mandatory, requiring a citizens' petition to call for an election, revealed divisions among the charter's supporters themselves.[52] Powell said that he supported the charter despite this new franchise law, explaining that it would be too costly and time consuming to obtain the necessary signatures for petitions. Harris, in contrast, argued that it solved the problem of endless elections while still allowing the people to call for a referendum if necessary.[53]

In spite of this difference of opinion, in the weeks before the charter election, Harris and Powell agreed that voters should reject the renewal sought by the Fort Worth Power and Light Company eight years before its current franchise expired. Reformers had long claimed that the real opponents of the charter were such corporations. Now the *Telegram* accused the Fort Worth Power and Light Company of trying to rush a renewal because the new charter would impose the 3 percent tax for the use of public property (the present charter charged no fee). Harris, Powell, the *Telegram*, and several of the civic leagues opposed the renewal, as did the voters of Fort Worth in the referendum of March 1907.[54]

In April, the new charter passed easily. With the establishment of the poll tax in 1902, only 5,184 of over 50,000 residents of the city were registered to vote by 1907. In the election, 84.3 percent favored the new charter.[55] Once the new commission charter was adopted, the city instituted a wave of reforms. In the first five years, it instituted a new purchasing system, created a new building code, adopted new accounting methods, and embarked on an array of public improvements, including the city's first playground.[56]

Oakland, 1907–1910: The Commission Plan and Southern Pacific Railroad

In the spring of 1907, when Fort Worth and other Texan cities were adopting commission charters, the Des Moines version of commission government, paired with the initiative, referendum, and recall, was attracting national attention. By summer, the *Bulletin of the League of American Municipalities* explained the details to its readers, largely elected officials. A wider audience learned of the new experiment through articles in popular magazines and newspapers. The *Chautauquan* told readers that the commission plan seemed to be "the 'way out' of the troubles of graft, corruption, spoils, politics, and general demoralization."[57]

With the passage of a home rule amendment in California that allowed cities to draft their own charters, residents of Oakland, still waging a decades-old struggle against the Southern Pacific Railroad Corporation, one of the biggest "interests" in the nation, turned to the Des Moines Plan. Oakland was an industrial seaport with a rapidly growing population, partly due to an earthquake in San Francisco in 1906, which sent 50,000 refugees to Oakland. In 1900, Oakland's population was 66,960; ten years later, it was 150,174, approximately 95 percent white.[58]

Efforts to secure commission government in Oakland provide another example of a movement led by reformers intent on destroying the hold of public service corporations on city politics. Yet their campaign also underscores the extent to which local business leaders were divided, with some supporting and others vehemently opposing commission government. In his second inaugural address, in 1907, Mayor Frank Mott, citing the new home rule amendment, declared that Oakland should elect a board of freeholders to frame a charter attuned to the needs of a growing city.[59] As mayor, Mott, a local businessman and founding member of the Chamber of Commerce, used his position to favor a variety of local businesses by granting franchises, tax breaks, and other forms of patronage, but he did not cross the line between what contemporaries referred to as "honest" and "dishonest" graft. Frustrated by his limited powers under the current charter, he hoped to institute a strong-mayor form of government. Mott, however, did not anticipate that reform-minded small-business owners and professionals in the Alameda County Progress Club (ACPC) would embrace charter revision as their own and spearhead an effort to bring commission government to Oakland.[60]

The ACPC, aided by the *Oakland Enquirer*, began a campaign to convince voters that a commission charter would create the modern structures essential for new services. The ACPC's leaders invited delegates of civic and labor organizations to form the Joint Charter Committee to draft a charter. Their invitation did not mention the commission plan but instead proposed specific reforms, mostly regarding new services such as a municipal market, free schoolbooks, and inspectors of milk, produce, plumbing, and electricity. Yet when the delegates met, the ACPC's leaders repeatedly spoke about the charters of Galveston and Des Moines.[61] Editorials in the *Enquirer* spread the message that such a charter was necessary for development. One contrasted Oakland's "entirely obsolete" charter with "progressive" commission charters, claiming that the "present charter . . . hampers the growth of the city."[62]

These editorials reveal the use of national reform discourse to persuade residents to support commission government. Several emphasized the use of the initiative, referendum, and recall, celebrating these measures as "progressive ideas" that made "city government more effective and more responsive to the will of the people." The *Enquirer* also reprinted excerpts from an article by Toledo's mayor Brand Whitlock. It began with a diatribe against charters that enabled "an oligarchy formed by a union of greedy politicians and greedy plutocrats" to prevent "the people of a city" from doing "anything for themselves" and ended with a call for commission government.[63] Such rhetoric framed the commission plan as part of a larger movement for democratization.

Attacks on the unjustness of special privileges granted to corporations resonated in Oakland, where the Southern Pacific Railroad Corporation had long controlled the city's waterfront and many of its railway lines. After the Civil War, western state and local governments, in need of transportation and capital, often granted railroad corporations favorable franchises, subsidies, and protections from regulation. By the close of the century, these corporations were powerful, often forming alliances with elected officials. In California, a campaign against the monopoly powers of Southern Pacific had been ongoing for decades.[64] In Oakland, Southern Pacific acquired ownership of the waterfront in the 1880s, profiting handsomely while providing little in return to the city. After a long legal battle, Southern Pacific was ordered to return the waterfront to the city, putting the railroad in the position of having to obtain a franchise to continue to use the property. The city had to decide whether to maintain control of the operation of the waterfront or to lease to Southern Pacific or Western Pacific, a competing transcontinental railroad.[65]

Reformers drew on widespread animosity toward Southern Pacific to generate support for a commission charter, depicting it as an instrument that would ensure that future franchises would not be given to corporations without securing profitable returns and establishing the right of the city to own the waterfront. Though Oakland's reformers advocated municipal ownership of utilities, they focused on control of the waterfront and streets and the regulation of railroad companies making use of these properties. In promoting charter reform, editorials in the *Enquirer* lamented that "the city has been almost absolutely divested of all possible sources of revenue other than license and direct taxation."[66]

Local business leaders were divided. In 1905, the director of the Merchants' Exchange charged that the Board of Trade (which would soon become the Chamber of Commerce) was controlled by Southern Pacific.[67] Two years later, relations between the two groups were still tense. Although the Chamber supported public ownership of the waterfront and welcomed new railroads, its officers felt that the continued presence of Southern Pacific was essential to Oakland's economy. The Merchants' Exchange, in contrast, would have preferred to see Southern Pacific leave the city.[68] When the ACPC invited delegates to a charter convention, promoting the commission plan as a tool to end "special privileges," the Merchants' Exchange was initially receptive.[69]

The ACPC also looked to unions as potential allies. Organized labor was politically powerful in Northern California. Progressive Republicans and

Democrats in the state legislature sought support for various reform measures, and labor leaders, in turn, bargained for favorable legislation.[70] In Oakland, the Progressive ACPC, Union Labor Party, and Socialist Party supported several shared causes, including the adoption of direct democracy and opposition to the franchise system.[71] When the Joint Charter Committee first met, supporters sought to convince delegates that a commission charter would achieve these ends. One member of the Building Trades Council and the legal committee of the ACPC envisioned a charter that would "give no opportunity for graft" and ensure "a Government for and by the people."[72]

In inviting delegates from "various representative bodies" to attend its first meeting, the ACPC's leaders likely hoped to form a coalition of civic, business, and labor organizations to circumvent unreceptive local officials.[73] Only sixteen, however, sent delegates: thirteen unions, one fraternal order, the Merchants' Exchange, and the Harbor League, which was dedicated to municipal ownership of the waterfront. Three months later, the Joint Charter Committee included twenty-four organizations: nineteen unions, four fraternal orders, and the Harbor League.[74] The Merchants' Exchange no longer attended meetings because the Chamber of Commerce had convinced the Exchange to focus on a joint campaign for consolidation of the cities of Alameda County. Many believed that consolidation would reduce taxes and stimulate economic growth, and the Chamber's leaders argued that consolidation should precede charter revision. In the coming months, as unions dominated the Joint Charter Committee, the Committee struggled to present itself as representative of all the people of Oakland.[75] Chairman Hugh Murrin maintained that charter reform should not be "a class fight" and that they "should represent, not the laboring class alone, but the business and professional men of Oakland."[76]

In an effort to rebuild the Joint Charter Committee's image, the ACPC turned to an authority on city government. William Carey Jones, professor of jurisprudence at the University of California, Berkeley, had written a version of the commission plan adapted to California's laws.[77] The *Enquirer* had covered Jones's work with a board of freeholders framing a charter in Berkeley, and the ACPC now invited Jones to deliver a talk to its own Joint Charter Committee.[78] In this talk, Jones said that commission-governed cities were "the only democratic city governments in the United States." Though he relied on the popular analogy of a business corporation with the residents of a city as stockholders, he also maintained that the inclusion of provisions for direct democracy made the commission plan analogous to a "town-meeting plan adapted to large populations."[79]

Within weeks the Committee published a proposed charter for Oakland, written largely by Jones, calling for commission government with strong provisions for direct democracy. It included strict regulations of franchises, requiring popular referenda for most grants, establishing a twenty-five-year maximum, and stipulating that the city had the right to purchase the plant or property of any corporation holding a franchise. It required that streetcar lines be open to use by multiple carriers and that rails be considered part of the streets themselves (and therefore the city's property). The *Enquirer* celebrated this document as the result of collaboration between Jones and those with "practical experience" on the Committee.[80]

With the publication of these proposals, opinion became increasingly polarized. Over the coming months, the Joint Committee and the ACPC undertook a petition drive calling for the election of a board of freeholders to frame a new charter. They submitted over four thousand signatures to Mott. Mott, however, did not ask the council to call for an election, citing the need to work for consolidation first and the expense of an election. In reality, powerful local interests, including Southern Pacific, public service corporations (several of which were members of the Chamber of Commerce), and liquor dealers, opposed the proposed charter's strict regulation of franchises and provisions for direct democracy. The *Oakland Tribune*, a conservative Republican newspaper and defender of Southern Pacific, published an editorial agreeing that consolidation was paramount and dismissing "new charter-makers" as "restless experimenters in governmental novelties who desire to impress upon the scheme all the fads and fancies that are the fungi of socialism."[81]

It was in this context that leaders of women's groups began to declare support for a charter. Echoing the views of the men who dominated municipal reform associations, they presented a charter as a tool to enact new governmental programs. A. Denison of the Equal Suffrage League and the Oakland Club claimed that "the adoption of modern ideas in city government" would yield "beneficial effects . . . in the way of better sanitation, better school facilities and better homes." Similarly, Minnie Rutherford of the Child Welfare League praised Berkeley's "model charter" when speaking on behalf of the establishment of juvenile courts.[82] In these ways, female leaders tied the adoption of structural reform to expanded programs in education, sanitation, housing, and juvenile justice.

Regardless of such sentiments, Mott held on to the petition, and as the weeks passed, the ACPC's leaders were increasingly angered by his inaction. T. F. Marshall, an owner of a small business and unofficial leader of the charter movement, wrote a public letter implicitly attacking Mott, the Chamber of Commerce, and the Merchants' Exchange for obstructing a reform supported by the fifty-six groups that now formed the Joint Charter Committee, as well as over four thousand residents. Mott decided to send the petition to the council without a recommendation, assuming that the council would not call for an election.[83] With the fate of the charter before the council, reformers worked to regain the support of the Merchants' Association and garner enough popular support to secure the necessary votes in the council. They organized meetings and spoke at improvement clubs and church groups, and the Enquirer renewed its editorial campaign.[84]

To sway the business community, the Enquirer printed numerous editorials arguing, to counter Mott, that a new charter would attract neighboring communities and help achieve consolidation.[85] Other editorials argued that a commission charter would improve popular control of public service corporations, enable the city to develop its holdings, and contribute to overall prosperity. One reprinted an article by Horace Deming, then chairman of the NML's executive committee, that appealed to "the aroused and intelligent patriotism of our businessmen" and claimed, "Good government is a vital, commercial asset."[86] In detailing future needs of the city, from the development of the waterfront to improvements in the transit system, other editorials maintained the need for "a modern and up-to-date charter."[87] Several suggested that only the "interests," "the recognized organs of graft," opposed the charter and sought "to defeat popular government in Oakland." They emphasized business support, noting that the Commercial Club of Des Moines and Chamber of Commerce of Berkeley promoted commission government.[88]

Though they were unable to secure a freeholder election that summer, their efforts were not in vain. The Merchants' Exchange supported the call for an election and sent representatives to appeal to the council. Nevertheless, after several heated public meetings, the council voted against the election in August 1908, claiming that it would be better to revise the charter after Oakland and surrounding towns voted on consolidation.[89] Yet when a consolidation vote drew near in the fall of 1909, some resisted joining a city that did not have a "modern" charter. To defuse such opposition, Mott, the council, the Chamber of Commerce, and the Merchants' Exchange pledged that if annexation passed, they would call for the election of a board of freeholders to frame a charter by the following summer. The ACPC and Joint Charter Committee now declared support for annexation. Less than a week later, annexation carried easily.[90]

Now that a new charter was unavoidable, almost every group publicly supported one and strategized to secure the election of freeholders sympathetic to their own interests. Leaders of the ACPC and Merchants' Exchange formed a new organization called the Civic League of Greater Oakland, calling for unions, civic groups, fraternal orders, and improvement clubs to send delegates to the Greater Oakland Charter Convention. As the convention's organizers were mindful of the consequences of labor's dominance on the Joint Charter Committee, several unions, though officially welcomed, were informally asked not to attend. In 1908, nineteen of twenty-four organizations sending delegates were unions; now, only twelve of eighty-three were.[91] Most unions refused to attend in protest and formed their own convention, the Union Labor Charter Convention. As the election neared, the Greater Oakland Charter Convention drafted a commission charter and nominated a slate of fifteen freeholders. The Union Labor Charter Conference drafted a list of demands for the charter and decided to back Mott's slate, which included four labor candidates. With the support of unions, Mott's ticket won most of the seats, but several candidates sympathetic to the original charter movement were also elected.[92]

The freeholders' charter emerged from extensive bargaining and suggests that Oakland's reformers were more concerned with franchise reform and direct democracy than with the commission form itself. The proposed charter was a commission charter in name only. Commission government called for the mayor and council to be replaced by five commissioners attending to their duties full time. Mott's representatives among the freeholders secured a charter that retained an elective mayor with wide appointive powers. The remaining four commissioners, who worked part time, were more subordinate department heads than commissioners. The original supporters of commission government were willing to accept these modifications in exchange for strict regulations of franchises and guarantees of the right to implement municipal ownership. Although not as far reaching as the charter proposed in 1908, the freeholders' charter provided for much stricter regulations of franchises than were currently in place and for the right of the city to own the waterfront and utility plants.[93]

Just as in Fort Worth, as the vote neared, a public controversy regarding a franchise renewal erupted, generating support for the charter. When Southern Pacific threatened to appeal the courts' decision returning ownership of Oakland's waterfront to the city, Mott had negotiated a compromise to prevent a continued legal battle. In September 1908, Southern Pacific agreed to renounce claims to ownership of the waterfront in exchange for a fifty-year franchise for 1,400 feet of frontage. Two years later, this agreement had yet to be formalized. Only when the vote on the charter was approaching did the railroad apply for franchises for the waterfront and a railway within the city.[94]

In protesting Southern Pacific's attempt to secure these last-minute franchises, representatives of organized labor and the Socialist Party advertised the new charter as a means to create greater popular control over public service corporations. The *Labor World*, a socialist newspaper in San Francisco, printed an editorial the previous spring attacking the prospect of a new charter and nonpartisan elections. It accused "the forces of Big business," including transit and utility companies, of "quietly working through the present city administration" and the Greater Oakland Charter Convention to advance their own "business interests."[95] Yet as the election neared, the *Labor World* did not print articles critiquing the charter. It did, however, print the platform of the Socialist Party, which called for direct democracy, home rule, and municipal ownership.[96] It continued to critique the current city government as beholden to Southern Pacific (figure 5.1). Moreover, in its extensive coverage of the efforts of unions and Socialists to block Southern Pacific's franchises, it repeatedly printed the demand that the matter be decided *when* the new charter became law, even though the election had not yet taken place.[97]

Though unions, Socialists, and others were unable to prevent the council from granting the franchise for the waterfront, they did prevent it from granting the railway franchise in December 1910.[98] That month, in an election marked by low turnout (roughly 40 percent), three-quarters of those who voted supported the charter. No group had actively campaigned for the charter because almost no group in Oakland opposed it.

FIGURE 5.1 Untitled political cartoon, *Labor World*

Labor World, November 26, 1910, 1.

The charter carried in every ward.[99] Even the Chamber of Commerce, long an opponent, now believed that the charter's adoption would contribute to prosperity and make Oakland more attractive to outsiders. In a pamphlet advertising the city published in 1911, the chamber noted the adoption of the commission charter, highlighting the value of direct democracy and popular votes on franchises.[100]

Worcester, 1913–1914: The Strength of Party Politics and State Regulation

In Worcester, reformers did not convince residents that a commission charter would improve city government. With a competitive two-party system and relatively effective state railroad commission, they were unable to form coalitions and galvanize voters angered by the franchise system as their counterparts had done in Fort Worth and Oakland. In the early twentieth century, Worcester was a manufacturing town with a range of industries, producing envelopes, wire, carriages, corsets, carpets, shoes, and much more.[101] Ethnic diversity among workers contributed to the Republican Party's strength in city politics, for the Democratic Party was so strongly associated with the Irish that Swedes, Russians Jews, and French Canadians tended to vote Republican.[102]

Despite the many differences among their campaigns for commission government, in all three cities mayors argued for the need to update their charters. In Worcester, Republican George Wright, head of the Wright Wire Company, became mayor in 1913.[103] He entered office envisioning city government as a corporation, proposing that Worcester needed a new charter to provide for the needs of a growing city. The current charter provided for a mayor and bicameral council and school committee elected by ward. There was no clear division between the executive and the legislative branches. The mayor appointed several important officials, but the councils appointed all department heads and many other officials.[104]

In contrast to California, cities in Massachusetts did not possess home rule with regard to charter making in 1913.[105] Local politicians had to appeal to the state legislature's Committee on Cities to amend charters. Yet despite these legal differences, Wright claimed that he hoped to "give the fullest opportunity to our citizens" to participate in the drafting of a new charter. He maintained that he had no specific agenda but did not think the present situation, with several competing groups petitioning the legislature for piecemeal changes, was the wisest course. Instead, he proposed that they thoroughly study and discuss the matter and then "go before the legislature with a practically united front." In a message delivered to Worcester's councillors, Wright recommended that they authorize him to appoint a committee of elected officials and twenty to thirty "representative citizens" to draft a new charter to be submitted to the state legislature and then a popular vote. Residents of Worcester were aware of events transpiring in other cities, and their attention quickly turned to commission government. In speeches to the council, Wright proposed many possible reforms for consideration, including, to name a few, instituting nonpartisan elections, creating a unicameral council, reconsidering which officials should be elected and which should be appointed, improving coordination among various departments, strengthening the power of the mayor, and adopting a commission form of government.[106] Unlike most eastern states, Massachusetts actually had seven commission-governed cities by 1912, though most were substantially smaller than Worcester.[107] The *Worcester Magazine* had printed several articles on the commission plan, urging readers to consider the experiences of other cities in the state operating under the plan.[108]

In spite of such attempts to promote commission government, opponents belittled it as either idealistic or autocratic. Though councillors claimed that they opposed Wright's plan only because it did not allow them a voice in the revision of the charter, many observers believed their real motivation was a dislike of commission government. Councillors initially considered the mayor's proposal, but after he announced his appointees to the commission, they tabled the bill.[109] According to one member of the Board of Aldermen, the mayor's commission consisted of members of "various idealistic organizations in Worcester" that would not be able to "see the practical side of city government."[110] Additionally, coverage of council meetings in local papers made it clear that several members feared the mayor's charter commission would adopt the commission plan, "an autocratic form of government." Democratic alderman H. H. O'Rourke even hyperbolically claimed that adopting commission government would lead to "bloodshed, loss of life and loss of property."[111] In the face of such opposition, efforts at reform stalled in 1913.

The issue emerged again the following year, when, as in Oakland, a group of reformers took over a reform initially proposed by a mayor. In January 1914, Wright, having received the largest plurality of any mayoral candidate in a contested election, again urged a reform of Worcester's charter.[112] Perhaps with the events of last year in mind, local papers and the councils mostly ignored Wright's plea.[113] Yet Worcester's Progressive Party, which had vocally supported Wright's earlier proposals, undertook its own effort to revise the city's charter, though perhaps not in the way that Wright envisioned.[114] At a meeting of the City Committee of the Progressive Party, members decided to file a bill with the state legislature requesting a new charter to establish a commission form of government, with five councillors elected in at-large, nonpartisan elections and direct democracy.[115] Whether the Progressives were attempting to circumvent local discussion was unclear. The following month, the state legislature's Committee on Cities came to Worcester for a public hearing. The *Worcester Telegram* accused the Progressives of attempting a "coup" and "hoping to catch the opposition asleep," and it urged opponents of the commission plan to attend the meeting.[116] The *Worcester Evening Gazette* dismissed this "fake story printed in The Telegram . . . about the Progressives trying to pack the meeting," claiming that it "was all rot." Yet the two newspapers agreed that the meeting, which was well attended, made clear that most residents did not want to adopt the commission plan, with only twenty-four of over five hundred people in attendance voting in favor of the proposed bill.[117] As a result, the Committee on Cities recommended that the petition to revise Worcester's charter be tabled, and the legislature agreed.[118]

The Progressive Party's political isolation contributed to this outcome. The party was never successful on the state level, and in Worcester itself Progressive candidates were decisively defeated in the election of December 1913.[119] Yet electoral defeats alone did not necessarily mean that Progressives' hopes for charter reform were doomed. In other cities, reform associations formed alliances—with major parties, labor unions, and/or commercial organizations—and were successful. Unions in the 1910s were not a strong force in Worcester's politics. Labor was relatively unorganized in the city, with ethnic divisions preventing greater unionization among industrial workers.[120] Worcester's business organizations, in contrast, were flourishing. The Board of Trade reorganized itself into a Chamber of Commerce in 1913. The Merchants' Association voted the next year to merge with the Chamber, which had become a powerful voice in city politics and active promoter of Worcester's commercial interests.[121] Had the Progressives courted such powerful allies, the outcome of their efforts to secure a commission charter might have been different.

Attempts to secure commission government also failed because most residents seem to have been generally satisfied with city government. The effectiveness of existing city government and the dynamics of local political conflict influenced the outcome of reform movements. Electoral fraud, political corruption (franchise and otherwise), and the poor provision of services created dissatisfaction, making voters more likely to support structural reforms.[122] In Worcester, such circumstances were largely absent. In making their case for commission government at the public hearing, the Progressive Party's leaders did not argue that the city's present government was corrupt or ineffective. According to the chair of the party's executive committee, "It is not our purpose to claim that there is any overwhelming demand for a change. We do not rest our case on general dissatisfaction with municipal government here." He added that though Worcester was "free from corruption and graft," adopting the commission plan would, as it had in three hundred other cities, create "more economical and efficient" government and yield lower taxes. Opponents, however, mocked the notion that Worcester should consider revising its charter with no evidence of "scandal."[123]

Satisfaction with Worcester's government was partly due to the effectiveness of state regulatory commissions. Massachusetts pioneered the regulation of railroads and other public service corporations with the creation of the Massachusetts Railroad Commission in 1869 (which had jurisdiction over municipal railways) and the Board of Gas and Electric Light Commissioners in 1885, both the first of their kind in the nation. Though later Progressives described these commissions as weak, armed more with advisory than compulsory powers, they provided relatively successful regulation for the day.[124] According to a paper presented to the NML in 1909 by the executive secretary of Massachusetts's Public Franchise League, the commissions had an "excellent record" of providing "impartial adjudication." As a result, there had not been any "gross scandals in connection with the public-service corporations of Massachusetts since . . . the [eighteen] eighties."[125]

Residents of Worcester likely agreed that the state railroad commission provided effective regulation. In February 1913, the *Gazette* published a scathing attack on the services provided by the Worcester Consolidated Street Railway Company, "a dilatory public services corporation," and urged Mayor Wright to rectify "the trolley situation." Adopting rhetoric used by critics of the franchise system throughout the country, Wright agreed that it was time for "the men behind the throne in the Consolidated, the men who are drawing big salaries and getting big, fat juicy dividends out of the Worcester riding public without returning anything like decent service" to "do something." The Board of Aldermen passed a resolution asking the city solicitor to petition the Massachusetts Board of Railroad Commissioners to investigate charges of inadequate provision of power, poor lighting and equipment, overcrowding on cars, and filthy conditions. The *Gazette* urged residents to write to the city solicitor detailing grievances "and arm him with a mass of facts that will compel the railroad Commission to act." The chairman of the Commission, however, responded within less than a month that it needed no additional proof, for it had sent its own inspector to Worcester to investigate the charges and the inspector had found them all to be true. The chairman emphasized that "the commission intends to remedy the conditions."[126] With such a commission acting to ensure the provision of adequate services, neither Mayor Wright nor the Progressive Party could argue that charter reform was needed to prevent "special privileges" and "corrupt bargains."

Despite the hopes of many union leaders, business leaders, politicians, and reformers, observers soon began to question whether commission government would deliver dramatic improvements. Early studies, as noted, found that initially residents were generally happy with commission government, which facilitated spending on public services.[127] Yet doubts quickly surfaced. One study published by the NML found that the measures of direct democracy were, in practice, not used often. By 1914, only 25 percent of the commission-governed cities with provisions for the initiative, referendum, and recall had used at least one of them.[128]

Another early assessment focused on administration and the kinds of new activities undertaken by commission-governed cities. Henry Bruère, codirector of the New York Bureau of Municipal Research, acknowledged improvements under the plan but hesitated to endorse it fully. He concluded that the "most conspicuous effect" was a marked increase in money spent on physical improvements that was "willingly borne" by residents who were more confident in their governments. At the same time, he maintained that most new programs resulted from "campaigns for commercial betterment," concluding that "the social welfare aim of the commission movement is chiefly a commercial welfare aim."[129]

Such sentiments begin to explain why many early studies characterized the commission plan as a tool of elite domination, but they may have confused outcomes with initial hopes. As this chapter demonstrates, diverse urban residents supported commission government during charter campaigns. At the same time, Bruère's early assessment of commission government in operation foreshadowed later studies that emphasize business dominance. These studies suggest that the plan failed to eliminate corruption. In Fort Worth, Oakland, and many other cities, the candidates elected as commissioners were not the disinterested civic leaders envisioned by reformers but rather the same type of party politician that had dominated city government under the mayor-council form. With individual commissioners in charge of specific administrative departments, logrolling, patronage, and even outright corruption continued.[130] Commission government, in short, would not be the culmination of the movement for good city government for it did not resolve many of reformers' primary concerns.

Bruère's appraisal not only identified the early limitations of commission government but also pointed to emerging shifts in reformers' agendas. He succinctly stated his own understanding of the purpose of urban reform: "to make city government a progressive and efficient instrument for promoting community welfare."[131] In some ways, this vision resembled that of the early NML, with concerns for "community welfare" echoing the goal of promoting the "public good." But Bruère's assessment differed in one essential way. He believed that the best way to achieve "good government" was not through charter revision and direct democracy. His interest in welfare was grounded in administrative efficiency as a tool for good government. He shared this belief in the potential of administrative efficiency with many leaders of the bureau movement, the next wave of urban reform.

6

"Whether Democracy and Efficiency Are Inherently Irreconcilable"

Professionalization and Expertise in Municipal Reform, c. 1905–1920

L eading scholars in the early field of municipal political science greatly admired the administration of German cities.[1] With the onset of World War I in Europe, many were forced to reconsider their fondness for German models and the increased efficiency they promised. In 1916, Charles Beard, then a professor of politics at Columbia University and supervisor of the Training School for Public Service at the New York Bureau of Municipal Research (NYBMR), declared "that the supreme public question of the hour is whether democracy and efficiency are inherently irreconcilable." The concept of the "expert administrator" had recently been popularized by political scientist and Harvard president A. Lawrence Lowell. Lowell argued for an extension of the professionalization of city government beyond legal training for city solicitors and medical training for city physicians. Real administrative reform, he believed, required more than an end to patronage. Control over the entire administration needed to be in the hands of professional, permanent experts. Lowell's ideas drew much attention, with Beard and many others debating how to implement such a system without sacrificing democratic governance.[2]

This question shaped the movement for urban reform on every level. Many historical accounts continue to assume that "good-government types sought efficiency rather than democracy."[3] Such assessments oversimplify the complex debates that took place among political scientists and reformers in national organizations and cities across the country. While most recognized that achieving both would be challenging, they maintained that it was possible to do so. This faith is perhaps best embodied in social scientist Mary Parker Follett's *The New State: Group Organization, the Solution of Popular Government* (1918). According to Follett, "The tendency to transfer power to the American citizenship, and the tendency toward efficient government by the employment of experts and concentration of administrative authority, are working side by side in American political life today. These two tendencies are not opposed."[4]

This chapter focuses on the ways that diverse Americans grappled with this challenge by exploring several trends that paralleled the rising interest in home rule, franchise reform, and commission government discussed previously. First, it begins with the emergence of a new type of urban reform organization: bureaus of municipal research. The founders of these bureaus portrayed their work as part of an effort to professionalize urban reform. Second, it examines the ways that leading political scientists discussed the relationship between expertise and reform, focusing on the work of Beard, Lowell, and William Bennett Munro, a political scientist at Harvard University. Like leaders of the bureau movement, these political scientists were committed to understanding cities by examining a broader array of the forces of "real" politics. Third, this chapter turns to the influence of the bureau movement and these trends in political science on the National Municipal League (NML). In these years, officers moved to make the NML more like bureaus and other professional organizations and less of a coalition of local voluntary organizations. Fourth, the chapter ends on the local level by examining a new movement for charter reform in Norfolk, Virginia. Promoters of a new charter promised that a variety of innovations would make it possible to balance efficiency and democracy.

In examining these four topics together, this chapter explores several shifts in the movement for urban reform. These shifts were gradual, marked by ambivalence and disagreement rather than certainty and unanimity. From the codirectors of the NYBMR to leading political scientists of the day to reformers in Norfolk, Americans struggled to increase efficiency while maintaining popular control. Their debates were closely tied to a continued desire to increase the scope of city government, but understandings of the purpose of an expanded city government were changing. Around the turn of the century, when reformers, union officers, socialists, and business leaders spoke of expanding functions, they generally focused on the provision of transportation and utilities. Spurred by popular outrage at the bribery and graft of the franchise system, they often framed proposed structural reforms as means to expand government without corruption.

In the new century, while many of these goals remained, the language used to describe them began to change. The vision of a city as a unified, organic entity, with citizens coming together to promote *the* public good, began to fade. For some, the image of a city as a business corporation came to the fore, providing efficient returns on taxpayers' money. For others, cities became agents of "social welfare," focused on enacting programs to ameliorate poverty and improve public health. For both groups, urban residents increasingly became "consumers" of services. Not only did the language used to describe expansion shift, so too did the means of achieving it. The NML's founders mostly argued that expanded home rule and charter provisions regarding elections and the respective powers of mayors and councils would create the necessary precursors for functional expansion. Now, reformers and political scientists focused more on administrative reform and increased efficiency to facilitate expansion.

Characterizations of cities as administrative service providers raised the question of who should control the provision and distribution of services. While political scientists debated the appropriate role of experts and public opinion in such control, most did not connect voting rights to an equitable provision of services. They largely neglected to consider whether a lack of involvement in decision-making processes would affect who received governmental services and what kinds of services governments opted to provide. Most textbooks on cities were silent on these issues; similarly, leaders of the NML and bureaus tended to discuss administrators as impartial experts who would address the needs of all residents equitably. A lack of consideration of this fact was closely related to their avoidance of controversial subjects in their published works. Given the fact that the woman suffrage movement was nearing its peak and the disfranchisement of African Americans was spreading, many Americans were clearly aware that electoral participation shaped the way that government treated different groups of citizens. Yet in their discussions of city politics, political scientists tended to avoid these issues. In contrast, when conducting studies of "real" politics in cities, the social scientists working on behalf of research bureaus sometimes found them impossible to ignore. When it came time to conduct a detailed investigation of Norfolk's government, the NYBMR's agents were forced to confront racial discrimination.

Efficiency as Reform: Bureaus of Municipal Research

> If, as Ambassador Bryce wrote, years ago, "Municipal government is America's most conspicuous failure," the cause, according to Mr. Bruère, is to be sought not in the corruption of men, but in the inefficiency of methods.
> —*Independent*, 1907[5]

Just as New Yorkers pioneered municipal reform associations in the 1890s with the formation of the City Club and allied good government clubs, they also initiated the municipal research bureau movement in the 1900s and 1910s. With the first election of a consolidated Greater New York approaching in 1897, officers of the City Club decided to take the lead in the organization of an urban reform party. The resultant Citizens' Union, which absorbed many of the good government clubs and collaborated closely with others, initially met with defeat. By 1901, however, it helped elect Seth Low mayor as a fusion candidate with the Republican Party.[6] Low's victory was viewed as a great triumph for reform, and his defeat two years later sparked disillusionment. In the aftermath, William Allen, head of the New York Association for Improving the Condition of the Poor, approached a leading figure in both the Association and the Citizens' Union about the formation of an alternative type of reform organization, one focused on the administration of city departments rather than the election of "good men" to office. As a result, in 1905, the Citizens' Union established the Bureau of City Betterment, and two years later, the Bureau became the independent New York Bureau of Municipal Research.[7] Word of this new instrument for achieving good city government rapidly spread through newspapers, magazines, and academic journals and at conventions of the NML and other national organizations.[8] By 1926, over forty cities maintained bureaus.[9]

The NYBMR's early leaders envisioned their organization as the key to improving city government permanently, contrasting their work with previous reform efforts. Just as proponents of charter revision in the 1890s often claimed that structural flaws rather than corrupt individuals were responsible for governmental failures, these leading figures of the "efficiency movement" now blamed inefficient administrative procedures rather than graft. They critiqued charter reformers' emphasis on representative rather than administrative structures as a failure to recognize that effective popular control depended not on electing "good men" but on securing the services of trained professionals. In one example, Henry Bruère, joint director of the NYBMR, argued that Fort Worth's successes under its new charter were due not to the adoption of the commission plan but rather to the institution of modern accounting. He claimed that "new devices of popular control"—including the recall, nonpartisan elections, direct primaries, and systems of preferential voting—had failed "to produce specially equipped candidates for office."[10]

His codirector Allen agreed, arguing in *Efficient Democracy* (1907) that "government cannot be good unless it is efficient, no matter how honest the official." Allen faulted leaders of "so-called reform movements" for failing to recognize the need for information regarding the functioning of administrative departments. Only when armed with "the facts," as provided by experts, would citizens be able to control city government.[11] He disputed the claim that the adoption of a commission charter could solve the problems posed by the franchise system. Speaking at a meeting of the League of American Municipalities in Norfolk, Allen declared, "Misgovernment in a democracy is due primarily to ignorance on the part of the general public as to official acts and community needs."[12]

With its passion for unearthing "facts" about the actual administration of government, the bureau movement drew on the realist impulse of political science, particularly as it pertained to the study of administration. Later commentators would describe the NYBMR as a conscious attempt to implement Frank Goodnow's distinction between political and administrative functions of government, citing his work and the bureau movement as foundations of the field of public administration.[13] Goodnow himself was directly involved in the founding of the NYBMR.[14] Municipal political scientists and the staff of the bureaus shared similar training and ideals. They employed the language of science and the concept of a politically neutral realm of administration to makes a space for themselves as impartial analysts of and active participants in city government. Bruère, Allen, and Frederick Cleveland, the joint directors of the NYBMR, all had graduate training and viewed themselves as social scientists applying their training to the real-world problem of administration.[15]

These three directors portrayed bureaus of municipal research as the embodiment of realist methodology of political science, undertaking scientific surveys in order to propose solutions rather than relying on theoretical visions of how government should function.[16] In 1908, Bruère, speaking at the annual meeting of the American Political Science Association (APSA), described bureaus as models "of the inductive method of political science" and "opposed to a static conception of political principles and ideals." Instead, they proposed, "on the basis of experience and contemporary social conditions," to produce "a new interpretation . . . of governmental ideals."[17] Similarly, in an article in *Political Science Quarterly*, Allen presented staff of the NYBMR as scientists involved in a larger effort to "promote efficient and economical municipal government" through "scientific methods of accounting and reporting" and the publication of "facts as to the administration of municipal government."[18]

The connection between political science and bureaus also existed on an institutional level. Within a year of the NYBMR's founding, Columbia University invited it to offer a course in "public business."[19] Soon the NYBMR set up its own Training School for Public Service to combine the theoretical training of academic social sciences with real-world, practical training for public service in governmental administration. Beard was impressed with the Training School. In 1913, in a report to the APSA and the American Economic Association, he concluded that "the Training School fulfills every requirement of a university" and even recommended that political science graduate students "spend a portion of their time at the Training School" while conducting doctoral research. Beard organized a "Politics Laboratory" at Columbia in 1911, and after resigning from Columbia, he became the director of the NYBMR's Training School.[20] Harvard instituted its own Bureau for Research in Municipal Government in the 1910s, and many state universities established bureaus as well.[21]

To assert their authority as trained experts, bureau leaders often criticized other municipal reform associations as inefficient and sometimes self-interested and portrayed bureaus as professional rather than voluntary organizations. One of the NYBMR's later directors celebrated bureaus as "pioneers in applied political science."[22] Though Allen believed that without civic organizations, elections alone could not make a democratic government "truly representative," he warned of "the importance of keeping foundations and all other volunteer activities in their places, as aids to and not obstructions to Democracy." He critiqued civic groups that promoted projects that did not benefit the entire community, even comparing the "secret lobbying or extensive advertising" of such "outside special interests" to "interference by 'politicians,' 'party managers,' and 'bosses.'"[23]

Notably, when Allen critiqued "civic agencies" that dominated city politics, he faulted them for "too often representing only a handful of men and women."[24] The inclusion of women reflects the awareness that Allen and other bureau leaders had of the roles of women's organizations in city politics. Bureaus of municipal research were unquestionably dominated by men, and, in the long run, procedural efficiency and cost saving became more of a focus than promoting social welfare.[25] In the early years, however, men like Allen and the small number of women involved in the bureau movement articulated a different vision of the potential of their work and women's contribution to the "efficiency movement."

Allen articulated these hopes most fully in *Woman's Part in Government: Whether She Votes or Not* (1911). He framed his discussion as part of his larger vision for promoting efficient citizen participation. Just as he critiqued all voluntary organizations for sometimes "obstructing" democracy, he wrote, "Women's organizations when inefficiently conducted may hamper government, just as efficient teamwork by women will always make efficient government easier." Allen maintained that much of what he wrote applied equally to men and women "because ninety-nine out of one hundred problems of government are sexless." He insisted that all citizens needed to focus on how they interacted with "government between elections" to accomplish the related goals of "improving government and accelerating social progress."[26] In doing so, Allen attempted to persuade readers that male and female residents shared common goals.

There was one crucial difference in men's and women's political participation that Allen could not ignore: most women could not vote, while most (white) men could. He addressed this fact directly, promoting one of the larger goals of the bureau movement: the need to focus less on elections and electoral structures and more on governance and administration. Striving to write objectively, Allen did not endorse or oppose enfranchising women, instead predicting that "the time is coming when women will not only be permitted but will be expected to vote." Yet he repeatedly maintained that voting was comparatively less important than citizens' work between elections. In a lengthy list of activities that made women "problem creators," he included the notion that "reform is a question of voting, rather than of getting things done." Though he discussed a variety of electoral reforms, from educational qualifications to proportional representation, he emphasized the limitations of electoral approaches: "The ballot cannot work 365 days in the year. Government must."[27] Allen thus suggested that a focus on governance rather than elections created greater opportunities for women.

As an example, he ended the book by celebrating "young women now training themselves for leadership and professional service in civic fields," specifically those working for the NYBMR.[28] Similarly, historian and activist Mary Ritter Beard (wife of Charles Beard) ended her own book *Woman's Work in Municipalities* by pointing to "the work of women in bureaus of municipal research in New York and elsewhere" as "evidence of the desire on the part of women for training in public service" and "woman's ability to adapt herself to the requirements of that training."[29] Thus, at the start, some hoped that the bureau movement would join men and women in a unified effort to improve the quality of municipal services.

In addition to the hope that bureaus would provide spaces for a few women to become trained professionals, early leaders also hoped that they would alter the relations among urban residents and city governments more generally. Allen's book on women's involvement faulted "citizens, male and female," for "ignorance" that led to "misgovernment and inefficiency."[30] Founders created bureaus to remedy this ignorance by replacing municipal reform associations as intermediaries among elected officials, administrators, and residents. An underlying premise of the bureau movement was that citizens were incapable of understanding the complexities of municipal administration on their own. According to Munro, who was also a leader in Harvard's Bureau for Research in Municipal Government, bureaus "take it upon themselves to act as public advisers in matters that are . . . too complicated and too technical for the public to understand and form opinions without assistance."[31] Charles Beard's textbook *American City Government* (1912) celebrated bureaus for encouraging "the public" to focus less on elections and more on "less spectacular but more important questions of city administration" (including the need to compel public service corporations "to fulfill more exactly the terms of their franchises").[32]

Though most supporters of bureaus expressed a desire to educate the public, they often did not agree on what it meant to do so. The primary backers of the NYBMR included some of the wealthiest Americans of the day, including John D. Rockefeller, Andrew Carnegie, and J. P. Morgan.[33] When Rockefeller attempted to dictate its agenda, the NYBMR's leaders were forced to consider what it meant to participate in city politics as impartial experts.[34] By the early 1910s, Rockefeller suggested that the NYBMR, among other changes, stop publishing weekly postcard bulletins to the public and, in Allen's words, end its "fight to secure democratic, progressive, informed management of New York City's school system."[35] Allen's politics were to the left of those of the other two directors. He viewed himself as a Progressive and a feminist. He was committed to public participation in governance, and he believed that a lack of information prevented the public from appreciating the true causes of misgovernment. Allen insisted that when provided with such information, most people would understand what needed to be done and join in the battle for good city government. Cleveland, in contrast, was less confident that the public, even when provided with information, would be able to comprehend increasingly complex administrative matters.[36] His ideal of citizen participation included wealthy elites determining "the welfare needs of the community" by funding "staffs of trained experts."[37] If asked to choose between efficient government to promote public welfare and democratic government to promote wider public participation, Cleveland would have chosen the former.

The Rockefeller Foundation preferred Cleveland's vision, as indicated in the reply of one of the trustees to Allen's report on public school administration. He suggested that the NYBMR should "confine its function to investigation, study and recommendation" and avoid "promotion, persuasion and agitation" in order to maintain "scientific detachment from partisan strife." Allen soon resigned in protest, and the NYBMR moved toward what an internal memo described as "the Cleveland point of view," emphasizing "the educational, as distinguished from the agitating or propagandist type of publicity" and cooperation "with the city administration, regardless of what political party was in power."[38] With Allen's resignation, the NYBMR began to focus more on technical and procedural details of administration, moving away from the original concern with the connection between the means and ends of government.[39]

Though the Rockefeller Foundation's influence is perhaps the most pronounced example of financial backers shaping a bureau's agenda, the phenomenon was not isolated. Bureaus did not rely on volunteers. They were staffed by paid professionals, which was essential to their goal of replacing volunteers with trained experts. One consequence was a greater reliance on donors. Bureaus required more funding than earlier municipal reform associations. In cities across the country, local commercial organizations were often the principal backers of bureaus, and, as a result, some questioned their professed impartiality.[40] Such connections also likely contributed to the increasing focus on savings for taxpayers.

In the early years, however, bureaus of municipal research, like many other types of reform associations, developed out of coalitions among those who believed that more efficient administration was necessary to expand the social welfare functions of government. Bureau leaders repeatedly insisted that they were interested in efficiency not as a tax-saving measure but rather as a means to increase the functional capabilities of cities. This perspective was not unique to the NYBMR. Lent Upson, director of the Dayton Bureau of Municipal Research, told an audience at the Toledo Commerce Club that "no city government has a right to be only economic and efficient. It must be the leader in community welfare."[41] Even Cleveland, the most conservative of the three codirectors, insisted that the purpose of democratic government was not to protect "private property" but rather to serve as "the welfare agency of the individual."[42]

Perhaps the most vocal proponent of this view of city government as an agency of social welfare was Bruère. He maintained that "the efficiency movement in cities grew out of recognition of the dependence of community welfare upon government activity." He proposed that when bureaus set out to "frame an efficient city program," they consider both "the work and service" currently undertaken and ways to meet "existing needs toward which community services have not as yet been directed."[43] In his study of commission government, Bruère expanded on his "conviction that only through efficient government could progressive social welfare be achieved." He provided an expansive list of the "simple prerogatives of citizenship," including the following:

- Personal and community healthfulness
- Equitable taxation for community benefits

- Purposive education
- Protection from exploitation by tradesmen, landlords and employers
- Prevention of injury to persons or property
- Adequate housing at reasonable rents
- Clean, well-paved, well-lighted streets
- Efficient and adequate public utility service
- Abundant provision for recreation
- Prevention of destitution caused by death, sickness, unemployment or other misfortune
- Publicity of facts regarding government's programs, acts and results.[44]

Yet Bruère's "prerogatives of citizenship" included only the right to receive certain services from city government. Bruère and others in the bureau movement thought of their work as democratic. At the time of its founding, the NYBMR claimed that it would simply "ascertain and publish facts concerning city needs and governmental means of protecting them; and to furnish information upon which the public may base sound judgment regarding problems of municipal government."[45] Allen later described bureaus as part of "a movement to make democracy a living, vital thing."[46] Yet over time, for many in the bureau movement, democracy became civic leaders acting for rather than with the wider public. In this model, citizens were largely consumers who had the right to have their needs met but not to participate in the determination of those needs.

Political Science, Reform, and Expertise

The affiliations of Beard, Lowell, and Munro demonstrate the strong connections between the early bureau movement and the discipline of political science. Beard, as noted, was a supervisor of the NYBMR's Training School for Public Service and a professor of politics at Columbia University. Munro was active in establishing Harvard's Bureau for Research in Municipal Government, which had close ties to the Department of Government.[47] Upon his retirement from the presidency of Harvard, Lowell became the chair of the Boston Municipal Research Bureau.[48] All three were also leading figures in not only the subfield of municipal politics but also the discipline of political science more generally, serving as presidents of the APSA.[49] Despite these similarities, differences in their scholarship underscore the complexity and seeming inconsistency of the views espoused by leading political scientists. They also demonstrate the diversity of views espoused by individuals who worked in the same field, attended the same conferences, and joined the same organizations.

Lowell is an especially paradoxical figure. He was born to an elite family in Boston and attended Harvard, attaining bachelor's and law degrees. After briefly practicing law, he turned his attention to political science, joining Harvard's faculty.[50] He later served as president from 1909 to 1933, when he was known for facilitating curricular reforms that allowed students a greater role in the determination of their fields of study, defending academic freedom during World War I, encouraging the admission of outstanding students from public schools throughout the country, and creating the Harvard Extension School, an open-enrollment program for area residents.[51] Yet today he is often remembered for prejudice and discrimination, including expelling African American students from dorms, limiting the admission of Jewish students, participating in an effort to purge homosexuals from Harvard, and working to distance Harvard from Radcliffe.[52]

As a political scientist, Lowell was known as part of the realist movement. Yet while his predecessors' interest in the "real world" of contemporary politics inspired them to become active in reform circles, Lowell's brand of realism was founded in part on his critique of reformers. Moreover, he differed from other leading figures by focusing on scientific and comparative rather than historical methods, and while he advocated administrative adaptations to meet the needs of a modern state, he adhered to a more limited vision of government as protector of individual liberty and private rights.[53] Lowell developed a functional understanding of politics based on an organic metaphor. In "The Physiology of Politics," his presidential address to the APSA in 1910, he defined a functional realism and applied it to urban reform. He suggested that political scientists study politics in the same way that physiologists studied organs: by examining their functions. He reminded listeners that they must study not "the functions [for] which the organs are intended" but rather "those which they actually do perform." He faulted studies of a number of topics, including "the reform of municipal government," for "treating mainly what ought to happen, rather than what actually occurs." One consequence was that, without information on "the actual workings of many political institutions," many "earnest men, overflowing with public spirit," wasted their energies on ineffectual reforms.[54]

In *Public Opinion and Popular Government* (1913), Lowell applied these convictions to defend the role of parties in American politics. Asserting that public opinion was not the result of reasoned deliberation, Lowell's book prefigured critiques of the public as irrational and incapable of understanding the complexities of modern government that became popular in the 1920s.[55] In exploring the constraints on public opinion, however, Lowell also provided an analysis of parties that drew on earlier realist interpretations of their role in the governmental system. Arguing for their necessity in a representative system, Lowell wrote that the "essential function" of parties "in any democracy" was "bringing public opinion to a focus and framing issues for the popular verdict." While acknowledging that the existing party system was flawed, he argued that its shortcomings resulted from "a perversion to improper ends of perfectly normal functions."[56] Unlike some of his contemporaries, Lowell did not believe that municipal reform associations or any nonpartisan organizations could replace parties as leaders of public opinion in American cities. Many of the leaders of reform associations hoped that these organizations would supplant parties in city politics, claiming that they, as disinterested leaders, would be better able to unite residents in the name of the public good. Initially, early members of the NML expressed similar sentiments.[57] The political scientists who participated in NML conferences in the 1890s portrayed it as apolitical as well. As noted, reflecting this vision of reform associations as above partisan motivations, the earliest textbooks on city politics did not analyze them as part of political systems.

By the end of the first decade of the twentieth century, textbooks included discussions of reform associations and other civic groups as parts of urban political systems, though they did so in very different ways. Munro and Beard were in many ways similar. Both wrote popular books on city politics. Both were professors of history and political science at elite institutions, and both were active in the NML and the research bureau movement. Beard was born to a middle-class family in Indiana, and he studied at DePauw, Oxford, and Columbia Universities before joining the faculty in 1904. He was perhaps best known for his pioneering work on the role of socioeconomic factors in politics. He was prolific and influential, independently writing forty-two books and coauthoring another thirty-five. His history books alone sold over eleven million copies in his lifetime, and he was involved in many Progressive reforms, including his work with the NYBMR.[58] Though Munro is much less well known today, he was also a prominent scholar at the time. Canadian by birth, he attended Queen's University in Ontario, the University of Edinburgh, and Harvard University. He went on to teach at Harvard for twenty-five years, a popular instructor known for engaging lectures. He wrote dozens of articles in popular magazines and twenty-six books, and he was known for philanthropic and civic work.[59]

Despite these similarities, their textbooks provided strikingly different assessments of the value of civic associations. In *The Government of American Cities* (1912), Munro highlighted the dangers and limitations of reform associations, warning that they could "be captured by active partisans." He also criticized "that legion of associations, clubs, leagues, federations, and so on which are chiefly civic in aim." Munro claimed that the "tangible results" of their efforts were "astonishingly meager" because they were inefficient. They spent too much on paid secretaries, did not cooperate with government when appropriate, and did not operate "in a business-like fashion." Not surprisingly, Munro portrayed bureaus of municipal research more favorably, as undertaking "thorough" studies of the "actual conditions" of their cities and then presenting "trustworthy information . . . to the ears of every citizen." Criticizing reformers for focusing on charter reform, he commended bureaus for turning to "internal organization" and "to the functioning mechanism of government."[60] In short, Munro presented bureaus as intermediaries between city governments and citizens that were superior to municipal reform associations.

In contrast, Charles Beard's *American City Government* portrayed civic organizations as effective mechanisms for citizen participation. Though Beard favorably assessed the contributions of bureaus of municipal research, he celebrated the participatory dimension of voluntary associations. He embraced a wider variety of groups as legitimate participants in city politics, including discussions of socialist parties and women's activism that were absent in Munro's text. He celebrated contributions made by women "in the organization and management of private civic associations," and he complimented the work of "associations and city clubs" more generally, writing that "through these organizations the citizen is able to voice continually his views on municipal administration and to bring pressure to bear upon public authorities." He expressed faith in these types of organizations to undertake endeavors that many contemporaries reserved for experts, including budgeting, appropriations, and "the undertaking of new functions."[61] In this way, Beard endorsed a model of governance that relied on the active participation of citizens through the institutions of civil society.

Lowell's assessment of civic associations was closer to Munro's than to Beard's, and his writings on the role of interests in democratic government partly explain his position. When he urged political scientists to observe "clubs, associations, organizations and institutions of all kinds" as part of his call to study "the actual working of government," he argued that members of such groups often behaved as machine politicians.[62] Lowell likely compared voluntary organizations to parties because he rejected one of their central assumptions. Most municipal reform associations continued to espouse a belief in a singular common good. Lowell, in contrast, rejected what he called the "Doctrine of the Harmony of Interests." He explained that, according to this older ideal, "everyone desires the same end, whether we call it the common will or the common welfare, and men differ only about the means of attaining that end." Lowell believed that by his own day, "even the strongest advocates of popular government have discovered . . . that the interests of all members of the community are not identical" and that "in many cases men seek to cloak selfish aims by arguments designed to prove that their own subjects will promote general prosperity."[63]

Within this framework, Lowell's explanation for the flawed nature of the party system did not rely on the common criticism that parties had become tools of "the interests" rather than "the common will." Instead, he argued that unlike residents of many other countries, Americans placed "an excessive burden" on parties, expecting them and their elected representatives to fill administrative offices and pass specialized legislation that was simply beyond the scope of their skills.[64] The solution that Lowell proposed, one that would solidify his position as one of the leading political scientists of the day, involved a greater reliance on "expert administrators in popular government."[65]

In advocating such a reliance, Lowell proposed removing many of the details of governance from popular decision-making processes. He argued that many Americans had lost their "faith in representative government as a universal means of solving political problems." The complexities of governance increased alongside the expansion of the scope of the state. In cities, where much expansion was occurring, Lowell suggested that neither voters nor mayors had the capacity to select the individuals best qualified "to construct the roads and bridges, direct the education, manage the finances, purify the water supply, or dispose of the sewage." In the business world and among professionals, a greater dependence on the advice of trained experts was widely accepted. Yet in government, because of "the democratic dislike of permanence of tenure" and "an insistence on equality," resistance remained strong. Regardless, Lowell insisted, "if democracy is to be conducted with the efficiency needed in a complex modern society it must overcome its prejudice against permanent expert officials as undemocratic." For Lowell, the decision to use experts was a matter of making use of "the best tools" available, and "the expert of high grade" was "the best living tool of modern civilization."[66]

Beard also believed in the need for greater dependence on experts, but he considered at greater length how to balance "democracy and efficiency." In "Training for Efficient Public Service" (1916), he argued that they were not "inherently irreconcilable" but that to join them Americans needed to stop attempting to copy European—particularly German—models, under which democracy was subordinated to efficiency, and create their own solutions. Building on Goodnow's distinction between political representatives who determined public policies and administrators who implemented those policies, Beard argued that the only expert that a democratic society "ought to tolerate is the expert who admits his fallibility, retains an open mind and is prepared to serve." Additionally, to democratize administrative staffing, Beard suggested that "civil service commissions should become less and less examining bodies and more and more training bodies." To underscore his priorities, he concluded, "There are many things in this world worse than very dirty streets, a high death rate and a larger percentage of crime. Anyone who is so overcome by a passion for efficiency and expertness that he is willing to sacrifice everything else for the sake of securing any kind of mere mechanical excellence has no message for democracy in America."[67]

In contrast, Lowell focused largely on achieving efficiency by distinguishing between the proper roles "of the layman and the expert," particularly when applied to municipal administration. He conceded the "need of cooperation and compromise between public opinion and expert knowledge" in some realms.[68] Yet in adhering to the common argument that "city government is essentially an administrative, not a legislative, concern," Lowell mostly did not address representative structures. Rejecting the applicability of the Jacksonian principle of rotation in office, he argued that "such a custom is quite out of place in the administration of a large modern city." The maintenance of public water supplies, the construction of bridges, and "the treatment of disease, pauperism and crime" were grounded in "the results of recent scientific discovery and mechanical invention" and "not matters with which even the most intelligent citizen" was familiar. According to Lowell, they could "be mastered only by special study or long experience" and "dealt with efficiently only by persons who have mastered them." As a result, he argued that reformers were mistaken in assuming that the election of "good citizens" rather than career politicians would improve city government, because even "the best elective officers" would be "helpless without good permanent administrators."[69]

Not only did Lowell devote little attention to how these "permanent administrators" might alter representative democracy, his writings in the 1910s also largely ignored two of the most significant and contentious political issues of the day: the movements to enfranchise women and disfranchise African Americans. In this instance, Lowell's, Beard's, and Munro's writings were quite similar. Just as leaders of bureaus of municipal research viewed themselves as neutral analysts, these political scientists attempted to maintain professional distance from controversial issues. As a result, in their scholarship on cities, they avoided matters pertaining to racial and gender discrimination.[70] When discussing critiques of immigrant voters as sources of urban corruption and misgovernment, both Beard and Munro characterized these views as exaggerated but still faulted "foreigners" and "aliens" for being easily manipulated by politicians.[71] When discussing the political rights of African Americans and women, they neglected to take positions. Both explained the real purpose of literacy tests. According to Munro, "The educational tests imposed by various states in the South are designed, not so much to purge the voters' lists of illiterates as to permit racial discriminations to be made without violating the letter of the federal constitution." Neither, however, directly condemned the practice.[72] Similarly, when they mentioned efforts to enfranchise women, they did not support or oppose them.[73] Lowell's omissions were even more striking. In a book focused on the appropriate role of "public opinion" in shaping "popular government," he referenced "woman suffrage" and a "recent effort to disfranchise negroes" only briefly and in the context of a broader discussion of the use of initiatives and referenda.[74] These silences demonstrate a reluctance to discuss controversial topics as part of a rising desire to write as objective scientists.[75]

Such silences did not go unnoticed. In one example, Mary Ritter Beard publicly critiqued Woodrow Wilson's five-volume *History of the American People* for ignoring women. Giving a speech titled "Woman's Work for the City" at the NML's 1914 convention, she claimed that readers of Wilson's work "would imagine that there had been no women in this part of the universe from the landing of the Pilgrims to the present day, for scarcely a mention of women can be found." She felt that this style of scholarship was a relic of the past, claiming that women were now writing their own histories. Drawing a parallel between scholarship and activism, she declared that women were no longer content to limit their activities to civic affairs and support for male politicians. Instead, according to Beard, they were demanding the right to vote.[76]

This context suggests that the silences of Charles Beard, Munro, and others do not reveal their true opinions on controversial matters, nor do they foreshadow the notable divergences in their futures. By the 1920s, Munro became an open skeptic of democracy, critiquing Americans for blindly accepting "formulas of democracy" as "gospel" despite government's irrationalities and inefficiencies. He supported the use of intelligence tests to remove "the lower ranks in the electorate" as necessary for "national self-preservation." He even expressed sympathy with the eugenics movement.[77] Beard, in contrast, marched with his wife in support of woman suffrage, aligning himself with the more radical wing of the suffrage movement. He became an influential public intellectual, known for his left-leaning views on the role of class struggle in American history, the dangers of laissez-faire individualism, and the importance of academic freedom.[78]

What, then, do their silences suggest? In many ways, political scientists attempted to describe existing systems while refraining from offering prescriptive statements regarding divisive topics. They seem to have thought that expertise and professionalism could transcend gender, racial, and class identity. Their omissions thus provide clues that help us discern what they believed to be the realm of acceptable disagreements. No political scientist, for example, openly discussed monarchical forms of government as reasonable alternatives to democracy. In contrast, the advisability of women and African Americans voting was open to debate.

From Natural Leaders to Trained Experts: The Transformation of the National Municipal League and Urban Reform

Despite their critiques of municipal reform associations, Lowell, Beard, and Munro were active not only in bureaus of municipal research but also in the NML. All three attended conventions, served on committees, and contributed to publications. Munro was an honorary vice president, and by 1929 Lowell was named to the "League's Honor Roll" for active membership for over twenty-five years.[79] Their willingness to be affiliated with the NML was due in part to efforts to reinvent its purpose. Though not all leaders had been equally committed to a participatory vision of urban democracy, in the 1890s and early 1900s the NML had provided a venue for lay reformers to come together and discuss problems facing their cities. Speakers at conventions repeatedly highlighted the goal of generating widespread involvement in urban reform through the network of affiliated organizations, hoping to spark a civic revival and deepen popular interest in city government. In the first two decades of the twentieth century, leading figures in the NML began to turn away from this vision, working to transform the NML into an organization for academics and other professionals, with a greater focus on technical and administrative matters.

Changes in membership provide the clearest evidence of these shifting goals. When discussing ways to increase membership in 1907, the executive committee informally decided to solicit members first "among the graduates from political science courses in educational institutions" and only second "among good government associations generally."[80] Although the NML was originally created as a federation of member organizations, a new constitution in 1911 allowed individuals to join as well. Within three years, members were overwhelmingly individuals rather than municipal reform associations, and libraries and universities even far outnumbered

TABLE 6.1 NML Membership, 1899, 1914

	NML members (1899)	NML members (1914)
Civic and reform associations	113[a] (88%)	110[a] (5%)
Commercial bodies	16 (12%)	47 (2%)
Individuals	0	1,923[b] (81%)
Public libraries and colleges/ universities/schools	0	240 (10%)
Departments of government	0	24 (1%)
Private corporations	0	17 (1%)
Other	0	3 (0.001%)
Total	129	2,364

Source: Data compiled from *Handbook of the National Municipal League* (Philadelphia: NML, 1914); sources listed for table 1.1.

[a] Two were identified as women's associations in 1900 and eight in 1914.

[b] 153 women; 1,770 men.

local groups (table 6.1). By 1919, the new constitution did not even mention organizations as a category of membership.[81] Political scientists praised this change.[82] The NML increasingly functioned as a venue for discussion among experts and the publication of authoritative literature that students and local political actors, who no longer attended conferences, could consult at libraries.

Several other decisions regarding activities and publications reflected changing goals. After 1910, the NML ceased referring to its annual meeting as a "conference for good city government" (it became an annual meeting) and publishing proceedings, replacing them with the *National Municipal Review*.[83] The *National Municipal Review* emulated academic journals such as the *American Political Science Review*.[84] While the proceedings had contained transcriptions of discussions and papers presented at the conference, the *Review* largely contained articles (presented as such, despite the fact that many were actually still speeches from the conference) and book reviews.[85] The NML also began publishing the National Municipal League Series—volumes of papers presented at conferences edited by political scientists—and issued fewer short pamphlets.[86]

Many political scientists favorably regarded the *Review*, and their involvement in its creation demonstrates that academics viewed the NML as a venue for scholarship. When offered the editorship, Munro wrote to

Lowell, "It seems highly desirable that this Review should be brought to Harvard if possible, for it would fit nicely with our new Bureau of Municipal Research and give us a marked advantage over other institutions in this field." Albert Bushnell Hart, chair of the Department of Government, concurred, writing to Lowell that when combined with their other work, "the editorship of the only real periodical in municipal government would reasonably give Harvard prestige above all other universities in this field."[87] Though Munro ultimately declined the offer and the NML's secretary became editor, two associate editors were political scientists: Beard and John Fairlie of the University of Illinois. In its first issue, the editors declared that the *Review* would not be "an organ of the League." Rather, it would "aim to present fairly and impartially the municipal programs of all parties and all organizations and to have technical matters treated by qualified experts."[88]

The NML's changing relationships with other organizations similarly reflected the aspiration to professionalize. The NML had attracted individual political scientists from its inception and in 1907 began official correspondence with the APSA. Over the coming decades, leaders of the two groups organized several joint events.[89] The NML had also long partnered with other national reform organizations such as the National Civil Service Reform League and the American Civic Association. These organizations, politically active but officially nonpartisan, aligned with the NML's vision of objective, unbiased reform.[90] Despite their shared interest in urban affairs, the NML never allied with the League of American Municipalities. Many leaders of the NML considered it, composed as it was of elected officials, a partisan organization.[91] Yet they eagerly sought to collaborate with professional organizations composed of appointed rather than elected officials, such as the American Association of Public Accountants and the City Managers' Association. Moreover, two organizations that sought to professionalize civic associations themselves developed out of NML conferences: the National Association of Civic Secretaries and the Governmental Research Association.[92] The NML's success in situating itself as a professional rather than civic association perhaps culminated with the invitation in 1918 to attend a convention to discuss the unique challenges faced by government during wartime, along with the APSA, the NYBMR, the City Managers' Association, the National Association of

Civic Secretaries, the Governmental Research Conference, and the Association of State Municipalities.[93]

Given these efforts to professionalize, it may seem surprising that in these same years the NML also actively sought alliances with middle- and upper-class women's voluntary organizations. In 1901, the NML's president suggested that woman suffrage was "a separate question" from which urban reformers should disassociate themselves; by 1918, the NML officially and unanimously voted to endorse it. In 1900, only 1.5 percent of the NML's member organizations were distinctively women's groups; by 1914, this figure had risen to 7 percent. Additionally, 8 percent of the 1,923 individual members were female in 1914 (table 6.1). This increase in membership was due in part to a decision in 1907 to form an official auxiliary committee of women. In these years, the NML also developed ties to the General Federation of Women's Clubs, and leaders from both organizations spoke at each other's conventions.[94]

Male and female reformers, even those from the same social class, often pursued distinctive political agendas. Not only did men dominate bureaus of municipal research and women dominate settlement houses, but male and female reform associations tended to interact with city government in different ways. For example, in Chicago, while the (men's) City Club primarily regarded the city as a place to conduct business, the Women's City Club primarily regarded it as a home. As a result, the former focused on ensuring that the city was run efficiently and economically, according to business principles, while the latter emphasized the role that it should play in promoting the welfare of all residents.[95] Women's groups often reached out to local officials to promote the expansion of government. In one example, in Fort Worth, in the midst of the male-run campaign to adopt the commission plan, the City Federation of Women's Clubs collaborated with the councils on several initiatives, inspecting cemeteries and requesting funds to hire a female police officer and improve public parks.[96]

Yet to emphasize only the differences among male and female reformers risks missing what they had in common. Settlement and charity work were not exclusively female domains, nor were municipal leagues and bureaus of municipal research exclusively male. Both types of organizations often shared a commitment to expanding the scope of activities undertaken by cities. When the leaders of the City Federation of Women's Clubs reached out to Fort Worth's council, they expressed their faith that city government could play a more positive role in the lives of urban residents. Neva Deardorff, assistant director of the Philadelphia Bureau of Municipal Research, celebrated such efforts, declaring that with "the change from the old ideal of as little government as possible to the new ideal of government as an active, positive agency of community welfare," women would take on even more important roles in local government.[97]

Though women did not generally present clubs as professional organizations, they largely escaped the accusations of self-interested partiality directed at predominantly male voluntary organizations. Partly, gendered ideals of women as morally superior protected women's groups from such criticisms. Yet women also made use of language suggestive of professional aspirations, describing themselves as impartial leaders who would bring specialized information to a wider public and shape public opinion. One president of the General Federation of Women's Clubs described the organization as "in no sense political" and as focused on "disseminating knowledge and arousing public sentiment."[98] Likewise, in *Woman's Work in Municipalities* (published by the NML), Mary Ritter Beard wrote that in "printing and circulating ordinances, discussing charters, asking citizens what they need, and helping to show them how their needs may be met," women "seek to arouse public opinion by explaining problems of government to the people."[99] Clinton Rogers Woodruff agreed, celebrating the "important function" of women's clubs "in the creation of public opinion."[100]

Though in the long run professionalization would marginalize women, many initially hoped that new public services and training programs offered by bureaus of municipal research would create opportunities for women. According to Deardorff, as government became more of "an active, positive agency of community welfare, the services of many kinds of people are being required. And among those new workers are women." She believed that hospitals, social services, juvenile courts, and many other new departments would require the employment of women.[101] Beard agreed, arguing that women had a "special aptitude . . . for certain municipal posts." She ended her book optimistically, predicting women's future contributions to "every need of modern municipal life" through training "to do high and efficient public service."[102]

Bureaus of Municipal Research, Efficiency, and Charter Reform in Norfolk, 1915

Political scientists and leaders of bureaus and the NML were not the only ones debating how to balance efficiency and democracy. In 1915, the *Virginian-Pilot and the Norfolk Landmark* reprinted an article from *Life* magazine. The article, entitled "Efficiency Not the Last Word," conceded its importance in technological and financial achievements, citing the recent completion of the Panama Canal, and acknowledging that an efficient government might be able to end poverty. But it cautioned those who seemed close to worshiping efficiency: "It will not do as a religion." Without accounting for "souls," appeals to efficiency could not meet the needs for "inspiration" and "dreams." It concluded that to end poverty, efficient governmental programs would have to "induce or compel all the common people—or enough of them—to obedience, diligence and patience. But to be obedient, diligent and patient under orders of a superior intelligence does not match at all with the American ideals, and never will."[103]

This article appeared around the same time that civic, business, and political leaders launched a campaign for a new charter. As in earlier charter campaigns, proponents claimed the existing system was antiquated. They also focused on problems with the existing franchise system and on the goal of providing improved services. Yet the discussions that took place in Norfolk in 1915 reveal that local political actors were now appealing to experts at unprecedented levels. Certainly, as noted earlier, in past campaigns local reformers cited the NML's work to justify their proposals. Mayors and other elected officials even attended meetings of the NML and other civic groups. By 1915, however, connections to external organizations had deepened. Not only did they send leaders to attend NML conventions, but promoters of a new charter—both reformers and elected officials—paid NYBMR representatives to come to Norfolk, investigate the city's government, and propose solutions. They also traveled around the country studying various forms of city government. The resulting conversations among professionals in bureaus, reformers, business leaders, elected officials, and residents all centered on the fundamental goal of creating a form of city government that was both efficient and democratic. They also revealed tensions regarding who was to be included in democratic decision-making. When business groups sought expert advice to support their plans, outside experts sometimes pointed to treatments of racial minorities they found troubling.

With World War I under way in Europe and the prospect of American entry looming, many residents had high hopes for the future. Norfolk's port was already an important center of commerce and transportation.[104] The war brought prospects for continued growth. In 1914, Norfolk's exports were valued at $9,500,000; by 1915, they had risen to $19,000,000.[105] Leaders of the Chamber of Commerce, founded in 1912, hoped to attract new industries.[106] The city council and mayor supported such plans, voting to spend $1,000 on advertising and work with the Chamber of Commerce, the Ad Club, and likeminded organizations to attract a naval base.[107]

These plans were hampered by a system of city government perceived as inadequate and inefficient. As discussed, the city was still governed by a mayor, bicameral council, and Board of Control (figure 6.1). Under this unwieldy system, with unclear lines of authority, the city seemed incapable

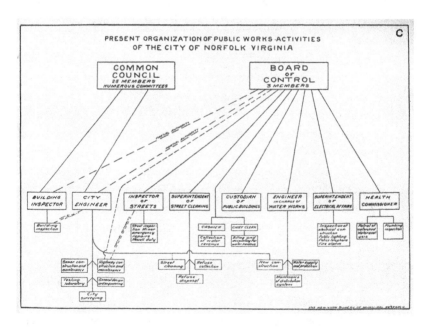

FIGURE 6.1 "Present Organization of Public Works Activities of the City of Norfolk Virginia"

New York Bureau of Municipal Research, "Present Organization of Public Works Activities in the City of Norfolk Virginia," *Report on a Survey of the City Government, Norfolk, Virginia* (1915).

of providing services desired by residents and businesses alike and solving pressing problems. The annexation of several suburban communities and the disfranchisement of African Americans weakened the strength of the Ring faction of the Democratic Party and enabled the opposing Citizens' Party to shift the agenda of city politics. While conflicting views on saloons, vice, and corruption had once dominated, by the 1910s concerns about services and expansion came to the fore. Older problems, such as the need to improve roads, schools, and the provision of gas and water, continued alongside new demands for public markets, docks, and playgrounds.[108] The council, which at times was unable to summon the necessary quorums to conduct business and fill vacancies, was facing many pressing questions.[109] Norfolk's per capita debt was high, the second highest of any southern city.[110] Residents were increasingly aware of and dissatisfied with the fact that they paid more for utilities and transportation than residents of other cities. In the near future, the city would have to decide whether to renew existing franchises or establish municipally owned plants.[111] As in other cities, many felt that the council was giving away too much in its dealings with public service corporations.[112]

While in other cities transit seemed to rouse the most anger, in Norfolk discontent focused on "the water problem." For years, the city had struggled to ensure the provision of adequate and reasonably priced water. By 1915, in the context of plans for expansion, business leaders demanded action. Together, the Chamber of Commerce and the Norfolk Ledger-Dispatch publicized the fact that Norfolk's residents paid far more for water than their counterparts in other cities. As a result, they argued that Norfolk would not be able to attract "big industries." The council wavered for months, passing first one ordinance to purchase several nearby lakes and then another to consider purchasing the existing Norfolk County Water Company.[113]

At this point, Councillor W. H. Sargeant connected the poor provision of services to the structure of Norfolk's government. Sargeant, a lawyer and longtime councillor, was active in reform circles outside Norfolk as president of the League of Virginia Municipalities.[114] In combining a critique of the council's handling of the water situation with a plea for the adoption of the commission plan, Sargeant claimed, "A form of city government which permits such an astounding state of affairs to exist unchecked should be remedied and replaced by some other more efficient mode of administering the city's affairs." He insisted that if Norfolk had a commission government, the problem would have already been resolved, while under the existing form, "this matter may continue until we are faced by some water famine."[115]

Sargeant was not alone in claiming that the poor provision of services derived from the limitations of the existing form of government. The Chamber of Commerce advocated a revision of Norfolk's charter as part of its efforts to attract new industries.[116] Early in 1915, various local groups, the Chamber, and the council all began discussing possible charter revisions.[117] Despite widespread agreement that changes were necessary, city officials and local civic leaders held very different views as to what form was best suited to Norfolk's needs. By February, a compromise seems to have emerged, with a decision to hold an election in August to elect a commission to draft a new charter.[118]

In the coming months, the two local newspapers and the Chamber of Commerce began a concerted campaign to persuade voters of the need for more efficient government. The editors of the *Virginian-Pilot and the Norfolk Landmark* and the *Norfolk Ledger-Dispatch* and the officers of the Chamber held similar political views, all Democrats and staunch proponents of Norfolk's expansion and commercial growth.[119] With the upcoming election, the newspapers publicized speeches and printed articles by proponents of a new charter. Notably, a common thread in most articles was appeals to experts. In March, they published articles about the activities of C. P. Shaw. Shaw, as noted, helped found the Norfolk Municipal League. A retired lieutenant commander in the navy, he was also on the councils of the National Civil Service Reform League and the American Proportional Representation League.[120] The first article detailed his speech before the Equal Suffrage League in neighboring Portsmouth favoring charter reform; the second, written by Shaw himself, cited Lowell, the Short Ballot Organization, the League of Virginia Municipalities, and the NML.[121] Shaw influenced a younger generation of Norfolk's reformers.[122] At least in part, he owed his influence to his connections and appeals to these groups.

The newspapers encouraged Norfolk's residents to follow the NML's lead. In April, the *Ledger-Dispatch* reminded readers that the previous fall, the council had sent two members to the NML's annual meeting to learn about new forms of government. When they returned, the councillors presented a report to the council, and the *Ledger-Dispatch* now reprinted lengthy excerpts. The editor described the NML's leaders as "men of national reputation, great learning . . . who have given unlimited time and study to the producing of a non-partisan business administration charter." The editor concluded, "That is what the National Convention of the Municipal League thinks. That is what the delegated councilmen sent at the expense of this city report. What do the people of Norfolk think?"[123]

The Chamber of Commerce undertook its own research on city government, sending a committee to visit Des Moines, Memphis, Dayton, and Springfield to study and compare different forms of government. The committee, armed with a list of seventy-five questions, set out to determine "the workings of city government," "the advantages of the new forms," and "any defects that may have developed." The local papers printed their findings in great detail, and the Chamber formally published them in a pamphlet entitled *For a Better Form of Government for the City of Norfolk*.[124] The Chamber was pleased when in July, the American City Bureau requested copies of the pamphlet to distribute to commercial bodies in other cities.[125]

At the same time, the Chamber and the newspapers brought leading experts to Norfolk to promote the need for greater efficiency and to assure citizens that greater efficiency did not necessarily mean a loss of democracy. The first was Leroy Hodges, who directed the Department of Municipal Efficiency and Administration for the Bureau of Applied Economics in Washington, D.C. (He later went on to work for the U.S. Tariff Board, U.S. Food and Drug Administration, and National Budget Commission and several groups devoted to tax and prison reform.)[126] Speaking before a crowd of nearly 350 in Norfolk, he made the case for the connection between efficient government and economic development: "Efficiency of government . . . [is] the first step toward enabling Norfolk to grasp the opportunities that [are] in reach."[127] The *Ledger-Dispatch* also reprinted a pamphlet by Hodges's Bureau of Applied Economics. While reformers previously had appealed to "citizens," this pamphlet addressed "taxpayers" interested in ensuring that their taxes were used efficiently and only for "the kind of public service which they sanction." The pamphlet demanded that they be involved in the solution "through a broader municipal-self-knowledge."[128] Hodges attempted to persuade voters that efficiency and popular control were not contradictory but compatible.

A second invited "Efficiency Expert" also promoted efficient government as democratic, but he did so somewhat differently, insisting that more efficient government would not only save money but also enable cities to address pressing social problems. With great fanfare, Lent Upson was invited to open the charter campaign, speaking at a mass meeting organized by the Chamber of Commerce. The papers described Upson as "an efficiency man of the National Cash Register Company" who was formerly the director of a bureau of municipal research in Dayton, Ohio.[129] He would go on to become one of the leading figures in the field of public administration.[130] At the meeting, Upson told listeners that Norfolk needed to adopt a new charter to ensure "a more business-like machine for handling the city's business." He credited Dayton's charter with creating a system that led to "increased efficiency and financial saving in every department, with every evidence that the people's money is being spent judiciously." He contrasted this system with "haphazard" methods that resulted in "carelessness" and "delays," and he specifically cited Norfolk's "water situation" as an example. Yet Upson also highlighted other gains, such as the creation of a "legal aid bureau for the deserving poor" and improvements in the public health department, including "free baby clinics and visiting nurses" that saved hundreds of lives.[131]

Despite these efforts, Norfolk did not get a commission to draft a new charter after the election. Of those who voted, 97 percent cast their ballots in favor of a charter commission, but under state law over half of qualified voters needed to turn out for election results to be valid. Turnout was only around 25 percent (2,068 voters). It is impossible to know with certainty why so few voted. Some suggested that opponents intentionally did not vote; others pointed to general apathy or the fact that the vote occurred in August, when many residents left the city.[132] There does seem to have been a general lack of interest in the election. The nine candidates nominated jointly by the Chamber of Commerce and Board of Trade ran unopposed, even though organized labor was active in other realms of city politics.[133] Moreover, while local leaders emphasized the provision of services and charter revision, a third issue also dominated Norfolk's politics: the disfranchisement of African American residents. Revisions to the state constitution in 1902 had already depleted African American voting rights. A complication emerged in Norfolk in 1915 when local Democrats disagreed about whether the Citizens' Party was a separate party or a faction of the

Democratic Party. At stake was the organization of a primary election, which led to the question of whether "colored voters" could be excluded.[134] In this context, the charter election seems not to have been a pressing issue for many.

Undeterred, boosters in the Chamber regrouped. A few days after the election, the editor of the *Virginian-Pilot and the Norfolk Landmark* commented that if the citizens of Norfolk did not care enough to vote for a charter commission, they were perhaps not ready for a government based on "economy and efficiency." He argued that without the active attention of "the so-called better classes of the citizenship," charters based on "concentrated authority and responsibility" could lead to corruption.[135] Perhaps following his advice, business leaders soon solicited members of the Chamber of Commerce and other commercial bodies to join a Norfolk Charter Association. Membership was open to "qualified voters of the city of Norfolk," which excluded women and most African Americans.[136]

Around the same time, the *Virginian-Pilot and the Norfolk Landmark* reminded readers that the campaign for efficiency was not over because the "specialists" from the NYBMR had arrived in Norfolk.[137] Several months earlier, when the campaign for a new charter began, the city council had hired the NYBMR to undertake an "investigation of the city's government." While a few questioned the need to hire "out-of-town experts," the councillors overwhelmingly supported the plan, voting for the funds at the same meetings where they discussed whether to renew franchises or pursue plans for municipally owned utility plants. The ultimate purpose of the investigation, however, was somewhat unclear, with some officials suggesting that it would simply improve their understanding of the operations of existing departments, others envisioning that it would lead to greater "economies," and still others claiming that it would help voters decide "what form of government" was most appropriate for Norfolk.[138] After the failed charter election, the *Virginian-Pilot and the Norfolk Landmark* celebrated the arrival of "highly trained" "investigators" and "specialists of city government," including "engineers, sanitary experts, accountants and sociologists." The newspaper reported that Director Frederick Cleveland promised that "every phase of the city government would be put under a microscopic examination by men who know and are trained to see."[139]

When the NYBMR issued its report three months later, perhaps unsurprisingly, it revealed many inefficiencies. Primarily, the report framed inefficiencies as problematic because they led to "the failure of the government to render enough service and service of a sufficiently high grade." It focused on overlapping and unclear jurisdictions, inadequate regulations, and poor communications with the public. Less directly, however, the report also suggested that the existing structures led to the unequal treatment of different groups of citizens. It highlighted the police department and city jails as particularly poorly run. While it did not discuss racism extensively, the unequal treatment of African Americans was evident. In the clearest example, it "severely censured" deplorable conditions in the jail for "colored children," contrasting these conditions with the less objectionable jail for "white children."[140]

The report also revealed that the city raised money by disproportionately and unfairly imposing fines on African Americans. The coverage in the *Virginian-Pilot and the Norfolk Landmark* noted that the report focused on the activities of the police department, police court, and justices of the peace. It explained that the report "attacks the fee system as the source of much of the inefficiency and many of the evils of city government" and "recommends the abolition of the justices of the peace, who, being paid by fees 'are naturally inclined' to issue warrants 'without cause.'"[141] It explained that the problem of issuing needless warrants was particularly apparent "with regard to cases affecting colored persons."[142] Articles from the *New Journal and Guide*, the local African American newspaper, confirmed the NYBMR's suggestion of racial discrimination in policing. Though this newspaper did not offer the same extensive coverage of city politics found in the *Virginian-Pilot and the Norfolk Landmark*, it reported numerous instances of police intimidation, spurious arrests, and unequal enforcement of laws in Norfolk and other Virginian cities. One article put it directly: the police were "unduly active in . . . operations against members of the race."[143] While cautiously and incompletely, the report suggests that the NYBMR's investigators pushed officials to confront some of the worst racial inequities in city government.

Although the NYBMR's report, following the lead of political science textbooks, did not seem to discuss the relationship between voting rights and the provision of services, the African American staff of the *Journal and Guide* articulated this connection clearly. An article that was also reprinted nationally in the *Crisis* detailed all the services that "colored rentpayers" did and did not receive from the city: education, but only through the seventh grade; streets, but no pavement for those streets; and police and fire protection in theory only, for "the policeman is on another beat and the fireman cannot reach his home on account of unpaved streets." The reference to rent payers suggests a challenge to property qualifications to vote, and the article directly connected disfranchisement to not receiving a "just proportion of municipal benefits in Norfolk."[144]

Despite such attempts to draw attention to the inequitable treatment of African Americans, subsequent newspaper coverage provides no real evidence that local officials attempted to end racial discrimination in the police department and courts. It does, however, provide abundant evidence that officials took the central recommendation of the NYBMR's report quite seriously: a reform of the city's charter to create a more efficient system to improve the overall provision of services. The report contained a section titled "Constructive Suggestions for Securing Increased Economy and Efficiency" that extensively discussed but never directly stated the purpose of such efficiency. It did not indicate a preference for municipal ownership or the sale of franchises to private service providers. Large portions were devoted to budgeting, reducing future debts, and improving purchasing methods. Notably, it more often referred to residents as "taxpayers" or "consumers" than as "citizens" or "voters." At the same time, the report discussed the creation of departments of public health and social welfare, the establishment of "infant welfare stations," and the employment of a food inspector.[145] In these sections and others, alongside calls for efficiency and savings, the report implicitly called for a wider sphere of government action.

What would be the role of residents in shaping the policies of this expanded city government? The NYBMR's investigators first recommended the formation of a research bureau in Norfolk to act as "an independent, unofficial citizen agency."[146] The additional proposals, however, suggest ambivalence. Some decreased demands on voters, recommending that many officials currently elected be appointed, but others proposed more elections in the form of popular referenda on budgets and major policy issues. Additionally, while the report neglected to comment on racial inequities in voting, it emphatically called for an end to the poll tax. It also called for an end to the ward system of electing councillors, claiming that such a system deprived minorities in wards of representation. It maintained that only a system of proportional representation would create "proper representation of the various classes and conditions" in the city.[147] The report thus contained hints of concerns about inequities and a recognition that there were diverse interests in Norfolk warranting representation.

Overall, the NYBMR followed the lead of the NML's *Municipal Program* by suggesting that the most important reform needed was the separation of legislative and administrative functions. The call for a new charter included proposed departmental reorganizations with a more logical grouping of functions. The major emphasis, however, was on the need to eradicate problems deriving from the large number of elected administrative officials and from the overlapping of administrative and legislative powers of the council and Board of Control. Its central recommendation was the election of a purely legislative council or commission and "the centralization of executive authority and responsibility in a single official" with the power to appoint all department heads and create a single budget. In describing such an authority, the report suggested that the title given such an administrator did not matter, noting that it was "immaterial whether he should be called a mayor or a city manager."[148]

Chapter 7 continues the story of charter reform in Norfolk in the context of rising interest in what would become known as the city manager plan. As this chapter has demonstrated, by the 1910s, many Americans concerned with city government focused on the need to balance efficiency and democracy, from social scientists in bureaus of municipal research and political science departments to reformers in the NML and cities like Norfolk. Many hoped that a greater reliance on experts would enable cities to meet the changing needs of urban populations, and some believed that professionalization would create new opportunities for women to become involved in city government. Yet while they maintained that experts could be controlled by an engaged citizenry wielding the ballot, they avoided discussing the denial of the ballot to women and African Americans. In doing so, though perhaps inadvertently, they made it easier for local politicians, reformers, and business leaders to draw on models of urban reform selectively, adopting some measures to promote efficiency while ignoring other measures to safeguard democracy. Chapter 7 begins to examine the consequences of these silences, turning to the city manager plan, the next phase of urban reform.

7

"The Transition to Government by Experts"

The Origins and Spread of Commission/ City Manager Government, 1912–1925

In December 1915, the same month that the New York Bureau of Municipal Research (NYBMR) suggested that a revised charter in Norfolk should include a centralized "executive authority" such as a city manager; the second Committee on Municipal Program of the National Municipal League (NML) finalized its work. This committee was appointed to revise the original *Municipal Program* adopted in 1899. In the new program, the NML endorsed what was described as the "commission manager," "city manager," and later "council manager" plan of government. It embodied A. Lawrence Lowell's call for expert control of governmental administration, providing for an elected commission or council to be granted all legislative powers and appoint a manager to head the administration.[1] Despite this immense administrative centralization, the NML proclaimed that, when paired with provisions for the initiative, referendum, and recall, the plan made possible "the largest measure of efficient, democratic government."[2]

The NML celebrated city manager government as the culmination of over twenty years of innovations, achieving many long-desired goals: a reduction in the number of elected officials, increased popular control, and the separation of politics and administration. In delegating administrative tasks to paid professionals, the NML promoted the plan as enabling a "broader and more diversified representation" of urban residents, including members of the working class, to serve on councils.[3] With over two thousand members voting at an annual meeting, the NML endorsed the manager plan in what would later be published as a *New Municipal Program*.[4]

Despite such public displays of support, this chapter's examination of the NML's discussion and presentation of the *New Municipal Program* highlights rising discord rather than consensus. While most of the NML's leadership agreed on the value of an appointed city manager as an administrative head, they disagreed on a growing number of other issues, including municipal ownership, direct democracy, and the nature of and need for the representation of groups in local politics and governance.

In several cases, their disagreements were part of the official record. Some members of the committee that drafted the *New Municipal Program* believed that certain features were essential for it to be democratic. Delos Wilcox continued to speak passionately on the need for home rule and municipal ownership, and William Dudley Foulke, then president of the NML, warned of the dangers of the manager plan's administrative concentration and unification of powers if adopted without other "principal features." For Foulke, who was also a prominent opponent of imperialism and supporter of civil service reform, woman suffrage, and civil rights for African Americans, these features included the election of councils by proportional representation, provisions for direct democracy, the establishment of civil service, and measures to ensure that politics did not enter into administrative matters.[5] Yet despite Foulke's convictions, his warnings appeared only in a footnote of the new program's model charter, which included provisions for direct democracy and proportional representation as recommendations endorsed by a majority—but not all—of the committee that wrote the *New Municipal Program*.[6]

At the same time, the omission of matters pertaining to gender and race reflected a continued avoidance of divisive topics. Following the lead of municipal political science textbooks, the new program, even in discussions of electoral institutions and representation, made no mention of African Americans or women. The absence of women elicited commentary from at least one prominent political scientist when Charles Beard commented on the gendered language of the new program. In a published review, after quoting a section on the qualifications required of each "man" to be appointed to head various administrative departments, Beard quipped,

"Evidently there are to be no women department heads in the League's scheme of things."[7] Such comments demonstrate an awareness of the potential implications of these omissions.

To explore the influence of national reformers and the consequences of their compromises and silences, this chapter pairs an examination of debates surrounding the creation of the *New Municipal Program* with accounts of the adoption of manager charters in Norfolk (1917) and Fort Worth (1924). On one level, interest in city manager government indicated an unprecedented level of influence of national leaders. Locally, supporters continued to cite figures in the NML and other leading municipal reform associations and political scientists. Additionally, both cities hired outsiders as their first city managers who were prominent national figures in the new profession, underscoring the nationalization of reform networks.

Yet, on another level, these two campaigns reveal a widening gap between the ideals put forth by national figures and the goals of charter advocates on the ground. While they continued to cite the NML's authority, local leaders drew on its work selectively. Nationally, reformers could not agree on the advisability of using systems of proportional representation to elect councils; in Norfolk and Fort Worth, no one seems to have considered proportional representation as a serious possibility, instead opting for councils elected at large. Nationally, the NML promised that provisions for direct democracy would offset the centralization of administrative power; locally, opponents of charter reform questioned whether these measures were workable in practice, suggesting that they only masked the loss of popular control created by a reduction in elective officers. While national reformers promised that city manager government was simultaneously more democratic and more efficient, local reformers focused more on efficiency and less on democracy.

Early academic studies accurately highlight the rising association of manager government with business interests, but this chapter's examination of two campaigns for manager charters reveals many added complexities. Reform campaigns were not democratic uprisings of "the people" advocating new charters to destroy corrupt machines, but they were also not simply efforts of calculating and unified elites working to control city governments. Chambers of commerce and other business groups unquestionably took the lead, but business leaders were far from united in these early campaigns. Labor leaders, while less supportive of city manager campaigns than they were of earlier movements for commission government, seem to have been similarly divided, as were elected officials. Most notably, however, labor leaders were simply less active in campaigns for manager charters.[8]

Just as class divisions do not seem to explain support or opposition in these two cities, nor do racial divisions. While the *New Municipal Program*'s authors and many political scientists preferred to avoid direct discussions of race, the records of local charter campaigns amply demonstrate its role in urban politics. In both cities, opponents portrayed city manager government as a threat to existing race relations, warning in Norfolk that "outside" experts might allow African Americans to vote, work in the civil service, and attend integrated schools. Supporters, however, responded with promises that a new charter would not alter existing racial hierarchies. In Fort Worth, leaders of both the pro- and anticharter forces were members of the Ku Klux Klan. Yet while charter debates reveal the salience of race, white political leaders' racial views do not seem to explain divisions among supporters and opponents of new charters.

What, then, explains why some voters favored city manager government while others vehemently opposed it? The most heated disagreements centered on the question of whether city manager government, even when paired with measures of direct democracy, was in fact democratic. At the same time, voices on both sides tended to agree on the inadequacies of existing forms of government in terms of the provision of services, and in both cities financial crises provided an impetus for moves to restructure city government.

To an extent, this focus suggests continuities with charter debates earlier in the century. Voters were angered by the poor provision of services and often blamed public service corporations. Political leaders often still appealed to the "people" to rise up against powerful "interests." Boosters promised that new charters were essential to improve services and infrastructure and thus promote growth. Yet there were also key differences. At the start of the century, critics of the franchise system often called for replacing it with municipal ownership, and many prominent supporters portrayed municipal ownership as a means for achieving a higher form of democracy and common purpose. In Norfolk and Fort Worth, concerns about franchises and the provision of services remained, but no one spoke of municipal ownership as a viable option. The rhetoric of democratic empowerment and communal purpose gave way to a framework of service provision for taxpayers. Some goals remained the same—urban residents still looked to city governments for clean water, paved streets, sewerage, education for their children, gas, electricity, and transportation. Increasingly, however, such discussions took place in the context of providing efficient returns on taxpayers' money and promoting economic development. In the end, the decision to support or oppose new charters seems to have come down to whether voters were persuaded that a city manager form of government would improve the provision of services. For some, this new framework was a move away from democratic commitments, yet for others, including disfranchised urban residents, consumer visions of citizenship—particularly those that appealed to taxpayers rather than voters—could be empowering.

City Managers as "Expert Servants": The "Commission Manager Plan" and the New Municipal Program, 1912–1919

Richard Childs, perhaps more than any other individual, drove the early movement for what was first called the commission manager plan. His initial prominence as a reformer stemmed from his leadership in the Short Ballot movement. Childs, an advertising executive and businessman from New York, graduated from Yale in 1904 and quickly became involved in reform. Though he cited James Bryce's The American Commonwealth and Lincoln Steffens's The Shame of the Cities as his inspirations, he was also influenced by political scientists.[9] Frank Goodnow, among others, had long argued for a shorter ballot. The "elective principle," Goodnow wrote in 1897, had been overused and misapplied to positions that required "skill" rather than "representation."[10]

For Childs, this issue became something of a crusade. When he first voted, he was dismayed that he knew nothing about most of the candidates. He initiated a campaign through the press and prominent civic associations to call attention to the need to shorten the ballot. In 1908, he sent a pamphlet that he had drafted on the short ballot to Goodnow, who replied,

"I fully agree with your view of the subject and have myself been preach-
ing this doctrine for the last ten or fifteen years."[11] Childs proposed that
no more than five offices appear on the ballot in any election so that the
average voter would not rely on partisan affiliations. When "the electorate votes only for men it knows," Childs promised, "we shall have real popular control, real democracy, and government that more accurately re-
sponds to public opinion." He organized the National Short Ballot
Organization, soliciting the support of prominent individuals, including
Woodrow Wilson, who agreed to serve as president.[12]

Childs turned his attention to urban reform, using similar methods to
promote his vision of the ideal form of city government. In 1909, the city
council of Staunton, Virginia, decided to pass an ordinance empowering a
"general manager" to undertake all executive and administrative duties
on behalf of the council. Childs read about Staunton's innovation and felt
it would work better paired with the smaller elected body of the commission plan. With the aid of one of Beard's graduate students, he drafted a
version of what he called the "commission manager plan," combining a
short ballot, with only commissioners elected, and an appointed "expert
administrator." As Childs explained, this manager was not to be involved
in politics but rather would operate as "simply the expert servant of the
commission." Childs later described his early promotional efforts:
"Papers . . . were gotten into various civic conventions and magazines;
and thus the idea was put on the map in a campaign which went on for ten
years under my personal and enthusiastic direction." The plan quickly attracted attention, adopted first in Sumter, South Carolina, in 1912 and
Dayton, Ohio, the following year.[13]

With these adoptions, the National Municipal Review reported that this
new form of government "continues to be watched with greatest interest
throughout the country."[14] Leaders of the NML themselves were paying
close attention, for the new plan had the potential to resolve a major dilemma for the organization. As noted, the spread of the commission plan
left the NML out of line with one of the most popular urban reforms of the
day. The NML's leadership tried to portray the popularity of commission
government as a positive reflection on their work. Secretary Clinton Rogers Woodruff even claimed that though there was "a slight difference as
to the form," "the commission form succeeded because it embodied certain fundamental principles of the Municipal Program."[15]

The commission manager plan appealed to political scientists and re-formers partly because it resolved what they believed to be the major lim-itation of commission government: its delegation of both legislative and administrative powers to elected commissioners. To assess this new vari-ation of the commission plan, the NML decided to reconvene the Commit-tee on the Operation of Commission Government in 1913. In 1911, this com-mittee had presented only a qualified endorsement of commission government for use in smaller cities because of its centralization of pow-ers and shortened ballot, cautioning of the dangers of combining politics and administration.[16] The same committee now issued a supplemental report, with a majority endorsing the variation: "The commission man-ager plan" permitted "expertness in administration at the point where it is most valuable, namely, at the head." It commended the plan for abandon-ing "all attempts to choose administrators by popular elections," which was "desirable" because voters were not qualified to "judge administrative ability."[17] In academic journals, political scientists concurred.[18]

That same year, Lowell articulated similar sentiments. As discussed, Lowell had long advocated a greater reliance on "expert administrators in popular government," focusing on cities in particular.[19] As early as 1908, he spoke at an NML conference on the need for "permanent officials" with "special training or long experience." Turning to commission government, Lowell later questioned the assumption that elected commissioners could lead administrative departments, claiming, "Election by popular vote is a very poor way of selecting expert administrators." While this view was fairly common, his extension of it to the original *Municipal Program* was novel. The authors of the *Municipal Program* provided for elected mayors to serve as administrative heads, believing that doing so removed administra-tion from the control of councils, which were policy determining and there-fore political bodies. Lowell now claimed that elected mayors could not en-sure that administrations were run by permanent staffs of professionals.[20]

Despite such criticisms, Lowell decided to become involved in the NML's work to promote his views. In 1911, the NML and the National Civil Ser-vice Reform League organized a joint committee to report on "the feasi-bility of putting and keeping in expert hands the administration of depart-ments of city government (streets, parks, water, etc.) requiring technical knowledge and skill," agreeing with Lowell that frequently changing de-partment heads was inefficient. Lowell did not serve on this committee but two years later agreed to serve on another committee to revise the *Municipal Program*.[21]

Yet not all political scientists were eager to serve on the committee to revise the original *Municipal Program*. As part of its efforts to present a strong public image, the NML's leadership did not announce any difficulties. Private correspondence, however, reveals that the executive committee initially hoped to convince five members of the original committee from 1897 to serve alongside five new members, and Woodruff was particularly interested in securing Goodnow's participation. Goodnow, however, turned Woodruff down.[22] Woodruff was the only individual to serve on both committees. The other eleven members were Childs, currently a member of the NML's executive committee; Lowell, currently a vice president; William Bennett Munro; three additional political scientists; and five leading urban reformers.[23] The NML portrayed the committee as both eminent and diverse, bringing "together intelligent citizens, holding varied and independent views."[24]

This type of public celebration of diversity partly served to frame disagreements in a positive light, for the record of the committee's work reveals an inability to reach consensus. There was unanimous support for the concept of a city manager and some degree of home rule, as proposed in a model charter and series of state constitutional provisions.[25] Yet the committee did not unanimously endorse several provisions, and there were several inconsistencies between the accompanying explanatory essays and the new program itself.

Prominent voices in the NML presented the lack of consensus as a mark of rising democracy, connecting the right of residents to draft charters with home rule. As discussed, the original *Municipal Program* defined home rule as the right to decide the scope of a city's activities. This definition allowed the NML to avoid taking a stance on that scope and municipal ownership. Yet the original *Municipal Program* maintained that the structures of city government should be uniformly defined by state laws.[26] As in the original *Municipal Program*, the *New Municipal Program* granted cities general rather than enumerated powers, allowing them to do anything not expressly prohibited by state law. But it also provided the right to draft charters locally.[27] The *New Municipal Program* thus rejected the need for "uniformity" and embraced "the idea of local freedom as to the forms of government."[28]

Publicly, the NML framed this move as consistent with continued support for home rule. According to Wilcox, it reflected an ongoing commitment "to define as well as to advocate the principle of municipal self-government."[29] Private correspondence, however, suggests another explanation. Goodnow, the strongest influence on the original *Municipal Program*, wrote in a 1909 textbook that both "functions" and "actual governmental organization" needed to be determined according to unique local conditions. He did not, however, openly disavow the *Municipal Program*, despite its call for uniform urban institutions. Yet in a letter to Horace Deming, who served as the chairman of the original committee, he wrote, "Further study . . . has led me to think that [the *Municipal Program*] has some serious defects and to believe that the question of municipal organization is not nearly as important a question as I formerly thought it was."[30] Goodnow—and other leading reformers—were beginning to question their ability to unearth and agree on universal forms of government. In short, home rule allowed the NML to mask the fact that prominent leaders had failed to agree not only on the scope of services but also on the institutional forms of city government.

Yet ongoing disagreements regarding municipal ownership were increasingly difficult to conceal. As detailed earlier, by the 1910s the NML promoted two contradictory positions. Some members expressed a preference for improved regulation of the existing system of granting franchises to private companies through state commissions, declaring municipal ownership unfeasible.[31] Others, including Wilcox, continued to advocate municipal ownership, arguing that state regulation would erode home rule.[32] The *New Municipal Program* and accompanying papers reflected a continued lack of agreement and resulting lack of clarity. Though Wilcox admitted that the NML "is not *yet* committed to the policy of municipal ownership and operation of all public utilities," he insisted that it "at least expresses a theoretical and ultimate bias in favor of municipal ownership."[33] Despite such claims, the *New Municipal Program* emphasized improved regulations, devoting nine sections to regulations and only one to municipal ownership, which discussed accounting methods. Support for municipal ownership appeared once, in a footnote.[34]

Regardless of the brief treatment of municipal ownership in the *New Municipal Program* itself, Wilcox's essay "The Franchise Policy of the New

Municipal Program" used the concept of expertise to defend the viability of municipal ownership and local control. Wilcox argued that "popular resentment against perpetual and long-term franchises and against the exploitation of the streets by public service corporations" had become "acute" and that, as a result, support for municipal ownership was "ascendant." Thus, according to Wilcox, in deference to home rule, the new program did not mandate municipal ownership but was designed to facilitate it. Additionally, he maintained that the "vitality of local self-government could not be more seriously threatened than by the complete centralization of the control of public utilities in the hands of state commissions." He concluded that in place of such commissions, cities, whether they opted for municipal ownership or granted franchises to public service corporations, needed to "develop their own experts." Wilcox thus attempted to draw on the popularity of expertise to propose a system to revitalize urban democracy under an expanded sphere of home rule.[35] The meaning of the concept "their own experts," however, remained unclear.

In contrast, there was consensus regarding what one committee member called "the distinguishing characteristic" of the new program: "the concentration of administrative powers and responsibilities in the hands of a city manager," who was "to be chosen by the council" and serve an indefinite appointment, removable only by the council if deemed necessary.[36] Yet while the committee agreed that councils should appoint managers and have legislative powers, they disagreed about how to elect councillors and resolve the underlying issue of the nature of group representation. The rising popularity of proportional representation among reformers suggested a shift away from consensus models and toward pluralist understandings of politics.[37] Yet an acceptance of pluralism was far from clear or universal.

All the committee members advocated nonpartisan local elections and the elimination of ward-based elections (except in the largest cities), but they differed as to whether they should be replaced by systems of proportional representation or at-large elections. As noted, the first *Municipal Program* favored at-large elections, though it included the option to adopt a system of proportional representation as part of home rule. In contrast, most of the authors of the *New Municipal Program* favored proportional representation, but the discrepancy between the explanatory essays and the model charter itself indicated disagreements. In his essay, committee member Mayo Fessler, secretary of the Board of Trade of Brooklyn, explained that the hare system, in which voters ranked candidates, was "preferred by a substantial majority." He presented the hare system first, then listed two "alternatives": at-large elections, with "elimination" primaries, and preferential voting.[38] The model charter, however, mentioned only at-large elections in the body, referring to "proportional representation" in the footnotes. Even more notably, while the 1916 edition explained the hare system and preferential voting in appendices, the 1919 edition omitted the appendix on the hare system, referencing it only in Fessler's essay, which included a list of objections to the system.[39] Moreover, even Fessler's strong statement regarding the need to represent "all elements and groups of opinion" was somewhat unclear. Though he repeatedly referenced the representation of groups ("each group of voters," "organized groups," and "like minded voters whether organized or not"), he did not specify what kinds of groups he envisioned participating.[40] Local political parties? Unions? Chambers of commerce? Women's clubs? Racial groups? Following the lead of many political science texts on urban politics, he left these questions unanswered.

Another disagreement centered on the use of the initiative, referendum, and recall as checks on the centralization of power in a small legislative body and appointed city manager. As Woodruff explained, "With the growth of the tendency to concentrate legislative and administrative powers in the hands of a steadily diminishing number of officials, one movement for popular control (the initiative, referendum and recall) has grown with almost equal rapidity and strength." He suggested that these features would act as a "safeguard" to ensure the proper functioning of "representative government."[41] But a minority of the committee did not agree. The sections on the initiative, referendum, and recall were not unanimously approved but rather "inserted by a majority vote of the committee."[42] The accompanying explanation of the new program did not provide a clear rationale as to objections.[43]

Lowell, who defined democracy as the promotion of public welfare rather than public participation, questioned the value of direct democracy. Speaking before a crowd of over two thousand at the NML's annual meeting in 1914, he highlighted the need for administrators "to deal with the vast amount of business to be transacted" and ensure that cities ran "smoothly, efficiently, and economically." Though he did not explain what this would encompass, elsewhere Lowell spoke of the potential of "expert knowledge" to generate "progress in civic welfare," and in this speech, he defined democratic government as "that which provides its citizens with the greatest amount of happiness." He did not highlight popular participation. Though he conceded the need for the "layman"—represented by an elected body—to "control the expert," he insisted, "If our people cannot control experts, they are not fit for self-government on the modern scale."[44] Though the final version of the *New Municipal Program* did not list the positions of individual committee members, privately Lowell commented that he did not "have much faith in the initiative, referendum, and recall or proportional representation" as tools to ensure popular control.[45]

For Childs, the short ballot was the means to achieve such control. He perceived himself to be an ardent supporter of democracy, and his understanding of democracy asked less of citizens. Supporters of the original *Municipal Program* hoped that it would create structures that would encourage urban residents to participate in city politics. In 1899, Deming had argued that no "scheme of city government" would improve urban conditions without developing "an effective and general interest among the voters themselves in the actual conduct of the public affairs of the city."[46] Childs, in contrast, dismissed the "old remedy" as "sound in theory, but unworkable in practice, for a wholesome citizenry has much else to do."[47] The *New Municipal Program* mentioned the importance of popular involvement once, in a footnote by Foulke warning that cities should not create the position of city manager without also adopting "the other principal features" because "the manager plan . . . might prove to be susceptible to perversion in the interest of a boss in cities with an undeveloped and inactive public opinion."[48]

As early as the 1910s, Childs and other leading reformers hinted at concerns that a similar "perversion" was happening when manager charters, particularly when paired with at-large rather than proportional elections, were enabling business groups to dominate city politics.[49] To an extent, however, some were willing to overlook the fact that business groups often initiated movements for charter reform, hoping that once these charters were adopted, other groups would see the merits of the plan and benefit accordingly. Additionally, Childs himself, regardless of his intentions, was partly responsible for the association of the manager plan with

business interests. In a later interview, he explained that he had intentionally chosen the term *city manager* to appeal to business leaders. According to the interviewers,

> As an advertising man, Mr. Childs was aware of the advantages of attrac-
> tive titles and catchwords. While framing the [first manager] charter, he
> considered titles like "executive secretary" and "civic secretary" for the
> administrative official. But he finally decided on the title of "city man-
> ager," in order to emphasize as much as possible the general similarity
> between the proposed position and that of the general manager of a busi-
> ness corporation.[50]

And yet the NML's leadership worked to challenge early associations of
manager government with business interests and instead promote it as
friendly to organized labor. As early as 1915, an NML publication on the
manager plan contained an entire chapter titled "Attitude of Labor and Socialism Toward the Commission Manager Plan." The fact that there were
some vocal labor leaders who vehemently opposed the adoption of manager charters was undeniable, but the chapter maintained that in operation, manager charters made it easier for laborers to be elected to representative bodies since they were no longer required to have administrative
skills to serve, and it detailed several examples of union members and
workers who became commissioners or councillors. Implicitly endorsing
a pluralist conception of politics, it argued that this outcome was "normal,
hopeful and fair" because labor was "a class needing representation."[51]
Throughout the 1920s, the NML's central office continued to collect and dis-
seminate information on labor unions that supported manager government. It also encouraged proponents of manager charters to seek out local labor leaders for support in their cities.[52]

Increasingly, the central purpose of the NML became its work for the
adoption of manager charters in cities throughout the country (figure 7.1).
The new program initially received far less attention than the first, partly
because of the outbreak of World War I, but its long-term influence was far
greater. Lowell later chaired the NML's Committee on City Manager as a
Profession in 1916; Childs was president of the NML from 1927 to 1931 and
was actively involved in the third, fourth, and fifth revisions of the program.[53] Ironically, while Woodruff described the new program as not "the

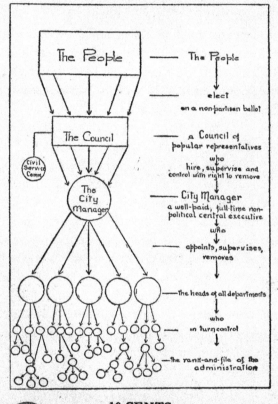

FIGURE 7.1 "The Story of the City-Manager Plan"

The Story of the City-Manager Plan: The Most Democratic Form of Municipal Government (National Municipal League, 1921).

last word, but the latest," the NML continued to endorse variations of manager government for over a hundred years.[54]

By the 1920s, however, some began to voice concerns that focusing so heavily on manager government and charter revision was potentially problematic. Following in the footsteps of Goodnow, Lowell, and Beard, Charles Merriam was one of the next prominent political scientists who became active leaders in urban reform circles and the NML.[55] In an article in the *National Municipal Review* in 1922, Merriam combined praise for past efforts with cautionary advice that reformers and political scientists did not yet possess a sufficient understanding of what he called "municipal behavior" to implement their visions. He credited the NML with beginning the "study of municipal government," pioneering a "model charter," and achieving many "practical improvement[s]."[56] Ten years earlier, Lowell and leaders of municipal research bureaus had called for less attention to politics and more attention to administration. Now Merriam, building on a rising interest in social psychology, called for greater attention to a new subject: "municipal behavior." He wrote, "Government does not consist in charters, ordinances and rules merely, but in the habits, dispositions, wishes, and tendencies of the urban population." He maintained that a lack of understanding of "the processes of social and political control conditioning public action" made politically active urban residents less likely to heed what political scientists viewed as "the precepts of experts in politics and administration respecting structure and procedure of government in cities."[57] In short, Merriam seemed to warn his readers that political scientists and reformers did not yet have a sufficient understanding of the forces that shaped urban political behavior to predict how urban leaders would respond to and make use of their proposals.

"The Autocracy of Irresponsibility": The City Manager Plan in Norfolk (1916–1919)

Less than two decades after Staunton's council hired the first manager, 375 cities had adopted this new plan of government. Political scientists like the University of Chicago's Leonard White eagerly studied these cities, asking how and why the plan was adopted. According to White's *The City Manager* (1927), communities followed an "almost identical" path. Business leaders, usually acting through a chamber of commerce, decided that "bad government" was hampering "the growth of their city." They were attracted to "the resemblance of the city-manager plan to their corporate form of business organization." Forming coalitions with other organizations, they led campaigns to revise charters and, when successful, typically secured the victory of sympathetic commissioners or councillors in the next election. White explained why this story was so often "repeated from one end of the country to another": "The persistence and effective agitation of . . . the National Municipal League has had a profound effect."[58]

Despite the NML's clear influence and support of many business leaders, charter reform in Norfolk deviated from White's pattern, revealing the widening gap between the ideals put forth by the NML and those of local charter advocates and also the central importance of a topic that the NML (and White) largely avoided: the role of race in urban politics.[59] Both supporters and opponents of city manager government appealed to the racial prejudice of white residents to gain their votes. Yet as in many other cities, perhaps the most decisive factor was a need to improve municipal services, an issue supported by diverse residents, from African American civic leaders to white businessmen.

Despite the failed attempt to revise Norfolk's charter in 1915, a variety of factors soon converged to create a more favorable climate for the city manager plan. As noted, the approach of World War I sparked interest in charter revision to create more efficient institutions that would improve municipal services and facilitate growth. In April of the same year, the Chamber of Commerce voted to send a committee to visit several cities to study and compare different forms of manager government, and, when the committee returned, the members unanimously endorsed the city manager plan.[60] Yet in August, an election for a board of freeholders to form a new charter failed because of low voter turnout.[61] Undeterred, business and political leaders continued their work. The Chamber formed the Norfolk Charter Commission to generate popular interest. Members at first discussed adopting the commission plan or reducing the size of the existing council when neighboring Portsmouth voted to adopt the manager plan. Several prominent supporters of a new charter were also working for the "consolidation" of Norfolk and Portsmouth, which partly explains rising interest in the manager plan.[62] The publication of the NYBMR's evaluation of Norfolk's government also contributed. Though the report did not specify only one plan, it described a new charter as the "greatest need" for Norfolk and proposed some kind of "centralized executive head," whether an elected mayor or appointed manager.[63] Around the same time, a change in state law (lobbied for by various politicians and Norfolk's Chamber of Commerce) allowed for charter revision based on a majority of voters participating in an election rather than a majority of registered voters.[64]

The United States' entry in World War I in April 1917 led many to agree that the time had come to restructure Norfolk's government. The Chamber viewed the war as an opportunity, campaigning to make Norfolk "one of the nation's greatest industrial centers."[65] The war brought rapid growth in the development of the naval yard, shipping, and manufacturing. This growth, coupled with a rising population, placed unprecedented demands on a city government already struggling to provide adequate services. There were shortages in housing, gas, electricity, and water, as well as a breakdown in the public transit system.[66] The police force struggled to deal with rising labor unrest and crime. Norfolk continued to be governed by a large bicameral council, a board of control, and an administrative system marked by often unclear and overlapping lines of authority. The Citizens' Party (one faction of the Democratic Party) actively promoted the need for a new charter, and the Ring (the other faction) was disorganized and divided, with several leaders supporting some of the Citizens' Party's proposals. In June, an election with low turnout established a commission to draft a new charter. Voters selected the Chamber's candidates, who quickly announced their support of city manager government.[67]

When the Charter Commission presented its work in the fall, supporters did not anticipate strong opposition. Both local newspapers favored the new charter, having long voiced dissatisfaction with existing public services and support for a smaller council.[68] The commissioners explained that the proposed charter "provides a centralized, executive administration through a city manager, who is directly responsible to, and removable by, the people's representatives, the council"; "provides a small council elected at large, representing the entire city as a whole, and responsible to public opinion by means of the initiative and referendum"; "furnishes, through the recall, a simple method of removing inefficient or corrupt officials"; and "safeguards the city in franchise matters." In short, they assured residents that their plan would create "a simple, direct and business-like form of government."[69]

Regardless of such characterizations of the "simple" benefits of the pro-posed charter, in the coming weeks, residents witnessed a confrontation between two deeply divided and contentious groups, groups that defy easy categorization. They organized public meetings in schools, in fraternal halls, and on street corners. Although women could not vote, they invited "ladies" to attend. They distributed thousands of leaflets and placed ad-vertisements in local papers. One side formed the Citizens' Union, celebrat-ing its membership of over five hundred "prominent business and profes-sional men," "representing every political party and faction."[70] The other side formed the League for Self-Government and Democracy at a meeting at the Real Estate Exchange, also touting a diverse membership.[71] A local newspaper corroborated these assertions, claiming that both organizations contained members of "every political party and faction."[72] The League countered by attacking charter supporters as tools of "corporate interests" that profited from franchises, charges that its opponents vehemently de-nied.[73] While there is evidence that representatives of the League reached out to local unions to promote opposition to the charter, coverage in the local papers reported that labor leaders neither supported nor opposed either campaign uniformly or actively.[74]

Regardless of union leaders' response, the League for Self-Government and Democracy portrayed the proposed charter as elitist, antidemocratic, and autocratic, focusing on the manager's powers and the election of coun-cillors at large rather than by ward. Leon Steele, who had recently run for mayor on the Citizens' Party's ticket, claimed that the manager plan had German origins (a serious charge during World War I) and sacrificed de-mocracy for efficiency.[75] At one meeting, opponents passed a resolution declaring that the charter was a "radical departure from the theory of democratic government" that would lead to "the people of Norfolk . . . surrendering prerogatives which have hitherto been their birthright."[76] One advertisement dismissed appeals to greater "efficiency" as an "excuse for tyranny and class government" that trampled on the rights of "poor men" and surrendered "human rights to wealth." The League connected at-large elections to these types of assertions, claiming that one section of the city could control the entire government and impose unequal taxes.[77]

In contrast, supporters echoed the NML's claims that the manager plan balanced efficiency and democracy by offsetting the powers of a small council and appointed manager with provisions for direct democracy.

Lieutenant C. P. Shaw, a retired naval officer who had been a leading reformer in Norfolk for decades, perhaps best articulated this vision. By the 1910s he was on the NML's advisory committee, attending annual meetings and offering feedback on drafts of the *New Municipal Program*.[78] He now declared his support for Norfolk's proposed charter: "For many years I have made a careful study of city charters, with the hope that Norfolk might someday adopt one which would combine the two elements of efficiency and democracy." He described the proposed charter as the realization of this hope. To counter claims that at-large elections would allow one ward to dominate unfairly, Shaw promised that a council of "five men elected at large" would "be representative of the whole city." He also maintained that the council, controlled by the people through "the powers of the initiative, referendum and recall," would make all policy decisions.[79]

The two groups also debated whether the provisions for direct democracy made the proposed charter democratic, focusing on the recall clauses. An advertisement signed by eighty-nine supporters of the new charter described the city manager as "selected by the Council, THE PEOPLE'S REPRESENTATIVES," who could be "REMOVED by them." It therefore promised, "Any autocratic assumption of authority by the City Manager can be speedily checked by the city council," and concluded, "We are now living under the AUTOCRACY OF IRRESPONSIBILITY."[80] Steele countered that the recall clauses were designed to be "absolutely inoperative." Another leading opponent declared that the provisions for direct democracy were "bunglesome rigamarole of red tape."[81]

Alongside debates about appointive managers and recall provisions, opponents played on racial tensions. At the start of November 1917, they claimed that an outsider would not be familiar with local conditions. In the coming weeks, they warned that the new manager might be from the western United States or even China.[82] A subtext was that an outsider might bring different ideas about race relations to Norfolk. The "antis" distributed circulars and published advertisements suggesting that manager government would lead to integrated schools. They reprinted a telegram purportedly from Dayton, Ohio, declaring, "WHITE AND COLORED CHILDREN TAUGHT IN THE SAME BUILDING AND SAME CLASS ROOM." The ad urged voters to reject the charter and "mixed schools."[83] Opponents thus suggested that "expert administrators" from other parts of the country would not simply implement policies determined by local councils but rather challenge existing race relations.

The opposition focused even more on the idea that the charter would enable African Americans to vote and gain access to civil service positions. The initial draft had provided for a nonpartisan primary before a nonpartisan general election, following the rationale that local elections should be decided without regard to national party platforms.[84] When opponents suggested that a primary was unnecessary, the Charter Commission agreed to omit it and hold one nonpartisan general election.[85] Yet the lack of a primary soon became a point of contention. Primaries run by the Democratic Party, expressly excluding African Americans, were perceived as legal.[86] It would be more difficult to exclude African Americans in a general election. J. Peter Holland, a businessman involved in real estate and publishing, told a crowd that "as soon as the primary laws are abolished, the negro problem, long held in check by the Democratic primary laws, will become a menace to white supremacy."[87] Holland claimed that the charter's adoption would enable African Americans not only to vote but also "to become eligible for positions under the city government."[88] The *Virginian-Pilot and the Norfolk Landmark* summarized the opposition's campaign as an effort to persuade voters that adopting the charter would "mean . . . a return to the dark days of reconstruction."[89]

With such rhetoric, opponents attempted to exacerbate racial divisions to generate hostility to the charter. Tensions among black and white workers had a long history in Norfolk and were rising. Economic opportunities drew African Americans to the city during the war, though they remained only slightly over 37 percent of the population. A 1914 state law allowed cities to enforce legalized residential segregation, which Norfolk's government enacted. White working-class residents attempted to keep African Americans out of their neighborhoods. African Americans held many lower-paying, unskilled jobs, and demands for improved pay and conditions grew alongside several African American unions. Relations with the city government were strained, with local police repressing striking workers.[90] In this context, opponents hoped that characterizing the charter as empowering African Americans would encourage white residents to reject it.

Moreover, the proposed shift from ward-based to at-large elections would diminish the political power of the few African Americans able to vote in Norfolk. With a voter registration drive by the local chapter of the National Association for the Advancement of Colored People, the number of qualified African American voters who had paid poll taxes rose from 131 in 1916 to 363 in 1917. Under the ward system, these voters, concentrated in a few districts, had the potential to influence elections. Indeed, African American voters had in the past provided crucial support for candidates of both the Ring and the Citizens' Party. Under an at-large system, African American voting power would be diluted. When the NYBMR recommended abolishing the ward system two years earlier, its report explicitly recommended instituting proportional representation to ensure minority representation on the council. The local press, however, largely ignored the recommendation, promoting at-large elections. And while they seem not to have made the claim publicly, supporters of at-large elections were undoubtedly aware of their potential effect on African American political power.[91]

Leaders of the Citizens' Union assured voters that a change in city government would not affect race relations. In advertisements and speeches, they maintained that the charter would not lead to integrated schools, assured voters that "THE CONSTITUTION OF 1902 SETTLED THE COLORED QUESTION IN VIRIGINIA," and attacked opponents for using "THE COLORED QUESTION . . . AS A POLITICAL WEAPON." One member declared his support for "helping the negroes to become better citizens," but most insisted that the charter would maintain the racial status quo.[92] In short, while opponents and supporters disagreed on much, their disagreements revealed a consensus among white political leaders that African Americans, under either charter, would have no political voice.

In the face of efforts to deny their rights, some African Americans sought alternate avenues to influence city government. They organized to challenge city segregation ordinances and the lack of police and fire protection, paved streets, sewers, drains, and parks in their neighborhoods. Despite rising disfranchisement, they formed organizations to appeal to the city.[93]

The *New Journal and Guide* (later *Norfolk Journal and Guide*) provides a glimpse into African Americans' views regarding Norfolk's government. The *Journal and Guide* was one of the leading African American newspapers in the South, circulating roughly four thousand copies per week. Editor P. B. Young was known as a follower of Booker T. Washington's philosophy of self-help and therefore as something of an accommodationist, but he actively opposed discrimination. He was instrumental in the formation of Norfolk's chapter of the National Association for the Advancement of Colored People, which protested not only lynching but also the poor condition of housing and streets in African American neighborhoods.[94] Copies of the newspaper from 1918 to 1920 are not accessible today, making it harder to determine how African American residents responded to charter debates.[95] But editorials in 1917 drew attention to a lack of municipal services, discussing housing, sanitation, and public health. One attacked "the city authorities" for ignoring "appeals" to pave "dirt roads . . . in the sections of the city where colored people live and own property." Another promoted the Monroe Ward Colored Civic League, formed to protest "intolerable conditions" and demand "justice at the hands of the city administration in the distribution of municipal improvements."[96]

Despite the lack of support displayed by the leaders of the Citizens' Union for African Americans' voting rights, they too focused on improving the provision of services. In the days before the election, they faulted the current system for creating rising debts without accompanying improvements and noted that many councillors supported a change. They promised that the system created by a new charter would ensure an adequate water supply, new public buildings, and a resolution to the "traction situation."[97] Echoing the stance of leaders of the bureau movement, they blamed a cumbersome and inefficient system rather than corrupt individuals for the failure to provide adequate services.

To buttress such claims, members of the Citizens' Union and their allies repeatedly cited prominent national experts. They reminded residents of the NYBMR's report, reprinted excerpts of academic articles, and solicited endorsements from secretaries of the American Civic Association, the National Civil Service Reform League, and the National Short Ballot Organization. At that time Childs was the secretary of the organization. His letter to the Citizens' Union, reprinted in the *Virginian-Pilot and the Norfolk Landmark* and read aloud at meetings by the Charter Commission's chair, promised that the proposed charter would create "flexible, responsible and effective government."[98]

The outcome of the election suggests that these arguments persuaded many. With a comparatively high turnout of 4,686 (fewer than 2,000 voted in a state election earlier in November, and approximately 5,500 voted in the August primary), the charter passed with 73 percent of the vote. Additionally, residents in one predominantly African American ward voted heavily for the charter. The *Virginian-Pilot and the Norfolk Landmark* claimed that the "labor vote was light" as a result of the effectiveness of the Citizens' Union in refuting the League for Self-Government and Democracy's racial pandering.[99]

After the election, the apparent lack of interest among labor leaders continued. Charter supporters now organized the New Charter League of Norfolk. After securing ratification by the state legislature, they selected a slate of five candidates to run in the first election under the new charter, which was unopposed. On election day, the *Virginian-Pilot and the Norfolk Landmark* claimed that "ninety-eight percent of Norfolk voters . . . have forgotten that there is an election." The same day, the paper detailed the Central Labor Union's efforts to secure state-level labor legislation and prepare for Labor Day celebrations; it made no mention of interest in the municipal election. International events also dominated the headlines, detailing battles in Europe. In this context, fewer than one thousand voters cast ballots for the council that would select Norfolk's first city manager.[100]

Business leaders were pleased with Charles Ashburner, the city manager selected by the council. Ashburner had served as the city manager in Staunton, Virginia—the first to hold the office in the nation—and was currently serving as manager of Springfield, Indiana.[101] In Norfolk, he would spearhead many improvements: municipal warehouses and docks, a grain elevator, a "rail-water terminal," and, addressing a perennial problem, "a new water system."[102] These achievements must have endeared him to businessmen, particularly boosters. A few months after arriving in Norfolk, he spoke at a meeting of the Chamber of Commerce–Board of Trade.[103] Within a few years, the organization celebrated Ashburner's achievements in *Norfolk's Governmental Achievement: Some Accomplishments of the Commission-Manager Plan in the Building of a Great Port and Industrial Center*. This promotional brochure depicted the new form of government as one that combined "the application of strict business methods to every phase of municipal governmental operation" and the promotion of "community welfare above politics," improving both "living conditions" and "business, industry and port commerce."[104]

It was not only business leaders who approved of Ashburner. African American leaders praised his efforts. The new form of government did initially seem to lead to greater provisions for African Americans, including new playgrounds, beaches, and recreational facilities.[105] In the *Journal and Guide*, Young highlighted Ashburner's personal role, praising him as "the friend and counselor of all creeds, classes and colors" and noting his efforts to obtain street improvements in "the Afro-American sections of the city."[106] The *Journal and Guide* also printed a speech that Ashburner gave supporting the allocation of $5,000 for an educational campaign to improve African American health.[107] Certainly, a wide variety of tensions remained, and disfranchised African Americans were unhappy to have to rely on white officials' paternalistic goodwill.[108] But in the early years, African American residents seemed to view city manager government as an improvement.

Yet Ashburner's administration certainly did not address all racial inequities. In 1915, the NYBMR had identified the "fee system," in which employees of the police department and courts were paid according to the number of warrants issued, as encouraging needless arrests, particularly among African Americans. The NYBMR's investigators recommended it be abolished immediately.[109] The new charter adopted in 1917 followed many of their other recommendations, but it was not until 1935 that the final remnants of this system seem to have been abolished.[110] While the city manager form of government may have lessened some inequities in services, many abuses remained.

"Democracy, Despite the Many Good Things in Its Favor, Is Not Efficient": The City Manager Plan in Fort Worth, 1924–1925

In the early 1920s, the Chamber of Commerce portrayed Fort Worth as a prosperous, harmonious, and growing city. In *Fort Worth, Texas: Where Golden West and Sunny Southland Meet*—a pamphlet intended to "sell" the city "to her own citizens as well as to outside business interests"—the Chamber detailed Fort Worth's inviting climate, civic resources, infrastructure, and industrial and agricultural interests, especially railroads, oil, and cattle. The pamphlet described the population of the city's "trade territory" in West Texas as homogenous: 96.8 percent native white, 2.1 percent foreign white, and 1.1 percent "Negro." When discussing residents of the city itself, the pamphlet claimed that "Fort Worth . . . has experienced less trouble with labor than any other city in the State."[111] In short, the Chamber promoted the city as ideal for potential investors.

The reality of life in the city was quite different, marked by racial and class tensions. The population of the city was 78.5 percent native white, 6.5 percent foreign white, and 15 percent African American.[112] In 1921, butchers walked out of local meat-packing plants as part of a national strike, and ensuing events resulted in mob violence and the lynching of an African American "scab."[113] In 1922, in neighboring Dallas, the Ku Klux Klan soundly defeated the reformist Dallas County Citizens' League, depicting opponents as elitist businessmen with Catholic sympathies.[114] By 1922, the Fort Worth Klan, established two years earlier, controlled the city's government.[115]

The Klan was a dominant force in Fort Worth's social, political, and economic life, but the exact nature and reach of its support remain unclear. Many historical accounts of the wider Klan aptly note (though perhaps overemphasize) that members were motivated by more than racism, highlighting nativism, patriotism, morality, anti-Semitism, and anti-Catholicism. In many locales, the Klan was part of mainstream life.[116] In Fort Worth, 5,000 hooded Klan members marched in one parade, and membership may have reached 6,500.[117] Many prominent individuals joined Klavern 101. The editor of the *Fort Worth Star-Telegram* was sympathetic, as was Mayor E. R. Cockrell, who may have been a member. Cockrell even tried to persuade African Americans to vote for him by promising that the Klan would defend the honor of white and African American women alike and not bother "any unoffending negro." William McDonald, an African American fraternal leader, businessman, and politician, supported Cockrell, regardless of his connections to the Klan.[118] In addition, while the state Chamber of Commerce denounced the Klan, in Fort Worth, the Klan used the local Chamber of Commerce building for lectures and shows.[119]

Opponents attempted to block the Klan's rise. After one man was tarred and feathered, the anonymous Committee of Good Democrats telegrammed the governor to demand an investigation, claiming that the local press was afraid to question the Klan.[120] Twelve anonymous businessmen formed the Anti–Ku Klux Klan, attacking the Klan as an "outlaw band" that terrorized black and white residents.[121] The next year, nearly thirty men openly joined the Citizens' League of Liberty of Fort Worth, which, like the Klan, requested to meet in the Chamber of Commerce's building. Despite the League's newspaper advertisements and meetings with as many as 1,500 attendees, the slate endorsed by the Klan won every seat in the municipal election in 1922.[122]

Regardless of possible ties to the Klan controlling the city's government, the Chamber initiated a campaign to revise Fort Worth's charter in the winter of 1923–1924. A financial crisis precipitated the move. Fort Worth spent $3,000,000 on improvements in 1923, paving roads, expanding waterworks, and constructing fire stations.[123] By December, the city's financial situation was dire, with an overdraft of nearly $1,000,000. Cockrell recommended collecting unpaid taxes, cutting expenses, and reducing the number of municipal employees. The Bureau of Civic Co-ordination of the Chamber, representing a collation of civic groups, proposed a different solution: a new charter.[124] Days later, a grand jury charged the city commission with "gross extravagance" and "bad business methods," particularly awarding contracts without competitive bidding.[125] By January, competing voices proposed a number of solutions, including a bond election to pay debts, a recall of all the commissioners, the mayor's resignation, and a new charter.[126]

This final option was popular among business leaders. Charter promoters promised that an efficient city manager form of government would simultaneously allow for increased services and lower taxes.[127] The city's bonded debt was over $11,500,000, with an additional deficit of $1,500,000. This state of affairs led the Chamber to organize the Fort Worth Nonpolitical Civic League and host a meeting attended by two thousand residents. One speaker framed reform as an "opportunity to establish a sound financial order." The meeting concluded with two resolutions, one to delay a bond election to cover existing debts and another to elect a commission to draft a city manager charter.[128] City officials and representatives from the Chamber struck a deal, with proponents of a new charter agreeing to support a bond election in exchange for the promise of a new charter. The bond passed, the city was later able to pay five hundred city employees, and an election for the Charter Commission was scheduled for April.[129]

As the election neared, residents considered who would draft the charter. The Klan was rumored to have decided to remain neutral. (Supporters of the charter, perhaps because Klan members currently held most city positions, carefully attacked the existing system rather than individuals.) The Chamber of Commerce organized the Citizens' Municipal League, which put forth a slate of candidates for the Charter Commission. The Chamber and its allies touted this group as "thoroughly representative of the varied interests of the city," including "seven merchants, six lawyers, five women, representing the various women's activities; three leaders of organized labor, two educators, two insurance men, two stockmen, one printer, and one of each of the following: Banker, lumberman, nurseryman, physician, general contractor, real estate man and retired capitalist." A few labor leaders disagreed and may have considered running an opposing ticket. Just before the election, representatives of twenty unions questioned "the manner in which the charter revision commission candidates were selected" and opposed their election.[130]

Despite such disagreements, the local newspapers largely supported charter revision. They often framed the issue using language reminiscent of older Progressive rhetoric about civic duty, even suggesting that the people's lack of interest in city affairs was partly responsible for the financial crisis.[131] Yet they also promoted city manager government by citing authoritative national experts, using rhetoric more in line with recent trends in urban reform. The Fort Worth Record claimed that "when the facts are placed before them," "the people of Fort Worth are for progress and sanity, for efficiency and economy."[132] These "facts" came from newspaper coverage of the growth of city manager government around the country: a survey by the City Managers' Association of over three hundred cities, a series on a recent adoption in Kansas City, and an endorsement by Woodrow Wilson.[133]

Such rhetoric seems to have been effective. In April, 10,044 people voted in the charter election, a much higher turnout than in the municipal election in 1922 when the Klan took over the city government (in which only 4,582 people voted). The opposition was disappointed, claiming that the citizens had "turn[ed] their government over to the Chamber of commerce and the newspapers." But with 65 percent of voters favoring a revision of the charter, the Charter Commission began its work.[134]

When the Commission first met, members continued to cite the authority of national experts. They began with "an exhaustive study of the city manager plan," acquiring copies of existing manager charters from a dozen cities, including Norfolk. They also obtained a copy of the NML's "model charter," expecting this "scientific" reference to be "a great aid." Though it ultimately decided not to, the Commission considered hiring political scientist A. R. Hatton as an adviser.[135] In citing these authorities, their central message remained the same: structural flaws in the existing charter were to blame for the present crisis, and an efficient manager charter would allow the city to provide more services at a reduced cost.[136]

In response to such rhetoric, supporters presented the proposed charter as an apolitical, scientific tool. After meeting for several months, the commissioners proposed a "council manager" government, with a nine-member council elected at large that appointed a city manager to serve as the "administrative head" of six major departments (health and welfare, finance, police, fire, engineering, and waterworks). It included provisions for a civil service; the initiative, referendum, and recall; a budget system; revised tax rates; competitive bidding for city contracts; and regulations of the sale of franchises.[137] Supporters formed the Citizens' Association for Civic Advancement. They described the charter as "non-political," dismissing opponents as "petty politicians" and "pie-counter demagogues" who only feared for their jobs.[138] In the coming weeks, they organized public meetings but refused requests to face their opponents, claiming that a debate would become "an exchange of personalities."[139]

Foes of the charter were frustrated by these refusals and charged the newspapers with bias, claiming that they were unable to promote their perspectives.[140] The *Record* and *Star-Telegram* were both owned by an open and active advocate of the charter.[141] While the *Fort Worth Press* also favored the charter, it devoted more extensive coverage to the opposition. As a result, the clearest record of conflicting views regarding the charter appeared in a series of letters entitled "The Charter, Pro and Con" in the *Press*.

The "pros" promised democracy and efficiency, increased services, and lower taxes.[142] The "cons" maintained that this was impossible. According to George Armstrong, a wealthy businessman in the gas, steel, and oil industries, "Democracy, despite the many good things in its favor, is not efficient; autocracy, despite the objectionable features, is efficient. Business is selfish and autocratic, and hence its efficiency; government is service for others and democratic, and hence its inefficiency. It is not fair for those gentlemen to claim the advantages of both."[143] By "autocratic," Armstrong was partly referring to the decision to appoint rather than elect the manager. While in Norfolk opponents focused on at-large elections and a small council as antidemocratic, Fort Worth already elected a commission of five at large. (There was a brief discussion of proportional representation, but the proposed charter retained at-large elections.)[144] Opponents therefore focused on an appointed manager as "destroying the fundamentals of democratic government," describing the manager as a "king," "dictator," or "czar."[145]

They also focused on the perennial issue of the franchise system. The connection to earlier reform movements was clearest in a speech given by former mayor T. J. Powell. In 1907, Powell had actively promoted charter reform as a means to improve franchise regulation.[146] In 1924, before an audience of three hundred that was meeting, ironically, in the Chamber of Commerce building, Powell spoke of himself as a passionate supporter of direct democracy. The proposed charter, he claimed, "kills the referendum and recall" and would "take away from the people the right to self-government." He explained that while voters currently needed five hundred signatures to submit an ordinance, they would need six thousand under the proposed charter. He also claimed that the charter decreased franchise regulations and favored corporations over the public interest in its revised tax system.[147]

A like-minded contributor to the *Press*'s series made the point more directly, arguing that "this new charter is the culmination of the trend of the public service corporations to dominate the city" and claiming that it no longer required "an adequate return on the special privileges granted them." He critiqued traction, gas, power, light, and telephone companies and ended with a plea to recognize city government as something more than a business matter, urging readers to remember that "the city presents a sociological problem, an economic problem and a political problem."[148] The opposition thus rejected the claims that city manager government was a mere matter of business efficiency. In this way, charter opponents in 1924 were similar to opponents in 1907. There was, however, one major difference. In 1907, Powell spoke passionately about municipal ownership as the ultimate solution.[149] Neither side seems to have considered this option in 1924.

In addition, in Fort Worth in the 1920s, criticisms of class biases were much more prominent. Opponents portrayed the manager not just as a "king" or a "czar" but also as a tool of business interests. At one meeting, Powell argued that the charter "arrayed class against class." Another speaker agreed that it favored "the rich classes over the masses."[150] As the campaign heated up, the attacks became more pointed, with opponents describing the plan as "'A silk stocking charter,' 'A monarchical charter,' 'A charter for the millionaires.'"[151] The opposition framed the charter as an effort of businessmen, working through the Chamber of Commerce, to take control of the city government.[152]

The pro-charter forces dismissed their opponents. The Citizens' Association for Civic Advancement maintained that the manager was not an "autocrat" but an administrator.[153] An editorial in the *Record* rejected claims that the manager would be a "czar" as "absurd."[154] In the series in the *Press*, former state senator R. L. Carlock of the Charter Commission explained that a manager was appointed by an elected council, representing the people's will. He added that changes in the initiative, referendum, and recall were in accordance with new state laws, and he maintained that the requirement of 20 percent of registered voters' names on a petition was lower than in many cities, which required 35 percent. He made similar arguments that changes in franchise regulations followed new state laws, promising that the new charter provided ample tools for the city to protect its interests.[155]

Critics also claimed that the "labor vote" heavily opposed the charter.[156] Did laborers oppose the charter, and was it biased against their interests? The pro-charter forces worked to dispel these claims and promote the charter among working-class residents, criticizing what they portrayed as efforts to foment class-based antagonism. Rev. Dr. J. Frank Norris, a leading fundamentalist in Texas, told his parishioners that the charter would promote public- and private-sector growth to benefit all classes.[157] The *Star-Telegram* quoted union leaders from around the country, claiming that "the new system draws its strongest advocates from the ranks of union labor."[158] The *Record* reported on a meeting of civic and business leaders at the Manufacturers and Retailers Association who decided to survey factory employees. Perhaps unsurprisingly, these leaders claimed that workers in forty-four of the forty-seven plants visited supported the charter as a "strictly a business proposition."[159] And to promote support, members of the press and the Citizens' Association for Civic Advancement framed the new charter as pro-labor because of the proposed treatment of municipal employees, highlighting civil service regulations, eight-hour days, standard pay, hazard insurance, pensions, and more.[160]

The "antis" countered that the focus on city employees was intended to distract working-class residents from the fact that the charter did not promote their interests. Armstrong portrayed the labor provisions as unfair to the "small taxpayer," asking why "city employees should fare better than the employees of private industry" and suggesting that the charter supporters should provide similar benefits for their own employees to "set an example."[161] (That Armstrong should make such a plea was ironic given that he was known for opposing unionization and even engaging in peonage with his own employees.)[162] An advertisement by charter opponents also claimed that it "raises the taxes of the laboring man and small home owner" and "reduces the taxes of the rich man and big corporations."[163] Opponents therefore claimed that laborers overwhelmingly opposed the charter, but the *Press*—the most balanced of the three papers—challenged such statements, concluding, "Union folks, like all other folks of the city, are divided."[164]

Though they featured extensive discussions of class, the newspapers rarely discussed race when covering charter debates. Unlike in Norfolk, opponents in Fort Worth almost never connected the charter with racial issues, though, notably, on a rare occasion (recorded in a newspaper) that a speaker did, he used similar language, warning that an "outsider" city manager might bring different ideas about race relations to the city: he might be a "Northern man . . . who has a negro wife."[165] Yet racial tensions were strong in Fort Worth in 1924. In November alone, at the height of the charter campaign, white residents of the Seventh Ward organized to ban African American residents, and the Klan building was bombed.[166]

Regardless, such animosities do not seem to have been decisive in determining voters' views of the charter, as suggested by the divergent positions of Klan associates. Prominent Klan leaders were active on both sides of the charter campaign. Armstrong, who vehemently critiqued the charter, publicly declared his sympathy for the Klan (and privately was an organizer). He later wrote books and pamphlets that promoted virulent anti-Semitism.[167] During the charter campaign, he faulted supporters for publicly speaking of business efficiency while privately promising both Klan members and Klan opponents that the charter would enable them to control the city government.[168] At the same time, some prominent Klan supporters actively campaigned for the charter, including reverends Norris and J. W. Underwood and Mrs. J. T. Bloodworth, a leader in the women's auxiliary to the Klan and mother of the Grand Dragon of the Klan in Texas. Norris and Underwood both spoke in favor of the charter, and Bloodworth joined the women's auxiliary to the Citizens' Association for Civic Advancement.[169] Yet representatives of the Association also reached out directly to Jewish voters. One spoke before the Council of Jewish Women.[170]

While appeals to Jewish voters were somewhat noteworthy given the activities of the Klan, appeals to women voters were not. Women now made up half of the electorate, and pro-charter forces worked to gain their support, largely using the tactics and rhetoric that characterized their campaign more generally. Building on existing networks of civic associations (in this case women's clubs), they organized "mass meetings" where representatives of the Citizens' Association for Civic Advancement spoke of the plan as "democratic" and "progressive" and dismissed opponents as "foolish" and "petty politicians."[171] Some tactics, however, also involved gendered language, such as the work of "college girls" pinning pro-charter buttons on supporters.[172] Yet even when using gendered language, they promoted their wider rational: the charter would put city government beyond the reach of politics.[173]

In spite of the rhetoric of both sides, the clearest division seems to have been based not on gender, race, class, or even reformers versus "the city gang" but rather on residence, with the strongest opposition coming from more suburban districts of the city.[174] In something of a parallel to African Americans in Norfolk, white suburbanites in Fort Worth protested that their neighborhoods lacked water, sewers, and fire protection. Despite the city's dire financial situation, in 1924 they organized to call for the issuance of a $1,000,000 bond to fund water and sewer extensions.[175] The mayor promised that a bond would be possible after the ratification of the charter.[176] The suburbanites did not want to wait. Leaders of suburban civic leagues claimed that pro-charter leaders had misled them, promising that a bond would be issued *before* the charter election. When city officials and charter supporters declared a bond impossible because of the city's poor credit, suburban leaders felt betrayed and joined forces with charter opponents. Together, they organized meetings at suburban civic clubs.[177] The *Star-Telegram* responded with an editorial maintaining that the charter was key to putting the city on a sound financial footing, making it possible to provide "water, sewer and fire protection service" to the suburbs.[178] The central message was that growth was impossible without charter reform.

This, in the end, was the major argument of the pro-charter forces. Their most consistent message was that the existing system's inefficiencies hampered growth and wasted taxpayers' money. As the election neared, one editorial in the *Record* argued that the financial crisis and inability to pay city employees was due "to defects in the charter." The present charter was "antiquated," while the city manager plan was "modern." To make the contrast clear, the editorial concluded that adopting the charter would "mark a new era" by "rescuing the city from its deplorable financial state," "substituting business efficiency for politics," "inviting new industries," "providing new ample safeguards over public utilities," "according fair treatment to all classes," and "providing for expansion in the suburbs."[179]

These messages seem to have resonated with many voters. With approximately 12,500 residents casting ballots, 56 percent voted for the charter.[180] In the weeks before the election, newspapers claimed that views on the charter varied among workers, city employees, and Klan members.[181] The election results suggested that they were correct, for while voters in most wards were divided, suburban districts largely rejected the charter. According to the *Record*, "Without a single exception the six suburbs that have clamored many months for sewer and water extensions, voted against the charter."[182] Despite all the factors at play, the question of the provision of services seems to have been decisive.

The first election under the new charter proceeded as in many other cities, with the slate of the Citizens' Association for Civic Advancement running on a platform of efficient and "businesslike" administration in the interests of taxpayers.[183] As in Norfolk, the new council in Fort Worth hired a prominent city manager from another city, selecting O. E. Carr. Carr was well known in city manager circles. He studied engineering at Allegheny College, worked in the Philippines, and returned to the United States to find employment in Cincinnati's public works department. He served as city manager in several cities before coming to Fort Worth. His background in engineering and his experience made him an attractive candidate, as did his reputation for courage and candor.[184]

Yet Carr's courage and candor sometimes bordered on belligerence and tactlessness, contributing to a confrontation with the Klan.[185] This confrontation underscores the extent to which city manager government was associated with taxpayers' interests. Carr initially assured residents that he would be the city's "hired man"—not a dictator—and would not shape policies.[186] He began by collecting unpaid taxes and reorganizing departments. He dismissed several employees who were members of the Klan, replacing them with men who did not live in Fort Worth. There were rumors of a recall of the council to protest these actions, but the Klan took more dramatic action, burning forty "indignation crosses" throughout the city. Carr denied that he had fired anyone because of association with the Klan, conceding that he was "in sympathy with the Ku Klux Klan in many circumstances." But he declared that his primary loyalty lay with the city's government, and he demanded the same of his employees. He explained, "The interest of the taxpayer dictates that the rules of honesty and economy must prevail. Economy can only come through the employment of efficient and experienced men." Maintaining that he would answer only to taxpayers and the council, he declared, "If the Knights of the Ku Klux Klan are to run the city Hall, there will be a new City Manager here."[187] The Klan's power in Texas was beginning to decline, and so, despite initial hesitations, several council members, the editor of the *Press*, and other civic leaders backed Carr.[188]

While Carr won this battle, he lost another. In the charter campaign, supporters repeatedly promised that increased efficiency would yield more services without higher taxes. Carr now presented a budget that included higher taxes. Explaining his rationale, he stated, "Future generations should not be burdened with taxes to pay for bonds issued for current improvements." The council disagreed, opposing tax hikes.[189] Who won? A year later, an article in the *City Manager Magazine* celebrated the "striking results" of Fort Worth's first year under city manager government, detailing improvements in "street widening and extensions, street paving, water, sanitary, and storm sewer extensions." The article also discussed new parks and swimming pools and overall improvements in the health department, stressing savings through reduced waste and increased efficiency. And yet, in what the author framed as a testament to the people's faith in the new regime, by a large majority, voters passed a bond of $7,659,000, "the largest bond issue ever voted for municipal improvements in any Texas city."[190] As in Norfolk, where remnants of the fee system remained into the 1930s, the change in charter did not lead to a full break with past practices, for though much changed in Fort Worth politics, much remained the same. In this case, the council—not the manager—dictated the course of public policy.

In the end, the stories of the adoptions of manager charters in Fort Worth and Norfolk reveal the complexities of city politics, challenging neat narratives of unified business leaders conspiring to disfranchise working-class and minority voters uniformly opposing new charters. They also demonstrate both the reach of the NML and the limitations of that reach, which were due in part to the compromises and optional features in the NML's model of manager government. With the *New Municipal Program*'s cautious and even ambiguous recommendations for proportional representation and direct democracy, local reformers were able to promote versions of the city manager plan with at-large elections and versions of direct democracy that opponents felt were inoperative in practice. What, then, were the longer-term consequences of the NML's advocacy and promotion of manager government? The final chapter turns to this question.

8

The Legacy of the Movement for Urban Reform

State Building and Popular Control

E ven in retirement, Clinton Rogers Woodruff, former secretary
of the National Municipal League (NML), stayed abreast of
trends in urban reform and remained a leading authority. He
appeared in the introduction of this book as a paradoxical figure, cited by
some as an elitist using reform as a guise for establishing business control
of government and by others as an ardent promoter of deliberative democracy. After stepping down as secretary, Woodruff remained active in public life, serving in Philadelphia as director of public welfare, on the library
board, and on the civil service commission. His additional civic commitments in the 1920s and 1930s suggest his support of the rights of diverse
groups, including his work for education for the blind, welfare for "men-
tally deficient and indigent persons," and legal aid for African Americans.[1]
His own biography embodied his vision of active engagement in public life.

In 1928, Woodruff reviewed early assessments of the city manager plan
for the *American Journal of Sociology*. He concluded that, true to his initial
hopes, manager charters increased popular trust and interest in government, which, in turn, facilitated a massive expansion of the scope of city
government. In one example, he quoted an official from Cincinnati on the
effects of their new manager charter: "Most remarkable is the change in
the attitude of the citizens towards their local government. Distrust and
opposition have given way to confidence, appreciation and cooperation."

In another, he presented an expansive list of Dayton's accomplishments during its first ten years of manager government, including not only decreases in costs and increases in administrative efficiency but also a wide range of new activities: "a free legal aid bureau," "a crime prevention bureau," "a bureau of policewomen," "a fire prevention bureau," "a home for dependent girls," "garbage collection," "medical inspection in the public schools," "a Civic Music League," "a complete food and dairy service," "a city-owned country club comprising 312 acres," and a new "city workhouse" on "a hundred-acre farm."[2] Over thirty years after the NML's founding, Woodruff continued to maintain that charter reform facilitated municipal expansion, and his list of achievements suggests a particular interest in social welfare programs.

Despite his overall optimism, Woodruff's review revealed hints of uncertainty. Much as he and others had claimed decades earlier, Woodruff still believed that political parties were largely to blame for problems faced by city government, maintaining that "90 percent of city government is administration" with no room for politics. Yet he offered this claim after detailing the case of Kansas City, where, under a new manager charter, partisan divisions and corruption remained, evidenced by the sale of a franchise to a street-railway provider under terms that favored the company. He then summarized the views of a critic from Cleveland, who insisted that manager charters would not create greater popular interest in city government or end the endemic corruption of the franchise system. The real solution for the latter problem, the critic maintained, was not the manager plan but rather "municipal ownership and operation of public service utilities." Woodruff conceded that the critic raised some "thoughtful" points but still concluded that "the plan is American, democratic and on the whole effective."[3] Through the 1930s, organized groups in cities across the country continued to argue that manager government would enable cities to improve existing functions and undertake new ones.[4] In short, Woodruff and many others continued to claim—at least publicly—that their movement had achieved its intended goals.

This final chapter explores the legacy of the movement for "good city government" by addressing whether many national reformers' major predictions about what structural reforms would accomplish were correct in the short and long run. Specifically, this chapter examines several interrelated claims:

- that cities with greater local autonomy from states (home rule) would be more likely to adopt reformed charters (by the 1930s, charters with city managers and provisions for nonpartisan, at-large elections)
- that cities with reformed charters would be more likely to enact programs of municipal ownership and/or expand the scope of city government through franchise reform
- that popular interest in city government and the accountability of elected officials would be enhanced by electing only small councils and appointing all other officials; replacing ward-based elections with either at-large elections or proportional representation; enacting strong provisions for direct democracy; and/or expanding municipal ownership
- that city managers would play purely administrative roles, not taking part in policy-making processes

To do so, this chapter explores ongoing debates and compromises in the NML in the 1920s and 1930s alongside several early academic studies of cities operating under city manager charters from the 1920s to the 1960s. It combines these sources with a quantitative analysis of the structures and functions of city government at the end of the period covered by this book. To investigate the first two predictions in the short run, I gathered data on the 310 cities with populations of thirty thousand or more in 1930. From the 1934 and 1935 installments of the *Municipal Yearbook* published by the International City Managers' Association (ICMA), I collected information on whether these cities had city manager, commission, or mayor-council forms of government; partisan or nonpartisan elections; elections by ward, at large, or a combination of the two; home rule laws; and municipal ownership. From the federal census, I gathered data on the size and ethnic and racial composition of urban populations. And from an earlier *Municipal Yearbook*, I located information on municipal ownership in 1902.[5] I ran simple logistic regressions to determine potential relationships among these variables. To investigate the latter two predictions in the long run (aggregate data for the 1930s are not available regarding electoral features), I draw on the findings of studies of urban politics by political scientists at the start of the twenty-first century. (Given that my goal is to present an overview of current views on urban politics rather than to engage in a scholarly debate, I leave the names of the authors of these studies in the footnotes. Readers interested in learning more about their work should look to those notes.)

This final chapter, in combination with the larger evidence base of this book (the internal debates and official publications of leading figures in the NML and municipal political science; accounts of reform in five cities), reveals much about the ultimate outcomes of the movement for urban reform. While some predictions were accurate, others led to very different results from those originally envisioned. In the short run, cities in states with home rule were much more likely to adopt reform charters. Cities with reform charters, however, were not more likely to adopt expansive programs of municipal ownership. In the long run, twenty-first-century scholarship demonstrates that predictions that shorter ballots and nonpartisan elections would increase popular interest and control of city government were wrong. They in fact tend to decrease interest and turnout, particularly among poorer and minority voters. Crucially, the features on which reformers compromised, agreeing only to "recommend" rather than require them as part of reform charters—municipal ownership, provisions for direct democracy, and proportional representation—all tend to increase turnout. These individual points regarding specific predictions can be quantifiably and empirically demonstrated. Together, they are also strongly suggestive of the overall consequences of the compromises and silences of urban reform. As this book has demonstrated, in order to promote reforms and present them as universally agreed on matters of expert, academic consensus, the NML's leaders compromised over and over, avoiding controversial topics and agreeing to disagree, often through professed deference to local choice.

By endorsing city managers, nonpartisan elections, and an end to ward-based elections without firmly stating that they must be paired with strong provisions for municipal ownership, direct democracy, and proportional representation, national reformers made it possible for local elites to selectively promote the features they favored. These elites presented reforms as democratic and universally endorsed by leading national authorities. Yet when new charters were adopted without the features that many figures in the NML, political science, and cities across the country suspected were essential for city manager government to function democratically, the resulting structures did not lead to greater popular control. For much of the twentieth century, they decreased electoral turnout, weakening the influence of poor and minority voters, which in turn enabled business elites to gain control of city governments. By midcentury, these elites largely opposed municipal ownership and social welfare programs, favoring local (and state and national) government that offered minimal regulations of private enterprise. Once in control, they implemented forms of state building perhaps closer to the visions of more conservative leaders such as James C. Carter, William Bennett Munro, and A. Lawrence Lowell but quite different from the visions of the more left-leaning voices in the movement for urban reform: NML leaders like Clinton Rogers Woodruff, Delos Wilcox, and Richard Childs; public intellectuals and activists like Frederic Howe, Albert Shaw, and Mary Ritter Beard; political scientists like Leo Stanton Rowe, Charles Beard, and Charles Merriam; and mayors like Samuel Jones, T. J. Powell, and Brand Whitlock. Rather than creating an expanded sphere of city government to promote public welfare, they instead ended up facilitating a continuation and expansion of the confusing array of public-private partnerships that have characterized much of American state building.

Home Rule, Charter Reform, and Municipal Ownership

The first major prediction was that home rule would enable urban residents to make choices about their governance that would differ from the choices of state legislatures. At first, some of the political scientists involved in the creation of the first *Municipal Program* (1899) argued that home rule should only include the right to determine the scope of activities undertaken, while charters should be uniform and fixed. As discussed earlier in the book, they believed that certain general principles of government should be determined by experts like themselves. But as the twentieth century progressed, the widespread popular association of home rule with the right to draft charters locally led the NML to change its position. The prediction then involved a sequence of two steps: that allowing cities greater home rule would result in revised city charters and that these revised charters, in turn, would lead to functional expansion. The first part of this prediction was correct. When compared with cities in states that controlled local charter making, cities in states with home rule were more likely to have adopted city manager charters with provisions for nonpartisan, at-large elections (tables 8.1–8.3). In short, by the 1930s,

TABLE 8.1 State Law and Mayor-Council, Commission, or Manager, 1935

	Mayor-council	Commission	Manager
Home rule	44.35%	18.55%	37.10%
Partial local control	46.85%	38.74%	14.41%
State control	65.33%	26.67%	8.00%

Sources: Data on state home rule laws for tables 8.1–8.3 from George Benson and Mary Benson, "Legal Classification of Cities by States," in *The Municipal Yearbook, 1935,* ed. Clarence Ridely and Orin Nolting (Chicago: ICMA, 1935). To simplify the presentation of data, I combined several of their subcategories: partial local control includes "optional charter provisions" and "freedom of choice between the three standard forms" and state control includes "rigid classifiers" that allowed "relatively little leeway to municipalities" and states that passed only "special charters." They listed only one category for home rule. Data on forms of government and methods of election in tables 8.1–8.3 from "Form of Government in the 310 Cities Over 30,000 in Population," in *The Municipal Yearbook, 1934,* ed. Clarence Ridely and Orin Nolting (Chicago: ICMA, 1934), 107–13.

TABLE 8.2 State Law and Partisan or Nonpartisan Elections, 1935

	Partisan	Nonpartisan
Home rule	29.03%	70.16%
Partial local control	30.63%	66.67%
State control	70.67%	28.00%

Note: Some rows do not add up to 100 percent because of the small number of cities that fell into other categories.

TABLE 8.3 State Law and Elections by Ward, Wards and at Large, or at Large, 1935

	Wards	Wards and at large	At large
Home rule	20.97%	16.94%	61.29%
Partial local control	24.32%	21.62%	54.05%
State control	29.33%	28.00%	41.33%

Note: Some rows do not add up to 100 percent because of the small number of cities that fell into other categories.

cities in states that allowed home rule with regard to charters were much more likely to adopt the reforms officially advocated by the NML.

Yet home rule varied so much by region that one might well ask whether variations in charter reform resulted from state home rule laws or regional variation. It would, however, be difficult to disentangle the influence of home rule and regional variation, for the two were intertwined. Evidence for regional variation in adoptions of Progressive reforms is clear. Western states were known as leaders in a variety of reforms, including woman suffrage, land conservation, juvenile courts, and child labor laws.[6] Laws providing for direct democracy were common in states west of the Mississippi, rare in the Northeast, and almost nonexistent in the South (only in Arkansas).[7] To an extent, the urban reform movement followed this pattern. On the local level, by the 1930s, there were clear regional variations in charter reform that largely paralleled regional variations in home rule. States in the West were most likely to allow cities greater autonomy, followed by the Midwest, the South, and, least likely, the Northeast. Following this pattern, cities in western states were most likely to adopt city manager charters, nonpartisan elections, and at-large elections, while cities in eastern states were least likely to. The evidence for the Midwest and South is a bit more complicated. In terms of nonpartisan elections, the South and Midwest were roughly the same and fell in between the extremes of the West and North, but the South was closer to the West in having higher levels of manager government and at-large elections, while the Midwest was closer to the North in having lower levels (tables 8.4–8.7). Today, elements of these variations remain, with cities in the West more likely to have council-manager government than cities in the North, South, and Midwest.[8]

Yet while regional variation is relatively easy to document empirically, the causes of this variation leave room for interpretation. In *City Politics* (1963), political scientists Edward Banfield and James Wilson offered what would become a widely influential theory regarding differences between reformed and unreformed cities. The former tended to be smaller, homogenous communities with native residents who largely adhered to a "middle-class ethos" based on "efficiency, impartiality, honesty," and a lack of personal favoritism; the latter tended to be larger, heterogeneous communities with residents who espoused an "immigrant ethos" based on neighborhood and personal loyalties and were less interested in abstract

TABLE 8.4 State Laws Regulating Cities by Region, 1935

	State control	Partial local control	Home rule
Northeast	66.7%	22.2%	11.1%
South (not D.C.)[a]	50.0%	37.5%	18.8%
Midwest[b]	8.0%	50.0%	50.0%
West	0.0%	45.5%	54.5%

Sources: Data on state home rule laws in table 9.4 from Benson and Benson, "Legal Classification of Cities by States." Regions from "Census Regions and Divisions of the United States," U.S. Census Bureau, accessed April 22, 2019, https://www2.census.gov/geo/pdfs/maps-data/maps/reference/us_regdiv.pdf.

[a] These numbers add up to more than 100 percent because Maryland was counted twice, as Baltimore had home rule but all other cities were under state control.

[b] These numbers add up to more than 100 percent because Missouri was counted twice, as Kansas City and Saint Louis had home rule and other cities had optional charter laws.

TABLE 8.5 Percentage of Cities with Mayor-Council, Commission, or Manager by Region, 1934

	Mayor-council	Commission	Manager
Northeast	63.30	24.77	9.17
South	27.94	30.88	41.18
Midwest	57.84	23.53	17.65
West	29.03	32.26	38.71

Sources: Data on forms of government and methods of election in tables 8.5–8.7 from "Form of Government in the 310 Cities." Regions from "Census Regions and Divisions."

Note: Some rows do not add up to 100 percent because of the small number of cities that fell into other categories.

and legal ideals.[9] On one level, statistical evidence from the 1930s supports parts of this theory. By the 1930s, cities with more immigrants (defined by the census as "foreign-born whites") were much less likely to adopt manager charters; larger cities were also less likely to adopt manager charters and at-large elections (appendix 1).[10] Later studies expanded on this distinction, offering more complex portraits of immigrant groups as heterogeneous and holding diverse values. One claimed that regional variation in fact stemmed from patterns of immigration from Europe, Asia, and Latin America that created several distinct political subcultures, some favoring the ideals of manager government, along with short ballots in non-

TABLE 8.6 Percentage of Cities with Partisan or Nonpartisan Elections by Region, 1934

	Partisan	Nonpartisan
Northeast	59.63	40.37
South	32.35	67.65
Midwest	31.37	68.63
West	12.90	87.10

TABLE 8.7 Percentage of Cities with Elections by Ward, Wards and at Large, or at Large by Region, 1934

	Wards	Wards and at large	At large
Northeast	28.44	26.61	44.95
South	17.65	13.24	66.18
Midwest	26.47	26.47	47.06
West	16.13	3.23	80.65

Note: Some rows do not add up to 100 percent because of the small number of cities that fell into other categories.

partisan, at-large elections, more than others. Immigrant settlement patterns, according to this view, explain the regional variations in reform.[11]

Today, scholars continue to promote similar ideas regarding the role of political cultures in relation to forms of city government.[12] Yet others directly reject cultural arguments, arguing instead for a variation of what is often referred to as a "diffusion" model, in which governments emulate changes made by other nearby governments.[13] For example, one study argues that "regional difference" in the adoption of commission and manager charters arose "not from social compositional differences of regions' cities but from some type of imitation or contagion effect as represented by the level of neighboring regional cities previously adopting reform government."[14] In this view, western and, in some cases, southern cities were more likely to adopt manager plans because their neighbors did so, not because of differences in their social or cultural characteristics. The higher levels of reformer charters, according to this view, might well have resulted from the fact that the first manager city was in Virginia and the first commission city in Texas.

Yet rather than focus on ethos, culture, or diffusion, others now maintain that institutions, both political and economic, better explain stark regional variations. For example, one influential study argues that there was more "regional receptivity" to many Progressive reforms in the West because parties were less entrenched, making it easier for opponents of patronage and party politics to garner voters' support.[15] Similarly, a study of state-level initiative, referenda, and recall laws argues that direct democracy's supporters were more successful in the West, where antimonopoly sentiment was strongest and parties were weakest, with anger at large corporations and the perceived collusion between government and business through favorable franchises, tariffs, and other "special privileges." In the East, parties were stronger and antimonopoly sentiment was weaker, while in the South, a wave of new state constitutions in the 1890s disfranchised not only African Americans but also many poor whites.[16] Others explain the popularity of commission and later manager government in the West and South by arguing for the centrality of two factors: the presence of fewer immigrants and the passing of restrictive suffrage laws that made voter turnout lower. According to this explanation, cities with strong party organizations that depended on immigrant voters were able to block urban reform. The fact that such cities existed largely in the Northeast and Midwest explains the regional variations.[17]

Certainly, many of these factors are not mutually exclusive, and the case studies in this book demonstrate that an additional factor—the ability of reformers to persuade voters that structural reform was a prerequisite for functional expansion—was also central. The argument that new charters were only adopted in cities with restricted electorates and low turnout is a provocative one, and it likely partly explains why reform charters were adopted in many cities in the South and West. This study, however, is based on aggregate county-level data on turnout in presidential elections, not on turnout in city elections. (Aggregates of data on city elections do not seem to exist for the early twentieth century.)[18] Yet we should not assume that presidential and municipal turnout were the same. Additionally, while they cannot provide quantitative evidence, the case studies in this book demonstrate over and over that elites did not uniformly support charter reforms and working-class and minority groups did not uniformly oppose them. Moreover, despite the unique elements in these cities' histories, in every case, advocates of new charters were more successful when they offered convincing arguments connecting charter revision to expanded municipal functions.

Timing is also central in understanding why and where this kind of argument was persuasive, and it partly explains regional variation. Smaller cities experiencing rapid growth had greater development needs. For example, by the late 1800s, local commercial organizations began to see securing public water supplies as key to competing with neighboring cities. And in the early twentieth century, cities in the Northeast and Midwest were generally more likely to have public water supplies, filtration systems, and sewers than cities in the South and West.[19] Cities in the Northeast and Midwest were also already long established, with political interests benefiting from the status quo, while cities in the Southwest and West were comparatively smaller and newer.[20] In this context, timing and sequencing were key.[21] In the Southwest, for example, not only were political parties weak, but urban reform was closely tied to economic development and industrialization. Local business leaders presented urban reform to voters as a way to draw badly needed investors to their cities. While suffrage restrictions partly explain the adoption of new charters, so too does the fact that remaining voters had good reasons to support reform.[22]

Services were an essential part of this type of argument, for outsiders were more likely to invest in cities with adequate utilities, transportation, and infrastructure. Charter revision, the expansion of government to provide such services, and economic development were closely interrelated in smaller and/or newer cities in the South and West. Municipal water, the only utility to become commonly provided through municipally owned plants, provides the clearest example of the major regional differences in service provision (tables 8.8 and 8.9). In 1902, 70.64 percent of northeastern

TABLE 8.8 Percentage of Cities with Municipal Ownership by Region, 1902

	Water	Gas	Electric lights	Street railways
Northeast	70.64	0.92	4.59	0.00
South	42.65	4.41	16.18	7.35
Midwest	55.88	0.98	19.61	7.84
West	45.16	0.00	6.45	9.68

Sources: Data on municipal ownership in 1902 from "Public and Private Ownership in Cities and Towns," in The Municipal Yearbook, 1902, ed. M. N. Baker (New York: Engineering News). Regions from "Census Regions and Divisions."

TABLE 8.9 Percentage of Cities with Municipal Ownership by Region, 1935

	Water	Gas	Electricity	Street railways	Ports	Airports	Markets	Abattoirs
Northeast	69.72	1.83	7.34	0.92	5.50	20.18	13.76	4.59
South	82.35	5.88	7.35	4.41	27.94	54.41	39.71	14.71
Midwest	76.47	1.96	15.69	3.92	9.80	40.20	24.51	2.94
West	77.42	3.23	19.35	12.90	35.48	67.74	9.68	3.23

Source: Data on municipal ownership in 1935 from "Directory and Governmental Data for the 960 Cities of Over 10,000 Population," in Ridely and Nolting, The Municipal Yearbook, 1935. Regions from "Census Regions and Divisions."

cities had municipally owned water plants, as did 55.88 percent of midwestern cities, while western and southern cities lagged behind at 45.16 percent and 42.65 percent, respectively. By 1935, this pattern was reversed, with southern cities now home to the largest percentage of municipally owned plants (82.35 percent), followed by western cities (77.42 percent), midwestern cities (76.47 percent), and northeastern cities (69.72 percent). In addition to the rising anger at the inadequate services provided by private corporations, urban boosters in chambers of commerce and other business associations viewed adequate water supplies as essential for growth.[23] Scientific advances led to clearer understandings of clean water's importance in preventing the spread of diseases, and prominent voices in urban public health believed that private companies would not reliably secure sanitary water.[24] And, as we have seen throughout this book, over and over, reformers promised that charter revisions would make municipal ownership possible. In this context, charter reform would likely be more popular in cities with a greater need for rapid expansion in service provision.

But as table 8.9 also demonstrates, despite claims that a new era of municipal ownership was imminent, water plants were the only form that became widespread. Gas, electricity, and public transportation continued to be provided largely through franchise contracts with private companies. Moreover, despite hopes that charter reforms would facilitate an expansion of municipal ownership, city manager government, nonpartisan elections, and at-large elections were not correlated with higher levels of municipally owned water, gas, electricity, transportation, ports, airports, markets, or abattoirs (appendix 2).

Even if cities with managers, nonpartisan elections, and at-large elections were not more likely to expand municipal ownership, they could have fostered state development in other ways. Yet there is no evidence that reformed cities spent more on infrastructure projects, a form of public ownership that was typically not labeled as such. A recent statistical study of the relationship between the structures of city government and spending on infrastructure (defined as water supplies, sewer systems, and roads) found that cities with manager and commission forms were *less* likely to spend money on infrastructure through the 1920s.[25]

Yet reformers were partly correct in one aspect of their predictions about municipal ownership: while manager government, nonpartisan elections, and at-large elections were not correlated with higher levels of municipal ownership, cities with home rule were much more likely to operate municipal airports and more likely to operate ports. Larger cities were also much more likely to operate municipal airports, more likely to operate ports, and somewhat more likely to operate municipal markets and transit systems (appendix 2). Notably, by the 1930s, airports were the second most common form of municipal ownership in all regions, and markets were the third most common in the Northeast, South, and Midwest. Why did municipal airports everywhere and markets in all regions but the West become more popular than municipal utilities and transportation?

In the 1910s and 1920s, several academics and left-leaning reformers continued to support municipal ownership, particularly through the Public Ownership League of America (POL), which was founded in 1917 with the NML's own Delos Wilcox as a vice president.[26] In some ways, the rhetoric of this organization's leaders echoed that of earlier proponents of municipal ownership, but it also differed in key ways, most notably by using the term *public* ownership rather than *municipal* ownership. They continued to rail against a corrupt system that allowed private corporations to benefit at the expense of the public, but they increasingly focused on national issues. Rather than critiquing public service corporations for bribing councils for franchises, they wrote about the national "Power Trust, in its mad effort to control the electrical energy of the nation[,] . . . buying up congressmen and senators, controlling the newspapers and magazines, polluting the source of education by placing school teachers on its payroll, editing text books for schools, corrupting legislators, and passing laws in its own interests."[27] Also, in 1919, the POL's president continued to use moralistic language, describing the organization's purpose as "spreading the gospel of Democracy and Social Justice."[28] Yet over the course of the 1920s, the POL's publications increasingly turned to the language of consumers' rights and cost savings to justify the effectiveness of public ownership.[29]

Characterizations of Americans as consumers in political discourse were on the rise in these years. From one perspective, depicting urban residents as "consumers" rather than "voters" or "citizens" was disempowering, related to a version of pluralism that depicted most people as inherently self-interested and suggested that political decisions needed to be left to impartial experts. As early as 1907, an early pluralist's account of a movement for municipal ownership of Chicago's streetcars argued that groups of urban residents acted according to material (rather than ideological) interests, more concerned with efficient transportation than with participating in decision-making processes.[30] According to this reasoning, consumerism undermined defenses of the civic capacities of urban voters. By midcentury, some political scientists discussed citizens as consumers who had the right to choose among commodified candidates but not to participate in any meaningful way in deliberative political processes. Politicians and administrators were to make decisions about public goods on behalf of—not alongside—a nation of citizen consumers.[31]

Yet from another perspective, consumer identities could empower citizens. In the first decades of the twentieth century, advertisers and other professionals drew on the work of social scientists and diverse American political traditions to popularize a new understanding of a national civic identity based on purchasing and consuming goods. While some critiqued consumer-citizens as self-interested, others viewed themselves as allies working with them to defend consumer rights.[32] Additionally, long before the famed lunch counter sit-ins of the 1960s, disfranchised African Americans engaged in consumer activism by boycotting segregated streetcars and creating black-owned businesses.[33] Describing urban residents as taxpayers and consumers receiving services in some cases fostered more inclusive outcomes. For example, in praising the efforts of the new manager in Norfolk, Virginia, to improve the streets in African American neighborhoods in 1921, African American journalist P. B. Young wrote, "We have no direct voice in the city government, but we pay our share of the taxation necessary to defray the expenses of city government, and we should always, therefore, on this account, have proper consideration."[34]

This focus on consumers provides one rationale for municipal markets' popularity. The term *market* encompassed several types of venues, including wholesale terminals for retailers, farmers' markets in permanent public buildings with stalls for rent, and mobile curbside carts. Promoters presented markets as cutting out middlemen between farmers and urban consumers, thus ensuring higher profits for the former and lower prices and higher-quality food for the latter, as well as more sanitary conditions for both.[35] Even in an era in which socialism was increasingly unpopular, municipal markets were not seen as such but rather were viewed as public facilities that did not infringe on private enterprise.[36] For example, in California, state courts ruled that public markets were a legitimate "municipal affair," therefore allowable under the state home rule law. The rationale was that "changed circumstances" altered the line "between public and private businesses," making markets legitimate "matters of public concern."[37] This decision was part of a wider trend, with a variety of public enterprises developed in cities pushing state courts to expand the accepted sphere of governmental endeavors.[38]

In part, characterizations of consumers as women in need of protection contributed to the greater acceptance of municipal markets. An article in *American City* in 1930 described consumers with clear markers of gender and class: "Mrs. Consumer" was frustrated by high delivery costs and desired only "the choicest" goods.[39] A book on markets in 1929 also expressed this vision, claiming, "It is true that the man of the family is the breadwinner, but the woman is the bread-buyer. Markets are built for women." This study presented the need for public markets as a matter of consensus among urban residents, claiming that women's organizations, central labor unions, chambers of commerce, and diverse civic bodies supported them.[40] In this view, markets not only protected women but also benefited a wide variety of groups, making cities more hospitable and likely to attract new residents.

Airports were even more closely associated with boosterism, and a variety of factors converged in the late 1920s and early 1930s to make municipal ownership widely accepted. At the end of World War I, the first landing fields began to appear, and they were locally financed through both public and private means. Initially, the major customers were the military and the U.S. Postal Service. Yet because neither had the finances to construct airports, they spearheaded campaigns to convince cities to finance them, portraying them as essential for economic growth. Federal laws, state laws, and the fact that most airports were not profitable further encouraged the turn to municipal ownership. Perhaps the most influential law was the Air Commerce Act of 1926, which defined airports as public ports, similar to the docks and harbors that were already usually accepted as local responsibilities, whether through public or private ownership (in contrast to railroad terminals, which were generally privately owned and operated). Political scientists and others justified public ownership of airports as a matter of fairness, arguing that private companies were less likely to treat all customers equally. Additionally, a desire to compete with other cities and promote growth made airports popular among local business groups. In Oakland, for example, the Chamber of Commerce, working with the military and the Postal Service, declared in 1917 that Oakland would become "the logical center for Pacific Coast air commerce." The Chamber identified a site, conducted a study, and presented its results to the Board of Port Commissioners; this work led to the construction of the Oakland Municipal Airport.[41] By 1926, an article in the *National Municipal Review* declared municipal ownership of airports to be "the most satisfactory method," and by the end of the decade, most local and national chambers of commerce agreed.[42]

Yet consumerism and boosterism alone cannot explain why municipal ownership of markets and ports was generally more common than other forms of municipal ownership. Utilities and transportation were arguably also public goods that, when provided to residents, would make cities more attractive to investors. One possibility is that Americans were more comfortable with publicly owned *spaces* than with publicly provided *services*. As voices in the POL pointed out when arguing for an expansion of public ownership, municipalities already owned and maintained parks, playgrounds, roads, libraries, and schools.[43] Such physical spaces, then and now, were in some ways taken for granted by the general public, not viewed as socialistic components of an expanding state. Airports and markets may have seemed more in line with these existing spaces.

Another possibility is that public ownership in these areas did not threaten vested interests in the same way that public ownership of utilities and transportation did. As noted, by the late nineteenth century, privately owned public service corporations were the most common means for providing utilities and transportation. Ending this franchise system and replacing it with a new one based on municipal ownership would end a profitable industry. Airports were a response to a new need for a service and therefore less likely to disrupt a profitable status quo. In the case of municipal markets, this form of public enterprise benefited small, local merchants and farmers in the early twentieth century. It was only later, with the advent of larger, national corporations and grocery stores, that municipal markets went into decline.[44] In other words, public markets began to fail when they challenged the profits of larger-scale private businesses. Therefore, markets and airports may have been the path to municipal ownership with the least resistance at the time. Timing, again, was key.

Public service corporations also actively worked to weaken popular support for municipal ownership, perhaps successfully. As early as the 1910s, utility companies undertook campaigns to sell stock to the urban residents who were their customers, promising a share in their profits. Across the country, local executives used this strategy as a response to the perceived threat of rising support for municipal ownership. Telephone, gas, electric, and streetcar companies created "customer stock ownership" programs. By the end of the 1920s, over two million Americans owned stock in utility and telephone companies, and, partly as a result, there was a decrease in popular distrust of public service corporations.[45]

Additionally, state laws regarding municipal financing created a major institutional barrier to new public endeavors in American cities. By the 1930s, even states that granted cities large measures of home rule in terms of charter making continued to regulate the amount of money that cities were allowed to borrow. While home rule cities were somewhat freer to experiment with municipal ownership, these regulations circumscribed their ability to do so.[46] Most states allowed cities to borrow relatively small amounts of money, often around 5 percent of the value of taxable municipal property, and many states required bonds to receive supermajorities in local elections for approval.[47] In short, despite evidence of widespread popular support for municipal ownership through the 1910s, state laws and courts remained obstacles.[48] Most cities would not have been able to afford multiple projects simultaneously. Given the need to choose, managers and councillors were probably more likely to push for the forms of public-sector expansion that were both accepted among voters and favorable to business interests.

Despite limited gains in municipal ownership, the provision of services through private companies had, overall, improved by the 1920s. Though far from uniform or unopposed, state-level regulation of public service corporations providing utilities and transportation in cities continued to grow in the 1930s.[49] On one level, the potential threat of municipal ownership likely pushed some companies to offer improved services at lower prices. On another, many reformers and politicians, when faced with obstacles to municipal ownership, may have decided to make do with improved municipal or state regulations. The New Municipal Program included recommendations for monitoring private companies more closely and securing more favorable franchises, with an option to terminate contracts every five years. It also called for more formal and detailed accounting, an essential component of the larger administrative reforms of the day. State-level regulatory bodies typically required uniform accounting methods in all cities, making it easier to compare private companies and hold them accountable.[50] In these ways, the focus on improved administrative methods and regulations helped address some of the worst inefficiencies and corruption. By midcentury, political scientists concluded that manager cities were largely less corrupt and more efficiently managed, ending the rule of machines and patronage politics.[51] In the short run, it seems that charter revision largely fostered a continuation and expansion of the form of state building on the local level that existed in the late nineteenth century: a reliance on private companies to provide public services through the sale of franchises. In doing so, charter revision also helped lay the groundwork for the development of the administrative and regulatory state.

Accountability, Electoral Structures, and Public Participation in Policy Formation and State Building

Many urban reformers predicted that charter reform would make city government more accountable and increase popular participation in local decision-making processes. The authors of the Municipal Program (adopted

in 1899) and the *New Municipal Program* (adopted in 1915) advocated powerful legislative councils to represent urban residents. Most also believed that
electing fewer people (particularly by appointing administrative positions)
would contribute to these goals. And while they may have disagreed about
the solutions, overall, they agreed that ward-based elections were problematic and should be replaced by either at-large elections or systems of
proportional representation. The compromises and ambiguities in the
NML's promotion of manager government in the 1920s and 1930s further
explain how and why, in the long run, many of the institutions created by
new charters did not achieve these goals.

On many levels, the NML seems to have been committed to the position
that proportional representation was necessary to ensure accountability in
the small councils associated with manager government. William Dudley
Foulke, known for his work on behalf of women's rights, civil service reform, anti-imperialism, and Russian freedom, was in 1914 president of not
only the Proportional Representation League (PRL) but also the NML, and
Richard Childs and Charles Beard served as officers in both organizations.[52]
With the inclusion of proportional representation in the *New Municipal Program*, the two organizations grew closer, holding joint meetings beginning
in 1929 and officially merging in 1932, when the *National Municipal Review*
began publishing materials previously printed in the *Proportional Representation Review*.[53] Childs continued to promote proportional representation
for decades, and in the 1960s he argued that it would ensure the representation of African American and Hispanic residents on councils.[54]

Despite this close association between the NML and proportional
representation—and between the NML and manager government—by the
1930s it was clear that manager government was not synonymous with proportional representation. Again, the NML was partly responsible. The *New
Municipal Program* presented proportional representation as essential to the
functioning of a manager form of government, though only a majority of
the program's authors agreed. The fourth revision of the municipal program (1933) included a model charter that continued to advocate proportional representation so that "voters [might] form their own natural constituencies" as the preferred option. Yet it also recommended an alternative
"system of non-partisan elections at-large," even though it was "not so accurately representative as proportional representation."[55]

Allowing for both methods seemed inconsistent, leading a recent scholar of pluralism to argue for "a growing incoherence in reform thought." In other words, proportional representation was associated with a pluralist view of politics, assuming the need for group representation; at-large elections were associated with the assumption that councillors could represent an entire community.[56] Certainly, on one level, the two systems were incompatible; yet their simultaneous endorsement likely reflected an inability of diverse reformers to agree rather than incoherence in the views of specific individuals. The decision to continue to include the option of at-large elections in the 1933 revision was another compromise. Eight of the seventeen committee members voted *against* including it, preferring to endorse only proportional representation. The secretary's records hint at the level of discord, with a plea that "the committee has already consumed more of its secretary's time and energy on this point than was justified."[57]

The question of how best to elect councils stemmed from debates about the appropriate political roles of groups in city politics. Advocacy of proportional representation is strongly associated with the rise of pluralist conceptions of political participation, and rightly so. Figures such as Arthur Bentley in the 1900s and Walter Lippmann in the 1920s published early and influential works, arguing that political actors were motivated by competing group interests rather than a singular public interest. Lippmann (who was on the council of the PRL) maintained that when individuals claimed to speak for the public interest, they were often promoting self-interested agendas. He therefore called for a reliance on experts to mediate among competing groups.[58] In this reading, pluralism—and proportional representation—was founded on a rejection of conceptions of "the public" and "the common good."

Yet some proponents of proportional representation seemed to reconcile a recognition of diverse interests and a continued belief in a higher common purpose. In 1893, one of the PRL's founders wrote of his hopes that legislative bodies that allowed for majority and minority representation would allow individuals to come together and "harmonize all social interests."[59] Twenty years later, another officer in the PRL wrote, "The way to foster mutual understanding and co-operation for the common welfare is to provide that all shades of opinion and interest shall be represented in the council justly."[60] In these views, support for proportional representation was compatible with a belief in an underlying, common good in American cities.

Regardless of reformers' intentions, in cities across the country (including Norfolk and Fort Worth), city manager government was largely associated with at-large elections and, by association, a rejection of the concept of legitimate, competing group interests. In 1940, Harold Stone, Don
Price, and Kathryn Stone published *City Manager Government in the United
States: A Review After Twenty-Five Years* based on visits to fifty cities operating under manager charters.[61] They largely avoided discussions of race and
ethnicity, and they implicitly rejected pluralism. They detailed several
"fundamental principles" espoused by most proponents of manager government, including "the idea that the most capable and public-spirited citizens should serve on the governing body as representatives of the city
at-large, to determine policies for the benefit of the community as a whole,
rather than for any party, faction, or neighborhood." They maintained that
the only real cleavages in city politics were between advocates of impartial administration and advocates of patronage, rejecting differences based
on "interests of any social or economic group."[62] They presented these
views as those of the supporters of manager government interviewed for
the project, and their overall tone and conclusions endorsed them.

In sharp contrast, over twenty years later, one of the next major studies of city government embraced pluralism in an account that was critical
of both manager government and its proponents. In *City Politics*, Banfield
and Wilson assessed the findings of roughly thirty reports from the Joint
Center for Urban Studies of the Massachusetts Institute of Technology and
Harvard University. A recognition and acceptance of conflicting interests
was central to their analysis.[63] They included a chapter analyzing African
Americans' lower levels of participation in city politics. They first offered
explanations based on racial stereotypes, but they also recognized that at-
large elections (instead of systems of proportional representation) made
it more difficult for African Americans to be elected on councils. They also
questioned the notion that expanding citizens' "knowledge about politics"
would solve urban problems because they maintained that problems resulted from disagreements, not lack of knowledge. While conceding that
administrative centralization under an appointed manager yielded certain
benefits, they rejected the claim that nonpartisan, at-large elections were
essential components of the manager form. They specifically faulted Stone,
Price, and Stone for neglecting to consider "the personal and class interest of reformers." Rather than viewing nonpartisan, at-large elections as

tools for securing the election of "capable and public-spirited citizens" interested in furthering "the benefit of the community as a whole," Banfield and Wilson suggested that they were tools "to put [reformers] and their kind into office." They also concluded that despite "the achievements of the [manager] plan in providing government that is honest, impartial, and efficient 'in the small,' *it is not clear that it has accomplished what its inventors mainly intended[:] . . . centralizing authority to make local government an effective instrument for carrying out the popular will.*"[64]

Debates about whether appointed managers should be involved in policy decisions followed a similar pattern, with compromises and ambiguities in official NML publications and explanations leading to deviations from reformers' original visions. As noted, in the 1910s, the earliest architects and promoters of the manager plan repeatedly maintained that managers, as unelected administrators, would not play any role in formulating public policies: the plan would separate politics and administration. Many envisioned it as a way to empower councils as strong legislative bodies. Yet Childs and other NML leaders contributed to interpretations that empowered appointed managers over elected councils, emphasizing the need to insulate managers' administrative powers from meddling councillors rather than to protect councils' political powers from meddling managers. The 1927 revision of the program contained a new section titled "Council Not to Interfere with Appointments or Removals" by managers but not a parallel section banning managers from interfering with councils' work.[65] The 1933 revision described the plan as a tool to destroy patronage by preventing councillors from making any administrative appointments other than those of managers. Though Childs passionately defended the city manager plan over the next forty years as a tool that would democratize city government, he sometimes promoted the plan as a means for ending patronage by decreasing councils' appointive powers.[66] In these ways and others, Childs and others implicitly framed the manager plan as disempowering elected officials and empowering appointed professionals.

Moreover, despite general agreement regarding the need to separate politics and administration in theory, this goal proved difficult to achieve in practice. Political scientist Leonard White's 1927 study of manager government provides insights into how this confusion played out locally, suggesting that charter commissions resisted attempts to disempower

councils. In summarizing his assessment of nearly one hundred manager charters, he emphasized the involvement of councils in administrative matters. He used Fort Worth as an example, noting that the council appointed not only the manager but also "the city secretary, the city
judge, the park board, the public recreation board, the board of equaliza-
tion, the city-plan commission, the art commission, and various advisory
boards." He therefore concluded that in Fort Worth, "the council wields
real political authority over many administrative officers," and he then
added that this "is still more true in Norfolk."[67] Despite the NML's suggestions, many promoters of manager government were initially not entirely
comfortable with delegating all appointive powers to city managers.

Yet White also emphasized the involvement of managers in political
matters. He underscored the general principle that managers were not supposed to be involved in politics, reprinting the ICMA's Code of Ethics
adopted in 1925. Among other provisions, the code required that managers not "take an active part in politics" and that they always remember
that "the council, the elected representatives of the people[,] . . . primarily determine the municipal policies." Despite the professed acceptance of
this theory, he detailed confusion surrounding its implementation in practice. Again discussing Fort Worth, he cited O. E. Carr as an example of a
manager who offered a subtle distinction: managers should not be involved
in council elections but should campaign for the adoption of "improvement
programs." Other managers agreed, adding that while managers should
not formulate policies, once councils determined courses of action, they
should support them publicly. White also claimed that many managers understood themselves to be more than administrators, expressing doubts
about the ability of elected councils to understand the overall best interests of cities. And despite his sympathy for the confusion as to their roles,
he concluded that an inability to separate politics and administration resulted in "evil results beyond measure" and that the involvement of managers in policy making was "the chief danger" of the new plan.[68] White's
early assessment, in short, reveals discomfort among political scientists
with the notion that appointed managers would assume policy-making
roles and a parallel desire to empower councillors, as elected representatives, to dictate policy.

Unlike White in 1927, Stone, Price, and Stone in 1940 entirely rejected
the premise that separating politics and administration represented a

division of powers. They believed that the unification—not separation—of powers was the chief feature of the plan. While early advocates often used business analogies to explain manager government, Stone, Price, and Stone were among the earliest to suggest a different model: a European, parliamentary model. They faulted the NML's leadership, in their promotional efforts, for emphasizing "the centralization of administrative duties in the city manager" to end patronage rather than "the unification of powers in the council." They claimed that urban reformers echoed this argument, resulting in a "failure to encourage leadership in the council."[69]

In this view, the NML and its affiliates failed to explain their understanding of the city manager plan effectively by neglecting to convey the central importance of strong city councils in ensuring popular control of government. As noted, the first *Municipal Program* (1899) called for centralizing administration in the office of the mayor *and* strengthening councils' legislative powers. Yet in the first decades of the twentieth century, urban reformers tended to promote what they called "strong-mayor" government, working to empower mayors at the expense of councils. Councils often lost power over financial decisions and administrative matters.[70] Stone, Price, and Stone later misrepresented the first *Municipal Program* as advocating a strong-mayor form of government. Their critique of the NML's work suggests that this same pattern occurred again in the 1920s and 1930s: despite the fact that the NML at first presented *commission manager* government as a means of creating powerful legislative commissions or councils that would then appoint managers, in cities across the country, *city manager* government was increasingly perceived as a way to create the independent power and authority of an appointed city manager.

Likewise, Stone, Price, and Stone critiqued leading figures in the NML for failing to communicate the proper role of city managers. They noted that Childs and others envisioned managers as apolitical public servants, working largely behind the scenes. In contrast, they argued that most Americans "could not be persuaded that [managers] should be . . . inconspicuous administrative officer[s]" and instead "expected them to be public figures," essentially demanding they become "civic leader[s]."[71] The implications were clear: the NML and affiliated political scientists may have succeeded in promoting the general idea of manager government and contributed to its adoption. Once adopted, however, they lost control of what they had created, and it became something many did not support.

By 1963, Banfield and Wilson agreed that the plan did not separate politics and administration, but they framed the significance of this conclusion quite differently. They conceded that most managers attempted to act as professional administrators and avoid political entanglements, but they suggested that the "invisible lines between 'submitting proposals' and 'making policy,' between 'exercising leadership' and 'engaging in politics,'" were often clear. Yet they also questioned the assumption that city government was largely a matter of administration rather than politics, and they rejected the claim that administration was apolitical: "The nature of the governmental system gives private interests such good opportunities to participate in the making of public decisions that there is virtually no sphere of 'administration' apart from politics."[72] In short, while Stone, Price, and Stone recognized that the division between politics and administration was often unclear, they pushed their readers to work toward this goal; Banfield and Wilson also recognized that the division was unclear but suggested that the goal itself was unattainable. Rejecting the notion of a public good and consequently that reformers could speak for that good, they rejected the notion that the purpose of city government was impartial administration for the public good.

In ensuing decades, scholars of public administration came to recognize and normalize city managers as playing "significant policy-making roles" in American cities.[73] Today, scholars in the field of public administration now widely accept that it is impossible to separate politics and administration completely and that managers have played a part in shaping public policies from the start. Many argue that managers do—and should—in some way act as "policy leaders," and some believe that they can simultaneously function apart from politics and still propose public policies.[74] In short, while early architects and promoters of the city manager plan promised voters that it was democratic because appointed managers would have purely administrative roles and not shape public policies, they were wrong.

Why does this matter? In part, the perception that managers play leading roles in the formation and implementation of public policies may decrease voter turnout. Reformers also predicted that electing only a small council would increase popular interest and control of government. The believed that if citizens voted for fewer people, they would know them as individuals and establish clearer lines of accountability. Yet by the 1960s, early statistical studies suggested that turnout was lower in cities with appointed managers rather than elected mayors and nonpartisan rather than partisan elections.[75] Today, there is evidence that appointing rather than electing officials, particularly the decision to appoint city managers rather than elect mayors, decreases turnout because people tend to vote when they feel that elections are consequential.[76] Moreover, the policy-making role of managers is potentially concerning in light of the continued gender gap in the management profession. As of 2012, women held roughly 12 percent of management positions, a figure that had remained the same for decades. In comparison with their male counterparts, female managers on average are more likely to value citizen input and community relations as part of decision-making processes.[77]

Similarly, while evidence as to whether at-large (as opposed to ward-based) elections increase or decrease turnout is mixed, it is clear that nonpartisan elections, particularly when held on separate days from local and national elections, draw fewer voters to the polls. (At-large elections, overall, make it more difficult for minorities to be elected but, in contrast, appear to make it easier for female candidates to be elected.)[78] Nonpartisan elections not only decrease turnout, they also tend to favor the election of Republicans, professionals, and business leaders, who in turn tend to be less responsive to the needs of minority residents.[79] As one recent review of scholarship on nonpartisan elections puts it, under "such systems, the unorganized and less attentive participate less and lose voice in the policy process, while policies align with the preferences of the better-off and business interests."[80] Even when controlling for partisanship and other variables, low turnout in local elections makes it more difficult for minority candidates to be elected.[81] In short, urban reformers were also wrong when they predicted that shorter ballots and nonpartisan tickets would lead to higher turnout and more informed voting that would, as a result, yield greater popular control over city government.

In contrast, they seem to have been right, at least in part, about the potential of direct democracy and proportional representation. Overall assessments of the use of the initiative and referenda vary widely, with many highlighting valid concerns that corporate and other interests use these tools to shape political outcomes.[82] Despite these limitations, the presence of ballot questions in local elections tends to deepen popular interest and raise voter turnout.[83] Additionally, a recent book on direct democracy in state-level elections finds that the Progressive advocates were correct: direct democracy has an educative effect. The book highlights the fact that Progressives supported direct democracy partly because they believed that it would encourage citizens to become more engaged and informed about public policies. It finds that "citizens living in states with frequent ballot initiatives are more motivated to vote, are more interested in and better informed about politics, and express more confidence in government responsiveness than do citizens living in noninitiative states" and that direct democracy "has a positive effect on political discussion."[84] Similarly, though scholars have long debated whether electing legislative bodies by proportional representation increases turnout, recent reviews of scholarship suggest that, on the whole, it does.[85] Many of the early promoters of manager government believed that elections by proportional representation and strong measures for direct democracy were essential for the city manager plan to function democratically, but they were willing to compromise to maintain a coalition, making these features recommended rather than essential. As noted, these compromises made it easier for business leaders to adapt the manager plan and adopt it without these features. While it is impossible to know with any certainty, the question remains: Would stronger inclusions of these features have been enough to offset the effects of appointed city managers and nonpartisan elections in order to achieve higher turnout and, in turn, greater popular interest and control?

Administration, Accountability, and State Building

In advocating forms of administrative insulation from political processes, urban reformers of the Progressive Era also contributed to the rise of one of the major forms of twentieth-century state building: public authorities. Many proponents of home rule and charter reform did not seek to circumvent existing institutions in order to achieve their ends but rather tried to change them directly. Others, however, worked to bypass rather than reform institutional impediments. In the early and mid-twentieth century, when faced with limitations on borrowing, city officials adapted to provide new services. Some local officials created new governmental entities that were not bound by debt restrictions, following the lead of state legislatures that had already established districts, commissions, and other entities to circumvent restrictions. While these state and local entities temporarily enabled government to meet needs, they also resulted in a labyrinth of confusing, overlapping jurisdictions that remain to this day. Other officials also financed new projects through a device that became known as revenue bonds. This approach relied on a legal doctrine that held that debt limits did not apply to revenue-generating endeavors because funds generated through fees could serve as collateral. The impact of these strategies was immense, establishing a system through which local and later state and national actors avoided barriers to public ownership. They laid the foundation for what today are known as public authorities, forms of quasi-public agencies with administrative and financial independence, including trusts, special districts, agencies, boards, commissions, and public corporations that blur the line between public and private enterprise and consequently are often not viewed by the public as part of government. In short, many left-leaning public officials who initially sought to regulate the economy to promote greater equality ended up contributing to the creation of public agencies in sectors such as banking and real estate that now arguably benefit special interests.[86]

Contemporary scholars view public authorities as a direct legacy of Progressive Era urban reform. According to *The Oxford Handbook of State and Local Government* (2014), public authorities were intended "to depoliticize administrative operations for the management of bridges, parks, housing, transportation and other infrastructure" as part of efforts "to separate politics from administration, just like the city manager form of government." It adds that Progressives "advocated [public authorities] over traditional governments because their structure incorporated business practices and expertise and . . . the managerial approach to public administration."[87]

Despite such assessments today, the NML and ICMA came out *against* early forms of public authorities by the 1930s. The NML's updated model charter in 1933 included the ICMA's list of "Objectionable Charter Provisions." It began with a warning that adopting charters with such adaptations might undermine manager government's fundamental objectives. First was a warning against the creation of *"independent boards or commissions and ex officio boards"* in the areas of "health, welfare, police, fire, utilities, public works, [and] parks" because they were "inconsistent with the spirit of council-manager government." Without direct control over the entire administration, managers could not coordinate efforts or be held accountable.[88] The early promoters of manager government desired the separation of administration and politics, but they firmly believed that popular accountability was essential. In the 1933 model charter, they directly warned that administrative boards that lacked accountability posed dangers.

By midcentury, more direct critiques of public authorities surfaced. In an article titled "Use and Abuse of Authorities" published in the *National Municipal Review* in 1953, one political scientist wrote that the proliferation of public authorities "alarmed many students and statesmen who fear that large chunks of government operations and responsibilities are being removed from democratic controls; there is the threat that a quasi-public government quite remote and unresponsive is developing." The article noted a sharp rise in the use of revenue bonds not subject to legal debt limitation to fund projects and the avoidance of "even minimum standards of personnel administration and technical competence" usually required for public projects. Additionally, the article highlighted a lack of democratic decision making and accountability arising from the delegation of too many decisions to administrators. A section entitled "The Nonpolitical Myth" cited decisions regarding the construction of roads, bridges, and public transportation to argue that such matters were political and needed to be open to "political discussions" because they were not matters that could be decided purely "in engineering and business terms."[89] Early urban reformers often argued that much urban governance was administrative rather that political and did not require popular input. By midcentury, some worried that the proliferation of public authorities was moving too many decisions to the administrative realm and that a form of state expansion was occurring, often invisible to the wider public, that lacked any real public control.

While this seemingly invisible form of government spread, opponents of government programs were becoming more vocal. By midcentury, local business leaders, known for their support of city manager government, tended to view limited regulation rather than public ownership as the appropriate role of government. The views of various chambers of commerce highlight a wider shift. As noted, particularly earlier in the twentieth century, business groups supported forms of municipal ownership that suited their interests. In some cases, local chambers of commerce collab-orated with city governments to establish new endeavors, including mu-nicipally owned service providers.[90] Even at midcentury, local business groups often supported government projects that benefited their own in-terests, including urban renewal and other building and infrastructure projects.[91] Yet as the century progressed, chambers of commerce increas-ingly opposed public ownership, including of light and power plants, rail-ways, parking, and more.[92]

By the 1960s, the Chamber of Commerce of the United States endorsed a "free enterprise system" over "government ownership," recommending limited government regulation only in cases in which it was "clearly re-quired by the public interest," preferably at the local or state rather than the federal level. In its statement *Policy Declarations*, although it allowed for some forms of public ownership (notably, for example, of water supplies), it included an expansive list of areas that should remain or become privatized. Conservation land, forests, national parks and monuments, recreation, com-munication, transportation, oil, natural gas, storage facilities, housing, and off-street parking were to be provided through private enterprise, "without hindrance, competition, or subsidization by government." (Despite such pronouncements, in other places the Chamber called for government fund-ing to promote private enterprise.)[93]

And yet despite the ascendance of such opposition to government pro-grams, public authorities have increased dramatically. Because of a lack of transparency and their diverse nature, it is difficult to determine their exact reach today. The increase in forms of debt is one indicator, with revenue-based debt increasing much more rapidly than general-obligation debt (fifty-six-fold v. fivefold, respectively). Public authorities are now re-sponsible for a larger share of tax-exempt bonds than local or state gov-ernments. Today, supporters and critics continue to debate the merits of this approach to developing governmental capacity. Proponents argue that public authorities have several advantages over standard governmental programs: they allow for long-term planning, promote economic develop-ment, produce revenue, and face less public resistance. Opponents dis-pute these claims and, echoing the *National Municipal Review*, argue that they are not accountable to voters. They add that they lead to the commer-cialization and fragmentation of public programs and do not effectively address questions of equity and justice. Yet despite these major limitations,

Americans with antigovernment leanings tend not to oppose public authorities because of their seeming invisibility.[94]

Similarly, many Americans tend not to perceive or oppose another largely unnoticed aspect of local government's expansion: increases in public-sector employees. From twenty-six per one hundred thousand Americans in 1947 to sixty-four per one hundred thousand in 2007, the ratio of local and state employees increased over 150 percent, while the number of federal employees decreased by one-third in the same period. At the start of the twenty-first century, roughly two of out every three public-sector employees work for local government. Sixty percent of all people employed by the government work in education and public safety, and these two functions are overwhelmingly the province of local government. Yet those who fear "big government" infringing on their rights tend to focus on the federal level more than the state or local level. Local public-sector employees are largely part of an accepted and, on one level, invisible component of governance.[95]

Despite this apparent acceptance, the late twentieth century was marked by privatization of local government and, in some ways, a return to the franchise system. Echoing wider efforts to decrease the size of government and augment free market competition, conservative local politicians argued that providing services through contracts with private firms would be more efficient and empower consumers by offering greater choices.[96] Yet by the early twenty-first century, the shift to privatization had slowed. As the ICMA's *Municipal Yearbook* (2014) summarizes, "Direct public service delivery continues to be the dominant form of local government service provision, accounting for 45% of delivery on average." Cities most often directly provide "police, fire, roads, parks and buildings maintenance, and land use planning" but rely on "for-profit delivery" companies for "vehicle towing, legal services, and commercial and residential solid waste." (Social services such as job training, child welfare, prisons, affordable housing, and mental health facilities are now commonly provided by "intermunicipal cooperation" or state government.) Echoing century-old debates, the ICMA raises concerns that this increased reliance on "private contracting" has not been accompanied by sufficient monitoring. Yet despite such concerns, it concludes that we have now achieved a "maturation of privatization," "with local leaders better able to grasp which services are appropriate for contract to private firms and which are not."[97]

Not all contemporary observers agree, with recent journalistic accounts of privatization offering very different interpretations. *Mother Jones* reports that poor administration, antiquated infrastructure, and rising debt at the municipal water plant led Pittsburgh to turn to what today is called a private management company. As part of cost-cutting efforts, this company cut staff and altered treatment plans, changes that many believe led to overcharging customers and dangerously high lead levels.[98] Even more starkly, the *New York Times* reports that in the aftermath of the 2008 financial crisis, many cities, finding themselves in dire financial situations, privatized emergency services, including ambulances and fire protection. Approximately 25 percent of American ambulance providers are now privately owned and operated. As a result of pressures to cut costs, 911 callers report late arrivals, unsanitary and unsafe vehicles, and sometimes no services.[99] More recently, in 2017 there were moves to privatize not only air traffic control, currently run by the Federal Aviation Administration, but also the ownership of airports. In April, the U.S. Transportation Department gave the City of Saint Louis permission to explore the possibility of privatizing its municipal airport.[100] These accounts echo the ICMA's concerns about a lack of regulation, but they challenge the notion that we have reached consensus regarding what services should be provided by the public and private sectors.

Today's scholars of urban politics, while assessing both benefits and drawbacks of these moves, tend to warn of their consequences. One recent study concludes that hopes that privatization would, through competition, lower costs for consumers have not been realized. Private firms compete to receive government contracts; once they possess contracts, more often than not, they have monopolies. It concludes, "While [contracting out] has increased the opportunity for consumer voice, there is a critical difference between consumer and citizen voice. Private markets segregate (by wealth, location, preference) whereas urban governments seek to integrate across the diversity of the city to create a more robust metropolitan region."[101] Scholars of public administration also warn that privatization runs against the norms of "procedural fairness, equal access or distribution to benefits, quality consistency, equal outcomes, and active citizen engagement processes."[102] In starker terms, another scholar argues, "We're reaching new lows in the public safety services we will help provide, especially in very poor cities. . . . [Private equity firms] . . . are not philanthropists."[103]

An additional consequence of privatization may be a weakening of political engagement. Many leading figures in the movement for urban reform believed that expanding municipal ownership would increase popular interest in government. They may have been right. The method for delivering services to urban residents shapes voter turnout. Today, when cities opt to provide services through private firms, following the franchise system model, voter turnout is lower. According to a recent study of city elections in California, "Each additional service provided by city staff ... (fire, police, library, sewerage, and garbage) ... is associated with approximately 1% higher turnout among registered voters." When voters perceive elected officials as directly involved in issues that affect their daily lives, they are more likely to go to the polls.[104] Additionally, when public services are provided through private companies, residents are not treated equally. Residents of poorer neighborhoods often receive inferior services.[105] Lower turnout among racial minorities leads to underrepresentation of minorities in city councils, which in turn contributes to inequitable distributions of services.[106] Yet while the prediction that municipal ownership would increase popular engagement was correct, many of the individuals in this book compromised on this subject. In the municipal programs, municipal ownership, like proportional representation and direct democracy, remained suggested rather than formally recommended.

How, then, should we assess the overall, long-term impact of the movement for urban reform? In part, its legacy lay in helping to lay the foundation for the regulatory agencies that would proliferate on the state and national levels later in the twentieth century. Unquestionably, many of the structural reforms, both political and administrative, that reformers advocated contributed to perceptions of declines in corruption and increases in efficiency that, in turn, helped cities improve the provision of services to residents. Many more (but not all) Americans have better access to clean water, utilities, and transportation than their counterparts living in cities in the 1890s. At the same time, despite the intentions of many of the leaders of this movement, their many compromises and silences contributed to the rise of the confusing and often inequitable mix of public and private programs that continues to characterize American government. Certainly, existing state laws made the path to municipal ownership more difficult, but as demonstrated, in the early twentieth century, there was widespread popular support—and even occasionally business support—for this form of state building.

By midcentury, through compromises on proportional representation, direct democracy, and municipal ownership and silences regarding race, the NML and its allies in political science aided in the promotion of forms of city government that enabled business groups to dominate urban politics. City manager government and nonpartisan, at-large elections made the election of business leader more likely; these leaders, in turn, favored a model of state development that promoted private enterprise through limited regulation, not an expansion of governmentally run (or supported) programs to promote public welfare. And as recent scholarship on the growth of the American state has demonstrated, the perception of limited government as neutral, benefiting no specific group and letting market forces determine outcomes, is inaccurate. The complicated intermingling of public and private that has characterized so much of nineteenth- and twentieth-century American state building creates programs that disproportionately benefit middle-class and wealthy Americans and neglect or even harm the poor and racial minorities.[107] Many politicians, labor leaders, reformers, and political scientists believed that home rule and charter reform would enable the popular will to be heard, which in turn would enable cities to expand their scopes to promote public welfare and put an end to the profits that private companies accrued through "special privileges." The reality of what happened was quite different.

Epilogue

The End of the Coalitions

At the start of the twentieth century, the leadership of the National Municipal League (NML) articulated a vision for the organization that combined impartial research and "militant" reform. In one example, Secretary Clinton Rogers Woodruff praised the NML's annual meeting for fostering "wider cooperation" among reformers throughout the country by creating a venue for political scientists and other experts to present their "careful and thoughtful" research. He also, however, highlighted "the militant character of the modern municipal movement." When discussing recent victories in the "battle" for "higher public life and cleaner politics," he celebrated the work of the "regular army of city clubs, municipal leagues, citizens' associations and civic federations," as well as "the volunteer corps of city parties and committees of various types." In other remarks, Woodruff proudly estimated that the NML's members included not only 1,348 individuals but also 135 organizations, representing roughly 60,000–70,000 people.[1] Woodruff envisioned the NML including both objective students of city politics and ardent supporters of specific reforms.

At the end of the 1920s, the NML's leadership was no longer sure that this combination was possible. Woodruff served as the NML's secretary and driving force for twenty-six years, stepping down in 1920.[2] After his departure, a new generation took the reins, and over the next decade, many voiced doubts about the NML's future. In 1931, the vice presidents and council, roughly half of whom were political scientists, met at the Union League Club in Chicago and discussed their concerns, asking, "What is the League's real function? Is it to be a militant reform organization, or a scientific research body, or a combination of both?" Frustratingly, the minutes do not indicate exactly how the vice presidents and council responded to these questions.[3]

An untitled memo in the surviving NML records marked "1931," however, provides an answer, and it suggests that individuals within the organization were concerned about the effects of compromises and efforts to be inclusive. The memo, containing questions either asked or answered by political scientist and NML secretary Russell Forbes, expressed grave doubts over the NML's purpose and future, offering a candid and often unflattering view of the organization. The memo partly focused on leadership, blaming Richard Childs for dominating the council and council members for a lack of real interest or participation (though notably it commended political scientists such as Charles Merriam and A. R. Hatton for their contributions). But the memo focused more on an underlying problem, asking, "What is the primary object of the League now? Propaganda or research, political or administrative? What is your program? What is the ultimate objective of the League?" The response recorded was, "We do not have a single objective, which is our greatest weakness as well as our greatest strength." Referring to recent conversations about the organization's future, the respondent highlighted divergent opinions regarding whether the NML should "do any research work on its own at all, or should . . . be only a propaganda body, taking whatever canned goods was [sic] handed to it that seemed good, opening it up and serving it to the assembled guests."[4]

The memo concluded that the lack of clear purpose made the NML ineffectual. Repeatedly, it noted that the NML's broad agenda made it "harmless" with "neither friends nor enemies," "a pallid organization that . . . has not aroused violent opposition or rabid support." In spite of political scientists' interest in further professionalizing the NML, the memo indicated that some critics felt that "all this scholarly, demagouged [sic] business isn't any good" and that the NML should engage in "propaganda work." Such voices harked back to a romanticized past when widespread corruption functioned as a clearer "evil" to combat, celebrating the "fire-eating" activism of Woodruff and other early leaders. The memo hinted that even though support of more controversial issues such as proportional representation might elicit opposition, "the program of the NML, as at present constituted, is so big and indefinite that it would be much better to stir up some antagonism. By doing so we would certainly rally more friends to our support."[5] In short, the memo suggested that in backing away from more active and "partisan" reform—but neglecting to become solely a research body—the NML had accomplished neither goal. The upshot was clear: it was not possible to combine "militant reform" and "scientific research."

Political scientists were also considering whether it was possible to combine research and reform as professional scholars. In the 1920s, early distinctions between "pure" and "applied" social science raised methodological and normative questions regarding the purpose of political science, particularly whether it was appropriate for scholars to be involved in reform movements. Before World War I, many political scientists' careers included activism and scholarship, and the members of the American Political Science Association (APSA) included not only professional academics but also lawyers, public officials, and reformers. After World War I, the lines between academic work and public engagement became more rigid with a rising interest in making political science more of a "genuine" science.[6] Critics of research bureaus and other forms of publicly engaged scholarship worried that pressure to produce results and provide practical advice prevented such work from being truly objective and scientific.[7] By midcentury, the line was firmer. In one example, political scientists Edward Banfield and James Wilson offered a critical account of a variety of reforms—the city manager plan, home rule, nonpartisan elections, and small councils—as well as the proponents of these reforms, specifically naming the NML and characterizing reformers as holding a narrow "middle-class political ethos." They also faulted earlier scholars for neglecting to consider "the personal and class interest of reformers."[8] In such accounts, political scientists distanced themselves from self-interested reformers lacking in objectivity.

In something of an ironic parallel, the very professionals created by the alliance between the NML and political science distanced themselves from both. While public administration was first regarded as a subfield of political science, its practitioners soon developed a separate professional identity and organizations.[9] Similarly, as early as the 1920s, political scientists voiced concerns that most city managers seemed uninterested in the insights of their discipline.[10] By the 1930s, city managers openly celebrated their lack of academic training, instead highlighting the value of their "practical" experiences.[11]

There were also tensions among city managers and reformers, even leaders of the NML. On one level, the NML was the national leader in the promotion of city manager government. From 1924 to 1927, the NML sold over forty-seven thousand copies of *The Story of the City-Manager Plan*, its most popular book. In these years, the national secretary answered over twelve thousand written inquiries. Many of these letters requested information in the midst of charter campaigns, during which local reformers asked for advice. In some cases, the NML sent speakers and even assisted in composing charters and other laws.[12] Yet on another level, while many local reformers continued to view NML publications and leaders as worthy of consultation, some city managers did not. An account of Childs's reception at a convention of city managers suggests that managers did not regard reformers as peers. After Childs spoke in favor of municipal ownership, pleading with managers to focus less on saving money and more on the "great new enterprises of service" of tomorrow, the managers were "not convinced" and "expressed themselves so contemptuously of the 'theorist'" that other attendees rose to his defense. In the end, according to the account, "Mr. Childs was told directly that theorists were not welcome at the meetings of the [International City Managers'] Association."[13] In short, despite their shared support of the general concept of city manager government, political scientists, reformers in the NML, and city managers themselves increasingly questioned not only what they had in common but also the value of their respective contributions to urban politics.

Debates about the relationship between research and reform, however, were not over. They have resurfaced in recent years, alongside ongoing discussions about the structures of city government. A brief look at some of the descendants of the subjects of this book highlights questions that continue to be relevant today. How should reformers and social scientists collaborate? How should they interact with business leaders and politicians? And how can scholars engage in public matters without compromising their objectivity and professionalism?

Most bureaus of municipal research are no longer in existence, but their legacy remains in the form of think tanks.[14] These associations, descendants of bureaus dedicated to the application of social science research methods, are now influential on the local, state, and national levels. Think tanks currently maintain influential positions in national policy making, having experienced rapid growth in the latter half of the twentieth century. They are now the primary institutions that bring the governmental, academic, political, economic, and media spheres into contact with one another. Some view them as effective mechanisms for competition among various groups vying to shape public policy in a pluralist society; others view them as a controlling mechanism employed by political and corporate elites. Today, many question their ability to achieve their professed goals of neutrality and originality, suggesting that they are constrained by their institutional ties to donors, politicians, and media outlets.[15]

The Brookings Institution is directly descended from the New York Bureau of Municipal Research.[16] Today, it presents itself using many of the same terms as its bureau predecessors, portraying its staff as neutral policy experts above financial or political motivation. Its declared "mission is to conduct in-depth research that leads to new ideas for solving problems facing society at the local, national and global level." Its website emphasizes "Brookings's commitment to institutional independence," noting that "the Institution does not take positions on issues."[17] It is not clear, however, that Brookings has achieved this mission. In 2016, an investigative journalism piece in the *New York Times* argued that the Brookings Institution and other think tanks are heavily influenced by the agendas of corporate donors. It revealed that think thanks often discuss potential findings of their studies, favoring donors' interests, before they conduct their research. As an example, the article detailed a program of the Brookings Institution to promote urban revitalization and economic development that was funded by private companies involved in real estate and commercial development in the cities of Philadelphia, Detroit, and San Francisco.[18] These current concerns regarding funding echo those in the early history of the New York Bureau of Municipal Research, when some leaders (privately) raised concerns that John D. Rockefeller and other wealthy donors were influencing the organization's agenda.[19] How can research remain neutral and objective in the face of donor influence?

The engagement of social scientists in public affairs remains a concern among academic political scientists as well. For over a hundred years, political scientists have debated the diverse approaches to improving our understanding of politics, employing state-centered, pluralist, behavioral, rational choice, and institutional methodologies, to name only a few. Embedded in these methodological debates are larger concerns regarding the appropriate relation between scholarship and public engagement.[20] The preface to a book on urban political institutions opens with a careful caveat that the authors' intention is not to promote any particular form, warning of a tendency "to confuse scholarly research and academic findings with advocacy or preference on the part of the scholars."[21]

Yet calls for a more engaged political science have resurfaced in the twenty-first century. The presidential addresses of the APSA provide one window into larger trends in the discipline. This presidency was first held by Frank Goodnow and later by several others who were deeply involved in the work of the NML or urban reform more broadly: Albert Shaw, James Bryce, A. Lawrence Lowell, Leo Stanton Rowe, Charles Merriam, Charles Beard, and William Bennett Munro. Regardless of their many differences, they largely agreed that political scientists should be actively involved in public debates. In 2003, Robert Putnam used his presidential address to the APSA to call for a return to "a greater public presence" of political science. He maintained that such a presence was an essential component of their "professional responsibility . . . to engage with our fellow citizens in deliberation." Putnam espoused many of the same goals as his Progressive forebears, some of whom he deeply admired: "My hero is the midwestern progressive of a century ago, seeking to learn from the experience of nonacademic reformers." Returning to a debate now a century old, he rejected a "need to choose between scientific rigor and public relevance," noting that the founders of the profession sought to achieve both. He recognized that "the tension between advocacy and disinterested expertise could threaten our academic credibility." But he argued that this risk is worth taking.[22]

In recognizing this danger, he partly echoed the individuals in the NML who worried that it was not possible to combine "scientific rigor" and "militant reform," but his remarks differed in one essential way. He noted that these early political scientists often "espoused what now seems a naive notion that science would provide 'one right answer' to social and political issues." As this book has demonstrated, the search for "one right answer" to good city government, and the silences required to agree on that answer, had serious consequences that are still with us today. Putnam called for a different vision for the future of the discipline, one that allows for contention and disagreement rather than consensus and compromise. He stated, "Since experts almost always differ, a more engaged discipline would be—should be—a more contentious discipline."[23]

The NML has experienced similar changes. Not wanting to be seen as a narrow organization focused only on municipalities rather than on democracy, civil society, and governance more broadly, the NML is now the National Civic League (NCL).[24] While the NCL today does not have the prominence of the NML one hundred years ago, a recent academic study of its work describes it as a "national forum and clearinghouse for discourse about cities and communities" staffed by "scholar-activists" working "to translate abstract theories of democracy into specific and workable democratic processes in cities."[25] As the study's findings suggest, while the NCL has been adapted to conform to twenty-first-century norms, many of the early Progressive ideals remain. Its website presents the NCL as a "nonpartisan, nonprofit organization" that offers "civic engagement expertise" and has been "a clearinghouse for information and other resources in the field of civic affairs since 1912." A focus on fostering public engagement continues, and it is now much more overtly inclusive. The NCL's mission is "to advance civic engagement to create equitable, thriving communities . . . by inspiring, supporting and recognizing inclusive approaches to community decision-making."[26] The goal of bringing diverse people together to discuss matters of common concern remains, with a different sense of the challenges involved. In one clear example, while the NML was once silent on racial matters, the NCL is now working with the W. K. Kellogg Foundation's initiative on Truth, Racial Healing, and Transformation. The initiative is intended to be "a comprehensive, national and community-based process to plan for, and bring about transformational and sustainable change, and to address the historic and contemporary effects of racism."[27]

The NCL is also still well known for the model city charters that it continues to revise and republish. After endorsing only the city manager plan for many years, in 1941 the NML opted to present two options: a mayor-council form and a council-manager form.[28] Yet the most recent iteration in some ways seems to be a return to the past: "The eighth edition of the

Model City Charter strongly endorses the council-manager structure of municipal government that was first proposed in 1915." It also continues to recommend proportional representation. Yet despite this asserted connection to the original form, the latest model now offers several optional modifications, including an alternative of having both an elected mayor and an appointed city manager.[29]

This framework reflects a recent blending of elements of charters once thought of as distinct. Today, many political scientists discuss "forms" (i.e., mayor-council v. council-manager) as separate from "a variety of other structural features," including, for example, nonpartisan elections.[30] It is not uncommon for mayor-council cities to implement civil service systems and allow elected mayors to appoint "chief administrative officers" who function much as managers. Similarly, council-manager cities sometimes have ward-based, partisan elections, and mayor-council cities sometimes have at-large, nonpartisan elections. These variations have led one recent study to conclude that "categorizing cities as mayor-council or council-manager had little real capacity to explain how cities were actually democratically structured, organized, and managed" and that adapted, hybrid cities are actually now more common.[31]

Yet other scholars reject this claim, arguing that fundamental differences between council-manager and mayor-council government remain.[32] Moreover, a recent study of charter revision in larger cities demonstrates that regardless of academic opinions, supporters and opponents of the two forms of government continue to characterize them as quite different, using many of the same arguments of their Progressive forebears. Are mayors strong leaders, or are they too easily corruptible and lacking in administrative skills? Do managers objectively act for the long-term good of entire communities, or are they too powerful and narrowly focused on efficiency? (Notably, this study finds that business leaders now largely prefer mayor-council forms rather than manager forms.)[33] The debates, it seems, are ongoing.

The fact that these debates endure suggests one of the most consequential institutional legacies of the urban reform movement: the inclusion of charter revision as a component of local self-government. The fact that Americans can and do continue to revise local charters is a direct and consequential legacy of the home rule movement. The concept of home rule remains contested today, with ongoing discussions regarding its appropriate scope and meaning. Some legal scholars argue that allowing municipalities too much autonomy has contributed to suburban sprawl, geographical inequalities, and a lack of metropolitan coordination and integration.[34] Yet others, while conceding the real challenges posed by suburban sprawl in metropolitan areas, counter that home rule is essential to American democracy in the twenty-first century, with its potential to promote popular participation in self-government, experimentation and innovation in public policy, and connections among local communities. The right to determine structures of city government is key to this kind of vision.[35]

In the early twenty-first century, roughly seventy-five cities hold referenda to change their forms of government each year, typically switching from council-manager to mayor-council or vice versa.[36] Toledo and Oakland recently returned to mayor-council government, after fifty-six and sixty-eight years of manager government, respectively.[37] Worcester, having rejected commission government in the 1910s, adopted a manager form of government in 1947, and though it has revised its charter several times since, it has opted to retain the manager form.[38] Norfolk has also elected to retain a manager form of government despite campaigns for a strong mayor charter, as has Fort Worth, though Fort Worth has returned to district elections.[39]

While Americans today might take this ability to revise city charters for granted, this right is not common. In most other countries, the forms of local government are fixed, imposed from above by federal laws.[40] In the context of continuing debates about the benefits and drawbacks of the many reforms that are the subject of this book, urban political actors today often attempt to create novel combinations to maximize the benefits while minimizing the costs. Like many urban reformers, they want cities that are both administratively efficient and responsive to popular demands. Interest in charter reform has experienced an ebb and flow throughout the twentieth century, but it continues today.[41] Renewed efforts at charter reform and robust scholarly exchanges about structures of city government demonstrate that, despite many differences, all agree that institutions matter. Electoral structures and the powers of appointed and electoral officials shape how people participate in city politics, the outcomes of elections, the behavior of local officials, and the creation and implementation of public policy.[42]

These, then, are perhaps the most important legacies: the tradition of engaging in public discussions about forms of city government, the legal right to make changes, and a vision of government that is malleable, able to be adjusted to address the problems not only of the twentieth century but also of the twenty-first and beyond. Many of the urban reformers and political scientists in this book, despite their differences of opinion, sincerely believed that the fate of American democracy resided in our cities. This rhetoric seems idealistic and even inflated today. Yet despite the increased importance of state, national, and international concerns, local government continues to be the most trusted branch of American government and the largest presence in our everyday lives. Urbanization is again on the rise, but so is political polarization, marked by an inability to engage in civil discourse and reach common ground. As Americans mobilize to address the problems of today, how will we form new organizations and new coalitions? How will we balance the need for compromise and consensus with the need for conviction?

Acknowledgments

I would not have been able to complete this project without the assistance of many individuals and institutions, and I am happy to have the opportunity to offer my sincere appreciation for all the help they have provided over many years.

For their assistance with my research, I thank the librarians, archivists, and additional staff members at the public libraries in Boston, Cambridge, Lincoln, and Worcester, Massachusetts; Norfolk, Virginia (and Norfolk City Hall); Oakland, California; and Toledo-Lucas County, Ohio; as well as at the archives and libraries of Harvard University (Harvard University Archives, Kennedy School Library, Lamont Library, Law School Library, and Widener Library), Johns Hopkins University (Milton S. Eisenhower Library), the University of Colorado Denver (Auraria Library), and the University of California, Berkeley (Bancroft Library).

For their generous funding of my research, I thank the Center for American Political Studies, Charles Warren Center for Studies in American History, and Fuerbringer Summer Faculty Grant Program, all at Harvard University.

For many years of stimulating conversations that shaped my thinking about the purpose of academia and the craft of writing, I thank all of my wonderful colleagues and students at the Princeton Writing Program, the Harvard College Writing Program, the Committee on Degrees in Social

Studies at Harvard College, the Master of Liberal Arts Program at the Harvard Extension School, and Project Pericles.

For the opportunity to share portions of this book as a work in progress and receive thoughtful feedback, I thank the organizers, panelists, and commentators of the Annual Meeting of the American Historical Association, the Annual Meeting of the Social Science History Association, the Biennial Conference of the Urban History Association, and the Policy History Conference, especially Amy Bridges, Christy Ford Chapin, Judge Glock, Joanna Grisinger, Patricia Hampson, Maribel Morey, Joel Rast, John Recchiuti, Kimberly Sims, Judith Spraul-Schmidt, Susan Sterett, Jessica Trounstine, Stephen Turner, Michael Willrich, and anyone I may have forgotten.

For their assistance with the publication process, I thank Bridget-Flannery McCoy, Stephen Wesley, Christian Winting, and the anonymous reviewers at Columbia University Press.

For their generosity in reading and commenting on portions of the final manuscript, I thank Caroline Light and Julie Reuben.

For their hard work and dedication to teaching, I thank all my teachers at the Lexington Public Schools, Swarthmore College, Trinity College Dublin, University College Cork, and Harvard University, especially Robert Bannister, Bruce Dorsey, Mary Keenan, Marjorie Murphy, Carol Nackenoff, Laurel Ulrich, and Rick Valelly.

For the most important teachers of all, I want to express my deep gratitude to the three individuals who have been with me from the very start of this project many years ago. Lizabeth Cohen, Jim Kloppenberg, and Theda Skocpol have provided unwavering support and mentorship. They are all inspiring teachers, colleagues, and scholars.

And last but not least, I want to thank my family for their love and support: my incredible extended family; my mother, Karen Liazos; my sister, Melissa Liazos; my husband, Tony Buendia, for his invaluable assistance with the statistical analysis in the appendices; my father, Alex Liazos, for his generous editing of the manuscript; and my children, Aleco, Georgia, and Marcelo, to whom this book is dedicated.

Appendix 1

Results of Simple Logistic Regressions with One
Nominal Variable (Forms of Government, 1934)
and Multiple Predictor Variables for Simple
Correlations

TABLE A1.1 Logistic Regression Analysis of Mayor-Council (nominal
variable)

Independent variable	Estimate	Standard error	Z value	Pr(>|z|)
1930 % white	1.509	1.233	1.224	0.221
1930 % immigrant	4.646	1.513	3.071	0.002**
1930 population/size	1.746	8.655	2.017	0.044*

Sources: Data for all appendices from George Benson and Mary Benson, "Legal Classification of Cities by States"; and "Directory and Governmental Data for the 960 Cities of Over 10,000 Population," in *The Municipal Yearbook, 1935,* ed. Clarence Ridely and Orin Nolting (Chicago: ICMA, 1935), 136–63, 164–87; "Form of Government in the 310 Cities Over 30,000 in Population," in *The Municipal Yearbook, 1934,* ed. Clarence Ridely and Orin Nolting (Chicago: ICMA, 1934), 107–13; Bureau of the Census, "Table 43: Per Cent Distribution by Color and Nativity, for Cities of 100,00 or More: 1930" and "Table 48: Sex, Color, and Nativity, for Cities 25,000 to 100,000," in *Abstract of the Fifteenth Census of the United States* (Washington, D.C.: Government Printing Office, 1933), 101–2, 108–12; and Bureau of the Census, "Table 12: Population of Cities and Other Urban Places Having, in 1930, 25,000 Inhabitants or More: 1900–1930," *Fifteenth Census of the United States: 1930,* vol. 1, *Population* (Washington, D.C.: Government Printing Office, 1931), 22–29.

Note: Significance codes: 0'***'; 0.001'**'; 0.01'*'; 0.05'.'; 0.1' '; 1.

TABLE A1.2 Logistic Regression Analysis of Commission

Independent variable	Estimate	Standard error	Z value	Pr(>|z|)
1930 % white	−1.650	1.195	−1.381	0.167
1930 % immigrant	−5.820	1.643	−0.354	0.723
1930 population/size	−9.993	8.526	−1.172	0.241

Note: Significance codes: 0'***'; 0.001'**'; 0.01'*'; 0.05'.'; 0.1' '; 1.

TABLE A1.3 Logistic Regression Analysis of Manager

Independent variable	Estimate	Standard error	Z value	Pr(>|z|)
1930 % white	3.872	1.231	0.3144	0.753
1930 % immigrant	−7.877	2.043	−3.856	0.00012***
1930 population/size	−1.422	1.261	−1.127	0.260

Note: Significance codes: 0'***'; 0.001'**'; 0.01'*'; 0.05'.'; 0.1' '; 1.

TABLE A1.4 Logistic Regression Analysis of Partisan Elections

Independent variable	Estimate	Standard error	Z value	Pr(>|z|)
1930 % white	1.599	1.210	1.321	0.186
1930 % immigrant	3.424	1.452	0.236	0.813
1930 population/size	3.353	2.468	0.136	0.891

Note: Significance codes: 0'***'; 0.001'**'; 0.01'*'; 0.05'.'; 0.1' '; 1.

TABLE A1.5 Logistic Regression Analysis of Nonpartisan Elections

Independent variable	Estimate	Standard error	Z value	Pr(>|z|)
1930 % white	−7.213	1.173	−0.615	0.539
1930 % immigrant	−1.374	1.448	−0.949	0.342
1930 population/size	2.341	2.475	0.095	0.925

Note: Significance codes: 0'***'; 0.001'**'; 0.01'*'; 0.05'.'; 0.1' '; 1.

TABLE A1.6 Logistic Regression Analysis of Ward Elections

Independent variable	Estimate	Standard error	Z value	Pr(>|z|)
1930 % white	5.134	1.475	0.348	0.728
1930 % immigrant	3.408	1.664	2.048	0.041*
1930 population/size	1.307	2.539	0.515	0.607

Note: Significance codes: 0'***'; 0.001'**'; 0.01'*'; 0.05'.'; 0.1' '; 1.

TABLE A1.7 Logistic Regression Analysis of At-Large Elections

Independent variable	Estimate	Standard error	Z value	Pr(>|z|)
1930 % white	−8.521	1.204	0.708	0.479
1930 % immigrant	−4.054	1.482	−2.736	0.006**
1930 population/size	−6.181	5.205	−1.188	0.235

Note: Significance codes: 0'***'; 0.001'**'; 0.01'*'; 0.05'.'; 0.1' '; 1.

TABLE A1.8 Logistic Regression Analysis of Combination of Ward and At-Large Elections

Independent variable	Estimate	Standard error	Z value	Pr(>|z|)
1930 % white	2.739	1.736	1.578	0.115
1930 % immigrant	1.140	1.715	0.822	0.411
1930 population/size	2.006	2.572	0.780	0.435

Note: Significance codes: 0'***'; 0.001'**'; 0.01'*'; 0.05'.'; 0.1' '; 1.

Appendix 2

Results of Simple Logistic Regressions with One Nominal Variable (Municipal Ownership, 1935) and Multiple Predictor Variables

TABLE A2.1 Logistic Regression of Abattoirs

Independent variable	Estimate	Standard error	Z value	Pr(>|z|)
1935 part. local control	NA	NA	NA	NA
1935 local control	−6.979	6.634	−1.052	0.293
1935 state control	2.126	5.886	0.361	0.718
1930 % white	−4.894	2.219	−2.206	0.027*
1930 % immigrant	1.541	3.539	0.436	0.663
1930 population/size	−4.074	1.142	−0.357	0.721
1934 mayor-council	1.299	1.834	0.007	0.994
1934 commission	1.354	1.834	0.007	0.994
1934 manager	1.373	1.834	0.007	0.994
1934 partisan	1.301	1.704	0.008	0.994
1934 nonpartisan	1.297	1.704	0.008	0.994
1934 wards	1.556	2.504	0.006	0.995
1934 at large	1.463	2.504	0.006	0.995
1934 wards/at large	1.526	2.504	0.006	0.995

Note: Significance codes: 0'***'; 0.001'**'; 0.01'*'; 0.05'.'; 0.1' '; 1.

TABLE A2.2 Logistic Regression of Airplane Landing Fields

Independent variable	Estimate	Standard error	Z value	Pr(>|z|)
1935 part. local control	NA	NA	NA	NA
1935 local control	1.248	3.598	3.469	0.001***
1935 state control	7.083	4.072	1.739	0.082
1930 % white	−1.248	1.388	−0.899	0.369
1930 % immigrant	−6.801	2.034	−3.344	0.001***
1930 population/size	8.343	1.894	4.405	1e-05***
1934 mayor-council	1.501	1.807	0.008	0.993
1934 commission	1.478	1.807	0.008	0.993
1934 manager	1.520	1.807	0.008	0.993
1934 partisan	1.313	1.531	0.009	0.993
1934 nonpartisan	1.332	1.531	0.009	0.993
1934 wards	1.933	1.931	0.010	0.992
1934 at large	1.960	1.931	0.010	0.992
1934 wards/at large	1.927	1.931	0.010	0.992

Note: Significance codes: 0'***'; 0.001'**'; 0.01'*'; 0.05'.'; 0.1' '; 1.

TABLE A2.3 Logistic Regression of Electric Distribution

Independent variable	Estimate	Standard error	Z value	Pr(>|z|)
1935 part. local control	NA	NA	NA	NA
1935 local control	7.676	1.300	5.907	0.555
1935 state control	1.024	1.385	7.393	0.460
1930 % white	−1.539	4.826	−3.189	0.975
1930 % immigrant	−7.620	8.110	−9.395	0.347
1930 population/size	2.825	9.228	3.061	0.760
1934 mayor-council	1.387	1.077	1.288	0.999
1934 commission	−1.111	1.091	−1.018	0.999
1934 manager	1.496	1.077	1.389	0.999
1934 partisan	−1.824	1.607	−1.135	0.999
1934 nonpartisan	−3.480	1.607	−2.165	0.999
1934 wards	1.828	1.974	9.261	0.999
1934 at large	1.560	1.974	7.901	0.999
1934 wards/at large	1.782	1.974	9.026	0.999

Note: Significance codes: 0'***'; 0.001'**'; 0.01'*'; 0.05'.'; 0.1' '; 1.

TABLE A2.4 Logistic Regression of Electric Plants

Independent variable	Estimate	Standard error	Z value	Pr(>|z|)
1935 part. local control	NA	NA	NA	NA
1935 local control	9.053	4.531	0.200	0.842
1935 state control	6.978	5.650	0.124	0.902
1930 % white	4.017	2.399	1.674	0.094
1930 % immigrant	−3.206	2.491	−1.287	0.198
1930 population/size	2.177	3.211	0.678	0.498
1934 mayor-council	2.084	1.707	0.122	0.903
1934 commission	−1.499	1.621	−0.092	0.926
1934 manager	−2.596	1.687	−0.154	0.878
1934 partisan	−2.121	1.749	−1.213	0.225
1934 nonpartisan	−1.474	1.686	−0.874	0.382
1934 wards	1.337	1.018	0.013	0.990
1934 at large	1.314	1.018	0.013	0.990
1934 wards/at large	1.303	1.018	0.013	0.990

Note: Significance codes: 0'***'; 0.001'**'; 0.01'*'; 0.05'.'; 0.1' '; 1.

TABLE A2.5 Logistic Regression of Gas Distribution

Independent variable	Estimate	Standard error	Z value	Pr(>|z|)
1935 part. local control	6.057	5.437	1.114	0.991
1935 local control	6.057	5.437	1.114	0.991
1935 state control	6.057	5.437	1.114	0.991
1930 % white	6.533	1.036	6.308	0.528
1930 % immigrant	−4.452	4.313	−1.032	0.302
1930 population/size	−4.585	4.086	−1.122	0.910
1934 mayor-council	−1.659	4.250	−3.902	1.000
1934 commission	−1.712	4.267	−4.011	1.000
1934 manager	2.562	4.250	6.029	1.000
1934 partisan	−2.602	4.240	−6.136	1.000
1934 nonpartisan	−7.371	4.235	−1.740	1.000
1934 wards	−4.745	2.554	−1.858	1.000
1934 at large	−2.985	2.541	−1.175	1.000
1934 wards/at large	−4.498	2.553	−1.762	1.000

Note: Significance codes: 0'***'; 0.001'**'; 0.01'*'; 0.05'.'; 0.1' '; 1.

TABLE A2.6 Logistic Regression of Gas Plants

Independent variable	Estimate	Standard error	Z value	Pr(>|z|)
1935 part. local control	NA	NA	NA	NA
1935 local control	1.044	9.050	1.154	0.249
1935 state control	3.852	1.086	0.355	0.723
1930 % white	−3.293	3.470	−0.949	0.343
1930 % immigrant	8.161	5.311	0.154	0.878
1930 population/size	3.212	3.497	0.919	0.358
1934 mayor-council	1.198	3.014	0.004	0.997
1934 commission	1.369	3.014	0.005	0.996
1934 manager	1.260	3.014	0.004	0.997
1934 partisan	1.265	2.841	0.004	0.996
1934 nonpartisan	1.307	2.841	0.005	0.996
1934 wards	1.627	4.254	0.004	0.997
1934 at large	1.500	4.254	0.004	0.997
1934 wards/at large	1.697	4.254	0.004	0.997

Note: Significance codes: 0'***'; 0.001'**'; 0.01'*'; 0.05'.'; 0.1' '; 1.

TABLE A2.7 Logistic Regression of Port Facilities

Independent variable	Estimate	Standard error	Z value	Pr(>|z|)
1935 part. local control	NA	NA	NA	NA
1935 local control	1.199	4.761	2.519	0.011*
1935 state control	6.667	5.231	1.275	0.202
1930 % white	−5.147	1.681	3.061	0.002**
1930 % immigrant	−5.076	2.655	−0.191	0.848
1930 population/size	1.500	5.799	2.587	0.00968**
1934 mayor-council	1.267	1.845	0.007	0.994
1934 commission	1.314	1.845	0.007	0.994
1934 manager	1.359	1.845	0.007	0.994
1934 partisan	1.276	1.666	0.008	0.994
1934 nonpartisan	1.239	1.666	0.007	0.994
1934 wards	1.633	2.322	0.007	0.994
1934 at large	1.567	2.322	0.007	0.994
1934 wards/at large	1.647	2.322	0.007	0.994

Note: Significance codes: 0'***'; 0.001'**'; 0.01'*'; 0.05'.'; 0.1' '; 1.

TABLE A2.8 **Logistic Regression of Public Markets**

Independent variable	Estimate	Standard error	Z value	Pr(>|z|)
1935 part. local control	NA	NA	NA	NA
1935 local control	2.417	3.597	0.672	0.502
1935 state control	−4.197	4.340	0.967	0.334
1930 % white	−2.636	1.427	−1.847	0.065
1930 % immigrant	−4.734	2.195	−2.157	0.031*
1930 population/size	1.072	5.241	2.045	0.041*
1934 mayor-council	1.448	1.492	0.010	0.992
1934 commission	1.391	1.492	0.009	0.993
1934 manager	1.476	1.492	0.010	0.992
1934 partisan	3.315	1.976	0.168	0.987
1934 nonpartisan	3.310	1.976	0.168	0.987
1934 wards	−1.631	1.397	−0.012	0.991
1934 at large	−1.660	1.397	−0.012	0.991
1934 wards/at large	−1.674	1.397	−0.012	0.990

Note: Significance codes: 0 '***'; 0.001 '**'; 0.01 '*'; 0.05 '.'; 0.1 ' '; 1.

TABLE A2.9 **Logistic Regression of Street Railways**

Independent variable	Estimate	Standard error	Z value	Pr(>|z|)
1935 part. local control	NA	NA	NA	NA
1935 local control	1.999	1.428	1.400	0.989
1935 state control	1.975	1.428	1.383	0.989
1930 % white	−1.599	3.483	−4.591	0.646
1930 % immigrant	−1.059	5.556	−1.907	0.849
1930 population/size	2.436	9.686	2.515	0.012*
1934 mayor-council	−1.660	1.254	−1.324	1.000
1934 commission	−2.086	1.254	−1.663	1.000
1934 manager	−2.146	1.254	−1.711	1.000
1934 partisan	−1.863	1.422	−1.310	1.000
1934 nonpartisan	−6.212	1.422	−4.367	1.000
1934 wards	1.831	1.604	1.142	0.999
1934 at large	1.956	1.604	1.220	0.999
1934 wards/at large	1.958	1.604	1.221	0.999

Note: Significance codes: 0 '***'; 0.001 '**'; 0.01 '*'; 0.05 '.'; 0.1 ' '; 1.

TABLE A2.10 Logistic Regression of Waterworks

Independent variable	Estimate	Standard error	Z value	Pr(>|z|)
1935 part. local control	NA	NA	NA	NA
1935 local control	7.767	3.991	1.946	0.052
1935 state control	−5.317	3.952	−1.345	0.179
1930 % white	−1.986	1.605	−1.238	0.216
1930 % immigrant	−1.473	1.874	−0.786	0.432
1930 population/size	3.001	1.791	1.675	0.094
1934 mayor-council	−1.492	1.648	−0.905	0.365
1934 commission	−1.080	1.614	−0.669	0.503
1934 manager	−1.585	1.657	−0.956	0.339
1934 partisan	8.866	1.508	0.588	0.557
1934 nonpartisan	1.448	1.466	0.988	0.323
1934 wards	3.015	1.837	1.641	0.101
1934 at large	1.994	1.773	1.125	0.260
1934 wards/at large	2.851	1.828	1.560	0.119

Publication Abbreviations

Fort Worth Press (FWP)
Fort Worth Record (FWR)
Fort Worth Star-Telegram (FWST)
Fort Worth Telegram (FWT)
Labor World (LW) (California)
Ledger Dispatch (LD) (Virginia)
New York Times (NYT)
Norfolk-Ledger Dispatch (NLD)
Norfolk Public Ledger (NPL)
Oakland Enquirer (OE)
Oakland Tribune (OT)
Toledo News Bee (TNB)
Toledo Union Leader (TUL)
Virginian Pilot (VP)
Virginian-Pilot and the Norfolk Landmark (VPNL)
Worcester Evening Gazette (WEG)
Worcester Magazine (WM)
Worcester Telegram (WT)

Notes

Introduction

1. U.S. Department of Justice, Civil Rights Division, *Investigation of the Ferguson Police Department* (U.S. Department of Justice, Civil Rights Division, March 4, 2015), https://www.justice.gov/sites/default/files/opa/press-releases/attachments /2015/03/04/ferguson_police_department_report.pdf.
2. John Eligon, "Ferguson Police Chief, Thomas Jackson, Steps Down," *New York Times*, March 11, 2015, https://www.nytimes.com/2015/03/12/us/ferguson-police -chief-thomas-jackson-steps-down-michael-brown.html?mcubz=0&_r=0; John Eligon, "Ferguson City Manager Cited in Justice Department Report Resigns," *New York Times*, March 10, 2015, https://www.nytimes.com/2015/03/11/us /ferguson-city-manager-resigns.html?mcubz=0.
3. "Norfolk City Government Is Under Searching Probe," *Virginian-Pilot and the Norfolk Landmark*, September 12, 1915, 20.
4. "City Charter Needs Radical Changes, Says Bureau Report," *Virginian-Pilot and the Norfolk Landmark*, December 22, 1915, 1, 8.
5. "City Charter Needs Radical Changes," 1, 8.
6. "Asks Justice for the Negro," *New Journal and Guide* (Norfolk, Va.), May 12, 1917, 1; "Subjected to False Arrest," *New Journal and Guide*, September 22, 1917, 1; "Norfolk Domestics Ask Better Wages," *New Journal and Guide*, October 6, 1917, 1.
7. U.S. Department of Justice, Civil Rights Division, *Investigation of the Ferguson Police Department*.
8. New York Bureau of Municipal Research, *Report on a Survey of City Government* (New York: Bureau of Municipal Research, 1915), 1:58.
9. U.S. Department of Justice, Civil Rights Division, *Investigation of the Ferguson Police Department*.

10. Ellis Paxson Oberholtzer, *The Referendum in American, Together with Some Chapters on the Initiative and Recall* (New York: Charles Scribner's, 1911), v–vi; George C. S. Benson and Mary Benson, "Legal Classification of Cities by States," in *The Municipal Yearbook* (Chicago: ICMA, 1935), 136–63.

11. John Fairlie, "America Municipal Councils," *Political Science Quarterly* 19, no. 2 (June 1904): 237–38.

12. "Form of Government in the 310 Cities Over 30,000 in Population," in *The Municipal Yearbook*, ed. Clarence Ridley and Orin Nolting (Chicago: ICMA, 1934), 107–13.

13. "Table 2: Cumulative Distribution of U.S. Municipalities," in *The Municipal Yearbook, 2014* (Washington, D.C.: ICMA Press, 2014); Evelina Moulder, "Municipal Form of Government: Trends in Structure, Responsibility, and Composition," in *The Municipal Yearbook, 2008* (Washington, D.C.: ICMA Press, 2008), 27–33; National League of Cities, "Municipal Elections," accessed April 5, 2019, http://www.nlc.org/municipal-elections; National League of Cities, "Partisan v. Nonpartisan Elections," accessed April 5, 2019, http://www.nlc.org/partisan-vs-nonpartisan-elections.

14. Frank Goodnow, "Political Parties and City Government Under the Proposed Municipal Program," Horace Deming, "Public Opinion and City Government Under the Proposed Municipal Program," and Delos Wilcox, "An Examination of the Proposed Municipal Program," in *A Municipal Program: Report of a Committee of the National Municipal League, Adopted by the League, November 17, 1899* (New York: Macmillan, 1900), 129–45, 156, 239, https://books.google.com/books?id=AWuijRhrVgQAC.

15. Richard Childs, "The Short Ballot Principle in the Model Charter," in *A New Municipal Program*, ed. Clinton Rogers Woodruff (New York: D. Appleton, 1919), 109–18, quote on 118.

16. Gerald Wright, "Charles Adrian and the Study of Nonpartisan Elections," *Political Research Quarterly* 61, no. 1 (March 2008): 13–16; Zoltan Hajnal and Jessica Trounstine, "When Turnout Matters: The Consequences of Uneven Turnout in City Politics," *Journal of Politics* 67, no. 2 (May 2005): 515–35; Zoltan Hajnal and Paul Lewis, "Municipal Institutions and Voter Turnout in Local Elections," *Urban Affairs Review* 38, no. 5 (May 2003): 645–68.

17. Mike Maciag, "Voter Turnout Plummeting in Local Elections," *Governing*, October 2014, http://www.governing.com/topics/politics/gov-voter-turnout-municipal-elections.html.

18. "Administration," City of Ferguson, accessed April 8, 2019, http://www.fergusoncity.com/58/Administration; Brian Schaffner, Wouter Van Erve, and Ray LaRaja, "How Ferguson Exposes Racial Bias in Local Elections," *Washington Post*, August 15, 2014, http://www.washingtonpost.com/blogs/monkey-cage/wp/2014/08/15/how-ferguson-exposes-the-racial-bias-in-local-elections/; Katie Sanders, "Ferguson, Mo., Has 50 White Police Officers and Three Black Officers, NBS's Mitchell Claims," *Tampa Bay Times Pundit Fact*, August 17, 2014, http://www

.politifact.com/punditfact/statements/2014/aug/17/andrea-mitchell/ferguson
-police-department-has-50-white-officers-t/.

19. Kathryn Doherty and Clarence Stone, "Local Practice in Transition: From Government to Governance," in *Dilemmas of Scale in America's Federal Democracy*, ed. Martha Derthick (New York: Cambridge University Press, 1999), 156.

20. Though my subjects used the word *municipal* to describe most topics related to city government (i.e., "municipal leagues," "municipal ownership," "municipal political science"), I also use the word *urban* (i.e., "urban reform," "urban politics," and "urban residents") when not quoting directly. I do so because the word *urban* resonates more with modern audiences interested in cities.

21. Samuel Hays, "The Politics of Reform in Municipal Government in the Progressive Era," *Pacific Northwest Quarterly* 55, no. 4 (October 1964): 157–69; James Weinstein, "Organized Business and the City Commission and Manager Movements," *Journal of Southern History* 28, no. 2 (May 1962): 166–82. Weinstein's article was later republished as "The Small Businessman as Big Businessman: The City Commission and Manager Movements," *The Corporate Ideal and the Liberal State* (Boston: Beacon, 1968), 92–116.

22. Perhaps the clearest example of their ongoing influence is James Connolly, *An Elusive Unity: Urban Democracy and Machine Politics in Industrializing America* (Ithaca, N.Y.: Cornell University Press, 2010). Connolly (192), citing Hays and Weinstein, writes,

Historians have not generally been inclined to acknowledge democratic impulses among municipal reformers. The good-government movement has instead served as the example par excellence of elitist Progressive reform. Scholars arrived at such a verdict with good reason. It is easy to match the names of men heading various reform groups with the listings of the Chamber of Commerce or the Social Register, and many of the structural reforms they pushed led to declining voter participation and less office holding among the lower classes.

Other major historical works that cite these two seminal texts include Glenda Gilmore, *Gender and Jim Crow: Women and the Politics of White Supremacy in North Carolina, 1896–1920* (Chapel Hill: University of North Carolina Press, 2013); Alex Keyssar, *The Right to Vote: The Contested History of Democracy in the United States* (New York: Basic Books, 2009); and David Roediger, *Working Toward Whiteness: How America's Immigrants Became White: The Strange Journey from Ellis Island to the Suburbs* (New York: Basic Books, 2006).

Major works in political science, political theory, and public administration that cite Hays and Weinstein include Guy Adams and Danny Balfour, *Unmasking Administrative Evil* (New York: M. E. Sharpe, 2014); Frank Fisher, *Democracy and Expertise: Reorienting Policy Inquiry* (New York: Oxford, 2009); and Joan Roelofs, *Foundations and Public Policy: The Mask of Pluralism* (Albany: State University of New York Press, 2003).

23. For example, see Todd Donovan, Christopher Mooney, and Daniel Smith, *State and Local Politics: Institutions and Reform, The Essentials* (Boston: Wadsworth, 2012), 270;

and Dennis Judd and Todd Swanstorm, *City Politics: The Political Economy of Urban America* (New York: Pearson Education, 2006), 74–75.

24. Amy Bridges, *Morning Glories: Municipal Reform in the Southwest* (Princeton, N.J.: Princeton University Press, 1997), 18–19, 30, 54–69. For examples of working-class or minority support of charter revision, see James Connolly, *The Triumph of Ethnic Progressivism: Urban Political Culture in Boston, 1900–1925* (Cambridge, Mass.: Harvard University Press, 1998), 77–104; Robert Burnham, "Reform, Politics, and Race in Cincinnati and the City Charter Committee, 1924–1959," *Journal of Urban History* 23, no. 2 (January 1997): 131–63; and Seth Scheiner, "Commission Government in the Progressive Era: The New Brunswick, New Jersey, Example," *Journal of Urban History* 12, no. 2 (February 1986): 157–79.

25. Amy Bridges and Richard Kronick, "Writing the Rules to Win the Game: The Middle-Class Regimes of Municipal Reformers," *Urban Affairs Review* 34, no. 5 (May 1999): 691–706. Bridges and Kronick argue that charter reforms were more successful in western and southern states where suffrage restrictions had been enacted, but they rely on data in *presidential* elections to posit a connection between low turnout and the adoption of reform charters (700). They acknowledge that they "do not provide evidence of the composition of municipal electorates in the Progressive Era" (693). Large-scale data sets on turnout in local elections in this period do not seem to exist, but one small set suggests that we cannot assume that presidential turnout paralleled local turnout. Banfield and Wilson compare turnout in mayoral and presidential elections from 1948 to 1952 in eighteen large cities, and there is no consistent relation between the two. Edward Banfield and James Wilson, *City Politics* (Cambridge, Mass.: Harvard University Press, 1963), 225. On the lack of aggregate data on local turnout, see Keely Wilczek, senior research and instruction librarian, Kennedy School of Government, email messages to the author, August 2017.

26. On the differences between political history and political science, see Julian Zelizer, "History and Political Science: Together Again?" and "What Political Science Can Learn from the New Political History," in *Governing America: The Revival of Political History* (Princeton, N.J.: Princeton University Press, 2012), 60–67, 90–103. On the influence of institutions in local politics, see Bridges, *Morning Glories*, 12–16; Richard Dilworth, ed., *The City in American Political Development* (New York: Routledge, 2009); and James Clingermayer and Richard Feiock, *Institutional Constraints and Policy Choice* (Albany: State University of New York Press, 2001).

27. David Nord, "The Politics of Agenda Setting in Late 19th Century Cities," *Journalism Quarterly* 58, no. 4 (1981): 565–74.

28. On the concept of a public sphere more generally, see Jürgen Habermas, *The Structural Transformation of the Public Sphere* (Cambridge, Mass.: MIT Press, 1991). On the concept of a "community of discourse" in urban life, see Thomas Bender, *Intellect and Public Life: Essays on the Social History of Academic Intellectuals in the United States* (Baltimore: Johns Hopkins University Press, 1993), 31–46.

29. See the tables in chapter 8 and the appendices.

30. For example, see Anirudh Ruhil, "Urban Armageddon or Politics as Usual? The Case of Municipal Civil Service Reform," *American Journal of Political Science* 47, no. 1 (January 2003): 159–70; David Knoke, "The Spread of Municipal Reform: Temporal, Spatial, and Social Dynamics," *American Journal of Sociology* 87, no. 6 (May 1982): 1314–39; Richard Bernard and Bradley Rice, "Political Environment and the Adoption of Progressive Municipal Reform," *Journal of Urban History* 1, no. 2 (February 1975): 149–75; and Raymond Wolfinger and John Osgood Field, "Political Ethos and the Structure of City Government," *American Political Science Review* 60, no. 2 (June 1966): 306–26.

31. See the tables in chapter 8.

32. A focus on cities of this size helps us to see beyond the story of urban reform told through the lens of only the largest cities, such as New York and Chicago, about which much has already been written. Moreover, it allows us to gain a fuller picture of the dynamics of charter revision, for reforms such as at-large elections and city manager plans were more likely to be adopted in medium-size and small cities.

33. Steven Blutza, "Oakland's Commission and Council-Manager Plans—Causes and Consequences: An Historical and Analytical Study" (PhD diss., University of California, Berkeley, 1978); *Charter, City of Worcester Massachusetts with Amendments to 1933* (n.p., n.d.); G. Curry, "Toledo's Fight for a City Manager," *National Municipal Review* 24 (April 1935): 202–5; chapter 7.

34. Wendy Hassett and Douglas Watson, *Civic Battles: When Cities Change Their Form of Government* (Highland Beach, Fla.: PrAcademics, 2007), iii, 20; James Svara and Douglas Watson, "Introduction: Framing Constitutional Contests in Large Cities," in *More than Mayor or Manager: Campaigns to Change Form of Government in America's Largest Cities*, ed. James Svara and Douglas Watson (Washington, D.C.: Georgetown University Press, 2010), 13.

    My approach is also informed by George and Bennett, who define a "case study approach" as "the detailed examination of an aspect of a historical episode to develop or test historical explanations that may be generalizable to other events." They note the importance of case selection in testing theories and argue that, despite potential dangers, selecting cases based on dependent variables "can serve the heuristic purpose of identifying the potential causal paths and variables leading to the dependent variable of interest." They describe the general value of the case study method in terms of "theory development," "testing hypotheses," and "fostering new hypotheses," particularly in terms of exploring "the hypothesized role of causal mechanisms in the context of individual cases" and "addressing causal complexity." They specifically note the value of the case method for historical institutionalists interested in "addressing qualitative variables, individual actors, decision-making processes, historical and social contexts, and path dependencies." In my research, controlling for population, I selected cities from different regions based on a dependent variable (whether they had adopted reform charters by the 1920s). I then set about exploring variables to investigate the complex causal mechanisms at play in decisions to adopt or reject proposed charters. Examining five case studies side by side enabled me to combine what George and Bennett call "within-case analyses" with "cross-case comparisons." Alexander George and Andrew Bennett, *Case Studies and Theory Development in the Social Sciences* (Cambridge, Mass.: MIT Press, 2005), 5, 7, 9, 19, 23.

35. For a study of outcomes, see Jessica Trounstine, *Political Monopolies in American Cities: The Rise and Fall of Bosses and Reformers* (Chicago: University of Chicago Press, 2008). Trounstine's detailed study provides strong evidence that reformers and machine politicians alike often acted in ways that ensured their own election and helped enact their policy agendas. She does not, however, consider either initial "motivations" or "unintended consequences" in her framework (32). In contrast, the difference between reformers' original intentions and the longer-term outcomes of their reforms is central to my analysis.

36. Kloppenberg writes, "I want to examine the theorists of social democracy and progressivism in part to disconnect their ideas from certain developments they could neither anticipate nor prevent.... Much of the criticism leveled against social democratic and progressive theorists, born of a coupling between the slick condescension accompanying hindsight and the easy imputation of unstated motives, reveals a failure of historical imagination masquerading as tough-minded savvy." James Kloppenberg, *Uncertain Victory: Social Democracy and Progressivism in European and American Thought, 1870-1920* (New York: Oxford University Press, 1986), 5.

37. Here, I follow John Buenker, who argues that a line of analysis that understands Progressivism as a movement marked by "shifting coalitions" rather than a monolithic or unified program had "the potential for reconciling most ... conflicting interpretations and of encompassing nearly all of the groups, values and programs that were plainly at work." John Buenker, untitled essay, in *Progressivism*, by John D. Buenker, John C. Burnham, and Robert M. Crunden (Cambridge, Mass.: Schenkman, 1977), 31.

38. Stephen Turner, "When Empathy Fails: Some Problematic 'Progressives' and Expertise" (paper presented at the American Historical Association Annual Meeting, New York, January 2015).

39. Rogers Smith, "The Progressive Seedbed: Claims of American Political Community in the Twentieth and Twenty-First Centuries," in *The Progressives' Century: Political Reform, Constitutional Government, and the Modern American State*, ed. Stephen Skowronek, Stephen Engel, and Bruce Ackerman (New Haven, Conn.: Yale University Press, 2016), 264–67.

40. John Leonard, ed., *Who's Who in Pennsylvania: A Biographical Dictionary of Contemporaries* (New York: L. R. Hamersly, 1908), 591–92; Leonard, ed., *Who's Who in Pennsylvania: A Biographical Dictionary of Contemporaries* (New York: L. R. Hamersly, 1904), 1:812–13; "Biographical Notices," *Municipal Affairs* 6, no. 2 (June 1902): 327. Some organizations include the Philadelphia Municipal League, Pennsylvania Ballot Reform Organization, American Institute of Civics, American Humane Union, Civil

Service Reform Association of Pennsylvania, Philadelphia Boys Club, American Park and Outdoor Art Association, Lake Mohonk International Arbitration Conference, American Young Men's Humane Union, American Friends of Russian Freedom, Italian Political Prisoners Aid Committee, and International Association for Labor Legislation.

41. Hays, "Politics of Reform," 160, 168.

42. Kevin Mattson, *Creating a Democratic Public: The Struggle for Urban Participatory Democracy During the Progressive Era* (University Park: Pennsylvania State University Press, 1998), 18.

43. Melvin Holli, *Reform in Detroit: Hazen S. Pingree and Urban Politics* (New York: Oxford University Press, 1969), xii–xiii, 161–70. Though most of Holli's book is about Detroit, he applies his distinction between social and structural reform more broadly in chapter 8. See also Martin Schiesl, *The Politics of Efficiency: Municipal Administration and Reform in America, 1880–1920* (Berkeley: University of California Press, 1977), 2–4.

44. Clinton Rogers Woodruff, "Municipal Progress in the United States, Recent," in *New Encyclopedia of Social Reform*, ed. William D. P. Bliss (New York: Funk and Wangalls, 1908), 795–800, quote on 799.

45. Clinton Rogers Woodruff, "Present Phases of the Municipal Situation," *National Municipal Review* 4, no. 1 (January 1915): 3.

46. Kenneth Fox, *Better City Government: Innovation in American Urban Politics, 1850–1937* (Philadelphia: Temple University Press, 1977), 100.

47. Ernest Griffith, *A History of American City Government: The Progressive Years and Their Aftermath, 1900–1920* (New York: Praeger, 1974), 173.

48. Gail Radford, *The Rise of the Public Authority: Statebuilding and Economic Development in Twentieth-Century America* (Chicago: University of Chicago Press, 2013), 72–88; Michael Willrich, *City of Courts* (New York: Cambridge University Press, 2003); Daniel Rodgers, *Atlantic Crossings: Social Politics in a Progressive Era* (Cambridge, Mass.: Belknap Press of Harvard University Press, 1998), 112–59.

49. David Nord, "The Victorian City and the Urban Newspaper," in *Making News: The Political Economy of Journalism in Britain from the Glorious Revolution to the Internet*, ed. Richard John and Jonathan Silberstein-Loeb (New York: Oxford University Press, 2015), 91–96.

50. For example, see Frederic Howe, *The City: The Hope of Democracy* (New York: Charles Scribner's, 1905), 158–76.

51. Paul Pierson, "Not Just What, but *When*: Timing and Sequence in Political Processes," *Studies in American Political Development* 14 (Spring 2000): 72–92.

52. H. George Frederickson, *The Adapted City: Institutional Dynamics and Structural Change* (New York: Routledge, 2003), 22–27; James Svara and Douglas Watson, "Introduction" and "Conclusion: Distinct Factors and Common Themes in Change of Form Referenda," in Svara and Watson, *More than Mayor or Manager*, 11–15, 304–16; Hassett and Watson, *Civic Battles*, ii, 4–7, 140–55.

53. For example, see Henry Bruère, "Efficiency in City Government," in *Efficiency in City Government*, ed. Clyde King (Philadelphia: American Academy of Political and Social Science, 1912), 1–22.

54. Kenneth Finegold, *Experts and Politicians: Reform Challenges to Machine Politics in New York, Cleveland, and Chicago* (Princeton, N.J.: Princeton University Press, 1995), 15, 24–25.

55. Camilla Stivers, *Bureau Men and Settlement Women: Constructing Public Administration in the Progressive Era* (Lawrence: University of Kansas Press, 2000); Maureen Flanagan, "Gender and Urban Political Reform: The City Club and the Woman's City Club of Chicago in the Progressive Era," *American Historical Review* 95, no. 4 (October 1990): 1032–50; Paula Baker, "The Domestication of Politics: Women and American Political Society, 1780–1920," *American Historical Review* 89, no. 3 (June 1984): 620–47.

56. Jane Addams, "Problems of Municipal Administration," *American Journal of Sociology* 10, no. 4 (January 1905): 428, 444; "Twentieth Annual Meeting of the National Municipal League," *National Municipal Review* 4, no. 1 (January 1915): 173.

57. For example, see Harold Stone, Don Price, and Kathryn Stone, *City Manager Government in the United States: A Review After Twenty-Five Years* (Chicago: Public Administration Service, 1940), 41; "Women Unite in Manager Campaign," *Oakland Post-Enquirer*, March 28, 1930, 28; and "Both Sides Perfecting Charter Fight Forces," *Fort Worth Star-Telegram*, November 18, 1924, 6.

58. On the value of membership in larger federations for American voluntary organizations, see Theda Skocpol, Marshall Ganz, and Ziad Munson, "A Nation of Organizers: The Institutional Origins of Civic Voluntarism in the United States," *American Political Science Review* 94, no. 3 (September 2000): 527–46.

59. Committee, "Preparatory Note," and L. S. Rowe, "A Summary of the Program," *Municipal Program*, xi, 160.

60. Delos Wilcox, "Municipal Home Rule and Public Utility Franchises," *National Municipal Review* 3 (January 1914): 13–27; Clyde Lyndon King, ed., *The Regulation of Municipal Utilities* (1912; repr., New York: D. Appleton, 1921), v–vi.

61. Mayo Fessler, "Electoral Provisions of the New Municipal Program," and "Report of the Committee on Municipal Program," in *New Municipal Program*, 101–7, 325, 329.

62. H. W. Dodds to the members of the Committee on Municipal Program, November 1, 1932, Folder 30, Carton 62, Series 4, National Municipal League Records, Archives of the Auraria Library, Denver.

63. Horace Deming, "Public Opinion and City Government" and James Carter, "Banquet Speeches," in *Proceedings of the Columbus Conference for Good City Government and Fifth Annual Meeting of the National Municipal League Held November 16, 17, 18 1899*, ed. Clinton Rogers Woodruff (Philadelphia: NML, 1899), 81–82, 86, 254, 273.

64. Clinton Rogers Woodruff, ed., *Proceedings of the Indianapolis Conference for Good City Government and Fourth Annual Meeting of the National Municipal League, Held November 30, December 1–2, 1898* (Philadelphia: NML, 1898), 146–47, 223–35, 252.

65. Michel-Rolph Trouillot, *Silencing the Past: Power and the Production of History* (Boston: Beacon, 1995), 26, 48–49.

66. For example, see Ralph Bunche, "The Negro in Chicago Politics," *National Municipal Review* 17, no. 5 (May 1928): 261–64; and Grace Abbott, "The Immigrant and Municipal Politics," in *Proceedings of the Cincinnati Conference for Good City Government and the Fifteenth Annual Meeting of the National Municipal League Held November 15, 16, 17, 18, 1909*, ed. Clinton Rogers Woodruff (Philadelphia: NML, 1909), 148–56. Word searches for "negro," "colored," and "immigrant" in both municipal programs on Google Books yields zero results, and a search for "women" yields one hit in each, neither pertaining to women's rights. See Woodruff, *New Municipal Program*; and *Municipal Program*.

67. Daniel Tichenor, *Dividing Lines: The Politics of Immigration Control in America* (Princeton, N.J.: Princeton University Press, 2002), 120; William Hixson, *Moorfield Storey and the Abolitionist Tradition* (New York: Oxford University Press, 1972), 134.

68. Mary Dietz and James Farr, "'Politics Would Undoubtedly Unwoman Her': Gender, Suffrage, and American Political Science," in *Gender and American Social Science: The Formative Years*, ed. Helene Silverberg (Princeton, N.J.: Princeton University Press, 1998), 65; Nancy Cott, "Two Beards: Coauthorship and the Concept of Civilization," *American Quarterly* 42, no. 2 (June 1990): 274–95.

69. "The Eleventh-Hour Audacity of J. Peter Holland," *Virginian-Pilot and Norfolk Landmark*, November 18, 1917, 9; "Assail Charter from All Angles," *Virginian-Pilot and Norfolk Landmark*, November 13, 1917, 7.

70. "We Are to Share in Street Improvements," *New Journal and Guide* (Norfolk, Va.), February 12, 1921, 4; "City Manager Aims to Better Living Conditions Among Colored Citizens," *New Journal and Guide*, March 12, 1921, 1.

71. Stivers, *Bureau Men and Settlement Women*; Helene Silverberg, "'A Government of Men': Gender, the City, and the New Science of Politics," in Silverberg, *Gender and American Social Science*, 156–84.

72. Mary Ritter Beard, *Woman's Work in Municipalities* (New York: D. Appleton, 1915), 319.

73. Suzanne Mettler and Richard Valelly, "Introduction: The Distinctiveness and Necessity of American Political Development," in *The Oxford Handbook of American Political Development*, ed. Richard Valelly, Suzanne Mettler, and Robert Lieberman (New York: Oxford University Press, 2016), 1–18.

74. Theda Skocpol, "Bringing the State Back In," in *Bringing the State Back In*, ed. Peter Evans, Dietrich Rueschemeyer, and Theda Skocpol (New York: Cambridge University Press, 1985), 3–37; Stephen Skowronek, *Building a New American State: The Expansion of National Administrative Capacities, 1877–1920* (New York: Cambridge University Press, 1982).

75. Brian Balogh, *A Government Out of Sight: The Mystery of National Authority in Nineteenth-Century America* (New York: Cambridge University Press, 2009), esp. 3–6, 219, 264–74; William Novak, "The Myth of the 'Weak' American State," *American Historical Review* 113, no. 3 (June 2008): 752–72.

76. Ira Katznelson, "On Diversity and the Accommodation of Injustice: A Coda on Cities, Liberalism, and American Political Development," in Dilworth, *City in American Political Development*, 246–57.

77. Balogh, *Government Out of Sight*, 3–6, 219, 264–74; Novak, "Myth of the 'Weak,'" 752–72.

78. Martha Derthick, introduction to *Dilemmas of Scale*, ed. Derthick, 3.

79. Herbert Croly, *The Promise of American Life* (1909; Boston: Northeastern University Press, 1989), 349.

80. Howe, *City*, 7–8, 158–76, 301–3.

81. In arguing for the importance of a coalition based on the connection between structural reform and functional expansion, I am emphatically not agreeing with the "functionalist" argument that the adoption of these types of charter reforms was in fact the only way that cities could undertake new programs but rather recognizing that a wide variety of contemporaries believed this to be true. *Functionalism* now largely refers to a paradigm in sociology and, to a lesser extent, political science popular in the mid-twentieth century that argued that social structures exist to perform functions that fulfill societal needs. Two seminal texts are Talcott Parsons, *The Social System* (New York: Free Press, 1951), and Kingsley Davis and Wilbur Moore, "Some Principles of Stratification," *American Sociological Review* 10, no. 2 (1944): 242–49.

    While they never identified themselves as functionalists, many municipal political scientists of the period increasingly discussed municipal government as an instrument for fulfilling certain functions to meet the needs of urban residents. One article published in 1968 even insisted that what political scientists then called functionalism was in fact "a continuation of the original paradigm" (380) initiated by the founders of political science in the 1890s, 1900s, and 1910s. See Martin Landau, "The Myth of Hyperfactualism in the Study of American Politics," *Political Science Quarterly* 83, no. 3 (September 1968): 378–99.

82. James Sparrow, William Novak, and Stephen Sawyer, introduction to *Boundaries of the State in US History*, ed. James Sparrow, William Novak, and Stephen Sawyer (Chicago: University of Chicago Press, 2015), 1–15.

83. Lincoln Steffens, *The Shame of the Cities* (1904; Mineola, N.Y.: Dover, 2004).

84. Radford, *Rise of the Public Authority*, 72–78.

85. Delos Wilcox, *The American City: A Problem in Democracy* (New York: Macmillan, 1904), 204, 226. On Wilcox, see David Nord, "The Experts Versus the Experts: Conflicting Philosophies of Municipal Utility Regulation in the Progressive Era," *Wisconsin Magazine of History* 58, no. 3 (Spring 1975): 224–27.

86. Charles Richardson, "Municipal Franchises," in Woodruff, *Proceedings . . . 1898*, 98; Frank Mann Stewart, *A Half-Century of Municipal Reform: The History of the National Municipal League* (Berkeley: University of California Press, 1950), 15, 19–20.

87. Robert Bremner, *George and Ohio's Civic Revival: The American Democratic Philosopher Inspired a Successful Fight Against Political Bossism, Ending Many Exactions of the System of Privilege*, ed. Will Lissner and Dorothy Lissner (New York: Robert Schalkenbach

Foundation, 1995), 101–3; Hoyt Landon Warner, *Progressivism in Ohio, 1897-1917* (Columbus: Ohio State University Press for the Ohio Historical Society, 1964), 31.

88. Samuel Jones, "Paper of Hon. Samuel M. Jones," in Woodruff, *Proceedings ... 1898*, 221, 227.

89. Radford, *Rise of the Public Authority*, 74.

90. Radford, 78–88.

91. Skocpol, Ganz, and Munson argue that throughout American history, voluntary associations have mediated between and among private individuals and the state, resulting in a system in which civil society, party politics, and government are intertwined. Skocpol, Ganz, and Munson, "Nation of Organizers," 529–33.

92. Elisabeth Clemens, "Lineages of the Rube Goldberg State: Building and Blurring Public Programs, 1900-1940," in *Rethinking Political Institutions: The Art of the State*, ed. Ian Shapiro, Stephen Skowronek, and Daniel Galvin (New York: New York University Press, 2006), 187–90, 197; Carol Nackenoff and Julie Novkov, "Statebuilding in the Progressive Era: A Continuing Dilemma in American Political Development," in *Statebuilding from the Margins: Between Reconstruction and the New Deal*, ed. Carol Nackenoff and Julie Novkov (Philadelphia: University of Pennsylvania Press, 2014), 1-2, 7–11, 18.

93. Joanna Grisinger, "The (Long) Administrative Century: Progressive Models of Governance," in Skowronek, Engel, and Ackerman, *Progressives' Century*, 360–64.

94. Laura Phillips Sawyer, *American Fair Trade: Proprietary Capitalism, Corporatism, and the "New Competition," 1880-1940* (New York: Cambridge University Press, 2018), 3.

95. William Novak, "The Public Utility Idea and the Origins of Modern Business Regulation," in *Corporations and American Democracy*, ed. Naomi Lamoreaux and William Novak (Cambridge, Mass.: Harvard University Press, 2017), 139–76, quotes on 139, 144, 161–62.

96. Rogers Smith, "Which Comes First, the Ideas or the Institutions?," in Shapiro, Skowronek, and Galvin, *Rethinking Political Institutions*, 109.

97. Rogers Smith, "Ideas and the Spiral of Politics: The Place of American Political Thought in American Political Development," *American Political Thought: A Journal of Ideas, Institutions, and Culture* 3 (Spring 2014): 127, 130.

Chapter 1. The Emergence of the Movement

1. Washington Gladden, "The Cosmopolis City Club: Why and How the Club Was Organized," *Century Illustrated* 45, no. 3 (January 1893): 396–98.

2. Gladden, 400.

3. Gladden, 404–6.

4. Entries by local groups in William Howe Tolman, *Municipal Reform Movements in the United States* (New York: Fleming H. Revel, 1895), 47–133, quotes on 62–63, 80.

5. David Karol, "Political Parties in American Political Development," in *The Oxford Handbook of American Political Development*, ed. Richard Valelly, Suzanne Mettler, and Robert Lieberman (New York: Oxford University Press, 2016), 478–79.

6. Theda Skocpol, Marshall Ganz, and Ziad Munson, "A Nation of Organizers: The Institutional Origins of Civic Voluntarism in the United States," *American Political Science Review* 94, no. 3 (September 2000): 527–46.

7. Examples include the National Popular Government League, National Short Ballot Association, National Civic Federation, National Birth Control League, National Child Labor Committee, National Conference on City Planning, and National Consumers' League.

8. Robert Burnham, "The Boss Becomes a Manager: Executive Authority and City Charter Reform, 1880–1929," in *Making Sense of the City: Local Government, Civic Culture, and Community Life in America*, ed. Robert Fairbanks and Patricia Mooney-Melvin (Columbus: Ohio State University Press, 2001), 76, 78.

9. Phillip Ethington, *The Public City: The Political Construction of Urban Life in San Francisco, 1850–1900* (Berkeley: University of California Press, 1994), 8–11; James Connolly, *An Elusive Unity: Urban Democracy and Machine Politics in Industrializing America* (Ithaca, N.Y.: Cornell University Press, 2010), 178–79.

10. Kevin Mattson, *Creating a Democratic Public: The Struggle for Urban Participatory Democracy in the Progressive Era* (University Park: Pennsylvania State University Press, 1998), 4–5, 8–9.

11. Jon Teaford, *The Unheralded Triumph: City Government in America, 1870–1900* (Baltimore: Johns Hopkins University Press, 1984), 193–94; David Israel Aronson, "The City Club of New York, 1892–1912" (PhD diss., New York University, 1975), 12–18; Frank Mann Stewart, *A Half-Century of Municipal Reform: The History of the National Municipal League* (Berkeley: University of California Press, 1950), 11.

12. Connolly, *Elusive Unity*, 32–33, 53–86; James Connolly, "From Ring to Machine: The Evolution of Urban Political Reform Language in Gilded Age America" (paper presented at the Boston Seminar on Urban and Immigration History, Boston, September 2003), 1–6, 12–20.

13. Robert Muccigrosso, "The City Reform Club: A Study in Late Nineteenth-Century Reform," *New York Historical Society Quarterly* 52, no. 3 (July 1968): 239.

14. Theodore Roosevelt, "Machine Politics in New York City," *Century* 33, no. 1 (November 1886): 74, 82.

15. Quoted in Edward Grosse, "The German-American Reform Union," in *The Triumph of Reform: A History of the Great Political Revolution* (New York: Souvenir, 1895), 185, 259.

16. Ari Hoogenboom, *Outlawing the Spoils: A History of the Civil Service Reform Movement, 1865–1883* (Urbana: University of Illinois Press, 1961), 186–89, 211; Frank Mann Stewart, *The National Civil Service Reform League: History, Activities, and Problems* (Austin: University of Texas, 1929), 26–28.

17. "Civil Service Reformers," *New York Times* (hereafter cited as *NYT*), August 12, 1881, 5.

18. "Civil Service Reform," *NYT*, November 11, 1881, 5.

19. Stewart, *National Civil Service Reform League*, 30–32, 41; Hoogenboom, *Outlawing the Spoils*, 211–13.

20. For examples of coverage of the NCSRL in newspapers, see "Civil Service Law," *Los Angeles Times*, December 30, 1884, 1; "Political Notes," *Atlanta Constitution*, August 12, 1883, 6; "Civil Service Reform," *Chicago Daily Tribune*, November 5, 1882, 10; and "Civil Service Reform Simple Simons," *Washington Post*, April 23, 1882, 1.

21. Sean Theriault, "Patronage, the Pendleton Act, and the Power of the People," *Journal of Politics* 65, no. 1 (February 2003): 61.

22. Tolman, *Municipal Reform Movements*, 7, 47–133. Tolman's 1895 study examines fifty-six organizations, but there were undoubtedly many more.

23. Clinton Rogers Woodruff, "A Year's Advance," in *Proceedings of the Columbus Conference for Good City Government and the Fifth Annual Meeting of the National Municipal League, Held November 16, 17, 18 1899*, ed. Clinton Rogers Woodruff (Philadelphia: NML, 1899), 171, 186.

24. Skocpol, Ganz, and Munson, "Nation of Organizers."

25. Aronson, "City Club of New York," 36–39, 75; "The Proper Work of the City Club," *Nation* 54, no. 1399 (April 21, 1892): 296–97.

26. Aronson, "City Club of New York," 52–62, 78–79.

27. Quoted in James Pryor, "The City Club," *Triumph of Reform*, 256.

28. Aronson, "City Club of New York," 66–70, 101, 115–17, 121, 133–35, 140, 146.

29. "Aimed at the Spoils System," May 19, 1894, 9; "For Better Rule in Cities," May 18, 1894, 8; "With a New Constitution," April 5, 1894, 4, all in *NYT*.

30. "A New Movement in Municipal Reform," *Chicago Daily Tribune*, August 21, 1892, 28; "A New Movement in Municipal Reform," *Century Illustrated* 44, no. 3 (July 1892): 474.

31. Tolman, *Municipal Reform Movements*, 98, 118.

32. E. M. Lyman, "The City Vigilance League, New York City," *Triumph of Reform*, 101.

33. Tolman, *Municipal Reform Movements*, 9. The book also includes thirteen "movements for civic betterment" and eight women's municipal reform groups in its survey. Of the fifty-six groups listed, forty-three (77 percent) were founded between 1891 and 1894.

34. Tolman, 47–133.

35. Gladden, "Cosmopolis," 398.

36. See *Constitution and By-Laws of the Central Labor Union of New York and Vicinity* (New York: Concord Co-operative, 1887), 3; *Constitution and By-Laws of the Central Labor Union of Philadelphia and Vicinity* (Philadelphia: New Era Cooperative, 1902), 3; and *Constitution and By-Laws of the Central Labor Union of Cleveland, O.* (Cleveland: Chas. Lezius, 1899), 1.

37. William Maxwell Burke, "History and Functions of Central Labor Unions," in *Studies in History, Economics, and Public Law*, ed. Faculty of Political Science at Columbia University (New York: Macmillan, 1899), 40–57; State Conference of Central Labor Unions of Massachusetts, *Report for 1889 of the Legislative Committee of the State Conference of Central Labor Unions* (n.p., n.d.).

38. "National Board of Trade," *Fort Worth Telegram*, January 13, 1903, 4; Kenneth Sturges, *American Chambers of Commerce* (New York: Department of Political Science of Williams College, 1915), 55–71; Robert Wiebe, *Businessmen and Reform: A Study of the Progressive Movement* (Chicago: Quadrangle Books, 1968), 18–19, 21–22, 33–41.

39. For examples from Worcester, Massachusetts, see *Act of Incorporation, Constitution and By-Laws of the Worcester Board of Trade* (Worcester: Chas. Hamilton, 1875), 3; "Board of Trade Banquet," *Worcester Spy*, March 25, 1893, 1; "Boards of Trade," *Worcester Spy*, February 22, 1893, 1–2; "At the Board of Trade," *Worcester Telegram*, January 10, 1893, 4; and "History of the Central Labor Union of Worcester and Vicinity," in *Official Souvenir for Grand Parade and Demonstration of the Combined Labor Bodies of Worcester and Vicinity* (Worcester: Central Labor Union and Building Trades Council of Worcester, c. 1891).

40. For example, see "Union Labor Men Want Municipal Ownership," *Virginian Pilot*, November 14, 1905, 7.

41. For example, see Georg Leidenberger, *Chicago's Progressive Alliance: Labor and the Bid for Public Streetcars* (DeKalb: Northern Illinois University Press, 2006), 88.

42. Amy Bridges, *Morning Glories: Municipal Reform in the Southwest* (Princeton, N.J.: Princeton University Press, 1997), 47–51. Bridges makes this argument for southwestern cities in this period.

43. For example, see Riverson Ritchie, "Commercial Organizations and Municipal Reform," in *Proceedings of the Louisville Conference for Good City Government and the Third Annual Meeting of the National Municipal League Held May 5, 6 and 7, 1897*, ed. Clinton Rogers Woodruff (Philadelphia: NML, 1897), 120–24.

44. Elisabeth Clemens, *The People's Lobby: Organizational Innovation and the Rise of Interest Group Politics in the United States, 1890–1925* (Chicago: University of Chicago Press, 1997), 1–4.

45. *Constitution and By-Laws of the Central Labor Union of New York and Vicinity*, 6.

46. Burke, "History and Functions," 87.

47. Ritchie, "Commercial Organizations and Municipal Reform," 120, 124.

48. Frederic Howe, "Cleveland's Education Through Its Chamber of Commerce," *Outlook* 83, no. 13 (July 28, 1906): 739–41.

49. Skocpol, Ganz, and Munson, "Nation of Organizers," 533. They argue that marginalized groups have sought to form voluntary associations as a means of achieving political power.

50. See Tolman, *Municipal Reform Movements*, 47–133, for many examples. This particular quotation comes from the constitution of the Good Government Club of Yonkers (99–100).

51. Tolman, 56–57, emphasis in original.

52. Tolman, 82–85; "The Week," *Nation* 56, no. 1438 (January 19, 1893): 40.

53. Richard McCormick, *The Party Period and Public Policy: American Politics from the Age of Jackson to the Progressive Era* (New York: Oxford University Press, 1986), 228–59.

54. Clifford Patton, *The Battle for Municipal Reform: Mobilization and Attack, 1875–1900* (Washington, D.C.: American Council on Public Affairs, 1940), 45. See also "Separate

City Elections," *Nation* 58, no. 1510 (June 7, 1894): 422–23; and "Separate Municipal Elections," *Century Illustrated* 37, no. 3 (January 1889): 472–73.

55. Clinton Rogers Woodruff, "The Progress of Municipal Reform, 1894–95," in *Proceedings of the Second National Conference for Good City Government Held at Minneapolis December 8 and 10, 1894 and of the Third National Conference for Good City Government Held at Cleveland May 29, 20 and 31, 1895*, ed. Clinton Rogers Woodruff (Philadelphia: NML, 1895), 311.

56. Moorfield Storey, "The Municipal Government of Boston," in *Proceedings of the National Conference for Good City Government, Held at Philadelphia, January 25 and 26 1894*, ed. Clinton Rogers Woodruff (Philadelphia: Municipal League, 1894), 4, 61–71; William Hixson, *Moorfield Storey and the Abolitionist Tradition* (New York: Oxford University Press, 1972).

57. Woodruff, "Progress of Municipal Reform," 311; Patton, *Battle for Municipal Reform*, 48–49.

58. "Minutes of the First Annual Meeting of the Board of Delegates of the National Municipal League Held in Cleveland, Ohio," in Woodruff, *Proceedings . . . 1895*, 195–98.

59. Skocpol, Ganz, and Munson, "Nation of Organizers," 531–42.

60. Woodruff, *Proceedings . . . 1894*, i–iv.

61. "Reform in City Government," *NYT*, January 27, 1894, 5.

62. Much like the NCSRL, the NML may have formed partly in response to an article in the *Nation*. See "The Week," *Nation* 57, no. 1478 (October 26, 1893): 298.

63. "A Review of Reform," *NYT*, August 7, 1884, 4.

64. Stewart, *Half-Century*, 13, 15, 119.

65. Stewart, *National Civil Service Reform League*, 9.

66. Aronson, "City Club of New York," 18–19, 52, 101; Stewart, *Half-Century*, 51, 76, 95, 119, 123, 233, 202–3, 206; Stewart, *National Civil Service Reform League*, 13–17, 36–37, 105, 174, 270–71; "The Month," *Good Government: Official Journal of the National Civil Service Reform League* 14, no. 12 (June 15, 1895): 161. See also "Civil Service Reform," *NYT*, November 2, 1882, 3; "Civil Service Reform," *NYT*, August 3, 1882, 3; and "Civil Service Reformers," 5.

67. Many state and local municipal leagues were also members of the NCSRL. See "Progress of the Reform," *NYT*, December 13, 1894, 16.

68. See "For Good City Government" 15, no. 5 (May 15, 1896): 61–62; "The Month," 161; "The National Municipal League" 14, no. 11 (May 15, 1895): 155–57; "Recruiting the National Municipal League" 14, no. 1 (July 15, 1894): 6; and "Proceedings of the National Municipal League" 14, no. 6 (December 15, 1894): 85–86, all in *Good Government: Official Journal of the National Civil Service Reform League*.

69. Carl Schurz, "The Relation of Civil Service Reform to Municipal Reform," in Woodruff, *Proceedings . . . 1894*, 8–9, 123–33; William Potts, "Civil Service Reform in City Government," in Woodruff, *Proceedings . . . 1895*, 67–68.

70. Stewart, *Half-Century*, 119.

71. Washington Gladden, "Influence Upon Officials in Office," in Woodruff, *Proceedings . . . 1894*, 162–63.

72. James Bryce, *The American Commonwealth*, vol. 2 (1888; repr., with an introduction by Gary L. McDowell, Indianapolis: Liberty Fund, 1995), 914.

73. Tolman, *Municipal Reform Movements*, 97–99.

74. Tolman, 79–80.

75. Tolman, 51–52.

76. Edmond Kelly, "The Municipal Government of New York," in Woodruff, *Proceedings . . . 1894*, 106; James Carter, "President's Annual Address," in Woodruff, *Proceedings . . . 1895*, 276.

77. John Butler, "A Plea for the Moral High Ground in Municipal Reform," in Woodruff, *Proceedings . . . 1894*, 231.

78. Mattson, *Creating a Democratic Public*, 4–5.

79. Connolly, *Elusive Unity*, 166–67. Connolly describes the Civic Federation of Chicago in similar terms.

80. Tolman, *Municipal Reform Movements*, 77–81; Gregory Powell, "Municipal Condition of Omaha," in Woodruff, *Proceedings . . . 1895*, 421; Isaac Milken, "Municipal Condition of San Francisco," in Woodruff, *Proceedings . . . 1895*, 452; "Municipal Reform Methods in Chicago," *Nation* 60, no. 1557 (May 2, 1895): 342–43; "Municipal Reform Methods in Chicago," *Nation* 70, no. 1822 (May 31, 1900): 411–12.

81. Maureen Flanagan, "Gender and Urban Political Reform: The City Club and the Woman's City Club of Chicago in the Progressive Era," *American Historical Review* 95, no. 4 (October 1990): 36.

82. Remarks by Wm. A. Giles of the Civic Federation of Chicago, in Woodruff, *Proceedings . . . 1895*, 18–19; Albion Small, "The Civic Federation of Chicago: A Study in Social Dynamics," *American Journal of Sociology* 1, no. 1 (July 1895): 80–81, 84. In its early years, the program of the Federation included wider philanthropic and labor-related concerns, but the specific problem of municipal government remained central.

83. Albion Small, "Civic Federation of Chicago," in Woodruff, *Proceedings . . . 1895*, 478.

84. "Civil Service Reformers." The conferences of the NCSRL, begun over a decade earlier, likely in part inspired this form of meeting. In 1881, the *New York Times* reported that a national civil service conference had been called to exchange "thoughts and ideas from different parts of the country on the subject of civil service reform," and the associations that came together at that conference decided to form the NCSRL.

85. "To Better Home Government," *NYT*, May 29, 1894, 2; "Reform in City Government."

86. Clinton Rogers Woodruff, ed., *Proceedings of the Third National Conference for Good City Government and the Second Annual Meeting of the National Municipal League, Held at Baltimore, May 6, 7 and 8, 1896* (Philadelphia: NML, 1896); Woodruff, *Proceedings . . . 1895*; Woodruff, *Proceedings . . . 1894*. In these years they also distributed thousands of pamphlets. In the first year alone, they distributed twenty-four thousand copies of their first four pamphlets. See Woodruff, "Progress of Municipal Reform," 304–12.

87. Woodruff, *Proceedings . . . 1896*, iv.
88. George Burnham Jr. and James Carter, quoted in Woodruff, *Proceedings . . . 1894*, 1–4.
89. Introduction to Woodruff, *Proceedings . . . 1894*, iv.
90. "The Week," *Nation* 58, no. 1492 (February 1, 1894): 76.
91. Clinton Rogers Woodruff, "A Year's Work for Municipal Reform," in Woodruff, *Proceedings . . . 1896*, 70; Stewart, *Half-Century*, 21.
92. Herbert Welsh, "Municipal Leagues and Good Government Clubs," in Woodruff, *Proceedings . . . 1895*, 146–53. Biographical information from David Pivar, "Theocratic Businessmen and Philadelphia Municipal Reform, 1870–1900," *Pennsylvania History* 33, no. 3 (1966): 297.
93. "Minutes of the First Annual Meeting of the Board of Delegates," in Woodruff, *Proceedings . . . 1895*, 194.
94. David Thelen, *The New Citizenship: Origins of Progressivism in Wisconsin, 1885–1900* (Columbia: University of Missouri Press, 1972), 168.
95. Clemens, *People's Lobby*, 184–234.
96. For example, see Flanagan, "Gender and Urban Political Reform," 1032–50.
97. Mary Mumford, "The Relation of Women to Municipal Reform," in Woodruff, *Proceedings . . . 1894*, 9–10, 134–43; Maria Sanford, "Woman's Work in Reform," in Woodruff, *Proceedings . . . 1895*, 40–44; C. A. Runkle, "Good City Government from a Woman's Standpoint," in Woodruff, *Proceedings . . . 1895*, 236, 500–507.
98. Tolman, *Municipal Reform Movements*, 168–69, 176–80.
99. An important contemporary essay on inquiry and knowledge was Charles Sanders Pierce's "The Fixation of Belief," *Popular Science Monthly* 12 (November 1877): 1–15. See also Thomas Haskell, *The Emergence of Professional Social Science: The American Social Science Association and the Nineteenth-Century Crisis of Authority* (Chicago: University of Illinois Press, 1977), 101–4.
100. This generalization did not, of course, apply to all those involved in municipal reform. Albion Tourgee, celebrated civil rights lawyer, addressed the NML's members at an 1894 convention on the subject of good citizenship: "The great value and truth of a democratic government is that it cannot be worked out by any preconceived theory; but going on from day to day we meet the day's problems and do our duty by finding some solution for them. We do not follow the cut and dried theory, but accomplish by our own devices what needs to be done." Speech by Albion Tourgee, "The Recruiting Sergeant in the Army of Good Citizenship," in Woodruff, *Proceedings . . . 1895*, 246.
101. Tolman, *Municipal Reform Movements*, 106–7, 110–12, 114–15.
102. For example, see Small, "Civic Federation of Chicago," 82, 100–102.
103. Tolman, *Municipal Reform Movements*, 91–93.
104. For example, see "The Month."
105. Membership data from sources listed in table 1.
106. Woodruff, *Proceedings . . . 1894*, 18–20.
107. Eldon Eisenach, *The Lost Promise of Progressivism* (Lawrence: University of Kansas Press, 1994), 5, 10, 17–18. Eisenach argues that the creation of national voluntary

associations was important to the nationalist element of Progressivism, with re-formers creating "parastate" institutions that "claimed to speak for and to estab-lish on a voluntary basis what they claimed to be the collective and the national community" (18).

108. These three were the League of American Municipalities, the American League for Civic Improvement, and the American Society of Municipal Improvements. See "Union of Civic Societies," *Independent* 54, no. 2821 (December 25, 1902): 3106.

109. James Carter, "President's Annual Address," in Woodruff, *Proceedings . . . 1896*, 44–45; Carter, "President's Annual Address," in Woodruff, *Proceedings . . . 1895*, 267.

110. *A Municipal Program, Report of a Committee of the National Municipal League, Adopted by the League, November 17, 1899, Together with Explanatory and Other Papers* (New York: Macmillan, 1900).

111. For example, see "The Week," *Nation* 58, no. 1492 (February 1, 1894): 76; and Storey, "Municipal Government of Boston," 61–71.

Chapter 2. "Saved by the Scholar"

1. "The Municipal Programme," *New York Times*, February 24, 1900, 6.

2. "Proceedings of the Louisville Conference and Third Annual Meeting," in *Proceedings of the Louisville Conference for Good City Government and the Third Annual Meeting of the National Municipal League Held May 5, 6, and 7, 1897*, ed. Clinton Rogers Woodruff (Philadelphia: NML, 1897), 7.

3. Frank Mann Stewart, *A Half-Century of Municipal Reform: The History of the National Municipal League* (Berkeley: University of California Press, 1950), 28–29; Lloyd Graybar, *Albert Shaw of the Review of Reviews: An Intellectual Biography* (Lexington: University of Kentucky Press, 1974), 16–29.

4. For example, see Clinton Rogers Woodruff, "The Municipal League of Philadel-phia," *American Journal of Sociology* 11, no. 3 (November 1905): 336–58; Clinton Rogers Woodruff, "The Nationalization of Municipal Movements," *Annals of the American Academy of Political and Social Science* 21 (March 1903): 100–108; Clinton Rog-ers Woodruff, "Philadelphia Street-Railway Franchises," *American Journal of Sociol-ogy* 7, no. 2 (September 1901): 216–33; Clinton Rogers Woodruff, "The Complexity of American Governmental Methods," *Political Science Quarterly* 15, no. 2 (June 1900): 260–72; and Clinton Rogers Woodruff, "Protection of Workingmen," *Annals of the American Academy of Political and Social Science* 14 (July 1899): 99–105.

5. "Members of the Association," *Proceedings of the American Political Science Associa-tion at Its Fifth Annual Meeting Held at Washington, D.C., and Richmond, Va., Decem-ber 28–31, 1908* (Baltimore: Waverly, 1909), 7–23.

6. "Proceedings of the Louisville Conference," 6–7.

7. Kenneth Fox, *Better City Government: Innovation in American Urban Politics, 1850–1937* (Philadelphia: Temple University Press, 1977), 59–62; Ernest Griffith, *A History of*

American City Government: The Conspicuous Failure, 1870-1900 (New York: Praeger, 1974), 272.

8. Helene Silverberg, "'A Government of Men': Gender, the City, and the New Science of Politics," in Gender and American Social Science: The Formative Years, ed. Helene Silverberg (Princeton, N.J.: Princeton University Press, 1998), 170–71.

9. James Connolly, An Elusive Unity: Urban Democracy and Machine Politics in Industrializing America (Ithaca, N.Y.: Cornell University Press, 2010), 198–99.

10. Frank Goodnow, Politics and Administration: A Study in Government (1900; repr., with an introduction by John A. Rohr, New Brunswick, N.J.: Transaction, 2003), 18.

11. "Preparatory Note," in A Municipal Program: Report of a Committee of the National Municipal League, Adopted by the League, November 17, 1899, Together with Explanatory and Other Papers (New York: Macmillan, 1900), xi.

12. Stephen Leonard, "The Pedagogical Purposes of a Political Science," in Political Science in History, ed. James Farr, John Dryzek, and Stephen Leonard (New York: Cambridge University Press, 1995), 67–74; David Ricci, The Tragedy of Political Science: Politics, Scholarship, and Democracy (New Haven, Conn.: Yale University Press, 1984), 66–70; Albert Somit and Joseph Tanenhaus, The Development of American Political Science: From Burgess to Behavioralism (Boston: Allyn and Bacon, 1967), 15–21, 42–48; Bernard Crick, The American Science of Politics: Its Origins and Conditions (Berkeley: University of California Press, 1959), xii, 21–36; R. Gordon Hoxie, A History of the Faculty of Political Science, Columbia University (New York: Columbia University Press, 1955).

13. John Dryzek and David Schlosberg, "Disciplining Darwin: Biology in the History of Political Science," in Farr, Dryzek, and Leonard, Political Science in History, 127–28; Dorothy Ross, The Origins of American Social Science (New York: Cambridge University Press, 1991), 261; Dwight Waldo, "Political Science: Tradition, Discipline, Profession, Science, Enterprise," in Political Science: Scope and Theory, ed. Fred Greenstein and Nelson Polsby (Reading, Mass.: Addison-Wesley, 1975), 28; Ricci, Tragedy of Political Science, 60–69; Somit and Tanenhaus, Development of American Political Science, 77; Martin Landau, "The Myth of Hyperfactualism in the Study of American Politics," Political Science Quarterly 83, no. 3 (September 1968): 383, 386, 390.

14. Somit and Tanenhaus, Development of American Political Science, 30–31.

15. Ross, Origins of American Social Science, 71, 260–65.

16. Waldo, "Political Science," 29–30; Somit and Tanenhaus, Development of American Political Science, 69–71.

17. James Bryce, The American Commonwealth, vol. 1 (1888; repr., with an introduction by Gary L. McDowell, Indianapolis: Liberty Fund, 1995), 1–10. Unless otherwise noted, citations refer to the 1995 edition.

18. Frederic Howe, The Confessions of a Reformer (1925; repr., Kent, Ohio: Kent State University Press, 1988), 3; Anna Haddow, Political Science in American Colleges and Universities, 1636-1900, ed. and intro. by William Anderson (New York: D. Appleton-Century, 1939), 249–50.

19. Bryce, *American Commonwealth*, vol. 2, 909–15, 1250–60.

20. Howe, *Confessions of a Reformer*, 3, 5, 8, 22, 28, 57.

21. Thomas Haskell, *The Emergence of Professional Social Science: The American Social Science Association and the Nineteenth-Century Crisis of Authority* (Chicago: University of Illinois Press, 1977), 101–4, 168–210.

22. Leonard, "Pedagogical Purposes," 67–74; Ricci, *Tragedy of Political Science*, 66–70; Somit and Tanenhaus, *Development of American Political Science*, 15–21, 42–48; Crick, *American Science of Politics*, xii, 21–36.

23. Fox, *Better City Government*, 38–39.

24. John Gunnell, "The Declination of the 'State' and the Origins of American Pluralism," in Farr, Dryzek, and Leonard, *Political Science in History*, 21.

25. Michael Frisch, "Urban Theorists, Urban Reform, and American Political Culture in the Progressive Period," *Political Science Quarterly* 97, no. 2 (Summer 1982): 299.

26. Leonard, "Pedagogical Purposes," 74–75.

27. Frisch, "Urban Theorists," 301–2. See also Gunnell, "Declination of the 'State,'" 21–23; Leonard, "Pedagogical Purposes," 74–75; Waldo, "Political Science," 30–32; Crick, *American Science of Politics*, 26.

28. Raymond Seidelman, *Disenchanted Realists: Political Science and the American Crisis, 1884-1984* (Albany: State University of New York Press, 1985), 45, 52.

29. Terence Ball, "An Ambivalent Alliance: Political Science and American Democracy," in Farr, Dryzek, and Leonard, *Political Science in History*, 44–47.

30. Woodrow Wilson, "Character of Democracy in the United States," *Atlantic Monthly* 64, no. 385 (November 1889): 577–88.

31. Ross, *Origins of American Social Science*, 279.

32. Waldo, "Political Science," 32–34.

33. Mary Dietz and James Farr, "'Politics Would Undoubtedly Unwoman Her': Gender, Suffrage, and American Political Science," in Silverberg, *Gender and American Social Science*, 68–69, 78–79.

34. Silverberg, "'Government of Men,'" 156–59.

35. Landau, "Myth of Hyperfactualism," 381–82.

36. Not until c. 1910 did textbooks on municipal political science begin to discuss voluntary associations in any depth. For examples of texts that largely ignored municipal reform associations, see Horace Deming, *The Government of American Cities: A Program of Democracy* (New York: G. P. Putnam's, 1909); L. S. Rowe, *Problems of City Government* (New York: D. Appleton, 1908); and John Fairlie, *Municipal Administration* (New York: Macmillan, 1901). For texts that contain isolated references to such groups, see Frank Goodnow, *City Government in the United States* (New York: Century, 1906), 135; Frank Goodnow, *Municipal Problems* (New York: Macmillan, 1897), 193; and Delos Wilcox, *The Study of City Government* (New York: Macmillan, 1897), 116.

37. Landau, "Myth of Hyperfactualism," 381–82.

38. Elisabeth Clemens, *The People's Lobby: Organizational Innovation and the Rise of Interest Group Politics in the United States, 1890-1925* (Chicago: University of Chicago Press, 1997), 1–4.

39. Frisch, "Urban Theorists," 295–315; Silverberg, "'Government of Men,'" 156, 169–70. Frisch presents political scientists' involvement in municipal reform as more ideologically motivated, while Silverberg presents it as more instrumental, serving their larger ambitions for professional development.

40. L. S. Rowe, "American Political Ideas and Institution in Their Relation to the Problem of City Government," in Woodruff, *Proceedings . . . 1897*, 75, 77–78.

41. L. S. Rowe, "Public Accounting Under the Proposed Municipal Program," in *Proceedings of the Columbus Conference for Good City Government and Fifth Annual Meeting of the National Municipal League, Held November 16, 17, 18, 1899*, ed. Clinton Rogers Woodruff (Philadelphia: NML, 1899), 104.

42. Stewart, *Half-Century*, 29; Deming, *Government of American Cities*; Horace Deming, "Municipal Nomination Reform," *Annals of the American Academy of Political and Social Science* 25 (March 1905): 1–15; Horace Deming, "A Municipal Program," *Annals of the American Academy of Political and Social Science* 17 (May 1901): 35–47.

43. "Proceedings of the Louisville Conference," 6–7.

44. "Proceedings of the Louisville Conference," 7–8, 16, 38.

45. "Report of the Committee on 'Municipal Program,'" in *Proceedings of the Indianapolis Conference for Good City Government and Fourth Annual Meeting of the National Municipal League, Held November 30, December 1–2, 1898*, ed. Clinton Rogers Woodruff (Philadelphia: NML, 1898), 2.

46. Introduction in Woodruff, *Proceedings . . . 1899*, iii; "Proceedings of the Fifth Annual Meeting," in Woodruff, *Proceedings . . . 1899*, 6.

47. "Proceedings of the Fifth Annual Meeting," 3, 45–47.

48. "Report of the Committee on 'Municipal Program,'" "Proposed Constitutional Amendment," and "Proposed Municipal Corporations Act," in Woodruff, *Proceedings . . . 1898*, 1–15, 16–24, and 25–52; "Proposed Constitutional Amendment" and "Proposed Municipal Corporations Act," in *Municipal Program*, 174–86, 187–224.

49. "Municipal Programme," 6.

50. Frank Goodnow, "The Tweed Ring in New York City," in James Bryce, *The American Commonwealth*, vol. 2 (New York: Macmillan, 1888), 335–53. Goodnow's chapter appeared only in the first edition of *The American Commonwealth* because it resulted in a libel suit. Bryce revised it, tempering its tone and bolder assertions, and included it in the third edition in 1910. See "Publisher's Note," in Bryce, *American Commonwealth*, vol. 2 (New York: Macmillan, 1995), xxxi.

51. Lurton Blassingame, "Frank J. Goodnow and the American City" (PhD diss., New York University, 1968), 9–11; Munroe Smith, "The Professional Life of Frank Johnson Goodnow," *Johns Hopkins Alumni Magazine* 2 (November 1913–June 1914): 277.

52. Blassingame, "Frank J. Goodnow," 9.

53. Fox, *Better City Government*, 25–39.

54. Smith, "Professional Life," 277.

55. Landau, "Myth of Hyperfactualism," 380–81.

56. Blassingame, "Frank J. Goodnow," 9–10.

57. Frank Goodnow, "Local Government in England," *Political Science Quarterly* 2, no. 4 (December 1887): 638–65; Frank Goodnow, "The English Local Government Bill," *Political Science Quarterly* 3, no. 2 (June 1888): 311–33.

58. Ross, *Origins of American Social Science*, 259; Blassingame, "Frank J. Goodnow," 78; R. T. Daland, "Political Science and the Study of Urbanism," *American Political Science Review* 51, no. 2 (1957): 494.

59. Quoted in Ross, *Origins of American Social Science*, 275.

60. Frank Goodnow, "Local Government in Prussia I," *Political Science Quarterly* 4, no. 4 (December 1889): 665–66; Frank Goodnow, "Local Government in Prussia II," *Political Science Quarterly* 5, no. 1 (March 1890): 150.

61. For example, see William Ivins, "Municipal Government," *Political Science Quarterly* 2, no. 2 (June 1887): 291–312.

62. Blassingame, "Frank J. Goodnow," 44, 53–54.

63. Frank Goodnow, *Municipal Home Rule: A Study in Administration* (New York: Macmillan, 1895), 15, 18, 43, 54, 229.

64. Anwar Hussain Syed, *The Political Theory of American Local Government* (New York: Random House, 1966), 94–98.

65. Frisch, "Urban Theorists," 304.

66. As noted in the introduction, in using the terms *structure* and *function*, I am not adopting or endorsing what later political scientists termed *functionalism*. Rather, I am using the terms as my historical subjects did.

67. Daniel Rodgers, *Atlantic Crossings: Social Politics in a Progressive Era* (Cambridge, Mass.: Belknap Press of Harvard University Press, 1998), 3–4, 112–13, 137. Rodgers's analysis amply highlights the importance of "European precedents" in providing "the American urban progressives a set of working, practical examples" in their efforts to expand the functions of municipalities. He claims that reformers minimized the importance of structure because the organization of European cities was completely different (143–44). While this assessment may apply to Shaw, it does not apply to Goodnow and others who emphasized the ways in which American and European cities were organized differently.

68. Blassingame, "Frank J. Goodnow," 14, 17.

69. Graybar, *Albert Shaw*, 84; "Presidential Address," *American Political Science Review* 1, no. 2 (February 1907): 177–86.

70. On Rowe, see Mark Berger, "Civilising the South: The U.S. Rise to Hegemony in the Americas and the Roots of 'Latin American Studies,' 1898–1945," *Bulletin of Latin American Research* 12, no. 1 (January 1993): 8–9, 36; "Report of the Academy Committee on the Sixth Annual Meeting," *Annals of the American Academy of Political and Social Science* 20 (July 1902): 295. Rowe's publications in popular journals were about Latin American politics, which in later years eclipsed his interest in municipal politics in the United States. For early examples, see L. S. Rowe, "The Era of Good Feeling in South America," *Independent* 68, no. 3068 (September 19, 1907): 686–91; and L. S. Rowe, "Significance of the Porto Rican Problem," *North American Review* 173, no. 536 (July 1901): 35–40.

71. L. S. Rowe, "The Problems of Political Science," *Annals of the American Academy of Political and Social Science* 10 (September 1897): 25, 38.

72. L. S. Rowe, "The Municipality and the Gas Supply, as Illustrated by the Experience of Philadelphia," *Annals of the American Academy of Political and Social Science* 11 (May 1898): 23.

73. L. S. Rowe, "The City in History," *American Journal of Sociology* 5, no. 6 (May 1900): 744–45.

74. Albert Shaw, *Municipal Government in Great Britain* (1895; New York: Macmillan, 1901), 8.

75. Quoted in Rodgers, *Atlantic Crossings*, 133.

76. Shaw, *Municipal Government in Great Britain*, vi–vii, 8, 304–5; Albert Shaw, *Municipal Government in Continental Europe* (1895; New York: Macmillan, 1906).

77. Shaw, *Municipal Government in Great Britain*, vii, 2, 18–19.

78. L. S. Rowe, review of *Municipal Government in Great Britain*, by Albert Shaw, *Annals of the American Academy of Political and Social Science* 5 (May 1895): 146–49; L. S. Rowe, review of *Municipal Government in Continental Europe*, by Albert Shaw, *Annals of the American Academy of Political and Social Science* 7 (May 1896): 116–17.

79. Frank Goodnow, review of *Municipal Government in Great Britain*, by Albert Shaw, *Political Science Quarterly* 10, no. 1 (March 1895): 172–73.

80. Frank Goodnow, review of *Municipal Government in Continental Europe*, by Albert Shaw, *Political Science Quarterly* 11, no. 1 (March 1896): 158–60.

81. Goodnow, *Municipal Home Rule*, 272.

82. L. S. Rowe, review of *Municipal Problems*, by Frank Goodnow, *Annals of the American Academy of Political and Social Science* 11 (March 1898): 116–18.

83. Goodnow, *Politics and Administration*, 18.

84. Dwight Waldo, *The Administrative State: A Study of the Political Theory of Administration* (New York: Ronald, 1948), 79. Woodrow Wilson was also a key figure. See Ross, *Origins of American Social Science*, 274–79.

85. Goodnow, *Politics and Administration*, 11, 16, 20–21.

86. Goodnow, 47–71; Frisch, "Urban Theorists," 308–11.

87. Frank Goodnow, "The Place of the Council and of the Mayor in the Organization of Municipal Government," *Municipal Program*, 75, 78–79.

88. Henry Jones Ford, "Politics and Administration," *Annals of the American Academy of Political and Social Science* 16 (September 1900): 1–2.

89. Frisch, "Urban Theorists," 303.

90. "Preparatory Note," *Municipal Program*, xi.

91. L. S. Rowe, "A Summary of the Program," *Municipal Program*, esp. 160, 163, 167–70.

92. Ross, *Origins of American Social Science*, 274.

93. Woodrow Wilson, "Bryce's American Commonwealth," *Political Science Quarterly* 4, no. 1 (March 1889): 159, 162–67.

94. Bryce, *American Commonwealth*, vols. 1–2, 572–75, 785, 794, 841.

95. Goodnow, *Municipal Problems*, 145–47, 170–71, 193–94.

96. Ross, *Origins of American Social Science*, 276.

97. Goodnow, *Politics and Administration*, 133–254. See also Goodnow, *Municipal Problems*, 258.

98. Goodnow, *Politics and Administration*, 133–254.

99. Goodnow, *Municipal Problems*, 194–208, 212–14.

100. Goodnow, 181–86.

101. "Summary of the Program," "Proposed Constitutional Amendments," and "Proposed Municipal Corporations Act," in *Municipal Program*, esp. 167–73, 176, 180–81, 204–24.

102. "Sixth Session," in Woodruff, *Proceedings . . . 1899*, 36.

103. *Proceedings of the National Conference for Good City Government, Held at Philadelphia, January 25 and 26 1894*, ed. Clinton Rogers Woodruff (Philadelphia: Municipal League, 1894).

104. "Proceedings of the Fifth Annual Meeting," 36–37.

105. Frank Goodnow, "Political Parties and City Government Under the Proposed Municipal Program," in Woodruff, *Proceedings . . . 1899*, 63–64.

106. Though Wilcox and John Fairlie, both students of Goodnow, were not official members of the committee, Frisch claims that they helped draft the program. They both wrote explanatory articles that were published with the program by the NML. See Frisch, "Urban Theorists," 303; John Fairlie, "Municipal Development in the United States," *Municipal Program*, 1–35; and Delos Wilcox, "An Examination of the Proposed Municipal Program," *Municipal Program*, 226–28, 239.

107. Silverberg, "'Government of Men,'" 171. For a favorable review of the program in a nonacademic publication, see "Municipal Programme," 6.

108. For examples of reformers writing to Goodnow for assistance, see George Cardwill (secretary of the New Albany Commercial Club) to Goodnow, November 26, 1906, and Thos. Cauldwell (Morristown Civic Association) to Goodnow, March 14, 1906, Folder "Ca," Box 3; C. S. Crandall to Goodnow, March 18, 1905, and Goodnow to C. S. Crandall, March 24, 1905, Folder "Coudert . . . ," Box 5; Sidney Dillon to Goodnow, May 23, 1907, Folder "Di (various) . . . ," Box 5; Thomas Ewing Jr. (Charter Commission of Yonkers) to Goodnow, October 27, 1904, Folder "Egbert . . . ," Box 6; W. F. Fitzgarrald (mayor of Marion, Iowa) to Goodnow, February 27, 1907, and Goodnow to W. F. Fitzgarrald, March 7, 1907, Folder "Fe-Fi," Box 6; Correl Humphry (secretary of the Utica Chamber of Commerce) to Goodnow, February 17, 1905, and Goodnow to Correll Humphry, February 21, 1905, Folder "Hov-Hy," Box 9; F. W. Lyman (Charter Commission of Minneapolis) to Goodnow, July 28, 1903, and Goodnow to F. W. Lyman, September 30, 1903, Folder "Little . . . ," Box 11; William Martin (Commission for the Revision of the Charter of the City of Newark) to Goodnow, June 1, 1907, Folder "Marsland . . . ," Box 11, all in Correspondence, Frank Johnson Goodnow Papers, Ms. 3, Special Collections, Milton S. Eisenhower Library, Johns Hopkins University, Baltimore. There are more examples of such letters in the Goodnow Papers. Moreover, the vast majority of the letters in this collection date from 1903 and later, and there were very likely

many more letters written to Goodnow regarding local efforts at charter reform before this date.

109. Smith, "Professional Life," 284.

110. Graybar, *Albert Shaw*, 91–202; Berger, "Civilising the South," 8–9, 36.

111. Fox, *Better City Government*, 63–64.

Chapter 3. The *Municipal Program* and Early Campaigns

1. "The National Municipal League," *Newport (R.I.) Daily News*, November 3, 1899, 3; "The Milwaukee Conference for Good City Government," *Fort Wayne (Ind.) Morning Journal-Gazette*, September 10, 1900, 4.

2. Clinton Rogers Woodruff, "A Year's Advance," in *Proceedings of the Columbus Conference for Good City Government and Fifth Annual Meeting of the National Municipal League Held November 16, 17, 18, 1899*, ed. Clinton Rogers Woodruff (Philadelphia: NML, 1899), 169.

3. Tso-Shuen Chang, *History and Analysis of the Commission and City Manager Plans of Municipal Government in the United States*, University of Iowa Monographs, Studies in the Social Sciences 6 (Iowa City: University of Iowa, 1918), 43–45; Frank Goodnow, *City Government in the United States* (New York: Century, 1904), 65–68.

4. Nancy Burns and Gerald Gamm, "Creatures of the State: State Politics and Local Government, 1871–1921," *Urban Affairs Review* 33, no. 1 (September 1997): 59–96.

5. Joseph McGoldrick, *The Law and Practice of Municipal Home Rule, 1916–1930* (New York: Columbia University Press, 1933), 2.

6. Clinton Rogers Woodruff, "The Advance of the Movement for Municipal Reform," and Josiah Quincy, "Paper Prepared by Mayor Quincy," in *Proceedings of the Indianapolis Conference for Good City Government and Fourth Annual Meeting of the National Municipal League, Held November 30, December 1–2, 1898*, ed. Clinton Rogers Woodruff (Philadelphia: NML, 1898), 115, 187.

7. "Proceedings of the Fifth Annual Meeting," in Woodruff, *Proceedings . . . 1899*, 4; Frank Mann Stewart, *A Half-Century of Municipal Reform: The History of the National Municipal League* (Berkeley: University of California Press, 1950), 28–29.

8. L. S. Rowe, "A Summary of the Program," in *A Municipal Program: Report of a Committee of the National Municipal League, Adopted by the League, November 17, 1899, Together with Explanatory and Other Papers* (New York: Macmillan, 1900), 160.

9. L. S. Rowe, "American Political Ideas and Institutions in Their Relation to the Conditions of City Life," in *Proceedings of the Louisville Conference for Good City Government and the Third Annual Meeting of the National Municipal League Held May 5, 6, and 7, 1897*, ed. Clinton Rogers Woodruff (Philadelphia: NML, 1897), 82.

10. Albert Shaw, "The City in the United States," in Woodruff, *Proceedings . . . 1898*, 82–83.

11. Frank Goodnow, "The Powers of Municipal Corporations," in Woodruff, *Proceedings . . . 1897*, 66.
12. Charles Richardson, "Municipal Voters," in Woodruff, *Proceedings . . . 1897*, 259–60.
13. "Paper of Mr. Delos F. Wilcox," in Woodruff, *Proceedings . . . 1898*, 193.
14. Riverson Ritchie, "Commercial Organizations and Municipal Reform," in Woodruff, *Proceedings . . . 1897*, 120, 122–24.
15. Quincy, "Paper Prepared by Mayor Quincy," 188. On Quincy's administration, see James Connolly, *The Triumph of Ethnic Progressivism: Urban Political Culture in Boston, 1900–1925* (Cambridge, Mass.: Harvard University Press, 1998), 26.
16. Samuel Jones, "Paper of Hon. Samuel M. Jones," in Woodruff, *Proceedings . . . 1898*, 220–21, 227.
17. Washington Gladden, "Reform in City Government," *New York Times*, November 26, 1899, 23.
18. Goodnow, "Powers of Municipal Corporations," 63; Shaw, "City in the United States," 88–89.
19. Rowe, "Summary of the Program," 162–65, 169–71.
20. "Constitutional Amendments," in *Municipal Program*, 176–85.
21. Shaw, "City in the United States," 82–85.
22. Frank Goodnow, "Political Parties and City Government Under the Proposed Municipal Program," in Woodruff, *Proceedings . . . 1899*, 73.
23. N. F. Hawley, "Paper of N. F. Hawley, Esq.," in Woodruff, *Proceedings . . . 1898*, 200.
24. N. F. Hawley, "Paper of N. F. Hawley, Esq.," in Woodruff, *Proceedings . . . 1898*, 201–2.
25. N. F. Hawley, "Paper of N. F. Hawley, Esq.," in Woodruff, *Proceedings . . . 1898*, 205.
26. "National Municipal League Records, 1890–1991: Guide to the Holdings," Auraria Library, February 1993, http://digital.auraria.edu/AA00004592/00001.
27. Woodruff, "Year's Advance," 171, 180–86.
28. Clinton Rogers Woodruff, "A Year's Municipal Development," in *Proceedings of the Milwaukee Conference for Good City Government and Sixth Annual Meeting of the National Municipal League Held September 19, 20, 21 1900 at Milwaukee, Wis.*, ed. Clinton Rogers Woodruff (Philadelphia: NML, 1900), 69–78, quote on 70.
29. Woodruff, "Year's Municipal Development," 72.
30. Portions of the discussion of Toledo in this chapter appear in Ariane Liazos, "'Ministering . . . to the Social Needs of the People': Samuel Jones, Strong Mayor, Government, and Municipal Ownership in Toledo, 1897–1904," *Journal of Economics and Sociology* 75, no. 1 (January 2016): 86–115.
31. Marnie Jones, *Holy Toledo: Religion and Politics in the Life of "Golden Rule" Jones* (Lexington: University of Kentucky Press, 1998), 109; Hoyt Landon Warner, *Progressivism in Ohio, 1897–1917* (Columbus: Ohio State University Press for the Ohio Historical Society, 1964), 11, 25–26, 107–9.
32. Marnie Jones, *Holy Toledo*, 118, 120–21; Samuel Jones, "What Can Woman Do Toward Good City Government," July 7, 1900, and "The Race Problem," September 16, 1899, Series Two, Samuel Milton Jones Papers, Toledo-Lucas County Public Library, Toledo (hereafter cited as Jones Papers).

33. Samuel Jones, "Patience and Education the Demands of the Hour," *Arena* 25 (May 1901): 544–46.

34. Robert Bremner, *George and Ohio's Civic Revival: The American Democratic Philosopher Inspired a Successful Fight Against Political Bossism, Ending Many Exactions of the System of Privilege*, ed. Will Lissner and Dorothy Lissner (New York: Robert Schalkenbach Foundation, 1995), 101–3; Warner, *Progressivism in Ohio*, 31.

35. Samuel Jones, "Paper of Hon. Samuel M. Jones," 220–27, quote on 221; Charles Richardson, "Municipal Franchises," in Woodruff, *Proceedings . . . 1898*, 94–100.

36. Samuel Jones, *The New Right: A Plea for Fair Play and a More Just Social Order* (New York: Eastern Book Concern, 1899), 286–88, 291–92, 317.

37. Bremner, *George and Ohio's Civic Revival*, 88, 105–6; Warner, *Progressivism in Ohio*, 24, 31.

38. Samuel Jones, "The New Patriotism: A Golden Rule Government for Cities," *Municipal Affairs* 3 (September 1899): 459–60.

39. Marnie Jones, *Holy Toledo*, 91–92.

40. Samuel Jones, *New Right*, 303.

41. Bremner, *George and Ohio's Civic Revival*, 64–65.

42. Brian Balogh, *A Government Out of Sight: The Mystery of National Authority in Nineteenth-Century America* (New York: Cambridge University Press, 2009), 6, 264–65.

43. Samuel Jones, *New Right*, 24, 299–300, 322; Samuel Jones, "New Patriotism," 460; Samuel Jones, "Municipal Expansion," *Arena* 21 (June 1899): 766.

44. Marnie Jones, *Holy Toledo*, 147, 155; Arthur DeMatteo, "The Progressive as Elitist: 'Golden Rule' Jones and the Toledo Charter Reform Campaign of 1901," *Northwest Ohio Quarterly* 69, no. 1 (1997): 14.

45. Woodruff, "Year's Advance," 177.

46. Samuel Jones, "Third Annual Message to the Common Council," August 14, 1899, 12–14, Series Two, Jones Papers.

47. Marnie Jones, *Holy Toledo*, 106–7, 121, 182–83.

48. DeMatteo, "Progressive as Elitist," 10; Bremner, *George and Ohio's Civic Revival*, 92.

49. DeMatteo, "Progressive as Elitist," 10.

50. "In Favor of New Charter," *Toledo Bee*, December 11, 1900, 1, 3; "The Mayor's Annual Message to Council," *Toledo Blade*, December 11, 1900, 10; Rowe, "Summary of the Program," 157–73.

51. Marnie Jones, *Holy Toledo*, 138.

52. "In Favor of New Charter," 1, 3; "Mayor's Annual Message to Council," 10.

53. Samuel Jones, "Third Annual Message," 14.

54. Samuel Jones, *New Right*, 386.

55. Jones is typically identified as a social rather than a structural reformer. See DeMatteo, "Progressive as Elitist," 8–10; Bremner, *George and Ohio's Civic Revival*, 16–17, 53–54, 112; Melvin Holli, *Reform in Detroit: Hazen S. Pingree and Urban Politics* (New York: Oxford University Press, 1969), 157–81. Jones's biographer rejects the characterization of Jones as solely a "social reformer," noting that he also pursued structural reforms. See Marnie Jones, *Holy Toledo*, 253.

56. Warner, *Progressivism in Ohio*, 17, 107–8; Clinton Rogers Woodruff, "Municipal Government in Ohio," *Yale Review* 12 (August 1903): 127–28; "Census Entitles Toledo to New Municipal Grading," *Toledo Bee*, December 6, 1900, 1–2.

57. Bremner, *George and Ohio's Civic Revival*, 128; DeMatteo, "Progressive as Elitist," 7, 16–17.

58. "Submitted by the Mayor," *Toledo Bee*, January 29, 1901, 1–3.

59. "Charter Commission Elects Leander Burdick President," *Toledo Blade*, March 11, 1901, 5; "Charter Commission Elects Another New Member," *Toledo Bee*, March 31, 1901, 2; "Permanent Officers Selected," *Toledo Bee*, March 10, 1901, 1, 8; "Discord Crops Out in the New Charter Commission," *Toledo Bee*, February 24, 1901, 1.

60. For example, see Elaine Naylor, *Frontiers: Port Townsend and the Culture of Development in the American West, 1850-1895* (Montreal: McGill-Queen's University Press, 2014), xii.

61. Jas. G. Riddick, "Norfolk's Public Institutions and Desirable Lines for Improvement," *Jamestown Exposition Edition of the Norfolk Dispatch* (Norfolk: Norfolk Dispatch Publishing Company, 1904), 123. On Riddick's background, see James Sidney Kitterman Jr., "Reformers and Bosses in the Progressive Era: The Changing Face of Norfolk Politics, 1880-1920" (master's thesis, Old Dominion University, 1971), 87.

62. "Norfolk Must Watch," *Norfolk Public Ledger* (hereafter cited as *NPL*), July 13, 1905, 4; Riddick, "Norfolk's Public Institutions," 120–23.

63. *A Record of the Common Council*, no. 20 (May 3, 1904–February 2, 1906): 153 (original copy located in City Hall, Norfolk); "Star Chamber Met Quick Death," *Virginian Pilot* (hereafter cited as *VP*), September 7, 1904, 1.

64. Chapter IV, Section 26, *The Ordinances of the City of Norfolk, VA, with the Amended Charter, Acts of Assembly Relating to City Government, and an Appendix* (Norfolk: Burke and Gregory, 1902), 21; Article VIII, Sections 119–20, *The Constitution of the State of Virginia Adopted by the Convention of 1901-2* (Richmond: n.p., 1902), 30–31.

65. Kitterman, "Reformers and Bosses," 67–96.

66. "Improving City Streets," *VP*, November 17, 1904, 3; "$42,278 Voted for Beautifying the City," *VP*, November 16, 1904, 1.

67. "Names Committees of Norfolk Chamber," *NPL*, January 25, 1906, 9. See also "Tentative Terms of Consolidation Fixed," March 30, 1905, 3; "Big Meeting Will Discuss Plan of Consolidation," March 24, 1905, 3; "Greater City Is Gaining Favor," March 22, 1905, 3; and "Municipal Bureau of Improvement Is Planned," September 18, 1904, 3, all in *VP*.

For the occupations of GGA councillors, see "Object to So Many Liquor Dealers on Ticket," *Ledger Dispatch* (hereafter cited as *LD*), May 15, 1906, 11. The Board of Trade and Retail Merchants' Association were similarly involved in local politics. See "Merchants Will Fight Light Co. in Council," *VP*, October 11, 1905, 3; and "Business Men Are to Confer," *NPL*, February 13, 1905, 7.

68. "Make the City Attractive," *VP*, October 3, 1905, 4.

69. "Union Labor Men Want Municipal Ownership," *VP*, November 14, 1905, 7.
70. Kitterman, "Reformers and Bosses," 94–95.
71. "Star Chamber Met Quick Death," 1; "Who Emasculated the City Charter?," *VP*, October 15, 1904, 4. For professions of members of the Charter Commission, see "Labor Candidate for Board of Control," *NPL*, March 19, 1906, 4.
72. "Unions Want Place on the Charter Commission," *VP*, September 15, 1904, 7.
73. "Labor's Proposition Was Rejected by the Common Councilmen," *VP*, October 5, 1904, 7; "Labor Gets No Man on New Charter Commission," *VP*, October 12, 1904, 3.
74. "Old Chairman of the Charter Commission," *VP*, November 15, 1904, 2.
75. "Charter Revision Commission's Big Task," *VP*, December 29, 1904, 3.
76. "With Bright Prospects the Municipal League Is Formally Organized," *VP*, March 17, 1905, 7.
77. "With Bright Prospects," 7; "Move to Stop Civic Corruption," *NPL*, October 30, 1905, 1; "Elects Officers, Plans Campaign," *NPL*, March 17, 1905, 2; "City League Enrolled 33 Members," *VP*, March 10, 1905, 1; "Municipal League Meeting Tonight," *VP*, March 9, 1905, 4; "Concerning a Municipal League," *VP*, March 1, 1905, 4; "Form Municipal League Is the Movement," *VP*, February 28, 1905, 3.
78. "National Municipal League's Convention," *VP*, March 23, 1905, 5.
79. "Form Municipal League," 3; "Writes Letter to the League," *NPL*, December 28, 1905, 6; "Shaw Scores Charter's Makers," *VP*, November 1, 1905, 2; "Meeting Called of Municipal League," *NPL*, October 14, 1905; "Referendum for Charter to Be Advocated," *VP*, September 14, 1905, 5.
80. "No Reply to Lieut. Shaw," *VP*, November 2, 1905, 5; "The Secret Sessions," *NPL*, November 4, 1905, 4.
81. "With Bright Prospects," 7; "Meeting Called of Municipal League," 1; "Shaw Scores Charter's Makers," 2; "Municipal League Will Not Attend Charter Meetings," *VP*, March 18, 1905, 5.
82. "No Reply to Lieut. Shaw," 5; "Shaw Scores Charter's Makers," 2; "Would Dispense with Secret Sessions," *VP*, August 13, 1905, 3.
83. Goodnow, "Political Parties and City Government," 77; Rowe, "Summary of the Program," 159–60; *Municipal Program*, 201–20. The program granted the mayor the power to appoint three or more individuals to a civil-service commission in charge of the regulation, examination, and appointment of all municipal officials except for departmental heads, who were appointed by the mayor.
84. Chang, *History and Analysis*, 43–45.
85. Rowe, "American Political Ideas," 79.
86. Harold Stone, Don Price, and Kathryn Stone, *City Manager Government in the United States: A Review After Twenty-Five Years* (Chicago: Public Administration Service, 1940), 4–5.
87. Goodnow, "Political Parties and City Government," 74.
88. "Constitutional Amendments," 180; "Proposed Municipal Corporations Act," in *Municipal Program*, 216, 219–20.

89. Horace Deming, "Public Opinion and City Government," *Municipal Program*, 154.

90. Rowe, "Summary of the Program," 167–68.

91. Goodnow, "Political Parties and City Government," 73; Horace Deming, "The Municipal Problem in the United States," *Municipal Program*, 57. Goodnow and Deming mentioned but did not explore these subjects at length.

92. Woodrow Wilson, "Government of the City: Prof. Wilson's Lectures at the Johns Hopkins University," February 26, 1896, in *The Papers of Woodrow Wilson*, vol. 9, *1896–1898*, ed. Arthur S. Link (Princeton, N.J.: Princeton University Press, 1971), 452.

93. Rowe, "Summary of the Program," 167–68.

94. Rowe, "American Political Ideas," 77.

95. Wilcox noted that there were two ways in which the program might not be considered democratic: it required that those elected to form a new city charter be "householders" and made no provision for the initiative or referendum. Yet the final version of the program omitted the requirement that framers be householders and added the option to adopt the initiative and referendum in the same section that allowed for minority or proportional representation to be adopted by local councils. "Constitutional Amendments," 180, 183–85; "Proposed Constitutional Amendment," in Woodruff, *Proceedings . . . 1898*, 19, 22; "Paper of Mr. Delos F. Wilcox," 193–94.

96. Deming, "Public Opinion and City Government," 151–56.

97. Rowe, "Summary of the Program," 168–69.

98. Deming, "Public Opinion and City Government," 146, 153–56.

99. "Urges Adoption of Cleveland Charter," *Toledo Bee*, April 28, 1901, 1–5; "If the People Want It," *Toledo Bee*, April 16, 1901, 1.

100. "Charter Opposition Becomes Apparent," *Toledo Blade*, October 14, 1901, 5; "Burdick Charged with Applying Gag Rule," *Toledo Bee*, October 13, 1901, 1, 8; "Claimed Gag Rule Was Applied," *Toledo Blade*, August 15, 1901, 5.

101. "New Charter as Planned by the Commission," *Toledo Blade*, October 5, 1901, 6.

102. "Now Up to Election Board," *Toledo Bee*, October 19, 1901, 3; "New City Charter," *Toledo Blade*, November 1, 1901, 1; "Charter Commissioners Who Oppose New Charter," *Toledo Bee*, November 1, 1901, 1.

103. "Charter Commissioners," 1; "Now Up to Election Board," 3; "These Persons Constitute the New Charter Commission," *Toledo Bee*, February 18, 1901, 2; "To Prepare a New Charter," *Toledo Bee*, February 17, 1901, 1.

104. Arthur Edward DeMatteo, "Urban Reform, Politics, and the Working Class: Detroit, Toledo, and Cleveland, 1890–1922" (PhD diss., University of Akron, 1999), 123; "Charter Commissioners," 1; "Likely to Knock the New Charter," *Toledo Bee*, October 21, 1901, 7.

105. L. W. Morris, "Judge Morris Points Out the Weak Points in the Instrument," *Toledo Blade*, October 25, 1901, 1, 6.

106. Julian Tyler, "Julian Tyler of the Commission Replies to Critics," *Toledo Blade*, October 31, 1901, 1.

107. L. W. Morris, "The One-Man Feature of the Proposed Charter," *Toledo Blade*, November 4, 1901, 6.

108. Morris unsuccessfully attempted to introduce an alternative charter that included a forty-five-member council elected by wards. "Charter Commissioners," 1; "The One That Was Not Read," *Toledo Bee*, October 17, 1901, 1, 3; "Charter Formally Adopted," *Toledo Bee*, October 17, 1901, 2; "Charter Adopted by Commission," *Toledo Blade*, October 17, 1901, 9.

109. Morris, "Judge Morris Points Out," 1, 6.

110. Tyler, "Julian Tyler of the Commission," 1.

111. DeMatteo, "Progressive as Elitist," 8, 20–21.

112. "Charter Discussed," *NPL*, February 10, 1906, 4.

113. "Mayor to Have Enlarged Powers," *VP*, November 25, 1905, 1.

114. "Board of Control Charter Finished," *NPL*, February 1, 1906, 1.

115. "Obtain Results on Police Force," *NPL*, September 14, 1905, 1; "Merit System Is Introduced," *NPL*, May 10, 1905, 1.

116. "Shaw Again Raps Star Chamber Meetings," *VP*, August 16, 1905, 3.

117. Goodnow, "Political Parties and City Government," 71.

118. "Negroes Will Apply to Serve as Police and Also as Firemen," *LD*, October 12, 1906, 1; "New Charter for Norfolk," *NPL*, March 10, 1906, 11; "Fight Charter in Legislature," *NPL*, February 17, 1906, 11. The city council later voted to create a civil service commission by ordinance, and Virginia's General Assembly amended Norfolk's charter accordingly. Soon after the charter took effect, two African Americans applied for municipal jobs.

119. "Don't Want the People to Elect," *NPL*, February 9, 1906, 9; "The New Charter," *NPL*, February 19, 1906, 4.

120. "Wants Finance Committeeman," *NPL*, February 11, 1906, 1.

121. "Wants Finance Committeeman," 1; "Board of Control Was Discussed," *NPL*, February 15, 1906, 11.

122. "New Charter," 4; "Fight Charter in Legislature," 11.

123. Kitterman, "Reformers and Bosses," 100–101.

124. Kitterman, 100–101.

125. "Labor Pleased with Results," *VP*, August 24, 1905, 5; "Labor Will Take Hand in State Politics," *VP*, August 6, 1905, 1.

126. "Board of Control," *NPL*, February 12, 1906, 4; "Report of the Committee on the Organization and Government of Cities and Towns" and "Article VII of the Constitution of the State of Virginia: The Organization and Government of Cities and Towns," reprinted in *Journal of the Constitutional Convention of Virginia* (Richmond: J. H. O'Bannon, 1901), 1–7, 29–35. The committee paraphrased Goodnow's explanation of the "the dual character of cities," indicating the influence of his conception of home rule. It did not, however, follow Goodnow and the *Municipal Program* in proposing a constitutional general grant of powers to cities.

127. "Legislature Will Amend New Charter," February 19, 1906, 10; "Real Charter Fight Tonight," February 26, 1906, 11; "People to Elect," February 27, 1906, 1, all in *NPL*.

128. *A Record of the Common Council*, no. 21 (February 6, 1906–September 3, 1906): 19, 36, 122–24; *A Record of the Select Council, Norfolk, VA*, no. 14 (January 10, 1905–August 31,

1906): 317–21, 323–24 (original copies located in City Hall, Norfolk); "Redist. Bill Now Up to Mayor," *VP*, August 9, 1905, 1–2; "Is It Goodbye to Old Fourth?," *NPL*, July 7, 1905, 12; "Redistricting Bill Passed Common Branch," *VP*, July 7, 1905, 1; "Identity of 4th Ward in Peril," *VP*, July 4, 1905, 1; Kitterman, "Reformers and Bosses," 81, 90–91.

129. Kitterman, "Reformers and Bosses," 81, 104. See also "The Fourth to the Rescue," July 8, 1905, 4; "Redistricting Bill Passed Common Branch," July 7, 1905, 1; "'Absurd,' Says Gwathmey of Umstadter's Opinion," November 29, 1904, 4; and "The Race Issue a National One," July 22, 1904, 4, all in *VP*.

130. Kitterman, "Reformers and Bosses," 104–6; "Declare Gerrymander Is Illegal and Want the Courts to Decide," *VP*, December 7, 1905, 1. See also "Failed to See All Norfolk Men," February 24, 1906, 1; "No Further Fight Against Injunction," January 31, 1906, 1, 10; "Caucus Endorsed Gerrymander Bill," December 6, 1905, 9; and "Redistricting Norfolk," December 6, 1905, 1, all in *NPL*.

131. "The Ring's Profession of Virtue a New Subterfuge," *LD*, May 14, 1906, 16.

132. "Candidates O.K. Says the League," May 15, 1906, 6; "Will Make All Replies Public," May 10, 1906, 6; "Candidates Are Preparing Replies," May 9, 1906, 1, 13; "Lines Are Drawn for the Board of Control," May 2, 1906, 1, 5; "Municipal League and the Board," May 1, 1906, 13, all in *LD*.

133. "Results of the Vote for Board of Control," *LD*, May 18, 1906, 11; "Complexion of New Councils," *LD*, May 18, 1906, 1.

134. For example, see "Satisfied Board on Boulevard," *LD*, October 23, 1906, 1; and "Provide for Boulevard," *LD*, August 22, 1906, 7.

135. Howard Lee McBain, *The Law and Practice of Municipal Home Rule* (New York: Columbia University Press, 1916), v.

Chapter 4. "The Franchise Problem"

1. For example, see "Municipal Ownership Elections," *Norfolk Public Ledger*, May 4, 1905, 9; "Democrats and Municipal Ownership," *Virginian Pilot*, April 15, 1905, 4; and "Municipal Ownership Carried Day in Chicago," *Virginian Pilot*, April 5, 1905, 9.

2. Lincoln Steffens, *The Shame of the Cities* (1904; Mineola, N.Y.: Dover, 2004), esp. 20–40.

3. Clinton Rogers Woodruff, "A Year's Municipal Progress," in *Proceedings of the Boston Conference for Good City Government and Eighth Annual Meeting of the National Municipal League Held May 7, 8 and 9, 1902*, ed. Clinton Rodgers Woodruff (Philadelphia: NML, 1902), 102–5.

4. Clinton Rogers Woodruff, "Municipal Progress in the United States, Recent," in *The New Encyclopedia of Social Reform*, ed. William D. P. Bliss (New York: Funk and Wangalls, 1908), 795–800.

5. For example, see Samuel Jones, *The New Right: A Plea for Fair Play and a More Just Social Order* (New York: Eastern Book Concern, 1899); Frederic Howe, *The City: The*

Hope of Democracy (New York: Charles Scribner's, 1905); and J. Warner Mills, "The Economic Struggle in Colorado," *Arena* 34, no. 191 (October 1905): 379–99.

6. Robert Bremner, "The Civic Revival in Ohio: Municipal Ownership and Economic Privilege," *American Journal of Economics and Sociology* 9, no. 4 (July 1950): 477.

7. William Novak, "The Myth of the 'Weak' American State," *American Historical Review* 113, no. 3 (June 2008): 769–71; Elisabeth Clemens, "Lineages of the Rube Goldberg State: Building and Blurring Public Programs, 1900–1940," in *Rethinking Political Institutions: The Art of the State*, ed. Ian Shapiro, Stephen Skowronek, and Daniel Galvin (New York: New York University Press, 2006), 196–208.

8. Carol Nackenoff and Julie Novkov, "Statebuilding in the Progressive Era: A Continuing Dilemma in American Political Development," in *Statebuilding from the Margins: Between Reconstruction and the New Deal*, ed. Carol Nackenoff and Julie Novkov (Philadelphia: University of Pennsylvania Press, 2014), 1–2; Gail Radford, *The Rise of the Public Authority: Statebuilding and Economic Development in Twentieth-Century America* (Chicago: University of Chicago Press, 2013), 72–88.

9. Joseph McGoldrick, *The Law and Practice of Municipal Home Rule, 1916–1930* (New York: Columbia University Press, 1933), 2–3.

10. Howe, *City*, 167.

11. John Fairlie, "Recent Extensions of Municipal Functions in the United States," *Annals of the American Academy of Political and Social Science* 25 (March 1905): 97–108.

12. Martin Melosi, *The Sanitary City: Urban Infrastructure in America from Colonial Times to the Present* (Baltimore: Johns Hopkins University Press, 2000), 119.

13. M. N. Baker, "Municipal Ownership and Operation of Waterworks," *Annals of the American Academy of Political and Social Science* 57 (January 1915): 279.

14. Eric Rauchway, *Blessed Among Nations: How the World Made America* (New York: Hill and Wang, 2006), 96–105; Melosi, *Sanitary City*, 123.

15. Fairlie, "Recent Extensions."

16. Frank Parsons, *The City for the People, or, The Municipalization of the City Government and of Local Franchises* (Philadelphia: C. F. Taylor, 1900), 1, 17–175, 218.

17. "Proceedings Eleventh Annual Convention of the League of American Municipalities," *Bulletin of the League of American Municipalities* 8, no. 4 (October 1907): 95–99; Frederic Howe, "Municipal Ownership in Cleveland," *Bulletin of the League of American Municipalities* 7, no. 1 (January 1907): 11–13.

Coverage of the conventions of the League of American Municipalities in the *New York Times* suggested that the organization leaned toward municipal ownership. See "Abuses Mayor Dunne," August 25, 1905, 1; "The Ideal City," October 11, 1903, 6; "Contract System Denounced," October 8, 1903, 3; "Municipal League Meets," December 13, 1900, 7; "League of Municipalities," September 22, 1899, 1; "Talked City Ownership," September 21, 1899, 7; "Municipal Ownership Question," May 7, 1899, 16; "To Discuss City Affairs," June 19, 1898, 15; and "League of American Municipalities," October 2, 1897, 3, all in *New York Times*.

18. League of American Municipalities, *10th Annual Convention of the League of American Municipalities Held at Chicago, September 26, 27 and 28, 1906* (Chicago: Kirchner, Meckel, 1906); "Municipal Control Opposed in League," *New York Times*, September 21, 1907, 8; "Non-Committal on M.O.," *New York Times*, September 29, 1906, 3.

19. Quoted in Clinton Rogers Woodruff, "The New Municipal Idea," in *Proceedings of the Buffalo Conference for Good City Government and the Sixteenth Annual Meeting of the National Municipal League Held November 14, 15, 16, 17, 1910*, ed. Clinton Rogers Woodruff (Philadelphia: NML, 1910), 40.

20. Edward Moffett, "The National Civic Federation Investigation," in *Proceedings of the Atlantic City Conference for Good City Government and the Twelfth Annual Meeting of the National Municipal League Held April 24, 25, 26, 27, 1906*, ed. Clinton Rogers Woodruff (Philadelphia: NML, 1906), 306.

21. *Report of the Delegates Representing the City of Hudson, N.Y. at the Eleventh Annual Convention of the League of American Municipalities Held at Norfolk, VA September 18-21, 1907* (Hudson: Bryan, 1907), 10. For the full report, see Commission on Public Ownership and Operation, *Municipal and Private Operation of Utilities, Report to the National Civic Federation*, pt. 1, vol. 1, *General Conclusions and Report* (New York: NCF, 1907).

22. John Fairlie, "Charter Tendencies in Recent Years," in *Proceedings of the Pittsburgh Conference for Good City Government and the Fourteenth Annual Meeting of the National Municipal League Held November 16, 17, 18, 19 1908*, ed. Clinton Rogers Woodruff (Philadelphia: NML, 1908), 204–11, quote on 211. On Fairlie's relationship with Goodnow, see Michael Frisch, "Urban Theorists, Urban Reform, and American Political Culture in the Progressive Period," *Political Science Quarterly* 97, no. 2 (July 1982): 303.

23. Howard Lee McBain, *The Law and Practice of Municipal Home Rule* (New York: Columbia University Press, 1916), v. For an example of outrage over "charter tinkering," see "Working for Better City Government," *New York Times*, June 23, 1893, 4.

24. Frederic Howe, *The Confessions of a Reformer* (1925; repr., Kent, Ohio: Kent State University Press, 1988), 1–6, 85–112.

25. Robert Bremner, *George and Ohio's Civic Revival: The American Democratic Philosopher Inspired a Successful Fight Against Political Bossism, Ending Many Exactions of the System of Privilege*, ed. Will Lissner and Dorothy Lissner (New York: Robert Schalkenbach Foundation, 1995).

26. Howe, *City*, 160–70.

27. Clinton Rogers Woodruff, "A Year of Municipal Advances," in *Proceedings of the New York Conference for Good City Government and the Eleventh Annual Meeting of the National Municipal League Held April 25, 26, 27 and 28, 1905*, ed. Clinton Rogers Woodruff (Philadelphia: NML 1905), 57–58.

28. Steffens, *Shame of the Cities*, 1–5.

29. Frederic Howe, "The Case for Municipal Ownership," *Proceedings of the American Political Science Association* 2 (1905): 89–94. See also Howe, *City*, 2–5. On Howe's friendship with Steffens, see Kenneth Miller, *From Progressive to New Dealer:*

Frederic C. Howe and American Liberalism (University Park: Pennsylvania State University Press, 2010), 92, 165, 241, 420–22.

30. Howe, "Case for Municipal Ownership," 90, 93–98.
31. Howe, *City*, 160–67, 313.
32. Howe, vii, x, xi.
33. Bremner, *George and Ohio's Civic Revival*, 40–43, 50–51.
34. Miller, *From Progressive to New Dealer*, 105, 110–12, 129.
35. Clinton Rogers Woodruff, review of *The City: The Hope of Democracy*, by Frederic Howe, *Yale Review* 15 (February 1907): 463–65.
36. For example, see Delos Wilcox, *Great Cities in America: Their Problems and Their Government* (New York: Macmillan, 1910), 13.
37. Arthur Williams, *Concerning Municipal Ownership* (n.p., 1905), 1–2.
38. L. S. Rowe, "Municipal Ownership and Operation—The Value of Foreign Experience," in Woodruff, *Proceedings . . . 1906*, 289–90; L. S. Rowe, "The Relation of Municipal Government to American Democratic Ideals," in Woodruff, *Proceedings . . . 1905*, 170–72.
39. Rowe, "Municipal Ownership," 284–86; Rowe, "Relation of Municipal Government," 174–75.
40. James Connolly offers a contrasting perspective. He examines the shift from political discourse that assumed the existence of a singular "common good" to pluralist conceptions of political participation that accepted and even embraced the heterogeneity of urban populations. He argues that there was a brief window in the 1890s when reformers began to include the diverse perspectives of immigrants and other working-class constituencies. However, he critiques Steffens and the NML in the *Municipal Program* (particularly in the call for at-large rather than ward-based elections) for retreating to a consensus model of urban politics that only allowed for a single "public interest" after 1900. James Connolly, *An Elusive Unity: Urban Democracy and Machine Politics in Industrializing America* (Ithaca, N.Y.: Cornell University Press, 2010), x, 191–208.
41. Rowe, "Relation of Municipal Government," 175.
42. "Banquet Speeches," in *Columbus Conference for Good City Government and Fifth Annual Meeting of the National Municipal League Held November 16, 17, 18 1899*, ed. Clinton Rogers Woodruff (Philadelphia: NML, 1899), 254.
43. Grace Abbott, "The Immigrant and Municipal Politics," in *Proceedings of the Cincinnati Conference for Good City Government and the Fifteenth Annual Meeting of the National Municipal League Held November 15, 16, 17, 18, 1909*, ed. Clinton Rogers Woodruff (Philadelphia: NML, 1909), 148–56, quotes on 154, 156.
44. "Wednesday Morning Session," in Woodruff, *Proceedings . . . 1909*, 51–52. For biographical information, see *State and Local Taxation: Fourth International Conference* (Columbus: International Tax Association, 1911): 5; Florence Levy, ed., *American Art Annual* 8 (1910–1911): 115; and J. Harris Aubin, *Register of the Military Order of the Loyal Legion of the United States* (Boston: Commandery of the State of Massachusetts, 1906), 30.

45. Wilcox, *Great Cities in America*, 9.

46. Kevin Mattson, *Creating a Democratic Public: The Struggle for Urban Participatory Democracy During the Progressive Era* (University Park: Pennsylvania State University Press, 1998), 18–19, 41–43.

47. Edward Ward, *The Social Center*, National Municipal League series (New York: D. Appleton, 1913), ix–x, 1; Clinton Rogers Woodruff, "Introduction," *The Social Center*, ix–x.

48. Jon Teaford, *The Unheralded Triumph: City Government in America, 1870–1900* (Baltimore: Johns Hopkins University Press, 1984), 107.

49. *Encyclopedia Britannica Online*, s.v. "Charles Joseph Bonaparte," last updated March 31, 2019, http://www.britannica.com/biography/Charles-Joseph-Bonaparte.

50. Charles Bonaparte, "The Field of Labor of the National Municipal League," in Woodruff, *Proceedings . . . 1905*, 43–47.

51. Clinton Rogers Woodruff, "The Year's Work," in *Proceedings of the Detroit Conference for Good City Government and the Ninth Annual Meeting of the National Municipal League Held April 22, 23 and 24, 1903*, ed. Clinton Rogers Woodruff (Philadelphia: NML, 1903), 79.

52. Clinton Rogers Woodruff, "A Year's Disclosure and Development," in *Proceedings of the Chicago Conference for Good City Government and the Tenth Annual Meeting of the National Municipal League Held April 27, 28 and 29, 1904*, ed. Clinton Rogers Woodruff (Philadelphia: NML, 1904), 117; Woodruff, "Year of Municipal Advances," 95–96.

53. "Round Table Luncheon Conferences, Cincinnati Business Men's Club, Tuesday, November 16, 1909," in Woodruff, *Proceedings . . . 1909*, 441–44.

54. On these two competing solutions generally, see David Nord, "The Experts Versus the Experts: Conflicting Philosophies of Municipal Utility Regulation in the Progressive Era," *Wisconsin Magazine of History* 58, no. 3 (Spring 1975): 219–36.

55. "Council Minutes, 1915," Folder 38, Carton 2, Series 1; "Committees and Projects, Franchises, 1911," Folder 25; and "Committee on Franchise Report," 1911, Folder 35, Carton 50, Series 4, National Municipal League Records, Archives of the Auraria Library, Denver.

56. Delos Wilcox, "The Street Car Crisis and the Way Out," *Municipal Railways in the United States and Canada Bulletin of the Public Ownership League of America* 18 (1922): 3–4.

    Wilcox remained a passionate advocate of municipal ownership throughout his career. He was also a vice president of the Public Ownership League of America in the 1920s and contributed to the *Bulletin of the Public Ownership League of America*. For more on Wilcox, see Frisch, "Urban Theorists," 303; and "Guide to the Delos Franklin Wilcox Papers," University of Chicago Library, 2006, https://www.lib.uchicago.edu/e/scrc/findingaids/view.php?eadid=ICU.SPCL.WILCOX.

57. "Committee on Franchise Report."

58. "Dr. Clyde L. King Dies Unexpectedly," *Reading Eagle*, June 21, 1937; "Clyde L. King Dies Suddenly," *Pittsburgh Press*, June 21, 1937; Clyde London King, "The Confer-

ence of American Mayors on 'Public Policies as to Municipal Utilities,'" *National Municipal Review* 4, no. 1 (January 1915): 91–93.

59. Clyde Lyndon King, ed., *The Regulation of Municipal Utilities*, National Municipal League series (1912; New York: D. Appleton, 1921); Delos Wilcox, "Municipal Home Rule and Public Utility Franchises," *National Municipal Review* 3, no. 1 (January 1914): 13–27, quote on 13.

60. Clyde Lyndon King, introduction to King, *Regulation of Municipal Utilities*, v–vi.

61. Clyde Lyndon King, "Municipal Ownership Versus Adequate Regulation," in King, *Regulation of Municipal Utilities*, 23–55, quotes on 49, 52. King conceded that state law should grant cities the right to own public utilities if residents so chose.

62. Joseph Eastman, "The Public Utilities Commission of Massachusetts," in Woodruff, *Proceedings . . . 1908*, 288–307, quotes on 302, 307.

63. Clyde Lyndon King, "The Need for Regulation," "Municipal Ownership Versus Adequate Regulation," and "The Need for Public Utility Commissions," in King, *Regulation of Municipal Utilities*, 19–20, 52–55, 185–207.

64. Howe, *City*, 171–74; Parsons, *City for the People*, 255–386.

65. Wilcox, "Municipal Home Rule," 15–17.

66. Delos Wilcox, *The Menace of Private Ownership of Municipal Utilities*, Leaflet No. 6 (New York: n.p., October 1923).

67. Nord, "Experts Versus the Experts," 219–36.

68. Clyde Lyndon King, *Lower Living Costs in Cities: A Constructive Programme for Urban Efficiency* (New York: D. Appleton, 1915), 3.

69. Delos Wilcox, *The American City: A Problem in Democracy* (New York: Macmillan, 1904), 201–26, quotes on 201, 206–7, 210, 226–27.

70. Arthur Edward DeMatteo, "Urban Reform, Politics, and the Working Class: Detroit, Toledo, and Cleveland, 1890–1922" (PhD diss., University of Akron, Ohio, 1999), 126–31; Wendell Johnson, *Toledo's Non-partisan Movement* (Toledo: H. J. Chittenden, 1922), 17–29.

71. Woodruff, "Year's Work," 73–74.

72. Brand Whitlock, "The Evil Influence of National Parties and Issues in Municipal Elections," in *Proceedings of the Providence Conference for Good City Government and the Thirteenth Annual Meeting of the National Municipal League Held November 19, 20, 21, 22, 1907*, ed. Clinton Rogers Woodruff (Philadelphia: NML, 1907), 193–208, quote on 206.

73. "Constitutional Amendments," *Toledo Blade*, August 26, 1912, 6; "The Fight on Home Rule Is Started," *Toledo Blade*, April 30, 1912, 2. At the time, Ohio's cities were governed by a municipal code and were only allowed to act on expressly granted powers. See "Independence of Ohio's Cities Is Up to Conders," *Toledo News Bee* (hereafter cited as *TNB*), April 25, 1912, 4; and "Near Home Rule," *TNB*, February 1, 1912, 6.

74. "Home-Rule in Sight," *Toledo Blade*, May 2, 1912, 6.

75. "A Charter for Freemen," *Toledo Blade*, August 31, 1912, 6. See also "Remember Home Rule," *Toledo Blade*, August 13, 1912, 6.

76. "Ohio Adopts New Constitution," *Toledo Union Leader* (hereafter cited as *TUL*), September 6, 1912, 1; "Open Battle for Con Con Amendments," *TNB*, August 13, 1912, 1; "Discuss New Constitution," *TUL*, May 24, 1912, 1; "Constitution Makers Finish Labors," *TUL*, May 17, 1912, 1; "Constitutional Convention Is On," *TUL*, January 12, 1912, 1; "The Constitutional Convention About to Begin," *Toledo Blade*, January 8, 1912, 8.

77. "Fight on Home Rule Is Started," 2; "For City Home Rule," *Toledo Blade*, January 26, 1912, 4; "Mayors Ask Home Rule," *Toledo Blade*, January 25, 1912, 4; "Toledo Secures Important Concession for Home Rule City," *TNB*, January 26, 1912, 7; "Whitlock and Schreiber Will Champion Cities," *TNB*, January 15, 1912, 2; Jack Tager, *The Intellectual as Urban Reformer: Brand Whitlock and the Progressive Movement* (Cleveland: Press of Case Western Reserve University, 1968), 137–38; Hoyt Landon Warner, *Progressivism in Ohio* (Columbus: Ohio State University Press for the Ohio Historical Society, 1964), 330–32.

78. "Toledo Secures Important Concession for Home Rule City," *TNB*, January 26, 1912, 7.

79. Warner, *Progressivism in Ohio*, 332; "Ohio Cities to Lead the Nation by Home Rule, Says Mayor," *Toledo Blade*, May 3, 1912, 1, 11; "Free Cities from Grasp of Privilege," *TNB*, May 1, 1912, 1.

80. "Ohio Cities to Lead Nation," 1, 11.

81. "Ohio Declares for Progress," *TNB*, September 4, 1912, 1, 2; "Toledo Unique Among Ohio Cities," *Toledo Blade*, September 4, 1912, 1; "Toledo Vote on Big Proposals," *Toledo Blade*, September 4, 1912, 1. The vote for the home rule amendment in Toledo was 13,749 to 2,501.

82. "Mayor Will Seek Facts for Charter," *TNB*, September 6, 1912, 1; "Mayor Plans New Charter Under Code," *TNB*, September 5, 1912, 1, 15; "Mayor Plans for New City Charter," *Toledo Blade*, September 6, 1912; Brand Whitlock to Marshall Sheppey, September 20, 1912, in *The Letters and Journal of Brand Whitlock*, ed. Allan Nevins (New York: D. Appleton-Century, 1936), 152–54.

83. Robert Crunden, *A Hero in Spite of Himself: Brand Whitlock in Art, Politics, and War* (New York: Alfred A. Knopf, 1969), 217–18, 225–27; Tager, *Intellectual as Urban Reformer*, 142–43. Whitlock also undertook this European tour for political reasons. Having declared that he would not run for reelection, the trip allowed him to avoid the fall election.

84. "Cities Abroad Are Keen for Owning Public Utilities," *TNB*, November 27, 1912, 1.

85. See "Liverpool Finds the Street Car Business Loaded with Profit," December 10, 1912, 1, 6; "Glasgow Has Snug Surplus from Its Own Plant for City Lighting," December 5, 1912, 1; "City Ownership of Telephones Is Big Thing for Glasgow," December 4, 1912, 1; "Mayor Tells How Glasgow Keeps Lean and Makes Money by It," December 3, 1912, 1; and "City Ownership of Street Car Line Has Given Glasgow Penny Fares, Good Service, and Increased Pay for Men," November 28, 1912, 1, 7, all by Brand Whitlock in *TNB*.

86. Brand Whitlock, "Germans Show Us How City Should Be Run," *TNB*, December 23, 1912, 1, 6. Other articles in this series include "Difficulties Mould Fine Civic

Spirit," December 24, 1912, 1; "Brussels' Motto: 'City Is the Citadel of Our Liberties,'" December 21, 1912, 1, 11; "Paris Offers Inspiration to City Builders," December 17, 1912, 1, 4; "Vast London Shameless in Her Failures," December 13, 1912, 1, 14; "Dublin's Behind Other Cities Because She Is Not Free," December 11, 1912, 1, 5; "City Ownership Should Succeed in This Country," November 26, 1912, 1, 2; "Mayor's First Letter," November 25, 1912, 1, all by Brand Whitlock in *TNB*.

87. "Officials to Discuss the City," *Toledo Blade*, January 22, 1913, 1; "Mayor Names Committee to Municipal League Meet," *Toledo Blade*, January 13, 1913, 1; "City Delegates Are Opposed to Model Charters," *TNB*, January 22, 1913, 1; "City League to Talk Charter at Coming Meeting," *TNB*, December 28, 1912, 1; "Mayor Starts on the Outlines of a New City Charter," *TNB*, December 9, 1912, 1. The Ohio Municipal League proposed to draft models of the federal plan, the commission plan, and the city manager plan for the state legislature to endorse as optional charters for cities to adopt.

88. "Mayor Plans for New City Charter," *Toledo Blade*, September 6, 1912, 1.

89. "Delay Charter Petitions a Week," January 16, 1913, 1; "Charter Petition out on Thursday," January 15, 1913, 1; "Petition for Charter," January 11, 1913, 1; "Toledo Prepares for New Charter," November 19, 1912, 13, all in *Toledo Blade*.

See also "Vote for Charter Does Not Commit City to Any Form," January 18, 1913, 1; "Prepare Prod for Council," January 15, 1913, 1; "Will People Have to Compel Council to Respect Their Wishes?," January 13, 1913, 1; "Prepare to Prod Councilmen Who Delay Action on Charter," January 10, 1913, 1, 5; and "Council Starts Move for a New City Charter," November 19, 1912, 4, all in *TNB*.

90. "Final Action on Charter Commission Due Monday," *Toledo Blade*, February 3, 1913, 1; "20 Citizens at Public Meeting," *Toledo Blade*, January 17, 1913, 19; "Let People Talk About a Charter," *Toledo Blade*, January 14, 1913, 11; "Few Come out to 'Mass Meeting' Council Called," *TNB*, January 17, 1913, 15; "Council Asks the Public Again to Discuss Charter," *TNB*, January 14, 1913, 1, 7.

91. "Why a New Charter?," *TUL*, February 7, 1913, 4.

92. "Toledo Test Suit Gets New Ruling from High Court," February 24, 1913, 24; "Vote on New Charter for Toledo Is Held Up Pending Test Suit Trial," February 11, 1913, 7; "Test Home Rule Power," February 10, 1913, 1; "Not Easy to Find Exact Duties of Charter Makers," February 6, 1913, 1; "Council Fixes Date When Citizens Can Vote on Charter Proposition," February 4, 1913, 1, all in *TNB*.

93. "Ohio Cities Are Denied Home Rule," *TUL*, May 9, 1913, 1; "Is Home Rule Amendment a Gold Brick," *Toledo Blade*, May 9, 1913, 1, 2; "'Home Rule' Doesn't Mean Anything Now According to City Solicitor Schreiber," *Toledo Blade*, May 7, 1913, 1; "Court Holds Home Rule in Not in Force," *Toledo Blade*, May 6, 1913, 1, 2; "Home Rule Section Made Worthless by Holding in the Theatres Case," *TNB*, May 6, 1913, 1.

94. "Charter Vote on November 4," July 15, 1913, 11; "Charter Vote to Be Taken Nov. 5," June 17, 1913, 1; "Mayor Urges Charter Election," May 13, 1913, 19; "Let This City Make Charter," May 8, 1913, 1, all in *Toledo Blade*.

See also "Council Orders Charter Election for November 4," July 15, 1913, 9; "New Charter Vote Fixed for Next Election," June 17, 1913, 1; and "Mayor Asks an Election on a Charter," May 13, 1913, 1, all in *TNB*.

95. David Anderson, *Brand Whitlock* (New York: Twayne, 1968), 46–48, 75; Tager, *Intellectual as Urban Reformer*, 129–31; Brand Whitlock, *On the Enforcement of Law in Cities* (1910; Indianapolis: Bobbs-Merrill, 1913), 3–4.

96. DeMatteo, "Urban Reform," 130–53.

97. Warner, *Progressivism in Ohio*, 447–48; Randolph Downes, "The Toledo Political-Religious Municipal Election of 1913," *Northwest Ohio Quarterly* 30 (Summer 1958): 137–63; Johnson, *Toledo's Non-partisan Movement*, 30–31.

98. "Whitlock Is Among 15 Charter Commissioners," *Toledo Blade*, November 5, 1913, 13; "It Looks like These for the Charter Board," *TNB*, November 5, 1913, 2. Isaac Kinsey was a candidate on both the Republican and the Independent tickets, and the Republicans won ten seats in addition to Kinsey's.

99. "Mayor to Leave City on Last Day of His Term," *TNB*, December 31, 1913, 2; "Whitlock Named Minister to Belgium," *Toledo Blade*, December 2, 1913, 1.

100. For a complete account of the debates of the Charter Commission, see *Journal of the Charter Commission of the City of Toledo* 1 (November 19, 1913)–29 (August 28, 1914). This journal can be found at the Toledo-Lucas County Public Library. See also "Mayor Believes the People Have Asked for a New Charter," *TNB*, January 9, 1913, 1; and "A Toledo Charter," *Toledo Blade*, September 7, 1912, 4.

See also "The Charter of the City of Toledo as Amended," in *The Toledo Code of 1919* (Toledo: n.p., 1920), 1–69; and *Proposed Charter for the City of Toledo, Prepared for the City of Toledo by the Charter Commission, Election Day—Tuesday, Nov. 3, 1914* (Toledo: Toledo Legal News Company, [1914]). This charter is bound and shelved with the *Journal of the Charter Commission of the City of Toledo* at the Toledo-Lucas County Public Library. It also contains proposals rejected by the commission. The charter was also published in the local papers and described in detail in numerous articles. See, for example, "Commissioners Explain Charter," *Toledo Blade*, September 21, 1914, 5; "Complete Draft of Proposed New Toledo Charter," *Toledo Blade*, July 10, 1914, 10–12; and "Charter Men Declare Code Progressive," *TNB*, July 10, 1914, 1, 2.

101. "City May Censor All Amusements," *Toledo Blade*, April 24, 1914, 8; "Dance Hall Regulation Asked in New Charter," *Toledo Blade*, March 28, 1914, 11.

102. J. Kent Hamilton, "New Charter Is a Big, Broad Measure," *TNB*, October 20, 1914, 6.

103. "Charter of the City," 37.

104. "Asks Recognition in New Charter Draft," *Toledo Blade*, December 12, 1913, 16; "Plan to Protect Labor in New Charter Draft," *Toledo Blade*, November 19, 1913, 2.

105. "Charter Board Is to Campaign," *TNB*, September 24, 1914, 9.

106. "The Question of Municipal Ownership," *TUL*, April 6, 1914, 4.

107. "Charter Advocates Believe Unionists' Views Are Unchanged," October 31, 1914, 2; "C.L.U. Decides to Oppose New Code for City," October 23, 1914, 12; "Unions Indorse Municipal Cars," April 10, 1914, 1; "Charter Framers Favor Election of a Council by Wards," February 20, 1914, 1, 2, all in *TNB*.

See also "Why Toledo Trades Unionists Opposed Proposed Charter," October 30, 1914, 1, 5; "Organized Labor Opposes the Proposed Charter," October 30, 1914, 2; "A Bosses' Charter," October 30, 1914, 8; and "The City Charter—a Joker," October 16, 1914, 4, all in *TUL*.

See also "Labor and the New Charter," *Toledo Blade*, October 26, 1914, 6; and "Adoption of Charter to Be Delayed Week," *Toledo Blade*, July 14, 1914, 1, 2.

The decision to allow the mayor to appoint all department heads also caused a division within the Charter Commission itself. See "Mayor's Right May Disrupt Charter Board," *TNB*, May 1, 1914, 9; and "Charter Board Deadlocks on Fundamentals," *Toledo Blade*, April 3, 1914, 8.

108. "Why Toledo Trades Unionists," 1, 5.

109. "C.L.U. Decides to Oppose," 12. Members of the Socialist Party were the most vocal critics of the charter. See "Attacks New Charter," *Toledo Blade*, October 28, 1914, 5; "20 Citizens at Public Meeting," *Toledo Blade*, January 17, 1913, 19; and "Few Come Out," 15.

110. "Answer Objection to Charter Rule," *Toledo Blade*, October 31, 1914, 2; "Strongly Indorse Charter," *TNB*, October 10, 1914, 10; "Devise New Idea of City Government," *Toledo Blade*, March 13, 1914, 1, 2.

111. Downes, "Toledo Political-Religious Municipal Election," 155. For more details on the history of the public battle with the Rail-Light Company, see DeMatteo, "Urban Reform," 126–28; Crunden, *Hero in Spite of Himself*, 220–23; and Tager, *Intellectual as Urban Reformer*, 132–39.

112. "Big Con Worried," *TNB*, March 6, 1914, 1, 2.

113. "Killits Upsets Low Fare Order," *TNB*, March 26, 1914, 1, 5; "Rail-Light Would Suspend 3-Cent Fair by Court Injunction," *Toledo Blade*, March 24, 1914, 1.

114. "Commerce Club Calls Meeting," *TNB*, March 31, 1914, 9; "City Will Reject Offer Made by Commerce Club," *Toledo Blade*, February 11, 1914, 1.

115. "Commerce Club Elects Trustees," *Toledo Blade*, September 16, 1914, 8; "New Citizen's Association Works on Franchise Draft," *Toledo Blade*, May 15, 1914, 1; "New Franchise Draft to Take Best of the Others," *TNB*, June 5, 1914, 1.

116. "Muny Election to Be Held Aug. 4, Is Board's Decision," *TNB*, July 18, 1914, 1; "Petition out Soon for City Car Ownership," *Toledo Blade*, May 15, 1914, 1.

117. "Plan a Long Franchise," October 2, 1914, 1; "Will Continue Fight on M.O. Program," August 5, 1914, 1; "The Citizen's Duty Next Tuesday," July 31, 1914, 6; "Suit Brought to Test Validity of a Muny Election," July 23, 1914, 1, all in *TNB*. A total of 10,597 people voted for bonds, and 9,409 voted against. Out of 37,000 registered voters, 20,006 participated in the election.

118. "Mayor Plans for New City Charter," *Toledo Blade*, September 6, 1912, 1.

119. "City Ownership Urged as Plank in New Charter," *TNB*, January 28, 1913, 5.

120. "Charter Opposes Exclusive Grants," *Toledo Blade*, May 29, 1914, 8; "Charter Men Support Every Popular Franchise Contention," *TNB*, May 22, 1914, 5. The final version of the charter presented to the voters banned exclusive franchises and grants of longer than twenty-five years, allowed for the city to purchase unexpired

franchises, and provided for municipal ownership by popular referenda. See "The New Charter on Franchises," *TNB*, October 27, 1914, 6.

121. "The Opportunity," *TNB*, October 17, 1914, 6; "Jones' Ideas in the Charter," *TNB*, October 12, 1914, 6.

122. "Renz Favors New Charter; Calls It Best," *TNB*, October 20, 1914, 11.

123. "The Charter Wins," *Toledo Blade*, November 4, 1914, 6; "New Charter to Make Great Change in City," *TNB*, November 4, 1914, 6. A total of 20,638 Toledoans voted for the charter and 15,908 against it.

124. Brand Whitlock, *Forty Years of It* (1914; Cleveland: Press of Case Western University, 1970), 333–56.

125. Wendell Johnson, "Toledo's Street Car Question Settled," *American City* 23, no. 6 (December 1920): 608–9.

126. William Novak, "The Public Utility Idea and the Origins of Modern Business Regulation," in *Corporations and American Democracy*, ed. Naomi Lamoreaux and William Novak (Cambridge, Mass.: Harvard University Press, 2017), 139–76, quote on 139.

Chapter 5. The Commission Plan

1. "The Des Moines Plan of City Government" 8, no. 1 (July 1907): 17–25; "Forms of City Government" 7, no. 3 (March 1907): 71–76; "Galveston's Civic Management" 7, no. 3 (February 1907): 50–52, all in *Bulletin of the League of American Municipalities*.

    See also "Spread of the Commission Plan," *Outlook* 89, no. 10 (July 4, 1908): 495; "Three Great Experiments," *Independent* 64, no. 3107 (June 18, 1908): 1409; "Government by Commission," *New York Times*, June 19, 1914, 12; "City Government by Commission," *Atlanta Constitution*, July 17, 1907, 6; "The Commission Plan," *Chicago Daily Tribune*, June 22, 1907, 8; and Bradley Robert Rice, *Progressive Cities: The Commission Government Movement in America, 1901-1920* (Austin: University of Texas Press, 1977), 19, xi–xix, 3–53.

2. For example, see Samuel Hays, "The Politics of Reform in Municipal Government in the Progressive Era," *Pacific Northwest Quarterly* 55, no. 4 (October 1964): 157–69; and James Weinstein, "Organized Business and the City Commission and Manager Movements," *Journal of Southern History* 28, no. 2 (May 1962): 166–82.

3. For example, see Rice, *Progressive Cities*, 12, 110; Seth Scheiner, "Commission Government in the Progressive Era: The New Brunswick, New Jersey, Example," *Journal of Urban History* 12, no. 2 (February 1986): 157–79; and Richard Miller, "Fort Worth and the Progressive Era: The Movement for Charter Revision, 1899–1907," in *Essays on Urban America*, ed. Margaret Francine Morris and Elliott West (Austin: University of Texas Press, 1975), 89–126.

4. Lincoln Steffens, *The Shame of the Cities* (1904; Mineola, N.Y.: Dover, 2004).

5. Harriet Lusk Childs, "The Rochester Social Centers," *American City* 5, no. 1 (July 1911): 19–20.

6. Michael Frisch, "Urban Political Images in Search of a Historical Context," in *Cities of the Mind: Images and Themes of the City in the Social Sciences*, ed. Lloyd Rodwin and Robert Hollister (New York: Springer Science Business Media, 1984), 218.

7. Frank Parsons, *The City for the People, or, The Municipalization of the City Government and of Local Franchises* (Philadelphia: C. F. Taylor, 1900), 17–18.

8. "News from the Class," *Iowa Alumnus* 7, no. 8 (October 1909): 228; John Steven McGroarty, *Los Angeles: From the Mountains to the Sea* (Chicago: American Historical Society, 1921), 272–73.

9. John Hamilton, *Government by Commission or the Dethronement of the City Boss* (1910; New York: Funk and Wagnalls, 1911), 86–91.

10. Charles Taylor, "Municipal Initiative, Referendum, and Recall in Practice," *National Municipal Review* 3, no. 4 (October 1914): 693–94.

11. Bureau of the Census, *Comparative Financial Statistics of Cities Under Council and Commission Government, 1913 and 1915* (Washington, D.C.: Government Printing Office, 1916), 9.

12. Rice, *Progressive Cities*, 72–76.

13. "Bradford, Ernest Smith," in *The National Cyclopaedia of American Biography* (Ann Arbor, Mich.: University Microfilms, 1970), 52:297.

14. Ernest Bradford, "A Comparison of the Forms of Commission Government in Cities," in *Proceedings of the Buffalo Conference for Good City Government and the Sixteenth Annual Meeting of the National Municipal League, Held November 14, 15, 16, 17, 1910*, ed. Clinton Rogers Woodruff (Philadelphia: NML, 1910), 247–48, 262.

15. "Ansley Wilcox," in *Biographical Record of the Class of 1874 in Yale College*, pt. 4, *1874–1909* (New Haven, Conn.: Tuttle Morehouse and Taylor, 1912), 236–39.

16. "Commission Government Luncheon," in Woodruff, *Proceedings . . . 1910*, 557–58, 564, 566–67.

17. *The Commission Plan and Commission-Manager Plan of Municipal Government: An Analytical Study by a Committee of the National Municipal League* (Philadelphia: NML, 1914), 2, 6–8.

18. *Commission Plan*, 8–12.

19. William Bennett Munro, *The Government of American Cities* (New York: Macmillan, 1912), 294–95, 305, 311.

20. Hamilton, *Government by Commission*, 64, 142; Benjamin Shambaugh, "Commission Government in Iowa: The Des Moines Plan," *Commission Government and the City-Manager Plan* (1911; Philadelphia: American Academy of Political and Social Sciences, 1914), 36.

21. Walter Cooper, "Objections to Commission Government," *Commission Government*, 187–88.

22. Frank Goodnow, *Politics and Administration: A Study in Government* (1900; repr., with an introduction by John A. Rohr, New Brunswick, N.J.: Transaction, 2003).

23. Clinton Rogers Woodruff, "Simplicity, Publicity and Efficiency in Municipal Affairs," *National Municipal Review* 2, no. 1 (January 1913): 3; Charles Beard, *American City Government: A Survey of Newer Tendencies* (New York: Century, 1912), 109. For

Beard's connections to Goodnow, see Clyde Barrow, *More than a Historian: The Political and Economic Thought of Charles A. Beard* (New Brunswick, N.J.: Transaction, 2000), 148; and R. Gordon Hoxie, *A History of the Faculty of Political Science at Columbia University* (New York: Columbia University Press, 1955), 106.

24. Hamilton, *Government by Commission*, 148.

25. Contemporaries were aware of this trend. See Woodruff, "Simplicity," 2.

26. Martin Shefter, *Parties and the State* (Princeton, N.J.: Princeton University Press, 1994), 169–79; Thomas Goebel, "'A Case of Democratic Contagion': Direct Democracy in the American West, 1890–1920," *Pacific Historical Review* 66, no. 2 (May 1997): 213–30.

27. Amy Bridges, *Morning Glories: Municipal Reform in the Southwest* (Princeton, N.J.: Princeton University Press, 1997), 18–19, 54–69. Bridges also suggests that reformers achieved greater success in cities in states with limited electorates, given that suffrage restrictions tended to disfranchise groups more likely to oppose reforms, such as organized labor and the working class.

28. Elaine Naylor, *Frontier Boosters: Port Townshend and the Culture of Development in the American West, 1850–1895* (Montreal: McGill-Queen's University Press, 2014), xii, 9–12.

29. Bureau of the Census, "Table 48. Population of Cities Having, in 1920, 25,000 Inhabitants or More," *Fourteenth Census of the United States Taken in the Year 1920*, vol. 1, *Population* (Washington, D.C.: Government Printing Office, 1921), 85; Miller, "Fort Worth," 90–91.

30. Rice, *Progressive Cities*, 19, 25; Tso-Shuen Chang, *History and Analysis of the Commission and City Manager Plans of Municipal Government in the United States*, University of Iowa Monographs, Studies in the Social Sciences 6 (Iowa City: University of Iowa, 1918), 105.

31. Miller, "Fort Worth," 92–93.

32. "Eleventh Annual Convention of the League of American Municipalities," *Bulletin of the League of American Municipalities* 8, no. 3 (September 1907): 82; League of American Municipalities, *10th Annual Convention of the League of American Municipalities* (Chicago: Kirchner, Meckel, 1906), front matter.

   The city of Fort Worth was a member of the League of American Municipalities. See correspondence and other items in Folder "July 1907, 2 of 2," Box "May–August 1907"; Folder "August 4, 1905," Box "June–August 1905"; Folder "July 7, 1905, 1 of 2," Box "June–August 1905"; Folder "February 3 and 17, 1905, 1 of 3," Box "January–May 1905"; and Folder "December 1, 1900," Box "September–December 1900," in Council Proceedings, Local History Collection of the Central Branch of the Fort Worth Public Library, Fort Worth (hereafter cited as Council Proceedings). This collection contains not council minutes but rather resolutions, contracts, petitions, letters from citizens, reports, messages from the mayor, etc.

33. T. J. Powell, "Right of Optional Referendum American Cities' Greatest Need," *Fort Worth Telegram* (hereafter cited as *FWT*), December 5, 1904, 4.

34. Miller, "Fort Worth," 91–98; mayor's veto, Folder "December 7, 1900," Box "September–December 1900," Council Proceedings; letter from committees appointed by the Fort Worth Building Trades Council and the Fort Worth Trades Assembly to the mayor and city council, November 2, 1900, "To the Present Board of Aldermen," and the report of the Charter Committee, Folder "November 16, 1900," Box "September–December 1900," Council Proceedings; charter resolution, Folder "May 4, 1900; May 7, 1900, 1 of 2," Box "May–August 1900," Council Proceedings.

35. "Council Accepts the Referendum," March 14, 1905, 2; "Trades Assembly Endorses Mayor," March 11, 1905, 2; "Mayor Vetoes Charter Action," March 7, 1905, 2; "Aldermen Vote Down Franchise Referendum," March 4, 1905, 2; "Final Action on Charter Changes," March 1, 1905, 2; "Charter Change to Be Reported," February 3, 1905, 2; "Charter Amendments Now in the Hands of Council Committee," January 7, 1905, 1; "Proposed Amendments to City's Charter," December 28, 1904, 1; "Citizens Plan Amendments," December 21, 1904, 5, all in FWT.

See also Miller, "Fort Worth," 102–4; Mayor T. J. Powell to the Hon. City Council, n.d., and Aldermen to John Montgomery, March 13, 1905, Folder "March 3 and March 13, 1905," Box "January–May 1905," Council Proceedings.

36. "Harris Wins Majority of 145," December 15, 1905, 1; "Lassiter and Progress," December 7, 1905, 4; "Big Meeting Held in Fifth Ward," December 6, 1905, 7; "Lassiter's Record from Laboring Man's Viewpoint," December 3, 1905, 14; "Fort Worth's Next Mayor," December 1, 1905, 4; "Lassiter Urges United Effort," November 25, 1905, 1; "Lassiter Opens City Campaign," November 21, 1905, 1; "Harris Attacks City Sprinkling," November 21, 1905, 2; "Lassiter out in Mayoralty Race," November 19, 1905, 12, all in FWT.

37. "Business Men Talk of Greater Fort Worth," FWT, November 6, 1906, 1; Taylor McRae, "How the Galveston Commission Works," FWT, March 2, 1906, 12. Copies of the FWT from March 5 to October 11, 1906, are not available, but presumably there were more articles on Galveston and commission government in these months.

38. "To the City Council," January 12, 1907, undated resolutions, and City Sect. Jno. Montgomery to Chief of Police Jas. Maddox, January 11, 1907, Folder "January 7, 11, and 21, 1907, 1 of 2," Box "January–April 1907"; various letters dated January 10, 11, and 14, 1907, to and from city officials, undated resolutions, charter amendments, and Mayor Harris's veto, Folder "January 7, 11, and 21, 1907, 2 of 2," Box "January–April 1907," Council Proceedings. This standoff was closely covered in the FWT. See "Council to Call Vote," February 27, 1907, 3; "No Opposition to New Charter," February 13, 1907, 7; "Charter Passes When It Passes," February 10, 1907, 6; "Council Talks of Vote," February 5, 1907, 2; "1,200 Petition for Election," February 3, 1907, 7; "People to Vote on New Charter," January 27, 1907, 9; "Mayor Vetoes Election Call," January 11, 1907, 6; "New Charter May Not Be Voted On," January 10, 1907, 3; "Busy Session of the City Council," January 8, 1907, 8; "Councilmen Will Contest Charter," December 29, 1906, 5; "Waggoman on New Charter,"

342 5. THE COMMISSION PLAN

December 21, 1906, 2; "New Charter Is Complete," December 16, 1906, 9; "Committee Will Discuss Charter," December 7, 1906, 2; "Council Will Write Charter," December 4, 1906, 5; and "Discussion of City Charter," October 12, 1906, 14, all in *FWT*. See also Miller, "Fort Worth," 106–11; and Henry Bruère, *The New City Government: A Discussion of Municipal Administration Based on a Survey of Ten Commission Governed Cities* (New York: D. Appleton, 1912), 40–68.

39. Miller depicts the charter campaigns of 1900–1907 as undertaken by an organized business community seeking to gain control of local government and implement a program of growth favorable to its own interests. He also portrays the democratic rhetoric of Powell and others as a deliberate facade. Miller, "Fort Worth," esp. 89–90, 93–94, 111, 114–15.

40. Bridges, *Morning Glories*, 18–19, 54–57.

41. "Board of Trade Protests Rates," February 16, 1907, 5; "Board of Trade Opposes Bills," February 2, 1907, 5; "People to Vote on New Charter," January 27, 1907, 9; "Committees of Board of Trade," January 24, 1907, 1; "Committee Will Discuss Charter," December 7, 1906, 2; "Now 459 Members Board of Trade," November 16, 1906, 2; "Showing Big Growth," November 7, 1906, 3; "Board of Trade President Busy," January 10, 1906, 3; "Will Ask Council for Improvement District," January 7, 1906, 1; "Committee Ready to Work," January 3, 1906, 8; "Issues Pamphlet," January 27, 1903, 1; "Committees for the Board," December 28, 1902, 4, all in *FWT*. Also see B. B. Paddock to T. J. Powell, June 9, 1905, Folder "July 21, 1905," Box "June–August 1905," Council Proceedings.

42. "Eighth Ward to Check Vote," March 30, 1907, 7; "Sixth Ward Supports; Third Opposes Charter," March 29, 1907, 7; "Charter Rally at City Hall," March 27, 1907, 1; "Civic Club to Rouse Voters," March 26, 1907, 6; "Mayor Addresses Fifth Ward Club," March 15, 1907, 12; "Gas Franchise Is Condemned," March 13, 1907, 10; "League Favors a Commission," January 23, 1907, 8; "Urge Voters to Pay Their Taxes," January 20, 1907, 13, all in *FWT*.

43. "Civic League Presents Argument for Charter," *FWT*, March 31, 1907, 4.

44. "Labor Will Vote on New Charter," March 1, 1907, 5; "26 New Members Trades Assembly," January 25, 1907, 5; "Union Members Prepare to Vote," January 7, 1906, 5; "Trades Assembly Endorses Mayor," March 11, 1905, 2; "Pay Poll Tax Is Advice of Trades Assembly," December 11, 1903, 8; "Labor Delegate Is in the City," January 9, 1903, 1, all in *FWT*.

45. "Mayor Indorses New Charter," March 3, 1907, 5; "New School Steps Taken," March 3, 1907, 1, 4; "City Finance in Good Shape," February 25, 1907, 5; "Finances of City Aldermen," November 17, 1906, 1, all in *FWT*.

46. "Santone After Water Plant," November 17, 1905, 2; Giovanni Conti, "Municipal Ownership Is Winning in Italy," October 1, 1905, 7; "What a City Can Do," November 14, 1902, 6; "Shows Profits of Municipal Ownership," November 4, 1902, 6, all in *FWT*.

47. "Mayor Powell out for Congressional Honors," *FWT*, February 11, 1906, 6; "Labor Delegate Is in the City," *FWT*, January 9, 1903, 1.

48. "Market House Deal Is Dead," November 20, 1906, 2; "City Council's Speedy Session," November 6, 1906, 10; "Council Votes for City Market House," February 4, 1906, 5; "Garbage Plant Offer Made," February 4, 1906, 2; "Population Is Nearly 52,000," December 5, 1905, 1; "Water Supply of Fort Worth," December 11, 1902, 6, all in *FWT*.

      See also petition, Folder "November 9, 1906, 1 of 2," Box "October–December 1906," and petition opposing a market house, Folder "November 9, 1906, 2 of 2," Box "October–December 1906," Council Proceedings.

49. "New Charter Is Complete," December 16, 1906, 9; "Charter of City Is Now Complete," December 14, 1906, 3; "Committee Met Monday Night," December 11, 1906, 6, all in *FWT*.

50. "Charter Complete," *FWT*, January 30, 1907, 12. For biographical information on Paddock, see "Showing of Big Growth," *FWT*, November 7, 1906, 3; and "The Civic League," *FWT*, November 26, 1904, 5.

51. "Plan Campaign for New Charter," *FWT*, March 31, 1907, 12; "Powell Dissects New City Charter," *FWT*, March 8, 1907, 5.

52. "Charter Complete"; "New Charter Is Complete." See also "Committee Hears Mayor's Troubles," January 13, 1907, 7; "Charter Committee," January 12, 1907, 8; "Officers May Be Recalled," December 12, 1906, 5; and "Committee Talks of New Charter," December 8, 1906, 5, all in *FWT*.

53. "Powell Dissects New City Charter"; "Mayor Indorses New Charter," *FWT*, March 3, 1907, 5.

54. "Ex-Mayors Talk to Civic League," March 16, 1907, 7; "Vote Down the Franchise," March 15, 1907, 1; "Franchise Extension in Hands of People," March 15, 1907, 1; "Gas Franchise Is Condemned," March 13, 1907, 10; "Citizens Alive to Gas Matter," March 12, 1907, 8; "Mayor Opposes New Franchise," March 7, 1907, 5; "Charter Was Juggled?," February 22, 1907, 1; "Want to Vote on Commission," January 31, 1907, 1; "Committee Hears Mayor's Troubles," January 13, 1907, 7, all in *FWT*.

55. "Citizens Vote for Commission," *FWT*, April 3, 1907, 4; "11,123 Paid Poll Tax in County," *FWT*, February 1, 1907, 1. Miller presents a different figure of 4,580 registered voters. Miller, "Fort Worth," 111.

56. Bruère, *New City Government*, 77, 128, 208, 239, 303.

57. "The Progress of Commission Government," *Chautauquan* 48, no. 1 (September 1907): 14–15; "The Spread of the Texas Idea," *Outlook* 86, no. 14 (August 3, 1907): 707–8; "The Des Moines Plan of City Government," *Bulletin of the League of American Municipalities* 8, no. 1 (July 1907): 17–25.

58. Steven Blutza, "Oakland's Commission and Council-Manager Plans—Causes and Consequences: An Historical and Analytical Study" (PhD diss., University of California, Berkeley, 1978), 5, 9, 19, 29; "California—Race and Hispanic Origin for Selected Large Cities and Other Places: Earliest Census to 1990," U.S. Census Bureau, accessed April 9, 2019, https://www.census.gov/population/www/documentation/twps0076/CAtab.pdf.

59. "Mayor Frank J. Mott Delivers Annual Message to Council," *Oakland Enquirer* (hereafter cited as *OE*), April 2, 1907, 10, 11.

60. Blutza, "Oakland's Commission," 4–9, 13.

61. Printed invitation from the Alameda County Progress Club, n.d., "Minutes of Joint Committee on New Charter for Oakland," n.d., and "Minutes of Joint Charter Committee," January 16, 1908, Folder "Oakland: Correspondence, Drafts, Literature," Box IV, William Carey Jones Papers, Bancroft Library, University of California, Berkeley (hereafter cited as Jones Papers). For the coverage of meetings in the local papers, see "New Charter to Be Their Slogan," *OE*, November 1, 1907, 6; and "Civic and Labor Bodies for New City Charter," *Oakland Tribune* (hereafter cited as *OT*), November 22, 1907, 17. Though both papers were Republican, the *Enquirer* was more Progressive than the *Tribune*, which typically sided with Southern Pacific. The *Enquirer* covered the campaign in greater depth. Blutza, "Oakland's Commission," 21, 27.

62. "Looking Forward to a New Charter," *OE*, November 1, 1907, 4.

63. "Features of the Des Moines Charter," *OE*, November 13, 1907, 4; Brand Whitlock, "Municipalities That Point the Way," *OE*, November 5, 1907, 7; "Looking Forward," 4.

64. Richard White, *"It's Your Misfortune and None of My Own": A New History of the American West* (Norman: University of Oklahoma Press, 1991), 367–70.

65. "Opportunity Is Knocking at Oakland's Door," *OE*, April 3, 1907, 1; Blutza, "Oakland's Commission," 9–12.

66. "Boosting for a New Charter," *OE*, November 4, 1907, 4.

67. Edgar Hinkel and William McCann, eds., *Oakland, 1852-1938: Some Phases of the Social, Political and Economic Development of Oakland, California* (Oakland: Oakland Public Library, 1939), 1:148–49.

68. Blutza, "Oakland's Commission," 31.

69. "Merchant's Exchange in Weekly Session," *OE*, November 6, 1907, 8; "Municipalities That Point the Way," 7; "New Charter to Be," 6.

70. Mary Ann Mason, "Neither Friends nor Foes: Organized Labor and the California Progressives," in *California Progressivism Revisited*, ed. William Deverell and Tom Sitton (Berkeley: University of California Press, 1994), 57–71.

71. "Platform of the Socialist Party of the State of California," *Labor World* (hereafter cited as *LW*), October 10, 1908, 4; "A Little Complaint," *LW*, May 16, 1908, 1.

72. "Minutes of Joint Charter Committee, Oakland, Cal., January 16, 1908," Folder "Oakland: Correspondence, Drafts, Literature," Box IV, Jones Papers; "Labor Will Help Framing New Charter," *OE*, February 2, 1910, 2; "To Discuss New City Charter," *OE*, February 5, 1908, 3.

73. I. Less to W.C. Jones, January 28, 1908, Folder "Oakland. correspondence, drafts, literature," Box IV, Jones Papers; Blutza, "Oakland's Commission," 21–25.

74. "To Discuss New City Charter," 3; "New Charter to Be," 6; Blutza, "Oakland's Commission," 24.

75. "Form Permanent Body to Secure Consolidation," June 4, 1908, 3; "Representatives of All Districts Interested to Discuss Consolidation," April 16, 1908, 1; "To Fight for Oakland Alone," November 14, 1907, 3, all in *OE*. See also Blutza, "Oakland's Commission," 32–36.

76. "Will Co-operate on New Charter," *OE*, December 20, 1907, 7; Blutza, "Oakland's Commission," 28.

77. Folder "Talk to Commonwealth Club Re: Berkeley Charter, n.d.," Box I, Jones Papers.

78. Correspondence between I. Less and Jones, Folder "Oakland: Correspondence, Drafts, and Literature," Box IV, Jones Papers; Blutza, "Oakland's Commission," 15–16. See also "To Discuss New City Charter," 3; "Prof. W. C. Jones Outlines Charter," *OE*, November 9, 1907, 8; and "Invite Prof. Jones," *OE*, November 8, 1907, 4.

79. Quotations from "What New Charter for the City Should Provide," *OE*, February 8, 1908, 3. See also "Provisions of a New Charter Discussed," *OT*, February 7, 1908, 2.

80. "Committee Frames Model for Municipal Charter," *OE*, February 28, 1908, 8; Blutza, "Oakland's Commission," 37–39.

81. "Four Thousand Voters Want Freeholders' Charter," May 26, 1908, 7; "To Present Petition for Election," May 1, 1908, 9; "Text of Charter Framed," April 27, 1908, 12; "Charter Framers to Make Talks," April 24, 1908, 1; "No Politics but a Non-partisan Effort," April 10, 1908, 1; "Charter Committee of the Alameda Progress Club Will Meet," April 9, 1908, 1; "New Charter Project Gaining Many Friends," March 27, 1908, 8; "Progress Club Plans Campaign," March 13, 1908, 12, all in *OE*. See also "A New Charter," *OT*, May 30, 1908, 6; and Blutza, "Oakland's Commission," 25–26, 42–44.

82. "Woman Praises City Charter of Berkeley," *OE*, August 8, 1910, 6; "To Present Petition," 9; "Clubwomen Ask That New Charter Be Adopted," *OE*, April 16, 1908, 9.

83. "The Charter Committee Ask Mayor to Return Petition," *OE*, June 26, 1908, 24; "Oakland's New Charter," *OE*, June 8, 1908, 3. See also Blutza, "Oakland's Commission," 44–48.

84. "To Hear Talk on New Charter," July 9, 1908, 2; "Church Federation to Hear of Charter," June 27, 1908, 2; "Charter Convention Is to Hold Meeting," June 24, 1908, 1; "Church Club Studies Municipal Charter," June 18, 1908, 8; "Present Charter Is Inadequate," June 15, 1908, 2, all in *OE*.

85. "Killing Every Prospect of a Greater Oakland," August 14, 1908, 4; "Why Berkeley Attracts," July 28, 1908, 4; "Work for New Charter and for Consolidation," July 16, 1908, 4; "A New Charter and Consolidation," June 4, 1908, 4, all in *OE*.

86. Horace Deming, "Civic Pride an Asset," *OE*, May 1, 1908, 8.

87. "Some Big Things for Oakland," *OE*, July 29, 1908, 4.

88. "Declare for a New Charter," November 8, 1907, 10; "Delay the Policy of Those Who Would Defeat the New Charter," August 1, 1908, 4; "The 'Interests' Oppose a New Charter," June 1, 1908, 4; "A Wise Policy for a City," April 11, 1908, 4, all in *OE*.

89. "Shall the Council Deny a Fundamental Right of Self-Government," August 3, 1908, 4; "Merchants' Exchange 'Recalls' Agent Gier," July 29, 1908, 6; "Citizens Ask Right to Vote," July 28, 1908, 2; "Merchants Favor New City Charter," July 22, 1908, 4; "Commercial Interests of the City Getting in Line for a New Charter," July 15, 1908, 4; "Asks Merchants' Exchange to Discuss New City Charter," July 15,

1908, 12, all in *OE*. See also "Merchants Are to Send Committee to Council," *OT*, July 22, 1908, 4; Hinkel and McCann, *Oakland*, 153–54; Blutza, "Oakland's Commission," 48–64.

90. "Annexation Carries," November 17, 1909, 1, 2; "Progress Club out for Bonds," November 12, 1911, 11; "City Council Pledges Oakland New Charter," November 2, 1909, 1, 3; "Five Cent Fare to All Annexed Districts," November 1, 1909, 7; "Mayor to Open Annexation Campaign," October 26, 1909, 9, all in *OE*. See also "Annexation Carries by Great Majority," November 17, 1909, 3; "Annexation Made Sure by Signing of Unique Pact," November 6, 1909, 1, 2; "Oakland's Pledge Sincere," November 4, 1909, 6; "Council Pledges New Charter," November 2, 1909, 9, all in *OT*.

91. "Charter Delegates Outline Their Plan," *OE*, March 18, 1910, 10; "To Frame Oakland's Charter," *OE*, February 25, 1910, 1, 2.

92. Five names appeared on both tickets. These five were all elected, as were eight from the mayor's ticket and two from the opposing ticket. "Total Official Returns Freeholders Election," *OE*, July 7, 1910, 2. See also "Mott Progressive Ticket," June 15, 1910, 2; "Progressive Ticket Assured of Election," June 13, 1910, 7; "Freeholders Nominees Fail to Respond," June 9, 1910, 20; "Mott Administration Freeholder Ticket," May 29, 1910, 15; "Oakland Freeholder Ticket," May 28, 1910, 1, 2; "Charter Meeting Completes Work," May 20, 1910, 16; "Charter Nominees Declare for Platform," May 13, 1910, 1, 5; "Charter Platform Is Ready," April 30, 1910, 11; "Union Men Talk of New Charter," April 14, 1910, 2; "Improvers Assemble," March 18, 1910, 13; "Clubs Take Preliminary Steps," February 25, 1910, 13; and "Union Men May Be Freeholders," February 25, 1910, 13, all in *OT*. See also Blutza, "Oakland's Commission," 110–58.

93. "Charter of the City of Oakland Prepared by the Board of Freeholders," *OT*, November 2, 1910, 22–26; "Charter of the City of Oakland Prepared by the Board of Freeholders," *OE*, October 24, 1910, 15–19; Blutza, "Oakland's Commission," 158–75.

94. "Franchise Worth $1,000,000," *OE*, November 17, 1910, 4; "The Steal Goes Through," *LW*, November 12, 1910, 2; Blutza, "Oakland's Commission," 68.

95. "Oakland's New City Charter," *LW*, June 3, 1910, 4.

96. "Platform of the Socialist Party," *LW*, October 8, 1910, 2; "Working Men, Rally to the Rescue of Oakland," *LW*, November 19, 1910, 2.

97. Harold Everhart, "The Power of Privilege," December 3, 1910, 3; "Oakland's Betrayal," November 12, 1910, 2; "The Steal Goes Through," November 12, 1910, 2; Harold Everhart, "Oakland's Golden Opportunity," November 5, 1910, 11; "Socialist Party Backs Up Everhart," October 29, 1910, 4, all in *LW*.

   Blutza suggests that the Socialist Party in Oakland supported the new charter but agreed not to do so publicly, recognizing that this would hamper its chances for success, but he does not have any sources for this claim. Blutza, "Oakland's Commission," 100–101, 112.

98. Blutza, "Oakland's Commission," 187–200.

99. "Adopt Charter by Big Vote," *OE*, December 9, 1910, 1; "Charter Vote December 8," *OE*, December 6, 1910, 1; "Charter Is Ratified by Big Vote," *OT*, December 9, 1910, 1, 2; "Charter Is Endorsed by All Voters," *OT*, December 8, 1910, 1, 4; Blutza, "Oakland's Commission," 182–83.

100. Pamphlet, "Alameda County—Oakland—1910-1919," County Pamphlet Files, Oakland History Room, Oakland Public Library, Oakland, 1911.

101. Albert Farnsworth and George O'Flynn, *The Story of Worcester Massachusetts* (Worcester, Mass.: Davis, 1934), 129, 140–41.

102. Richard Abrams, *Conservatism in a Progressive Era: Massachusetts Politics, 1900-1912* (Cambridge, Mass.: Harvard University Press, 1964), 51; Charles Washburn, *Industrial Worcester* (Worcester, Mass.: Davis, 1917), 314.

103. "The City Government for 1913," *Worcester Magazine* (hereafter cited as *WM*) 16, no. 1 (January 1913): 10–12; Washburn, *Industrial Worcester*, 200–201, 241.

104. Ronald Petrin, "Ethnicity and Urban Politics: French-Canadians and Worcester, 1895–1915," *Historical Journal of Massachusetts* 15, no. 2 (June 1987): 146; Thomas O'Flynn, "The City Government," in *The Story of Worcester Massachusetts* (Boston: Little, Brown, 1910), 132–34; *Charter and Ordinances of the City of Worcester, 1911* (Worcester, Mass.: Blanchard, [1911?]); *Second Inaugural Address of Honorable George M. Wright, Mayor of Worcester, Massachusetts, January 5, 1914* (Worcester, Mass.: Commonwealth Press, 1914), 3, 30; *Inaugural Address of Hon. George M. Wright, Mayor of Worcester, Mass., January 6, 1913* (Worcester, Mass.: Belisle, 1913), 7.

105. Massachusetts did not adopt an optional city charter law until 1915. Chang, *History and Analysis*, 136.

106. "Go Over to Next Year," *Worcester Telegram* (hereafter cited as *WT*), March 14, 1913, 3; "City Council Meeting, February 3, 1913," *WM* 16, no. 3 (March 1913): 88; "Mayor Wright Wants More Light on Any City Charter Changes," *Worcester Evening Gazette* (hereafter cited as *WEG*), February 4, 1913, 1; "Mayor Suggests Charter Changes for Worcester," *WEG*, February 4, 1913, 3; "Commission Government for Worcester Will Be Considered," *WT*, February 4, 1913, 1, 4.

107. Rice, *Progressive Cities*, 117.

108. "The Commission Plan," *WM* 13, no. 5 (May 1910): 141; "Commission Government: How It Works Out in Our Neighboring City of Haverhill," *WM* 13, no. 5 (May 1910): 126.

109. "Mayor's Appointments for Charter Committee Tabled," May 13, 1913, 1; "Opposition to Scope of Plan," May 5, 1913, 1, 2; "Order Adopted for a Committee to Consider Changes," March 18, 1913, 1, 4, all in *WT*. See also "Aldermen Lay on Table Commission," May 13, 1913, 16; "City Charter Commission Is Held Up," May 10, 1913, 1; "Order Passed to Name Committee," March 18, 1913, 10; "Move on Foot to Kill New Charter Plans," March 15, 1913, 2; and "Committee Votes for Commission on Charter," February 28, 1913, 3, all in *WEG*.

110. "Charter Plan Opposition Is Looming Up," *WEG*, May 2, 1913, 1, 2. For the names of those appointed by the mayor, see "City Council," *WM* 16, no. 5 (May 1913): 155;

"Mayor Names 20," *WT*, April 29, 1913, 1; and "Mayor Wright Appoints Commission," *WEG*, April 29, 1913, 16.

111. "Charter Plan Opposition," 1, 2; "Order Passed to Name Committee," 10; "Order Adopted for a Committee," 1, 4.

112. *Second Inaugural Address*, 30; "Second Inaugural of Mayor George M. Wright," *WM* 17, no. 2 (February 1914): 53; "City Charter," *WT*, January 6, 1914, 11.

113. For example, the following articles on the mayor's speech neglected to mention Wright's call for charter revision: "Second Inaugural"; "Mayor's Inaugural Address Dissected," *WT*, January 14, 1914, 8.

114. "Progressives Favor New Charter Plan," *WT*, February 14, 1913, 10.

115. "New Charter Wipes Out City Council," *WEG*, February 20, 1914, 1, 19; "Petition in House," *WT*, January 22, 1914, 7; "Progressives for Commission Form," *WT*, January 16, 1914, 3; "Progressives Elect Officers," *WEG*, January 16, 1914, 13.

116. "Coup in Favor of Government by Commission," *WT*, February 20, 1914, 1, 2.

117. "Commission Gov't for Worcester Strongly Opposed," *WEG*, February 21, 1914, 2; "But 24 out of Over 500 for Commission Government," *WT*, February 21, 1914, 1, 5.

118. "Goes Over Until 1915," *WT*, February 28, 1914, 4; "Committee for Delay," *WT*, February 26, 1914, 4.

119. Abrams, *Conservatism in a Progressive Era*, 285–86; "City Election," *WM* 17, no. 1 (January 1914): 22.

120. Bruce Cohen, "The Worcester Machinists' Strike of 1915," *Historical Journal of Massachusetts* 16, no. 2 (Summer 1988): 154–56.

121. "Come to Worcester," February 13, 1914, 3; "Housing Survey," January 17, 1914, 1; "Legislative Delegation," January 3, 1914, 2; "Membership Campaign of Worcester Chamber of Commerce," May 3, 1913, 1; "Chamber of Commerce Is Formed by Board of Trade," February 1, 1913, 1; "Board of Trade to Take Action Tonight," January 31, 1913, 1, 3; "Board of Trade's Development Plans," January 20, 1913, 16, all in *WT*.

122. For another example, see Scheiner, "Commission Government," 157–58, 168.

123. "But 24 out of Over 500," 1, 5; "Commission Gov't for Worcester," 2; "Progressives Elect Officers," 13.

124. Abrams, *Conservatism in a Progressive Era*, 5–8.

125. Abrams, 59–60; Joseph Eastman, "The Public Utilities Commissions of Massachusetts," in *The Regulation of Municipal Utilities*, ed. Clyde London King (1912; New York: D. Appleton, 1921), 280, 292, 294.

126. "All Charges Against Consolidated True," March 14, 1913, 1; "Mr. Citizen, It's Up to You," February 21, 1913, 1; "City Council Orders Consolidated Probe," February 18, 1913, 1; "Mayor Probes Consolidated" 8, February 8, 1913, 1; "Public in No Temper to Wait Longer for Consolidated," February 7, 1913, 1, all in *WEG*.

127. *Commission Plan*, 2, 6–8; Bureau of the Census, *Comparative Financial Statistics*, 9.

128. Charles Taylor, "Municipal Initiative, Referendum, and Recall in Practice," *National Municipal Review* 3, no. 4 (October 1914): 693–94.

129. Bruère, *New City Government*, 84–87.

130. Bridges, *Morning Glories*, 79–81, 104–5; Rice, *Progressive Cities*, 96–99; Blutza, "Oakland's Commission," 207–10; Bruère, *New City Government*, 97.
131. Bruère, *New City Government*, xii.

Chapter 6. Professionalization and Expertise in Municipal Reform

1. For example, see Frank Goodnow, "Local Government in Prussia, I," *Political Science Quarterly* 4, no. 4 (December 1889): 648–66; and L. S. Rowe, "Municipal Ownership and Operation of Street Railways in Germany," *Annals of the American Academy of Political and Social Science* 27, no. 1 (January 1906): 37–65.
2. Charles Beard, "Training for Efficient Public Service," *Annals of the American Academy of Political and Social Science* 64, no. 1 (March 1916): 215; A. Lawrence Lowell, "Expert Administrators in Popular Government," *American Political Science Review* 7, no. 1 (February 1913): 46, 51–59.
3. Quotation from James Connolly, *An Elusive Unity: Urban Democracy and Machine Politics in Industrializing America* (Ithaca, N.Y.: Cornell University Press, 2010), 222. For an earlier, extended iteration, see Martin Schiesl, *The Politics of Efficiency: Municipal Administration and Reform in America, 1800-1920* (Berkeley: University of California Press, 1977).
4. Mary Parker Follett, *The New State: Group Organization, the Solution of Popular Government* (New York: Longmans, Green, 1918), 174–75.
5. "The Bureau of Municipal Research," *Independent* 58, no. 3080 (December 12, 1907): 1444.
6. David Israel Aronson, "The City Club of New York" (PhD diss., New York University, 1975), 281–89, 380–82.
7. John Louis Recchiuti, *Civic Engagement: Social Science and Progressive-Era Reform in New York City* (Philadelphia: University of Pennsylvania Press, 2007), 27–33; Jane Dahlberg, *The New York Bureau of Municipal Research: Pioneer in Government Administration* (New York: New York University Press, 1966), 5–17; Norman Gill, *Municipal Research Bureaus: A Study of the Nation's Leading Citizen-Supported Agencies* (Washington, D.C.: American Council on Public Affairs, 1944), 12–15.
8. For example, see Edward Sait, "Research and Reference Bureaus," *National Municipal Review* 2, no. 1 (January 1913): 48–55; Henry Bruère, "The Bureau of Municipal Research," *Proceedings of the American Political Science Association* 5 (1908): 111–21; and "For a Bureau of Municipal Research," *Chicago Daily Tribune*, December 24, 1908, 8.
9. Dahlberg, *New York Bureau*, 66.
10. Henry Bruère, "Efficiency in City Government," in *Efficiency in City Government*, ed. Clyde King (Philadelphia: American Academy of Political and Social Science, 1912), 17. See also Henry Bruère, *The New City Government: A Discussion of Municipal*

Administration Based on a Survey of Ten Commission Governed Cities (New York: D. Appleton, 1912), 103.

11. William Allen, *Efficient Democracy* (New York: Dodd, Mead, 1907), x, 1, 280–85.

12. Allen paraphrased in "Chadwick Favors Trained Mayors," *New York Times*, September 20, 1907, 6.

13. Charles Beard, "Administration, a Foundation of Government," *American Political Science Review* 34, no. 2 (April 1940): 232–33.

14. Clyde Barrow, *More than a Historian: The Political and Economic Thought of Charles A. Beard* (New York: Transaction, 2000), 13.

15. Dahlberg, *New York Bureau*, 7–9; Recchiuti, *Civic Engagement*, 103–7.

16. For more on the survey method, see Camilla Stivers, *Bureau Men and Settlement Women: Constructing Public Administration in the Progressive Era* (Lawrence: University of Kansas Press, 2000), 76–81; and Dahlberg, *New York Bureau*, 53–64. Dahlberg (42) also describes the influence of Frederick Taylor.

17. Bruère, "Bureau of Municipal Research," 111.

18. William Allen, "Instruction in Public Business," *Political Science Quarterly* 23, no. 4 (December 1908): 607.

19. Allen, 605.

20. Beard as quoted in Recchiuti, *Civic Engagement*, 109–10; Stivers, *Bureau Men and Settlement Women*, 104.

21. One of Harvard's Bureau for Research in Municipal Government's key publications was Nathan Matthews, *Municipal Charters* (Cambridge, Mass.: Harvard University Press, 1914). For financial records of the Harvard bureau, see Folder 904, Series 1919–1922; Folders 14, Series 1917–1919; Folder 78, Series 1914–1917; and Folder 726, Series 1909–1914, Records of the President of Harvard University, Abbott Lawrence Lowell, 1909–1933, Harvard University Archives, Cambridge, Massachusetts (hereafter cited as Records of the President).

    For bureaus affiliated with other universities, see Charles McCarthy, "Preliminary Report of the Committee on Practical Training for Public Service," *Proceedings of the American Political Science Association* 10 (1913): 307–10; and T. B. Elbridge, "State Bureaus of Municipal Research and Information," *Journal of Social Forces* 1, no. 1 (November 1922): 47–48.

22. Luther Gulick, "Voluntary Organizations That Promote Better Government and Citizenship," *Annals of the American Academy of Political and Social Science* 105 (January 1923): 71–75.

23. William Allen, *Universal Training for Citizenship and Public Service* (New York: Macmillan, 1917), 87–90.

24. Allen, 89.

25. Stivers argues that predominantly male bureaus used the "masculine" language of science and professionalism to counterbalance efforts to introduce "feminine" concerns with morality and social welfare into the administration of municipal government. Stivers, *Bureau Men and Settlement Women*, 3–11, 75. Yet Schacter correctly notes that early leaders also focused on welfare, working to expand the ca-

pacity of government to improve the lives of urban residents. Hindy Lauer Schachter, "Settlement Women and Bureau Men: Did They Share a Useable Past?," *Public Administration Review* 57, no. 1 (January–February 1997): 93–94.

26. William Allen, *Woman's Part in Government: Whether She Votes or Not* (New York: Dodd, Mead, 1911), v, vii.
27. Allen, vi, 5, 28–29, 83.
28. Allen, 337.
29. Mary Ritter Beard, *Woman's Work in Municipalities* (New York: D. Appleton, 1915), 336–37; Schachter, "Settlement Women and Bureau Men," 93–94.
30. Allen, *Woman's Part*, 87.
31. William Bennett Munro, *The Government of American Cities* (New York: Macmillan, 1912), 377.
32. Charles Beard, *American City Government: A Survey of Newer Tendencies* (New York: Century, 1912), 78–79.
33. Recchiuti, *Civic Engagement*, 114–15.
34. Recchiuti, 113–23; Stivers, *Bureau Men and Settlement Women*, 41–45, 72–73.
35. Quoted in Stivers, *Bureau Men and Settlement Women*, 42–43.
36. Recchiuti, *Civic Engagement*, 105–7; Stivers, *Bureau Men and Settlement Women*, 70–72.
37. Frederick Cleveland, *Organized Democracy: An Introduction to the Study of Politics* (New York: Longmans, Green, 1913), 104.
38. Quoted in Recchiuti, *Civic Engagement*, 118–20.
39. Stivers, *Bureau Men and Settlement Women*, 33.
40. For example, see Bruère, "Efficiency in City Government," 19; Gill, *Municipal Research Bureaus*, 17–21; and "For Municipal Research Bureau," *Toledo Blade*, July 21, 1914, 4.
41. "Dayton Manager Describes System," *Toledo Blade*, April 6, 1914, 7.
42. Frederick Cleveland, "The Need for Coordinating Municipal, State and National Activities," in King, *Efficiency in City Government*, 24.
43. Bruère, "Efficiency in City Government," 6–8.
44. Bruère, *New City Government*, 2, 100, 124.
45. Quoted in Dahlberg, *New York Bureau*, 34.
46. Quoted in Dahlberg, 32.
47. Helene Silverberg, "'A Government of Men': Gender, the City, and the New Science of Politics," in *Gender and American Social Science: The Formative Years*, ed. Helene Silverberg (Princeton, N.J.: Princeton University Press, 1998), 174–75.
48. "Municipal Research Bureau, 1934–41," Boxes 57–59, Series IV, Papers of Abbott Lawrence Lowell, Harvard University Archives, Cambridge, Massachusetts.
49. "APSA Presidents: 1903 to Present," American Political Science Association, accessed April 10, 2019, http://www.apsanet.org/ABOUT/Leadership-Governance/APSA-Presidents-1903-to-Present.
50. Encyclopedia.com, s.v. "Abbot Lawrence Lowell," accessed April 10, 2019, http://www.encyclopedia.com/topic/Abbott_Lawrence_Lowell.aspx.

51. "A(bbott) Lawrence Lowell," Harvard University, accessed April 10, 2019, http://www.harvard.edu/about-harvard/harvard-glance/history-presidency/abbott-lawrence-lowell.

52. Morton Keller and Phyllis Keller, *Making Harvard Modern: The Rise of America's University* (New York: Oxford University Press, 2007), 52; Simon Vozick-Levinson, "Writing the Wrong: A. Lawrence Lowell," *The Crimson*, November 3, 2005, http://www.thecrimson.com/article/2005/11/3/writing-the-wrong-a-lawrence-lowell/; "It's Complicated: 375 Years of Women at Harvard," Radcliffe Institute for Advanced Study, accessed April 10, 2019, https://www.radcliffe.harvard.edu/schlesinger-library/exhibition/its-complicated-375-years-women-harvard.

53. Dorothy Ross, *The Origins of American Social Science* (Cambridge: Cambridge University Press, 1991), 290–97.

54. A. Lawrence Lowell, "The Physiology of Politics," *American Political Science Review* 4, no. 1 (February 1910): 2–3.

55. Ross, *Origins of American Social Science*, 296.

56. A. Lawrence Lowell, *Public Opinion and Popular Government* (New York: Longmans, Green, 1913), 70, 99.

57. *Proceedings of the Second National Conference for Good City Government Held at Minneapolis, December 8 and 10, 1894 and of the First Annual Meeting of the National Municipal League and of the Third National Conference for Good City Government Held at Cleveland, May 29, 30 and 31, 1895*, ed. Clinton Rogers Woodruff (Philadelphia: NML, 1895), 225.

58. Barrow, *More than a Historian*, 1–23.

59. Harvey Eagleson, *William Bennett Munro, 1875–1957* (Pasadena: Anderson, Ritchie and Simon, 1959).

60. Munro, *Government of American Cities*, 367–82. Munro's treatment of national organizations, specifically the NML and the American Civic Association, was less critical (360–61).

61. Charles Beard, *American City Government*, 75–87.

62. Lowell, "Physiology of Politics," 2, 10.

63. Lowell, *Public Opinion*, 29–30.

64. Lowell, 105–6.

65. Lowell, "Expert Administrators in Popular Government."

66. Lowell, 46, 51–55. A similar treatment of this topic can be found in Lowell, *Public Opinion*.

67. Charles Beard, "Training for Efficient Public Service," 215–18, 220.

68. Lowell, *Public Opinion*, 289.

69. Lowell, "Expert Administrators in Popular Government," 56–59.

70. Silverberg, "'Government of Men,'" 158. Despite this avoidance, ideas about race were central to the development of the discipline. See Jessica Blatt, *Race and the Making of American Political Science* (Philadelphia: University of Pennsylvania Press, 2018).

71. Charles Beard, *American City Government*, 25; Munro, *Government of American Cities*, 12, 183.

72. Munro, *Government of American Cities*, 113–14, 119; Charles Beard, *American City Government*, 54.

73. Charles Beard, *American City Government*, 54; Munro, *Government of American Cities*, 123.

74. For example, see Lowell, *Public Opinion*, 169, 205–6.

75. Mary Dietz and James Farr, "'Politics Would Undoubtedly Unwoman Her': Gender, Suffrage, and American Political Science," in Silverberg, *Gender and American Social Science*, 78.

76. "Points to Wilson's Silence on Women," *New York Times*, November 20, 1914, 6.

77. Munro quoted in Eagleson, *William Bennett Munro*, 17–23, quotes on 19–20, 22.

78. Nancy Cott, "Two Beards: Coauthorship and the Concept of Civilization," *American Quarterly* 42, no. 2 (June 1990): 274–95.

79. Frank Mann Stewart, *A Half-Century of Municipal Reform: The History of the National Municipal League* (Berkeley: University of California Press, 1950), 63–64, 74–75, 92, 96, 103–5, 119, 136, 140, 142, 207–8.

80. Executive Committee Minutes, November 19, 1907, Folder 73, Carton 1, Series 1, National Municipal League Records, Archives of the Auraria Library, Denver (hereafter cited as NML Records).

81. Stewart, *Half-Century*, 183. Executive Committee Minutes indicate that they considered several alternatives regarding the composition of the membership, including promoting a network of good government clubs in colleges and universities and organizing membership by states. April 23, 1903, Folder 70, and April 26, 1905, Folder 71, Carton 1, Series 1, NML Records.

82. Albert Bushnell Hart to A. Lawrence Lowell, November 24, 1911, Folder 733, Series 1909–1914, Records of the President.

83. From 1894 to 1910, the proceedings were the major NML publication. Stewart, *Half-Century*, 152, 182.

84. W. B. Munro to A. Lawrence Lowell, April 26, 1911, Folder 738, Series 1909–1914, Records of the President.

85. For example, compare Woodruff, *Proceedings . . . 1895*, with *National Municipal Review* 1 (1912).

86. Stewart, *Half-Century*, 150–52. Selected volumes in this series include the following: Clyde Lyndon King, ed., *The Regulation of Municipal Utilities* (New York: D. Appleton, 1921); Edward Fitzpatrick, ed., *Experts in City Government* (New York: D. Appleton, 1919); Clyde King, ed., *Lower Living Costs in Cities: A Constructive Programme for Urban Efficiency* (New York: D. Appleton, 1915).

87. A. Lawrence Lowell to Albert Bushnell Hart, April 29, 1911, Folder 733, Records of the President; Hart to Lowell, April 28, 1911, and W. B. Munro to Lowell, April 26, 1911, Folder 738, Series 1909–1914, Records of the President; May 25, 1911, Folder 23, Carton 3, Series 2, NML Records.

88. Title page of the *National Municipal Review* 1 (1912).

89. November 21, 1917, Folder 40, Carton 2, and January 24, 1907, Folder 73, Carton 1, Series 1, NML Records. See also Stewart, *Half-Century*, 79, 103–4, 164–65.

90. On the National Civil Service Reform League, see Frank Mann Stewart, *The National Civil Service Reform League: History, Activities, and Problems* (Austin: University of Texas, 1929). On the American Civic Association, see "American Civic Association," *Chautauquan* 39, no. 5 (July 1904): 496; November 19, 1907, Folder 73, Carton 1, Series 1, NML Records; and Stewart, *Half-Century*, 131.

91. January 7, 1902, Folder 69, Carton 1, Series 1, NML Records; Stewart, *Half-Century*, 162.

92. April 19, 1916, Folder 39, and April 17, 1914, Folder 37, Carton 2; January 24, 1907, Folder 73, Carton 1, all in Series 1, NML Records. See also Stewart, *Half-Century*, 162.

93. April 19, 1919, Folder 42, and April 24, 1918, Folder 41, Carton 2, Series 1, NML Records.

94. April 24, 1918, Folder 41, and November 21, 1917, Folder 40, Carton 2, Series 1; April 25 and 26, 1906, Folder 72, Carton 1, Series 1; February 18, 1905, Folder 20, Carton 3, Series 2, all in NML Records. See also Stewart, *Half-Century*, 167–68; and *Proceedings of the Rochester Conference for Good City Government and Seventh Annual Meeting of the National Municipal League Held May 8, 9, 10, 1901*, ed. Clinton Rogers Woodruff (Philadelphia: NML, 1901), 38.

95. Maureen Flanagan, "Gender and Urban Political Reform: The City Club and the Woman's City Club of Chicago in the Progressive Era," *American Historical Review* 95, no. 4 (October 1990): 1032–50.

96. "Council Session Was a Busy One," December 18, 1906, 3; "Police Matron May Be Given by Council," August 14, 1904, 21; "City Council," August 6, 1904, 6; "Chief Rea Favors Employment of a Matron," July 8, 1904, 8, all in *Fort Worth Telegram*. See also Mrs. John Sawyer and Mrs. A. H. McCarty to the Hon. Mayor and City Council, December 14, 1906, and Sawyer to the Hon. Mayor and City Council, November 22, 1906, Box "Council Proceedings, October–December 1906," Council Proceedings, Local History Collection, Central Branch, Fort Worth Public Library, Fort Worth.

97. Neva Deardorff, "Women in Municipal Activities," *Annals of the American Academy of Political and Social Sciences* 56 (November 1914): 75; Stivers, *Bureau Men and Settlement Women*, 10, 142.

98. Sarah Platt Decker, "The Meaning of the Woman's Club Movement," *Annals of the American Academy of Political and Social Science* 28 (September 1906): 6.

99. Mary Ritter Beard, *Woman's Work in Municipalities*, 319.

100. Josiah Strong et al., "Men's Views of Women's Clubs," *Annals of the American Academy of Political and Social Science* 28 (September 1906): 88.

101. Deardorff, "Women in Municipal Activities," 75.

102. Mary Ritter Beard, *Women's Work in Municipalities*, 328, 336–37.

103. "Efficiency Not the Last Word," *Virginian-Pilot and the Norfolk Landmark* (hereafter cited as *VPNL*), February 7, 1915, 6.

104. Bruce Field, "Norfolk in Wartime: The Effect of the First World War on the Expansion of a Southern City" (master's thesis, East Carolina University, 1978), 5–12.

105. James Sidney Kitterman Jr., "Reformers and Bosses in the Progressive Era: The Changing Face of Norfolk Politics, 1890–1920" (master's thesis, Old Dominion University, 1971), 130–31.
106. "Norfolk Chamber of Commerce," *Norfolk-Ledger Dispatch* (hereafter cited as *NLD*), January 1, 1915, 1; "Industrial Fund Planned for City," *VPNL*, May 19, 1915, 1–2.
107. "$1,000 Available to Advertise Norfolk," *NLD*, April 20, 1915, 1–2.
108. Kitterman, "Reformers and Bosses," 129–33.
109. "Try Again to Hold Meeting of Council," *VPNL*, August 12, 2015, 3.
110. New York Bureau of Municipal Research, *Report on a Survey of the City Government, Norfolk, Virginia* (New York: NYBMR, 1915), 88–90.
111. "Aldermen Insist on Repeal of Drug Law," *NLD*, April 14, 1915, 8.
112. "Council Lacks Nerve, Said Speaker," *NLD*, March 9, 1915, 2.
113. "Declares Council Is Inconsistent," *VPNL*, September 26, 1915, 8.
114. William Stewart, *History of Norfolk County, Virginia and Representative Citizens* (Chicago: Biographical, 1920), 544; "News of the Societies," *Municipal Journal and Public Works* 37, no. 18 (1914): 640.
115. "Declares Council Is Inconsistent," 8.
116. "Norfolk Chamber of Commerce," *NLD*, January 1, 1915, 1.
117. "Government by Commission of Five," *NLD*, January 28, 1915, 9.
118. "Three Plans Presented," *NLD*, February 13, 1915, 14.
119. Field, "Norfolk in Wartime," 6–7.
120. "Officers of the American Proportional Representation League," *Proportional Representation Review* 3, no. 47 (July 1918): 15; "Officers of the League Elected for 1915–1916," in supplement, *Good Government* 33 (January 1916): 24.
121. C. P. Shaw, "The City Manager Plan of Municipal Government," *VPNL*, March 28, 1915, 51; "Ladies to Hear of City Manager Plan," *VPNL*, March 21, 1915, 14 (Portsmouth Section).
122. Robert MacMillan, "City Manager Government in Norfolk, Virginia" (PhD diss., University of Alabama, 1948), 41.
123. "City Manager Plan," *NLD*, April 24, 1915, 6.
124. For example, see "Chamber Committee's Report," June 6, 1915, 11; "Chamber Committee's Report," June 3, 1915, 5; "Committee Leaves for Western Cities," May 13, 1915, 3; "Will Investigate City Governments," May 11, 1915, 4; and "Charter Commission of Chamber Holds Meeting," May 4, 1915, 2, all in *VPNL*. The chamber recommended a city manager charter, as will be discussed in chapter 7.
125. "Unexpected Demand for Cty [*sic*] Government Books," *VPNL*, July 18, 1915, 4.
126. "Leroy Hodges to Be Speaker," *Cavalier*, May 23, 1932, 1, 3.
127. "Speakers Give Reasons for New Charter," *VPNL*, August 13, 1915, 1, 14.
128. "Municipal Efficiency," *NLD*, March 31, 1915, 6.
129. "Speakers Give Reasons," 1, 14.
130. "Lent Upson Lecture," Department of Political Science, Wayne State University, accessed April 10, 2019, http://clas.wayne.edu/PoliticalScience/Lent-Upson-Lecture.

131. "City Manager Plan Discussed by Upson," *VPNL*, August 9, 1915, 4; "Speakers Give Reasons," 1, 14.

132. MacMillan, "City Manager Government in Norfolk," 43–44; Kitterman, "Reformers and Bosses," 134; "Apathy Defeats Movement," *VPNL*, August 21, 1915, 1, 3.

133. "Nine Candidates Have Clear Field," *VPNL*, August 1, 1915, 7; "Candidates Send Replies to Labor Union's Questions," *VPNL*, August 2, 1915, 5.

134. "Colored Voters Barred," June 1, 1915, 3; "No Decision on Colored Voters," May 28, 1915, 1, 15; "Statement on Primary Law," May 4, 1915, 2; "Believe 7,000 Voters Qualified," May 2, 1915, 5, all in *VPNL*.

135. "Friday's Vote," *VPNL*, August 22, 1915, 6.

136. "Norfolk Charter Body Approved," *VPNL*, October 2, 1915, 1–2; "Charter Body Will Be Organized Today," *VPNL*, October 1, 1915, 3.

137. "Norfolk City Government Is Under Searching Probe," *VPNL*, September 12, 1915, 20.

138. "Aldermen Insist on Repeal of Drug Law," April 14, 1915, 8; "Prepare Petitions for New Government," March 3, 1915, 3; "Municipal Matters," February 25, 1915, 3; "Investigation of the City's Government," January 19, 1915, 3; "Would Investigate City's Government," January 9, 1915, 2, all in *NLD*.

139. "Norfolk City Government," 20.

140. "City Charter Needs Radical Changes," *VPNL*, December 22, 1915, 1, 8; "Many Recommendations Made by Municipal Bureau," *VPNL*, December 22, 1915, 8, 13.

141. "City Charter Needs Radical Changes," 1, 8.

142. "Too Many Arrests Made in Norfolk," *VPNL*, December 27, 1915, 3.

143. "Asks Justice for the Negro," May 12, 1917, 1; "Subjected to False Arrest," September 22, 1917, 1; "Norfolk Domestics Ask Better Wages," October 6, 1917, 1, all in *New Journal and Guide* (Norfolk, Va.).

144. Reprinted as "TAXES: Who Pays Them," *Crisis* 10, no. 1 (May 1915): 22–23.

145. New York Bureau of Municipal Research, *Report on a Survey*, 31–35, 37–40, 48, 73–79.

146. New York Bureau of Municipal Research, 7–8.

147. New York Bureau of Municipal Research, 58, 61, 63, 69.

148. New York Bureau of Municipal Research, 57–59.

Chapter 7. "The Transition to Government by Experts"

1. *A Model City Charter and Municipal Home Rule as Prepared by the Committee on Municipal Program of the National Municipal League* (Philadelphia: NML, 1916), 11–14, 29–30.

2. Clinton Rogers Woodruff, "The Municipal Program: Old and New," in *A New Municipal Program*, ed. Clinton Rogers Woodruff (New York: D. Appleton, 1919), 25.

3. Woodruff, "Municipal Program," 17–20, quote on 20.

4. William Dudley Foulke, *A Hoosier Autobiography* (New York: Oxford University Press, 1922), 98.

5. Harold Stone, Don Price, and Kathryn Stone, *City Manager Government in the United States: A Review After Twenty-Five Years* (Chicago: Public Administration Service, 1940), 19–20; Foulke, *Hoosier Autobiography*.

6. "Preface," vii; Mayo Fessler, "Electoral Provisions of the New Municipal Program," 101; and "The Model Charter," 325, 329, 334, all in Woodruff, *New Municipal Program*.

7. Charles Beard, review of *A Model City Charter and Municipal Home Rule*, *American Political Science Review* 10, no. 3 (August 1916): 604.

8. The labor movement more generally experienced setbacks in the 1920s. See Irving Bernstein, *The Lean Years: A History of the American Worker, 1920-1933* (Boston: Houghton Mifflin, 1960), 83–143.

9. Bernard Hirschhorn, *Democracy Reformed: Richard Spencer Childs and His Fight for Better Government* (Westport, Conn.: Greenwood, 1997), 22.

10. Frank Goodnow, *Municipal Problems* (New York: Macmillan, 1897), 181–86, quotes on 181, 186.

11. Frank Goodnow to Richard Childs, December 16, 1908, and Childs to Goodnow, December 15, 1908, Folder "Ce-Ch," Box 3, Collection 3, Frank Johnson Goodnow Papers, Ms. 3, Special Collections, Milton S. Eisenhower Library, Johns Hopkins University, Baltimore (hereafter cited as Goodnow Papers).

12. John Porter East, *Council-Manager Government: The Political Thought of Its Founder* (Chapel Hill: University of North Carolina Press, 1965), 4–5, 43–54; Richard Childs, *Short-Ballot Principles* (Boston: Houghton Mifflin, 1911); Richard Childs, "Ballot Reform: Need of Simplification," *Proceedings of the American Political Science Association* 6 (1909): 69–71; Richard Childs, "The Short Ballot," *Outlook*, July 17, 1909, 635.

13. Robert Bradley Rice, *Progressive Cities: The Commission Government Movement in America, 1901-1920* (Austin: University of Texas Press, 1977), 100–107; excerpts of 1931 interview in Frank Mann Stewart, *A Half-Century of Municipal Reform* (Berkeley: University of California Press, 1950), 219–20; Richard Childs, "The Theory of the New Controlled Executive Plan," *National Municipal Review* 2, no. 1 (January 1913): 79; *Loose-Leaf Digest of Short Ballot Charters: A Documentary History of the Commission Form of Municipal Government*, ed. Charles Beard (New York: Short Ballot Organization, 1911), 61001–7.

14. H. S. Gilbertson, "The City Manager Plan," *National Municipal Review* 2, no. 3 (July 1913): 472.

15. Woodruff, "Municipal Program," 14.

16. *The Commission Plan and Commission-Manager Plan of Municipal Government: An Analytical Study by a Committee of the National Municipal League* (Philadelphia: NML, 1914), 2, 6–12.

17. *Commission Plan*, 16–23. Committee member Ernest Bradford dissented from this final report.

18. For example, see Herman James, "The City Manager Plan," *American Political Science Review* 8, no. 4 (November 1914): 602–13.

19. A. Lawrence Lowell, "Expert Administrators in Popular Government," *American Political Science Review* 7, no. 1 (February 1913): 56–59.

20. A. Lawrence Lowell, "Permanent Officials in Municipal Government," in *Proceedings of the Pittsburgh Conference for Good City Government and the Fourteenth Annual Meeting of the National Municipal League Held November 16, 17, 18, 19, 1908*, ed. Clinton Rodgers Woodruff (Philadelphia: NML, 1908), 215–22; Lowell, "Expert Administrators in Popular Government," 59–62.

21. "Experts in Municipal Government," 1911, Folder 30, Carton 50, Series 4, National Municipal League Records, Archives of the Auraria Library, Denver (hereafter cited as NML Records); A. Lawrence Lowell to A. B. Hart, December 20, 1913, Folder 1229, Arthur Brigham to A. Lawrence Lowell, December 6, 1911, and draft of the Report on the Selection and Retention of Experts in Municipal Service, November 1911, Folder 730, Series 1909–1914, Records of the President of Harvard University, Abbott Lawrence Lowell, 1909–1933, Harvard University Archives, Cambridge, Massachusetts (hereafter cited as Records of the President).

22. Correspondence between Woodruff and Goodnow, February 5, 1913, December 3 and 5, 1912, and November 27, 1912, Folder "Woodruff, Clinton Rogers," Box 19, Collection 3, Goodnow Papers.

23. Stewart, *Half-Century*, 50–51, 216–17; Woodruff, "Municipal Program," 22; Woodruff, *New Municipal Program*, vii–viii, 21–23; *Model City Charter*, 5.

24. C. C. Williamson, review of *A New Municipal Program*, ed. Clinton Rogers Woodruff, *National Municipal Review* 8, no. 6 (August 1919): 442–43.

25. *Model City Charter*, 7–53.

26. *A Municipal Program: Report of a Committee of the National Municipal League, Adopted by the League, November 17, 1899, Together with Explanatory and Other Papers* (New York: Macmillan, 1900).

27. Woodruff, *New Municipal Program*, 302–7.

28. Delos Wilcox, "The Franchise Policy of the New Municipal Program," in Woodruff, *New Municipal Program*, 178.

29. Wilcox, 173.

30. Frank Goodnow, *Municipal Government* (New York: Century, 1909), 41–43; Frank Goodnow to Horace Deming, March 24, 1909, Folder "Deming, Horace E. . . . ," Box 5, Collection 3, Goodnow Papers; Stewart, *Half-Century*, 29.

31. Clyde Lyndon King, ed., *The Regulation of Municipal Utilities* (1912; New York: D. Appleton, 1921), v–vi.

32. Delos Wilcox, "Municipal Home Rule and Public Utility Franchises," *National Municipal Review* 3, no. 1 (January 1914): 13–27.

33. Wilcox, "Franchise Policy," 177, 188, emphasis is mine.

34. Woodruff, *New Municipal Program*, 354–60; *Model City Charter*, 46–50.

35. Wilcox, "Franchise Policy," 173, 176–79, 188, 194–96. For more on this perspective, see David Nord, "The Experts Versus the Expert: Conflicting Philosophies of Municipal Utility Regulation in the Progressive Era," *Wisconsin Magazine of History* 58, no. 3 (Spring 1975): 234–36.

36. Herman James, "Administrative Organization," in Woodruff, *New Municipal Program*, 119–20.

37. James Connolly, *An Elusive Unity: Urban Democracy and Machine Politics in Industrializing America* (Ithaca, N.Y.: Cornell University Press, 2010), 212–13.
38. Fessler, "Electoral Provisions," 95–103.
39. Woodruff, *New Municipal Program*, 96–104, 307–9, 364–66; *Model City Charter*, 11–12, 54–59.
40. Fessler, "Electoral Provisions," 95–103.
41. Clinton Rodgers Woodruff, "The Initiative, Referendum, and Recall," in Woodruff, *New Municipal Program*, 159–61.
42. Fessler, "Electoral Provisions," 101; "A Model Charter," in Woodruff, *New Municipal Program*, 325, 329; *Model City Charter*, 18, 21, 24.
43. Woodruff, "Initiative, Referendum, and Recall," 169.
44. A. Lawrence Lowell, "Administrative Experts in Municipal Government," *National Municipal Review* 4, no. 1 (January 1915): 28–31; A. Lawrence Lowell, "Experts in Municipal Government and the New Model Charter," in Woodruff, *New Municipal Program*, 28–45; "Progress in City Government," *Outlook* 108, no. 14 (December 2, 1914): 750.
45. A. Lawrence Lowell to Charles Fassett, March 9, 1915, Folder 552, "Municipal Government," Series 1914–1917, Records of the President.
46. Horace Deming, "Public Opinion and City Government Under the Proposed Municipal Program," in *Proceedings of the Columbus Conference for Good City Government and Fifth Annual Meeting of the National Municipal League, Held November 16, 17, 18, 1899*, ed. Clinton Rogers Woodruff (Philadelphia: NML, 1899), 77, 85.
47. Childs, "Short Ballot Principle in the Model Charter," in Woodruff, *New Municipal Program*, 112.
48. Woodruff, *New Municipal Program*, 334; Stone, Price, and Stone, *City Manager Government*, 19–20.
49. Hirschhorn, *Democracy Reformed*, 73; Lent Upson, "Letting City-Manager Charters Grow," *National Municipal Review* 8, no. 8 (October 1919): 567–71.
50. Stone, Price, and Stone, *City Manager Government*, ix.
51. Harry Toulmin, *The City Manager: A New Profession* (New York: D. Appleton, 1915), 155–69, quotes on 157.
52. "Suggested Procedure When Undertaking to Secure and Support City Manager Government in a City," 1929, Folder 6, Carton 63, Series 2, NML Records.
    The central office collected newspaper clippings with examples of organized labor supporting manager government. Clippings, Folder 1, Carton 68, Series 5, NML Records. The NML then publicized such findings. For example, see *The Story of the City-Manager Plan: The Most Democratic Form of Municipal Government*, supplement to the *National Municipal Review* (February 1921): 2, 11, 16–18.
53. Stewart, *Half-Century*, 65–67, 75, 206, 218; "Council Minutes," November 23, 1916, Folder 39, Carton 2, Series 1, "Administrative Records, 1894–1989," NML Records.
54. *Model City Charter*, 8th ed. (Washington, D.C.: National Civic League, 2003); Woodruff, "Municipal Program," 24–25.

55. On Merriam's activism, see Barry Karl, *Charles E. Merriam and the Study of Politics* (Chicago: University of Chicago Press, 1974), 61–83; Stewart, *Half-Century*, 207, 223–30.

56. Charles Merriam, "The Next Step in the Organization of Municipal Research," *National Municipal Review* 11, no. 3 (September 1922): 274–81, quotes on 274–75, 279.

57. Merriam, 279.

58. Leonard White, *The City Manager* (Chicago: University of Chicago Press, 1927), ix–x.

59. White mentioned African Americans only twice, both times in passing. Searches for "colored" and "negro" in *The City Manager* on Google Books, https://books .google.com/books/about/The_City_Manager.html?id=vr9EAQAAIAAJ.

60. *For a Better Form of Government for the City of Norfolk, Virginia* (Norfolk: Chamber of Commerce, 1915), 5; "Will Investigate City Governments," *Virginian-Pilot and the Norfolk Landmark* (hereafter cited as *VPNL*), May 11, 1915, 4.

61. "Apathy Defeats Movement for Charter Change," *VPNL*, August 21, 1915, 1, 3.

62. "Say Consolidation Not Yet Blocked," December 14, 1915, 3; "Meeting Monday on Consolidation," November 14, 1915, 11; "Portsmouth for City Manager," November 3, 1915, 8; "Charter Commission to Meet Wednesday," October 19, 1915, 3, all in *VPNL*.

    The city council voted in 1916 to reduce its size from forty to twenty-five. See "Board Concurs in Reduction of the Council," *VPNL*, January 12, 1916, 1; and "Smaller Council Item up Tonight," *VPNL*, January 4, 1916, 5.

63. "City Charter Needs Radical Changes, Says Bureau Report," *VPNL*, December 22, 1915, 1, 8; "Many Recommendations Made by Municipal Bureau," *VPNL*, December 22, 1915, 8, 13; New York Bureau of Municipal Research, *Report on a Survey of the City Government, Norfolk, Virginia* (New York: NYBMR, 1915), 58.

64. "Matthews City Charter Bill Passes House," *VPNL*, February 9, 1916, 1; Robert Mac-Millan, "City Manager Government in Norfolk, Virginia" (PhD diss., University of Alabama, 1948), 44–45.

65. "Greater Norfolk Is Vividly Painted," *VPNL*, September 22, 1917, 1.

66. Lenoir Chambers and Joseph Shank, *Salt Water and Printer's Ink: Norfolk and Its Newspapers, 1865–1965* (Chapel Hill: University of North Carolina Press, 1967), 298; Bruce Field, "Norfolk in Wartime: The Effect of the First World War on the Expansion of a Southern City" (master's thesis, East Carolina University, 1978), 28, 31; James Sidney Kitterman Jr., "Reformers and Bosses in the Progressive Era: The Changing Face of Norfolk Politics, 1890–1920" (master's thesis, Old Dominion University, 1971), 130–32.

67. "Charter Election on November 8," *VPNL*, September 7, 1917, 4; Kitterman, "Reformers and Bosses," 117–35; MacMillan, "City Manager Government," 46–47.

68. Chambers and Shank, *Salt Water*, 298, 304–5.

69. "Charter Betters City Government," September 25, 1917, 10; "Make Aggressive Charter Fight," September 20, 1917, 4; "Charter Fight On," October 29, 1917, 4, all in *VPNL*.

70. "Prominent Men Favor Charter," November 2, 1917, 8; "Citizens' Union Outlines Work," October 24, 1917, 5; "Citizens Union Formed to Fight for New Charter," October 20, 1917, 1, 8; "Charter Body to Be Organized," September 30, 1917, 5, all in *VPNL*.

71. "Street Meetings Against Charter," November 11, 1917, 3; "Mass Meeting Tuesday Night," November 11, 1917, 5; "Charter Opponents Line Up for a Fight," November 10, 1917, 3; "Organized Fight Against Charter," November 2, 1917, 2, all in *VPNL*.

72. "Charter Champions Highly Optimistic," *VPNL*, November 5, 1917, 5.

73. "Corporate Interests and the New Charter," *VPNL*, November 17, 1917, 2; "Norfolk People Vote on Charter Change Tuesday," *VPNL*, November 18, 1917, 1, 12; "Charter Betters City Government," 10.

74. "New Charter Adopted by Majority of 2,181," *VPNL*, November 19, 1917, 1; "Kizer Endorsed by Central Labor Union," *VPNL*, November 13, 1917, 7.

75. "Street Meetings Against Charter," 3; "Assail Charter from All Sides," *VPNL*, November 9, 1917, 3.

76. "Organized Fight Against Charter," 2.

77. "Attention!," *VPNL*, November 11, 1917, 23.

78. MacMillan, "City Manager Government," 41; Stewart, *Half-Century*, 51–52.

79. "Why I Favor the New City Charter," *VPNL*, November 9, 1917, 3.

80. "Attention!," *VPNL*, November 9, 1917, 7.

81. "Assail Charter from All Angles," *VPNL*, November 13, 1917, 7; "The New City Charter, Article IV," *VPNL*, September 29, 1917, 6.

82. "Both Sides Hold Charter Meetings," *VPNL*, November 15, 1917, 9; "Street Meetings Against Charter," 3; "Organized Fight Against Charter," 2.

83. "Stop! Look and Listen!," *VPNL*, November 20, 1917, 7; "Final Broadside Fired Last Night," *VPNL*, November 19, 1917, 3.

84. "The New City Charter, Article III," *VPNL*, September 28, 1916, 6.

85. "Primary Clause Eliminated," *VPNL*, October 7, 1917, 5.

86. Michael Perman, *Struggle for Mastery: Disfranchisement in the South, 1888-1908* (Chapel Hill: University of North Carolina Press, 2001), 299–320.

87. "Assail Charter from All Angles"; "Entry and Exit of Virginia Daily," *Fourth Estate*, November 28, 1920, 31.

88. "Charter Campaign Continues Lively," *VPNL*, November 16, 1917, 3.

89. "Norfolk People Vote," 1, 12.

90. Earl Lewis, *In Their Own Interests: Race, Class, and Power in Twentieth-Century Norfolk, Virginia* (Berkeley: University of California Press, 1991), 30–33, 46–48, 56, 68–69, 76.

91. Peyton McCrary, "Race and Municipal Reform in the Progressive Era: The Adoption of At-Large Elections in Norfolk, Virginia, 1914-1918," in *The Struggle for Equality: Essays on Sectional Conflict, the Civil War, and the Long Reconstruction*, ed. Orville Vernon Burton, Jerald Podair, and Jennifer Weber (Charlottesville: University of Virginia Press, 2011), 240–47.

92. "Able Arguments for the Change," November 18, 1917, 7; "Mr. Voter," November 18, 1917, 4; "The Eleventh-Hour Audacity of J. Peter Holland," November 18, 1917, 9, all in *VPNL*.

93. Lewis, *In Their Own Interests*, 30, 79, 80–81, 85, 229; Henry Lewis Suggs, *P. B. Young, Newspaperman: Race, Politics, and Journalism in the New South, 1910–1962* (Charlottesville: University Press of Virginia, 1988), 14, 32–33.

94. Lewis, *In Their Own Interests*, 3; Suggs, *P. B. Young*, 23–25, 31.

95. Lewis, *In Their Own Interests*, 258.

96. "The Dirt Roads of Norfolk," July 21, 1917, 4; "Movement for Better Streets," March 24, 1917, 1; "Better Streets Movement," January 27, 1917, 4; "Decreasing the Death Rate," January 20, 1917, 4, all in *Norfolk Journal and Guide*.

97. "Why I Favor the New City Charter," November 14, 1917, 2; "Government by Deficit," November 18, 1917, 49; "Warning to Voters," November 19, 1917, 2, all in *VPNL*.

98. "New City Charter Highly Commended," November 19, 1917, 3; "Commendations for Proposed Charter," November 18, 1917, 5; "Attention!," November 14, 1917, 9; "Captain Taylor Speaks," November 14, 1917, 1, 7, all in *VPNL*.

99. "Vote Throughout Norfolk Section," *VPNL*, November 7, 1917, 3; "New Charter Adopted," 1; McCrary, "Race and Municipal Reform," 246.

100. "Smallest Vote in Many Years," June 12, 1918, 4; "Central Union Makes Plans for Labor Day," June 11, 1918, 3; "Not Many Thrills Looked for in Election Day," June 11, 1918, 2; "Organization to Keep Hands Off," December 11, 1917, 3; "Organize New Charter League," November 24, 1917, 3, all in *VPNL*.

    For an example of European coverage, see "In Violent Attack French Retake Belloy, Genlis Wood and Heights," *VPNL*, June 12, 1918, 1.

101. "Ashburner Will Draw $9,000 as City's Manager," *VPNL*, July 3, 1918, 2; "Ashburner May Come to Norfolk as City Manager," *VPNL*, June 19, 1918, 2.

102. White, *City Manager*, 90–97.

103. *The Sixth Annual Report of the Chamber of Commerce-Board of Trade of Norfolk, Virginia, December 31, 1919* (n.p., n.d.), 1, 9.

104. *Norfolk's Governmental Achievement: Some Accomplishments of the Commission-Manager Plan in the Building of a Great Port and Industrial Center* (Norfolk: Chamber of Commerce, n.d.), 2.

105. Lewis, *In Their Own Interests*, 82–83.

106. "Change in City Administration," *New Journal and Guide* (Norfolk, Va.), June 30, 1923, 10; "We Are to Share in Street Improvements," *New Journal and Guide*, February 12, 1921, 4.

107. "City Manager Aims to Better Living Conditions Among Colored Citizens," *New Journal and Guide* (Norfolk, Va.), March 12, 1921, 1.

108. Lewis, *In Their Own Interests*, 82.

109. "City Charter Needs Radical Changes"; "Many Recommendations Made."

110. *Annual Report of City Manager, Norfolk Virginia, Fiscal Year Ended December 31, 1935* (Norfolk, 1936), 11.

111. *Fort Worth, Texas: Where Golden West and Sunny Southland Meet* (Fort Worth: Chamber of Commerce, 1923), 1, 8, 10, https://texashistory.unt.edu/ark:/67531/metapth41337/.

112. Campbell Gibson and Kay Jung, *Historical Census Statistics on Population Totals by Race, 1790 to 1990, and by Hispanic Origin, 1970 to 1990, for Large Cities and Other Urban Places in the United States*, Population Division Working Paper 76 (Washington, D.C.: U.S. Census Bureau, February 2005), https://www.census.gov/population/www /documentation/twps0076/twps0076.pdf.

113. Barry Sandlin, "The 1921 Butcher Workmen Strike in Fort Worth" (master's thesis, University of Texas at Arlington, 1988).

114. Kevin Portz, "Political Turmoil in Dallas," *Southwestern Historical Quarterly* 119, no. 2 (2015): 148–78.

115. Charles Alexander, *The Ku Klux Klan in the Southwest* (Lexington: University of Kentucky Press, 1965), 127.

116. Nancy MacLean, *Behind the Mask of Chivalry: The Making of the Second Ku Klux Klan* (New York: Oxford University Press, 1994), xii; Kenneth Jackson, *The Ku Klux Klan in the City* (New York: Oxford University Press, 1967), xi–xii; Alexander, *Ku Klux Klan*, xv–xvii.

117. "Thousands See 5,000 Klansmen March," *Fort Worth Star-Telegram* (hereafter cited as *FWST*), February 17, 1922, 1; Jackson, *Ku Klux Klan*, 239.

118. Elizabeth Turner, *Lone Star Pasts: Memory and History in Texas* (College Station: Texas A&M Press, 2007), 130–31; Victoria Buenger, *Texas Merchant: Marvin Leonard and Fort Worth* (College Station: Texas A&M Press, 1998), 63; William Bundy, *Life of William Madison McDonald, Ph.D.* (Fort Worth: Bunker, 1925), 266–67.

119. David Mark Chalmers, *Hooded Americanism: The History of the Ku Klux Klan* (Chicago: Quadrangle Books, 1968), 42; Alexander, *Ku Klux Klan*, 50; Lacie Ballinger, "Ku Klux Klan in Fort Worth" (unpublished paper, Fort Worth, 1997), 11, 13 (copy in Fort Worth Public Library); "Club-Klan Row Settled," *Fort Worth Press* (hereafter cited as *FWP*), November 8, 1924, 4; "Klan Play Wins Praise Here at Chamber," *FWST*, March 16, 1924, 8; "Klan Composed of Leaders in City," *FWST*, April 23, 1922, 8; "Terror Reign Seen If Klan Is Allowed to Exist," *FWST*, May 9, 1922, 7; "Business Meeting Condemns K.K.K.," *Dallas Morning News*, October 16, 1921, 1; "Fort Worth to Hear K.K.K. Speaker at 8 P.M. Saturday at Chamber," *FWST*, August 8, 1921, 1.

120. "'Democrats' Wire to Neff Asks Secret Probe of Klan," *FWST*, July 8, 1921, 4.

121. "Anti-Ku Klux Ready to Give 'Dose' to Klan," *FWST*, August 26, 1921, 4.

122. "Vote Is Lightest in History of City," November 8, 1922, 17; Will Sargent, "Letters from the People," November 6, 1922, 15; "To the Democrats of Tarrant County," July 21, 1922; "Fist Fights Develop at Anti-Klan Meet," July 18, 1922, 6; "1,500 Persons at Anti-Klan Meeting," June 25, 1922; "Klan Asked to Divide Time with Antis," April 21, 1922, 26, all in *FWST*.

123. "1923 Brings Biggest Year in History of Fort Worth," *FWST*, December 4, 1923, 1.

124. "City Expenses to Be Slashed" and "Resolutions Urge Revision of Fort Worth Charter," *Fort Worth Record* (hereafter cited as *FWR*), December 21, 1923, 1; "Cockrell Predicts Tax Raise," *FWST*, December 19, 1923, 1.

125. "Gross Extravagance Charged to City Commission by Grand Jury," *FWST*, December 28, 1923, 1, 3.

126. "What Is Best for Fort Worth?," *FWST*, January 16, 1924, 1.

127. "Improve City's System First," *FWR*, December 31, 1923, 6.

128. "Purge City Politics," *FWR*, January 16, 1924, 1; "Fort Worth Non-political League Is Launched," *FWR*, January 16, 1924, 2.

129. "Fort Worth's Bank Credit Will Be Restored Today," *FWR*, April 17, 1924, 1; "City Hall to Receive Funding Bonds Within Week," *FWR*, March 20, 1924, 1; "1,500 Citizens Hear Speakers," *FWR*, January 22, 1924, 1, 2; "Charter Election Is Called," *FWST*, January 21, 1924, 1; "Mayor Opposed Bond Delay," *FWST*, January 16, 1924, 1, 2.

130. "Who Drafted the Charter?," December 2, 1924, 8; "50 Union Men Oppose Charter Amendment," April 13, 1924, 1, Sect. 2; "Mayor Asks All to Vote Tuesday," April 13, 1924, 1, Sect. 2; "City Manager or Commission Manager or Council Manager Plan," April 11, 1924, 19; "No More Names Expected," March 28, 1924, 11, all in *FWST*.
    See also "City Apathetic," March 27, 1924, 5; "City Manager Idea Discussed," February 3, 1924, 7; and "City Manager Plan Approved," February 2, 1924, 4, all in *FWR*.

131. "Vote Tuesday," *FWST*, April 9, 1924, 10; "Know About the Charter Question," *FWR*, April 8, 1924, 1; "City Government Is Citizens' Job," *FWST*, January 19, 1924, 4.

132. "Fort Worth Goes Ahead," *FWR*, April 16, 1924, 20.

133. "City Manager Plan," *FWST*, April 6, 1924, 7, Sect. 2; "Ability of City Manager Theory Shown in Survey," *FWST*, March 23, 1914, 5; "City Manager Plan Approved," *FWR*, February 2, 1924, 4; "Portland Tries Manager Plan," *FWR*, January 15, 1924, 18.

134. "Fort Worth Votes Charter Change," *FWR*, April 16, 1924, 1; "Primary Vote Is Lightest in History of City," *FWST*, November 8, 1922, 17.

135. "Expert Offers Services," *FWR*, May 23, 1924, 13; "Charter Work Will Be Open," *FWR*, April 22, 1924, 5; "Election Is Unlikely Before Fall," *FWST*, April 20, 1924, 1; Stone, Price, and Stone, *City Manager Government*, 24.

136. "Critics Call Old Charter Civic Cancer," December 5, 1924, 2; "More Efficiency or Higher Taxes," July 4, 1924, 13; "Metropolitan City Needs New Charter," April 10, 1924, 1, all in *FWR*.

137. Charter Commission, *Draft of the Proposed New Charter for the City of Fort Worth* (n.p., 1924) (copy in the Fort Worth Public Library).

138. "Gossip Over Manager Is Called 'Rot,'" December 2, 1924, 1, 2; "Charter Crusaders Drive," November 30, 1924, 15; "Politics Banned from Campaign," November 23, 1924, 17, all in *FWR*.

139. "Many Meets on Schedule," *FWR*, December 7, 1924, 1, 2; "Statement to the Public," *FWP*, December 1, 1924, 2; "The Charter, Pro and Con," *FWP*, November 28, 1924, 4.

140. "Speakers Flay Charter Plan," *FWR*, December 7, 1924, 3; "Charter Foes Active," *FWP*, November 13, 1924, 1.

141. David Stokes, *The Shooting Salvationist: J. Frank Norris and the Murder Trial That Captivated America* (Hanover, N.H.: Steerforth, 2011), xi, 31, 61–64; "Officials to Attend Mass Meeting," *FWST*, January 15, 1924, 1, 2.

142. "Charter Plan Is Democratic," *FWR*, December 8, 1924, 8; "The Charter, Pro and Con," *FWP*, November 28, 1924, 4.

143. Bryan Burrough, *The Big Rich: The Rise and Fall of the Greatest Texas Oil Fortunes* (New York: Penguin, 2009), 103, 209; "The Charter, Pro and Con," *FWP*, November 26, 1924, 2; "Personal Notes," *American Gas Engineering Journal* 108 (June 22, 1918): 15.

144. Charter Commission, *Draft of the Proposed New Charter*, 8–9; "9-Man Council Charter Plan," *FWR*, June 6, 1924, 1; "Portland Tries Manager Plan," *FWR*, January 15, 1924, 18.

145. "Vote Against the Carlock Charter," *FWST*, December 9, 1924, 9, Sect. 2; "The Charter, Pro and Con," *FWP*, December 5, 1924, 2; "City Charter Attacked," *FWP*, November 14, 1924, 3.

146. For example, see T. J. Powell, "Right of Optional Referendum American Cities' Greatest Need," *Fort Worth Telegram*, December 5, 1904, 4.

147. "City Charter Attacked"; "New Charter Favors Classes Over Masses," *FWST*, November 14, 1924, 23.

148. "The Charter, Pro and Con," *FWP*, December 8, 1924, 2.

149. Powell, "Right of Optional Referendum."

150. "City Charter Attacked"; "New Charter Favors Classes."

151. "Speakers Flay Charter Plan."

152. "Rival Camps Line Up Forces," *FWST*, December 7, 1924, 9, Sect. 2.

153. "Politics Banned from Campaign," *FWR*, November 23, 1924, 17.

154. "Charter Plan Is Democratic," 8.

155. "The Charter, Pro and Con," *FWP*, November 26, 1924, 2; "The Charter, Pro and Con," *FWP*, November 25, 1924, 2.

156. "Rival Camps Line Up Forces."

157. Stokes, *Shooting Salvationist*, 67; "Gossip Over Manager."

158. "Labor and the City Manager," *FWST*, November 21, 1924, 12.

159. "Industry Here to Aid Charter," *FWR*, November 27, 1924, 6; "Leaders Plan Charter Drive," *FWR*, November 26, 1924, 7.

160. "Working Men Should Vote on Charter," *FWR*, December 9, 1924, 1; "Unions Urged by Meacham to Support Charter," *FWST*, December 6, 1924, 2; "Gossip Over Manager," 1, 2; "Workers Poll on Charter Sentiment Planned," *FWST*, November 26, 1924, 3.

161. "Taxation Plan of Charter Is Target" *FWST*, December 7, 1924, 9, Sect. 2.

162. Harold Rich, *Fort Worth: Outpost, Cowtown, Boomtown* (Norman: University of Oklahoma Press, 2014), 172.

163. "Vote Against the Carlock Charter," 9.

164. "Charter Vote Is Expected to Total More than 10,000," *FWST*, December 10, 1924, 1, 6; "Voters Divided on Charter," *FWP*, December 8, 1924, 1.

165. "Citizens Hear City Manager Plan Praised," *FWR*, December 9, 1924, 5.

166. "Seventh Ward Puts Ban on Negroes," *FWST*, November 19, 1924, 20; "Chief Ferguson Believes Blaze Incendary [*sic*]," *FWP*, November 6, 1924, 1.

167. Burrough, *Big Rich*, 103, 209; "Tax Features of Charter Draw Armstrong's Ire," *FWST*, November 30, 1924, 1, 6; "Business Meeting Condemns K.K.K.," *Dallas Morning News*, October 16, 1921, 1.

168. "The Charter, Pro and Con," *FWP*, November 26, 1924, 2.

169. Stokes, *Shooting Salvationist*, 14; "Charter Vote to Be Urged from Pulpits," *FWR*, December 7, 1924, 18; "Gossip Over Manager"; "Both Sides Perfecting Charter Fight Forces," *FWST*, November 18, 1924, 6; "Club-Klan Row Settled," 4; "Minister Lauds Ku Klux Klan in Sermon," *FWST*, February 6, 1922, 11. See also "Charity by Day, Punishment by Night: The Ku Klux Klan in Fort Worth," *Hometown by Handlebar* (blog), November 8, 2018, http://hometownbyhandlebar.com/?p=12678.

170. "Charter Crusaders Drive."

171. "It's Every Woman's Duty," *FWR*, December 8, 1924, 1; "Women Hear of New Charter," *FWP*, December 5, 1924, 6; "Clubwomen to Discuss New Charter," *FWR*, November 30, 1924, 5.

172. "College Girls Aid Crusade," *FWR*, December 11, 1924, 13.

173. "Need Is Seen for Revision," *FWR*, December 5, 1924, 1.

174. "Voters Divided on Charter"; "Approach of Charter Vote Stirs City Hall," *FWR*, December 9, 1924, 6.

175. "$1,000,000 Bond Election to Be Asked," *FWR*, July 13, 1924, 1.

176. "$1,000,000 Bond Issue Seen," *FWR*, October 30, 1924, 13.

177. "The Charter, Pro and Con," December 9, 1924, 2; "Charter Foes Call Meeting," November 17, 1924, 3; "More Charter Opposition," November 14, 1924, 10; "Charter Foes Active," November 13, 1924, 1, all in *FWP*.

    See also "Mayor Opposes City Bond Election," November 17, 1924, 1; "Officials Claim Suburb Needs Hinge on New Charter," November 14, 1924, 1, 8; "Suburbs Will Be Asked to Oppose Charter," November 13, 1924, 14, all in *FWST*.

178. "The Suburbs and the Charter," *FWST*, November 20, 1924, 12.

179. "Up to Citizens to Try Charter," *FWR*, December 11, 1924, 20.

180. "New Charter Declared Effective Wednesday," *FWST*, December 17, 1924, 1.

181. "Approach of Charter Vote," 6; "Voters Divided on Charter," 1.

182. "Charter Triumphs by 1,420 Margin," *FWR*, December 12, 1924, 1.

183. "Vote for a Bigger and Better Fort Worth," *FWST*, April 7, 1925, 1; "'Citizens' Urge Full Vote," *FWST*, April 6, 1925, 2.

184. White, *City Manager*, 115–16.

185. White, 117–20.

186. "Mr. Carr States Ideals," *FWR*, May 4, 1925, 8.

187. White, *City Manager*, 118; "'Klan Cannot Run City Hall,'" *FWP*, August 3, 1925, 1, 3; "'Klan Won't Run City Hall,'" *FWST*, August 3, 1925, 1, 3; "Carr to Ignore Klan Protest," *FWST*, August 1, 1925, 1, 2; "Klan Seeks City Council Recall," *FWP*, August 1, 1925, 1.

188. Stokes, *Shooting Salvationist*, 73; Alexander, *Ku Klux Klan*, 222; "Pike Citizens Back Carr," *FWP*, August 7, 1925, 2; "Carr's Regime Indorsed by League," *FWST*, August 7, 1925, 17; "Police Are Told Not to Discuss Klan-Carr Tilt," *FWST*, August 5, 1925, 4; "Klan-Carr Tilt to Be Passed by Council," *FWST*, August 4, 1925, 19.

189. "Carr Explains City Taxes," August 31, 1925, 1; "Councilmen Oppose Tax Rate Increase," August 29, 1925, 1; "City in Need of Money," August 27, 1925, 1, all in *FWP.*
190. C. W. Koiner, "Fort Worth and the City Manager Plan," *City Manager Magazine* 8,
no. 11 (1926): 19–21.

Chapter 8. The Legacy of the Movement for Urban Reform

1. "Clinton Rogers Woodruff," *New York Herald Tribune*, January 25, 1948, 40; Joseph
Rainey, "Abolition of Legal Aid by City," *Philadelphia Tribune*, October 27, 1932, 1;
"Welfare Bond Issue Endorsed by Bishops," *Philadelphia Tribune*, July 5, 1928, 14.
2. Clinton Rogers Woodruff, "The City-Manager Plan," *American Journal of Sociology*
33, no. 4 (January 1928): 599–613, quotes on 603–4, 606.
3. Woodruff, 607–12.
4. Harold Stone, Don Price, and Kathryn Stone, *City Manager Government in the United
States: A Review After Twenty-Five Years* (Chicago: Public Administration Service,
1940), 28, 259.
5. Data for all appendices from George Benson and Mary Benson, "Legal Classification of Cities by States" and "Directory and Governmental Data for the 960 Cities
of Over 10,000 Population," in *The Municipal Yearbook, 1935*, ed. Clarence Ridely
and Orin Nolting (Chicago: ICMA, 1935), 136–63, 164–87; "Form of Government in
the 310 Cities Over 30,000 in Population," in *The Municipal Yearbook, 1934*, ed. Clarence Ridely and Orin Nolting (Chicago: ICMA, 1934), 107–13; Bureau of the Census,
"Table 43: Per Cent Distribution by Color and Nativity, for Cities of 100,00 or More:
1930" and "Table 48: Sex, Color, and Nativity, for Cities 25,000 to 100,000," in *Abstract of the Fifteenth Census of the United States* (Washington, D.C.: Government
Printing Office, 1933), 101–2, 108–12; Bureau of the Census, "Table 12: Population of
Cities and Other Urban Places Having, in 1930, 25,000 Inhabitants or More: 1900–
1930," in *Fifteenth Census of the United States: 1930*, vol. 1, *Population* (Washington,
D.C.: Government Printing Office, 1931), 22–29; and "Table XVIII: Public and Private Ownership in Cities and Towns," in *The Municipal Yearbook, 1902*, ed. M. N.
Baker (New York: Engineering News), xxxv–liv.
6. Walter Nugent, *Progressivism: A Very Short Introduction* (New York: Oxford University Press, 2009), 63–73.
7. Thomas Goebel, "'A Case of Democratic Contagion': Direct Democracy in the
American West, 1890–1920," *Pacific Historical Review* 66, no. 2 (May 1997): 213–30.
8. H. George Frederickson, Gary Johnson, and Curtis Wood, *The Adapted City: Institutional Dynamics and Structural Change* (Armonk, N.Y.: M. E. Sharpe, 2004), 44–45.
9. Edward Banfield and James Wilson, *City Politics* (Cambridge, Mass.: Harvard University Press, 1963), 46.
10. Regional variation may partly explain these findings. Cities in the Northeast had
the lowest percentage of manager charters at 9.17 percent and by far the highest
density of immigrants at 21 percent of the region's total population. In contrast,

cities in the South had the highest percentage of manager charters at 41.18 percent and the lowest density of immigrants at 1 percent of the region's total population. For data on immigrant populations by region, see Bureau of the Census, "Table 3: Population of the United States, by Divisions and States: 1790–1930" and "Table 30: Total and White Population by Nativity and Parentage by Divisions and States: 1930," in *Abstract of the Fifteenth Census*, 10, 85.

11. Frederickson, Johnson, and Wood, *Adapted City*, 45–46; Daniel Elazar, *The American Mosaic: The Impact of Space, Time, and Culture on American Politics* (Boulder, Colo.: Westview, 1994), 229–94.

12. James Svara and Douglas Watson, introduction to *More than Mayor or Manager: Campaigns to Change Form of Government in America's Large Cities*, ed. James Svara and Douglas Watson (Washington, D.C.: Georgetown University Press, 2010), 5–6.

13. On the scholarship on "the regional diffusion model," see Frances Stokes Berry and William Berry, "Innovation and Diffusion Models in Policy Research," in *Theories of the Policy Process*, 3rd ed., ed. Paul Sabatier (Boulder, Colo.: Westview, 2014), 307–62.

14. David Knoke, "The Spread of Municipal Reform: Temporal, Spatial, and Social Dynamics," *American Journal of Sociology* 87, no. 6 (May 1982): 1314–39.

15. Martin Shefter, *Political Parties and the State: The American Historical Experience* (Princeton, N.J.: Princeton University Press, 1993), 169–94.

16. Goebel, "'Case of Democratic Contagion.'"

17. Amy Bridges and Richard Kronick, "Writing the Rules to Win the Game: The Middle-Class Regimes of Municipal Reformers," *Urban Affairs Review* 34, no. 5 (May 1999): 691–706.

18. Bridges and Kronick. On the lack of aggregate data on local turnout, see Keely Wilczek, senior research and instruction librarian, Kennedy School of Government, email messages to the author, August 2017.

19. Martin Melosi, *The Sanitary City: Urban Infrastructure in America from Colonial Times to the Present* (Baltimore: Johns Hopkins University Press, 2000), 119–21, 145, 151.

20. Raymond Wolfinger and John Osgood Field, "Political Ethos and the Structure of City Government," *American Political Science Review* 60, no. 2 (June 1966): 326.

21. On timing more generally, see Paul Pierson, "Not Just What, but *When*: Timing and Sequence in Political Processes," *Studies in American Political Development* 14 (Spring 2000): 72–92.

22. Amy Bridges, *Morning Glories: Municipal Reform in the Southwest* (Princeton, N.J.: Princeton University Press, 1997), 53–68.

23. Melosi, *Sanitary City*, 119–23.

24. Martin Melosi, *Precious Commodity: Providing Water for America's Cities* (Pittsburgh: University of Pittsburgh Press, 2011), 58–63.

25. James Rauch, "Bureaucracy, Infrastructure, and Economic Growth: Evidence from U.S. Cities During the Progressive Era," *American Economic Review* 85, no. 4 (September 1995): 968–79. In contrast, cities that had adopted civil service systems were *more* likely to spend money on infrastructure.

26. *Proceedings, Public Ownership Conference Held in Chicago November 15, 16, 17, 1919* (Olivia: MNL Renville County, 1919), cover page, 3.

27. J. F. Christy, *The Power Trust vs. Municipal Ownership*, comp. Harry Lee Williams (Chicago: Public Ownership League of America, 1929), 9.

28. *Proceedings, Public Ownership Conference*, 9.

29. Christy, *Power Trust*, 11, 162.

30. Georg Leidenberger, *Chicago's Progressive Alliance: Labor and the Bid for Public Streetcars* (DeKalb: Northern Illinois University Press, 2006), esp. 128–29.

31. Kevin Mattson, *Creating a Democratic Public: The Struggle for Urban Participatory Democracy in the Progressive Era* (University Park: Pennsylvania State University Press, 1998), 2–3.

32. Charles McGovern, *Sold American: Consumption and Citizenship, 1890–1945* (Chapel Hill: University of North Carolina Press, 2006), 3–9.

33. Lizabeth Cohen, *A Consumers' Republic: The Politics of Mass Consumption in Postwar America* (New York: Alfred Knopf, 2003), 42–44.

34. "We Are to Share in Street Improvements," *New Journal and Guide* (Norfolk, Va.), February 12, 1921, 4.

35. James Mayo, "The American Public Market," *Journal of Architectural Education* 45, no. 1 (November 1991): 41–42; Arthur Goodwin, *Markets: Public and Private, Their Establishment and Administration* (Seattle: Montgomery, 1929), 16–18; "Establishment and Operations of Municipal Public Markets," *Monthly Review of the U.S. Bureau of Labor Statistics* 5, no. 1 (July 1917): 131–35.

36. Mayo, "American Public Market," 42.

37. "Municipal Corporations: Municipal Home Rule: Municipal Market as a Public Purpose," *California Law Review* 11, no. 6 (September 1923): 446–48.

38. Gail Radford, *The Rise of the Public Authority: Statebuilding and Economic Development in Twentieth-Century America* (Chicago: University of Chicago Press, 2013), 78–83.

39. "Public Markets as a Problem of the Farmer and His City Cousin," *American City* 42 (March 1930): 117–18.

40. Goodwin, *Markets*, 55–59.

41. Janet Bednarek, *America's Airports: Airfield Development, 1918–1947* (College Station: Texas A&M University Press, 2001), 3–66; Board of Port Commissioners, City of Oakland, *Oakland Municipal Airport* (Oakland: n.p., 1928), 5–6; Corps of Engineers, U.S. Army, *Shore Control and Port Administration: Investigation of the Status of National, State, and Municipal Authority Over Port Affairs* (Washington, D.C.: Government Printing Office, 1923), 136–40.

42. Austin Macdonald, "Airport Problems of American Cities," *Annals of the American Academy of Political and Social Science* 151, no. 1 (October 1, 1930): 221; Charles Whitnall, "Municipal Airports," *National Municipal Review* 15, no. 2 (1926): 104–7.

43. Carl Thompson, *Municipal Ownership: A Brief Survey of the Extent, Rapid Growth and the Success of Municipal Ownership Throughout the World* (New York: B. W. Huebsch, 1917), 1–10.

44. Mayo, "American Public Market," 55–56.

45. Daniel Robert, "Customer Stock Ownership as Monopoly Utility Political Strategy in the 1910s and 1920s," *Enterprise and Society* 18, no. 4 (December 2017): 893–920.

46. James McGoldrick, *Law and Practice of Municipal Home Rule* (New York: Columbia University Press, 1933), 342–43.

47. Radford, *Rise of the Public Authority*, 83–84.

48. Ernest Griffith, *A History of American City Government: The Progressive Years and Their Aftermath, 1900-1920* (New York: Praeger, 1974), 86–87.

49. For example, see Orren Hormell, "State Regulation of Public Utilities, 1938–1938," *American Political Science Review* 32, no. 6 (December 1938): 1123–39.

50. Griffith, *History of American City Government*, 85–99.

51. Frederickson, Johnson, and Wood, *Adapted City*, 49–51.

52. Kathleen Barber, *A Right to Representation: Proportional Election Systems for the Twenty-First Century* (Columbus: Ohio State University Press, 2000), 32–40; William Dudley Foulke, *A Hoosier Autobiography* (New York: Oxford University Press, 1922).

53. Frank Mann Stewart, *A Half-Century of Municipal Reform* (Berkeley: University of California Press, 1950), 99–100.

54. Bernard Hirschhorn, *Democracy Reformed: Richard Spencer Childs and His Fight for Better Government* (Westport, Conn.: Greenwood, 1997), 111–12.

55. Committee on Municipal Program of the National Municipal League, *A Model City Charter with Home Rule Provisions Recommended for State Constitutions* (New York: NML, 1933), 2–3, 8–9.

56. James Connolly, *An Elusive Unity: Urban Democracy and Machine Politics in Industrializing America* (Ithaca, N.Y.: Cornell University Press, 2010), 213.

57. H. W. Dodds to the members of the Committee on Municipal Program, November 1, 1932, Folder 30, Carton 62, Series 4, National Municipal League Records, Archives of the Auraria Library, Denver.

58. Connolly, *Elusive Unity*, 213–15; Barber, *Right to Representation*, 37.

59. John Commons, "Proportional Representation," *Proportional Representation Review* 1, no. 1 (September 1893): 8–11.

60. C. G. Hoag, "The Representative Council Plan in Ohio," *Equity Series* 15, no. 1 (January 1913): 80.

61. Stone, Price, and Stone, *City Manager Government*, v; H. W. Dodds, review of *The City Manager*, by Leonard White, *Annals of the American Academy of Political and Social Science* 138 (July 1928): 184–85; Henry Hodges, review of *City Manager Government in Nine Cities* and *City Manager Government in the United States*, by Harold Stone, Don Price, and Kathryn Stone, *Annals of the American Academy of Political and Social Science* 212 (November 1940): 258.

62. Stone, Price, and Stone, *City Manager Government*, 236, 240–41.

63. A seminal text that offered a pluralist interpretation of urban politics was published two years earlier. Robert Dahl, *Who Governs? Democracy and Power in an American City* (New Haven, Conn.: Yale University Press, 1961). Dahl's study of New Haven does not examine proportional representation, the NML, or the model charters.

64. Banfield and Wilson, *City Politics*, 3, 171–72, 186 (emphasis mine), 293–312.
65. Committee on Municipal Program of the National Municipal League, *A Model City Charter with Home Rule Provisions Recommended for State Constitutions* (New York: NML, 1927), 34.
66. Hirschhorn, *Democracy Reformed*, 74–77.
67. Leonard White, *The City Manager* (Chicago: University of Chicago Press, 1927), 161, 166.
68. White, *City Manager*, 197, 283–91, 301–2.
69. Stone, Price, and Stone, *City Manager Government*, 23–24, 249–57.
70. Griffith, *History of American City Government*, 51–54.
71. Stone, Price, and Stone, *City Manager Government*, 4–5, 72–75.
72. Banfield and Wilson, *City Politics*, 1–2, 173–74.
73. For example, see Richard Stillman, *The Rise of the City Manager: A Public Profession in Local Government* (Albuquerque: University of New Mexico Press, 1974), 3.
74. Yahong Zhang and Richard Feiock, "City Managers' Policy Leadership in Council-Manager Cities," *Journal of Public Administration Research and Theory* 20, no. 2 (April 2010): 461–76; Patrick Overeem, "The Value of the Dichotomy: Politics, Administration, and the Political Neutrality of Administrators," *Administrative Theory and Praxis* 27, no. 2 (June 2005): 311–29; James Svara, "The Myth of the Dichotomy: Complementarity of Politics and Administration in the Past and Future of Public Administration," *Public Administration Review* 61, no. 2 (March–April 2001): 176–83; Robert Montjoy and Douglas Watson, "A Case for Reinterpreted Dichotomy of Politics and Administration as a Professional Standard in Council-Manager Government," *Public Administration Review* 55, no. 3 (May–June 1995): 231–39.
75. Robert Alford and Eugene Lee, "Voting Turnout in American Cities," *American Political Science Review* 62, no. 3 (September 1968): 796–813.
76. Zoltan Hajnal and Paul Lewis, "Municipal Institutions and Voter Turnout in Local Elections," *Urban Affairs Review* 38, no. 5 (May 2003): 658–59.
77. LeAnn Beaty and Trenton Davis, "Gender Disparity in Professional City Management: Making the Case for Enhancing Leadership Curriculum," *Journal of Public Affairs Education* 18, no. 4 (January 2012): 617–32; Richard Fox and Robert Schuhmann, "Gender and the Role of the City Manager," *Social Science Quarterly* 81, no. 2 (June 2000): 604–21.
78. Jessica Trounstine and Melody Valdini, "The Context Matters: The Effects of Single-Member Versus At-Large Districts on City Council Diversity," *American Journal of Political Science* 52, Issue 3 (July 2008): 554–69; Neal Caren, "Big City, Big Turnout? Electoral Participation in American Cities," *Journal of Urban Affairs* 29, no. 1 (February 2007): 31–46; Hajnal and Lewis, "Municipal Institutions and Voter Turnout."
79. Craig Wheeland, Christine Palus, and Curtis Wood, "A Century of Municipal Reform in the United States: A Legacy of Success, Adaptation, and the Impulse to Improve," *American Review of Public Administration* 44, no. 4 (July 2014): S15; Gerald

Wright, "Charles Adrian and the Study of Nonpartisan Elections," *Political Research Quarterly* 61, no. 1 (March 2008): 13–16.

80. Wright, "Charles Adrian," 15.

81. Zoltan Hajnal and Jessica Trounstine, "Where Turnout Matters: The Consequences of Uneven Turnout in City Politics," *Journal of Politics* 67, no. 2 (May 2005): 515–35.

82. Daniel Smith and Caroline Tolbert, *Educated by Initiative: The Effects of Direct Democracy on Citizens and Political Organizations in the American States* (Ann Arbor: University of Michigan Press, 2004); Thomas Goebel, *A Government by the People: Direct Democracy in America, 1890–1940* (Chapel Hill: University of North Carolina Press, 2002); Daniel Smith and Joseph Lubinski, "Direct Democracy During the Progressive Era: A Crack in the Populist Veneer?," *Journal of Policy History* 14, no. 4 (2002): 349–83.

83. Hajnal and Lewis, "Municipal Institutions and Voter Turnout," 649, 658.

84. Smith and Tolbert, *Educated by Initiative*, xi–xxii, 1–30, 136–48, quote on 138.

85. Benny Geys, "Explaining Voter Turnout: A Review of Aggregate-Level Research," *Electoral Studies* 25, no. 4 (2006): 637–63, 650–51; Shaun Bowler, David Brockington, and Todd Donovan, "Election Systems and Voter Turnout: Experiments in the United States," *Journal of Politics* 63, no. 3 (August 2001): 902–15.

86. Radford, *Rise of the Public Authority*, 1–16, 82–87, 157.

87. Suzanne Leland and Holly Whisman, "Local Legislatures," in *The Oxford Handbook of State and Local Government*, ed. Donald Heider-Markel (New York: Oxford University Press, 2014), 431–33.

88. *Model City Charter* (1933), 101–6, quotes on 102–3.

89. Joseph McLean, "Use and Abuse of Authorities," *National Municipal Review* 42 (October 1953): 438–44.

90. J. N. Sletten, "Municipal Ownership of Water Plant Secured in Adrian," *American City* 23 (November 1920): 529; Stone, Price, and Stone, *City Manager Government*, 42.

91. Banfield and Wilson, *City Politics*, 261–64.

92. Remarks of Henry K. Evans, Chamber of Commerce of the United States, before the National Parking Association, Cincinnati, Ohio, October 2, 1952 (typescript original at the Loeb Library, Harvard University); *Re-privatizing Public Enterprise* (Washington, D.C.: Chamber of Commerce of the United States of America, 1952); Hoboken Chamber of Commerce, *The Hoboken Case: A Warning to Other Municipalities of the Dangers of Public Ownership* (Hoboken, N.J.: n.p., 1944); New York Chamber of Commerce, *A Statement in Opposition to the Establishment of a Municipal Power and Light Plan in New York City and to the Creation of Municipal Power Authorities* (New York: n.p., 1936).

93. *Policy Declarations Adopted by Members of the Chamber of Commerce of the United States of America, 1966/67* (Washington, D.C.: Chamber of Commerce, 1967), 28–29, 99–105, 109, 111, 121, 126, 141.

94. Leland and Whisman, "Local Legislatures," 431–33; Radford, *Rise of the Public Authority*, 2–16.

95. Adam Sheingate, "Why Can't Americans See the State?," *Forum* 7, no. 4 (2009): 5–14.

96. Mildred Warner, "Privatization and Urban Governance: The Continuing Challenges of Efficiency and Integration," *Cities* 29 (2012): S38–S43.

97. George Homsy and Mildred Warner, "Intermunicipal Cooperation: The Growing Reform," in *The Municipal Yearbook, 2014* (Washington, D.C.: ICMA Press, 2014), 58–61.

98. Julia Lurie, "This Major City's Drinking Water Was Fine. Then Came the Private Water Company," *Mother Jones*, October 26, 2016, http://www.motherjones.com /environment/2016/10/private-water-pittsburgh-veolia/.

99. Danielle Ivory, Ben Protess, and Kitty Bennett, "When You Dial 911 and Wall Street Answers," *New York Times*, June 25, 2016, https://www.nytimes.com/2016 /06/26/business/dealbook/when-you-dial-911-and-wall-street-answers.html.

100. David Shepardson, "St. Louis Wins U.S. Approval to Explore Airport Privatization," Reuters, April 24, 2017, http://www.reuters.com/article/us-missouri -airport-privatization-idUSKBN17Q0VA.

101. Warner, "Privatization and Urban Governance," S41.

102. Jing Wang and Erica McFadden, "The Absence of Social Equity Measurement in Municipal Service Privatization: Are Residents Feeling Dumped On?," *State and Local Government Review* 48, no. 1 (2016): 22–23.

103. Quoted in Ivory, Protess, and Bennett, "When You Dial 911."

104. Hajnal and Lewis, "Municipal Institutions and Voter Turnout," 658.

105. Wang and McFadden, "Absence of Social Equity Measurement."

106. Hajnal and Trounstine, "Where Turnout Matters," 530–32.

107. Brian Balogh, *A Government Out of Sight: The Mystery of National Authority in Nineteenth-Century America* (New York: Cambridge University Press, 2009), 397.

Epilogue

1. Clinton Rogers Woodruff, preface, remarks, and "The Battle for Betterment," in *Proceedings of the Providence Conference for Good City Government and the Thirteenth Annual Meeting of the National Municipal League, Held November 19, 20, 21, 22, 1907*, ed. Clinton Rogers Woodruff (Philadelphia: NML, 1907), iv, 20, 95.

2. Frank Mann Stewart, *A Half-Century of Municipal Reform: The History of the National Municipal League* (Berkeley: University of California Press, 1950), 206; William Dudley Foulke, *A Hoosier Autobiography* (New York: Oxford University Press, 1922), 98.

3. "Minutes of the Meeting of the Vice Presidents and Council of the National Municipal League," February 21–22, 1931, "Council Minutes 1930–1939," Folders 48–55, Carton 2, Series 1, National Municipal League Records, Archives of the Auraria Library, Denver (hereafter cited as NML Records).

4. Untitled 1931 memo, "History—Miscellaneous Statements," Folders 10–13, Carton 4, Series 2, NML Records. On Forbes, see "Russell Forbes Made Purchase Commissioner," *New York Herald Tribune*, December 30, 1933, 28.

5. Untitled 1931 memo, "History—Miscellaneous Statements."

6. Dwight Waldo, "Political Science: Tradition, Discipline, Profession, Science, Enterprise," in *Political Science: Scope and Theory*, ed. Fred Greenstein and Nelson Polsby (Reading, Mass.: Addison-Wesley, 1975), 41–50.

7. Barry Karl, *Charles E. Merriam and the Study of Politics* (Chicago: University of Chicago Press, 1974), 119–22.

8. Edward Banfield and James Wilson, *City Politics* (Cambridge, Mass.: Harvard University Press, 1963), 141–42, 171–72.

9. Waldo, "Political Science," 41–50.

10. Leonard White, *The City Manager* (Chicago: University of Chicago Press, 1927), 148–50, 166.

11. Clarence Ridley and Orin Nolting, *The City-Manager Profession* (Chicago: University of Chicago Press, 1934), 39–43, 59–70, 82–106.

12. "Secretary's Report to the Thirty-Third Annual Meeting of the National Municipal League, November 1, 1927," "Secretary's Reports," 1927–1929, Folders 11–13, Carton 1, Series 1, NML Records.

13. White, *City Manager*, 148–50, 166.

14. A few exceptions include the Boston Bureau of Municipal Research, the Municipal Research and Services Center, and the Worcester Regional Research Bureau. See http://bmrb.org; http://mrsc.org; and http://www.wrrb.org.

15. Thomas Medvetz, *Think Tanks in America* (Chicago: University of Chicago Press, 2012), 5–16, 55–70.

16. Jonathan Kahn, *Budgeting Democracy: State Building and Citizenship in America* (Ithaca, N.Y.: Cornell University Press, 1997), 165–67.

17. "About Us," Brookings Institution, accessed April 10, 2019, https://www.brookings.edu/about-us/.

18. Eric Lipton and Brooke William, "How Think Tanks Amplify Corporate America's Influence," *New York Times*, August 7, 2016, https://www.nytimes.com/2016/08/08/us/politics/think-tanks-research-and-corporate-lobbying.html; Julie Hirschfeld David, "Trump Backs Air Traffic Control Privatization," *New York Times*, June 5, 2017, https://www.nytimes.com/2017/06/05/us/politics/trump-privatize-air-traffic-control.html.

19. John Louis Recchiuti, *Civic Engagement: Social Science and Progressive-Era Reform in New York City* (Philadelphia: University of Pennsylvania Press, 2007), 113–23.

20. John Dryzek, "Revolutions Without Enemies: Key Transformations in Political Science," *American Political Science Review* 100, no. 4 (November 2006): 487–92.

21. H. George Frederickson, Gary Johnson, and Curtis Wood, preface to *The Adapted City: Institutional Dynamics and Structural Change* (Armonk, N.Y.: M. E. Sharpe, 2004), xii.

22. Robert Putnam, "APSA Presidential Address: The Public Role of Political Science," *Perspectives on Politics* 1, no. 2 (June 2003): 249–55.

23. Putnam, 253.

24. "History of the National Civic League," National Civic League, November 11, 2014, http://www.nationalcivicleague.org/history-of-the-national-civic-league/.

25. Lenneal Henderson, "The Civic Index: Theory, Practice and Learning Across American Cities," *Administrative Theory and Praxis* 25, no. 3 (September 2003): 371–72.

26. "Mission and Vision," National Civic League, accessed May 29, 2019, https://www.nationalcivicleague.org/mission-and-vision/; "Our Work," National Civic League, accessed May 29, 2019, https://www.nationalcivicleague.org/our-work/; "About Our Resources," National Civic League, accessed May 29, 2019, https://www.nationalcivicleague.org/resource-center/.

27. "Truth, Racial Healing, and Transformation," National Civic League, accessed May 29, 2019, https://www.nationalcivicleague.org/truth-racial-healing-transformation/.

28. Frederickson, Johnson, and Wood, *Adapted City*, 17.

29. Craig Wheeland, Christine Palus, and Curtis Wood, "A Century of Municipal Reform in the United States: A Legacy of Success, Adaptation, and the Impulse to Improve," *American Review of Public Administration* 44, no. 4 (July 2014): 13S–14S; "Model City Charter, 8th Edition," National Civic League, accessed April 10, 2019, http://www.nationalcivicleague.org/model-city-charter-8th-edition/; National Civic League, *Model City Charter: Defining Good Government in a New Millennium*, 8th ed. (Washington, D.C.: National Civic League, 2003), iii, 40–41.

30. James Svara and Douglas Watson, "Introduction: Framing Constitutional Contests in Large Cities" and "Conclusion: Distinct Factors and Common Themes in Change of Form Referenda," in *More than Mayor or Manager: Campaigns to Change Form of Government in America's Large Cities*, ed. James Svara and Douglas Watson (Washington, D.C.: Georgetown University Press, 2010), 4–5, 307–8.

31. Frederickson, Johnson, and Wood, *Adapted City*, 4.

32. Wheeland, Palus, and Wood, "Century of Municipal Reform," 15S–16S; Douglas and Svara, "Introduction," 4–5; Wendy Hassett and Douglas Watson, *Civic Battles: When Cities Change Their Form of Government* (Boca Raton: PrAcademics, 2007), 10.

33. Svara and Watson, "Introduction," 13–15; Svara and Watson, "Conclusion," 320–21.

34. David Barron, "Reclaiming Home Rule," *Harvard Law Review* 116, no. 8 (2003): 2257–66.

35. Richard Briffault, "Home Rule for the Twenty-First Century," *Urban Law* 36 (2004): 253–72.

36. Hassett and Watson, *Civic Battles*, ii.

37. Hassett and Watson, 10.

38. Laura Porter, "April 25, 1951: McGrath begins 34-year stint at city manager," *Worcester Telegram*, July 11, 2016, accessed May 29, 2019, https://www.telegram.com/news/20160711/april-25-1951-mcgrath-begins-34-year-stint-as-city-manager; "Quick Facts," The City of Worcester, accessed May 29, 2019, http://www.worcesterma.gov/quick-facts.

39. "A Noisy Distraction on Norfolk Mayor," *Virginian Pilot*, February 22, 2008, https://pilotonline.com/opinion/editorial/a-noisy-distraction-on-norfolk-mayor/article_ffe8d657-43fb-5beb-83b2-4b721257e6ae.html; "City Government,"

City of Fort Worth, Texas, accessed April 10, 2019, http://fortworthtexas.gov
/government/.

40. Hassett and Watson, *Civic Battles*, 1; Svara and Watson, "Introduction," 1–2.

41. Frederickson, Johnson, and Wood, *Adapted City*, 3–16; Svara and Watson,
"Introduction."

42. James Clingermayer and Richard Feiock, *Institutional Constraints and Policy Choice:
An Exploration of Local Government* (Albany: State University of New York Press,
2001), 1–6; Svara and Watson, "Conclusion," 319–20.

Index

Abbott, Grace, 122–23

accountability: Bryce and, 74; city manager government and, 267; commission government and, 140, 141, 143; direct democracy and, 91; Goodnow and, 75; mayors and, 81, 104; proportional representation and, 257; short ballots and, 241, 263; spoils system and, 41; of state-level administrative commissions, 127

Addams, Jane, 14–15

administration: city manager government and, 241, 261, 263; city-state relations and, 72; experts in, 173, 175; Goodnow and, 55, 65, 71–72, 147, 186; mayor and professional, 82, 98, 210; mayor-council government and, 81; political scientists and, 54, 71–72; politics distinct from, 54, 71–72, 263. *See also* public administration; state-level administrative commissions

administrative centralization: city manager government and, 259; direct democracy and, 206; Lowell on, 204; NML on, 262; in Norfolk, 106–7; in Toledo, 101, 102, 103

administrative efficiency: Bruère and, 170; voting rights and, 173

African American votes: at-large system and, 223–24, 259; city manager plan and, 223–24; in Norfolk, 18–19, 199–200, 207, 223, 225–26; ward system and, 224

African Americans: Ashburner and, 226–27; charter reform and, 5, 6; civil service and, 223; unions for, 223. *See also* disfranchisement of African Americans

airports: municipal ownership of, 250, 251, 253–55, 270; in Oakland, 254; World War I and, 253–54

Alameda County Progress Club (ACPC), 157, 160, 161, 162; unions and, 158–59

Allen, William, 174, 181; on civic groups, 176–77; NYBMR and, 175–76, 179; politics of, 179; on proportional representation, 178; on woman suffrage, 177–78; on women's groups, 177

American City, The (D. Wilcox), 23

American Commonwealth (Bryce), 28, 44, 74; Goodnow and, 64, 317n50; influence of, 57–58

American political development (APD), 6, 19, 20, 24, 25